Communications
in Computer and Information Science   284

Stefan Oppl   Albert Fleischmann (Eds.)

S-BPM ONE - Education and Industrial Developments

4th International Conference, S-BPM ONE 2012
Vienna, Austria, April 4-5, 2012
Proceedings

 Springer

Volume Editors

Stefan Oppl
Johannes Kepler University Linz
Department of Business Information Systems
Communications Engineering
Freistaedterstrasse 315
4040 Linz, Austria
E-mail: stefan.oppl@jku.at

Albert Fleischmann
Metasonic AG
Münchner Strasse 29
Hettenshausen
85276 Pfaffenhofen, Germany
E-mail: albert.fleischmann@metasonic.de

ISSN 1865-0929   e-ISSN 1865-0937
ISBN 978-3-642-29293-4   e-ISBN 978-3-642-29294-1
DOI 10.1007/978-3-642-29294-1
Springer Heidelberg Dordrecht London New York

Library of Congress Control Number: 2012934506

CR Subject Classification (1998): H.3.5, H.4, J.1

Typesetting: Camera-ready by author, data conversion by Scientific Publishing Services, Chennai, India

Printed on acid-free paper

Springer is part of Springer Science+Business Media (www.springer.com)

Preface

Starting from 2009, S-BPM ONE has traditionally brought together scientists and practitioners from the field of subject-oriented business process management. This tradition not only was reflected in the lively interactions at the conference itself but has also always been visible in the variety of published contributions, ranging from formal models for business process modeling to evaluations of end-user applications in business and education.

We are proud that this year's S-BPM ONE was able to continue and even strengthen the tradition of facilitating the discourse of researchers, developers, educators and practitioners. For the first time, the contributions to S-BPM ONE 2012 are published in two distinct volumes, reflecting the rising awareness of subject-oriented business process management in academia as well as industry and education.

In all, 19 contributions that were selected from the practically oriented submissions to the conference are included in these adjunct proceedings. All the papers published in this volume have gone through the same rigorous peer-review process as the papers published in the LNBIP 104 proceedings. We would like to thank the members of the Program Committee for providing high-quality feedback on the papers included in this volume and the authors for sharing their expertise and experiences with the S-BPM community.

Finally, we cordially thank Alfred Hofmann and Leonie Kunz from Springer for their assistance and support during the preparations of this volume.

April 2012

Stefan Oppl
Albert Fleischmann

Organization

Executive Committee

Conference Chair

Christian Stary   Johannes Kepler University Linz, Austria

Organizing Chair

Stefan Oppl   Johannes Kepler University Linz, Austria

Organizing Committee

Stefan Oppl (Chair)	Johannes Kepler University Linz, Austria
Dominik Wachholder	Institute of Innovative Process Management, Germany
Werner Schmidt	Ingolstadt University of Applied Sciences, Germany

Program Committee

Christian Stary (Chair)	Johannes Kepler University Linz, Austria
Franz Barachini	BIC-Austria, Austria
Thomas Bahlinger	FH Nürnberg, Germany
Reza Barkhi	Virginia Tech, USA
Noureddine Belkhatir	University of Grenoble-LIG France, France
Freimut Bodendorf	University of Erlangen-Nürnberg, Germany
Yeong-Long Chen	National Chiao Tung University, Taiwan
Anke Dittmar	University of Rostock, Germany
Peter Forbrig	University of Rostock, Germany
Alexander Gromoff	Moscow National Research University, Higher School of Economics (HSE), Russia
Lutz Heuser	AGT Group (R&D) GmbH, Germany
Ebba Thora Hvannberg	University of Iceland, Iceland
John Krogstie	Norwegian University of Science and Technology, Norway
Florian Lautenbacher	SysTec-CAx GmbH, Germany
Juhnyoung Lee	IBM T.J. Watson Research Center, USA
Christopher Lueg	University of Tasmania, Australia
Tansel Özyer	Ekonomi ve Teknoloji Üniversitesi, Turkey
Carlos Pedrinaci	The Open University, UK
Stefan Reinheimer	BIK GmbH, Germany
Gustavo Rossi	LIFIA. F. Informatica, UNLP, Argentina

Gabriele Saueressig	University of Applied Science Würzburg-Schweinfurt, Germany
Werner Schmidt	Ingolstadt University of Applied Sciences, Germany
Detlef Seese	Karlsruhe Institute of Technology, Germany
Robert Singer	FH Joanneum Graz, Austria
Renate Strazdina	Ernst&Young Baltic SIA, Latvia
Alexandra Totter	ByElement GmbH, Switzerland
Eric Tsui	The Hong Kong Polytechnic University, China
Gerrit van der Veer	Open University Netherlands, The Netherlands
Nikolas Vidakis	Technological Education Institution of Crete, Greece
James Weber	St. Cloud State University, USA
Cornelia Zehbold	Ingolstadt University of Applied Sciences, Germany
Erwin Zinser	FH Joanneum Graz, Austria

Sponsoring Institutions

Metasonic AG, Pfaffenhofen-Hettenshausen, Germany
VALIAL Solution GmbH, Ilmmünster, Germany
Infomedia Services G.m.b.H., Vienna, Austria
Competence Center on Knowledge Management, JKU, Linz, Austria
IANES (Interactive Acquisition, Negotiation and Enactment of Subject-Oriented
    Business Process Knowledge) – EU FP 7 Marie Curie IAPP
Reiner ConsSys, Cham, Switzerland
Format Werk GmbH, Gunskirchen, Austria

Table of Contents

A Current Assessment of the Quality and State of the Art of Process Management

A Discussion of Results from a Recent Survey

Thomas J. Olbrich and Norbert Kaiser

taraneon Process TestLab
Office Saarbruecken, Pfaffenkopfstrasse 21M, 66125 Saarbruecken, Germany
{thomas.olbrich,norbert.kaiser}@taraneon.com

Abstract. During the second half of 2011 we conducted a survey into the quality and state of the art of business process management. The survey results – based on face to face interviews as well as responses to an online questionnaire from 150 companies – provide a good indication of the challenges companies are facing when designing, implementing and operating processes. In this paper we present an overview of the main results and provide some discussion of their implications.

Keywords: Process quality, design defects, implementation errors, training and education.

1 Introduction

In a keynote presentation in 2010 we put forward the argument that while available functional capabilities of business process management systems (BPMS) had vastly increased over the past 10 years, this development has not been mirrored in the capabilities of companies to make use of BPMS[2] in the sense of

- creating processes more swiftly, more efficiently, with fewer errors,
- of implementing said processes to a higher level of satisfaction from the point of view of the business users
- operating and running the processes with an inherent management component.

In order to validate these points of view, the taraneon Process TestLab in close cooperation with the University of Applied Sciences Koblenz (FH Koblenz) decided to conduct an in-depth study into current practices in enterprises. The objectives of the study were to

- identify current approaches to designing, implementing and operating business processes
- elicit survey participant assessments of the perceived quality of these tasks
- identify general areas of concern but also to
- derive – where possible – best-practice approaches.

S. Oppl and A. Fleischmann (Eds.): S-BPM ONE 2012, CCIS 284, pp. 1–15, 2012.

2   Formal Approach

In May 2011 we set out by collecting a large number of questions dealing with a vast range of aspects of process quality in several brainstorming sessions. Out of the nearly 200 questions covering process quality on several layers of detail, a discussion arose on the sematic interpretation of the term 'process quality'. It was then decided not to formulate a definition of the term but to design the questionnaire in such a way as to allow the survey participants to fall back on their own understanding of the term while at the same time ensuring that the way in which questions were put would allow us to create common ground between the participants.

The initial draft list was then filtered down to around 35 questions which were refined in order to make them as specific and easy to understand as possible. Once the final list had been created, it was used as a guideline during face to face interviews with representatives from a number of enterprises. The objective was to test the questions with regard to how they were understood by the interviewees and also the check if aspects arose out of the interviews that might lead to a revision of the questionnaire. The answers to the questions gained during the interviews were later on added to the bulk of responses from the online version of the survey.

Thought was then given to identifying potential participants. To ensure that a preselection based on existing client relationships should not influence the outcome of the survey it was decided to 'market' the survey using social network sites such as LinkedIn, Xing as well as using forums such as conferences to inform interested parties about the option to participate.

At the same time, a team of students from the FH Koblenz set up a survey site with an online version of the questionnaire in German and English language. The site was opened to receive participant input in mid-October 2011 and remained open for 5 weeks. Every week, the survey organizers would use the available marketing channels to call for further participation.

Even though the survey website offered the functionality for participants to formally register by name and affiliation, it was decided to keep this on a voluntary basis.

3   Survey Participation: Structure and Analysis

Altogether, 150 representatives from enterprises, public and private institutions participated in the survey by providing answers, though not all participants answered all questions. Rather than forcing participants to provide answers on issues on which they had no knowledge which might then lead to inappropriate overall results, it had been decided to allow participants to skip questions. On average however, questions were answered by 84 participants.

3.1   Geographical Spread

While the survey did not specifically ask participants their location, the choice between the German and English language version of the questionnaire does at least give some indication of the balance between German language participants (Germany, Switzerland and Austria in the main) and non-german language participants. Of the 144 respondents, 88% choose to use the German language survey while 12% used the English version.

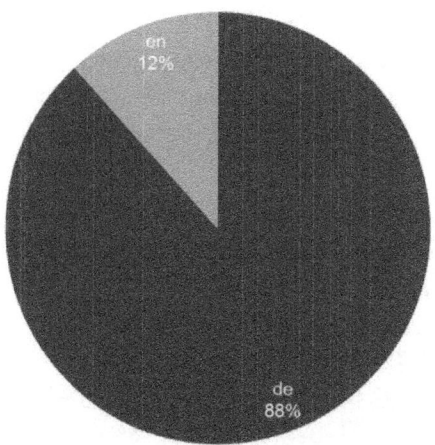

Fig. 1. Usage of survey language

3.2   Industry Spread

The next figure gives an indication of the type of industry participants belong to. Although 58% of respondents come from the service, financial and telecommunication industry, it should be noted that this does not imply that these sectors view process quality issues with a higher degree of concern than other sectors.

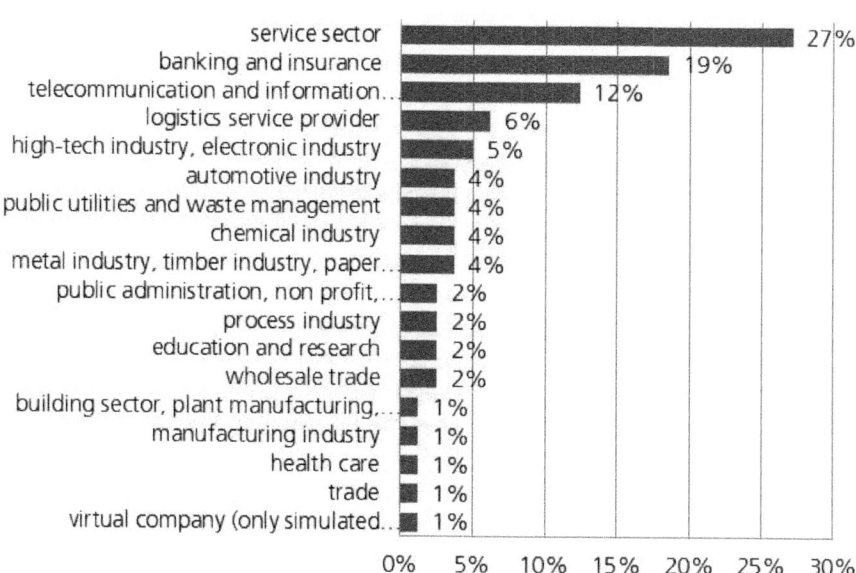

Fig. 2. Industry spread

3.3   Company Size and Annual Turn-Over

Also of interest may be the size of companies responding. Rather surprisingly participants came from across the spectrum from very small companies to large, multinational enterprises.

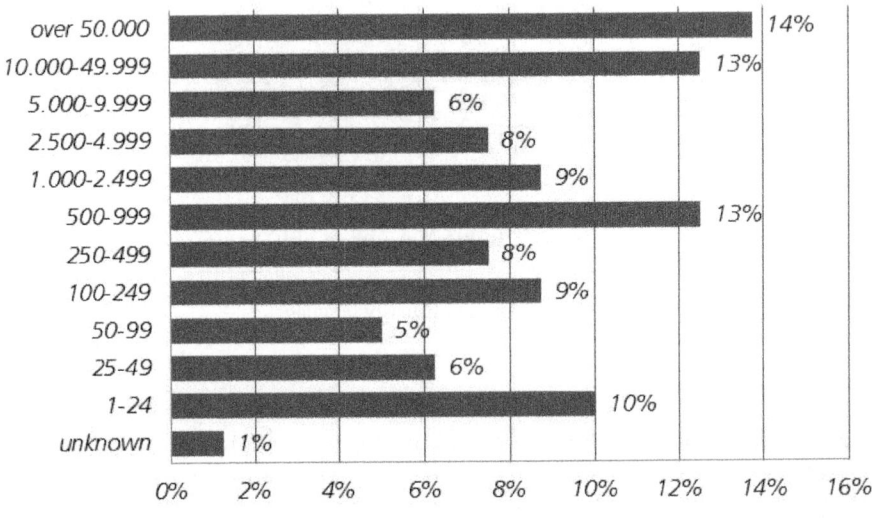

Fig. 3. Company size

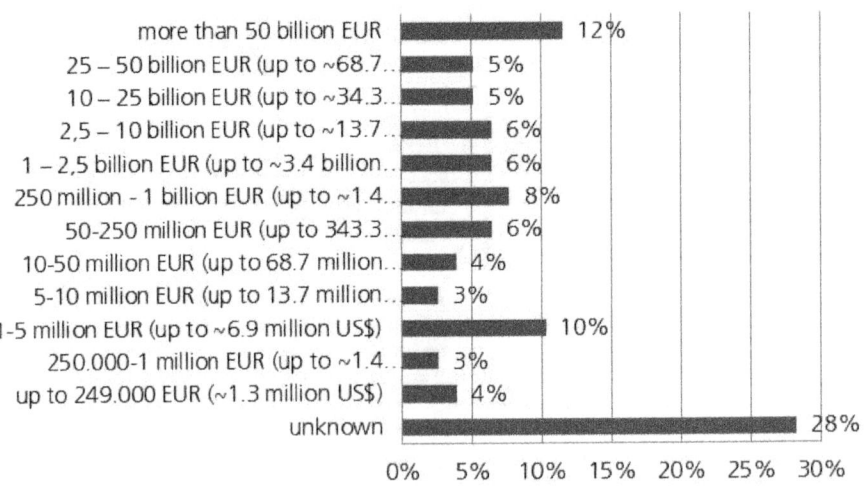

Fig. 4. Annual company turn-over

3.4   Role of Respondents

Next we asked respondents to indicate which role (level of hierarchy) they hold within their company. With 48% indicating that they hold a position as manager of a department or above, we feel that this shows that BPM generally does hold a position as a topic of interest for senior management – contrary to what is usually described as a difficulty in obtaining management buy-in.

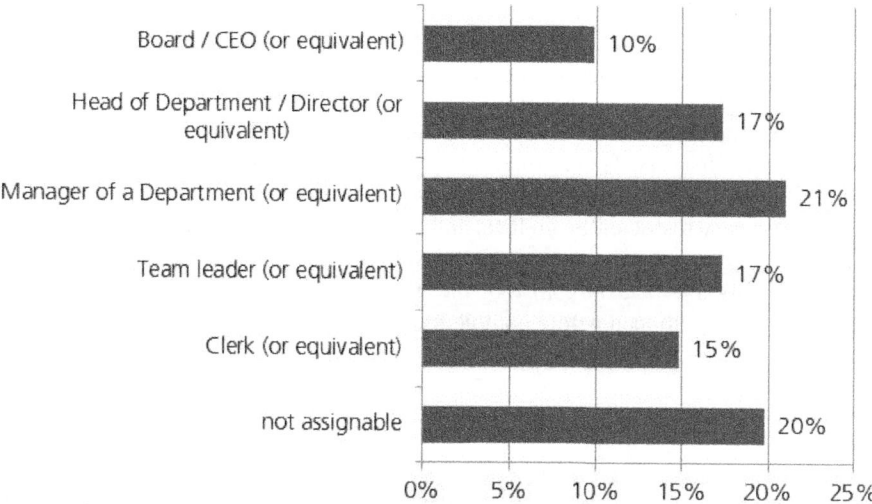

Fig. 5. Role of respondents/Level of hierarchy

4   Relative Level of Success

Asked to indicate the perceived or actual success of their company in relation to their market competitors, 45% of participants responded by saying that their company had been more or significantly more successful than their competitors over the past 3 years.

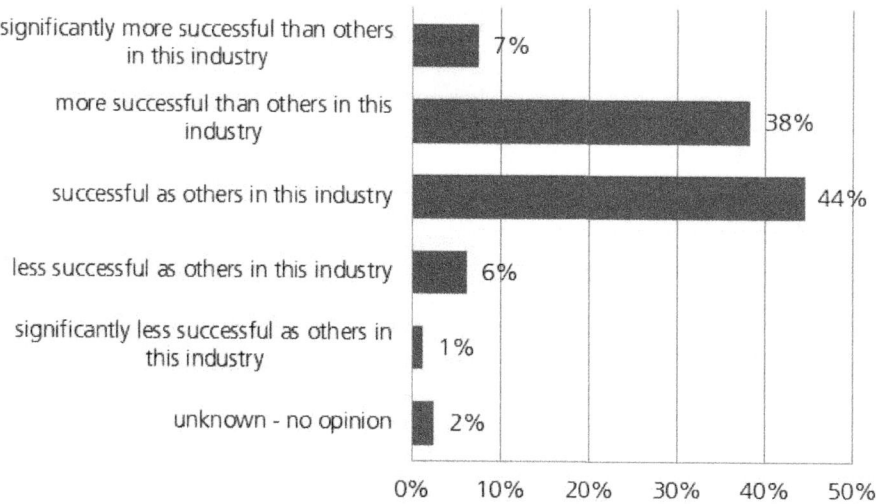

Fig. 6. Relative company success

5   Quality of Processes

In this section of the questionnaire the main focus of the questions concerned visible issues with regards to process quality.

5.1   Overall Success Rate of Process Related Projects

One of the most prominent questions we asked dealt with the level of success of process related projects. These projects usually include a set of target objectives to be reached through a new or changed process in addition to which the projects them- selves are usually restricted by budgets and timeframes. Given that business processes from a design, implementation and operating perspective are not a new phenomenon, it seems remarkable that only 46% of these projects fully reach their objectives and that even 18% are stopped before completion.

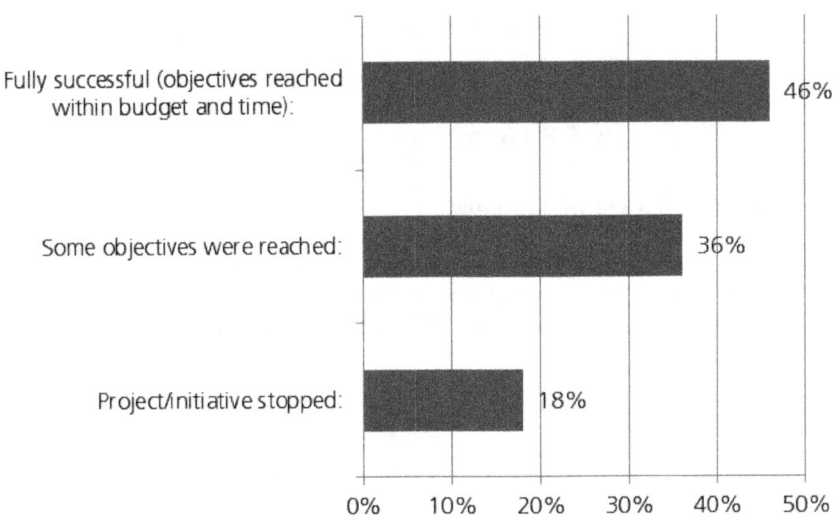

Fig. 7. Success rate of process related projects

5.2   Level of Process Defects

Of those projects that delivered results up to an operational stage, the survey was interested in the quality as in this case defined by the scope of corrective efforts re- quired post-project to correct defects in order to make the process operational. In keeping the overall low success rate of process related projects in general, some 37% of project results (i.e. processes) required major or even fundamental changes before they could be utilized and put into operations.

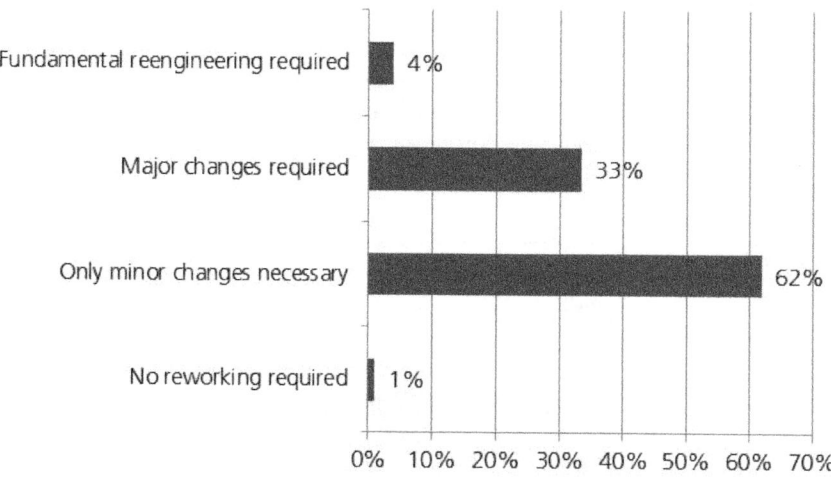

Fig. 9. Scope of corrective efforts post-project

The fact that 37% of projects require major re-work is also reflected in the amount of time companies need to invest in addition to the original project time-frame. As figure 10 shows, 43% of companies need to invest at least 15% of the initial project time to 'repair' the results delivered through the original project before the processes can be operated.

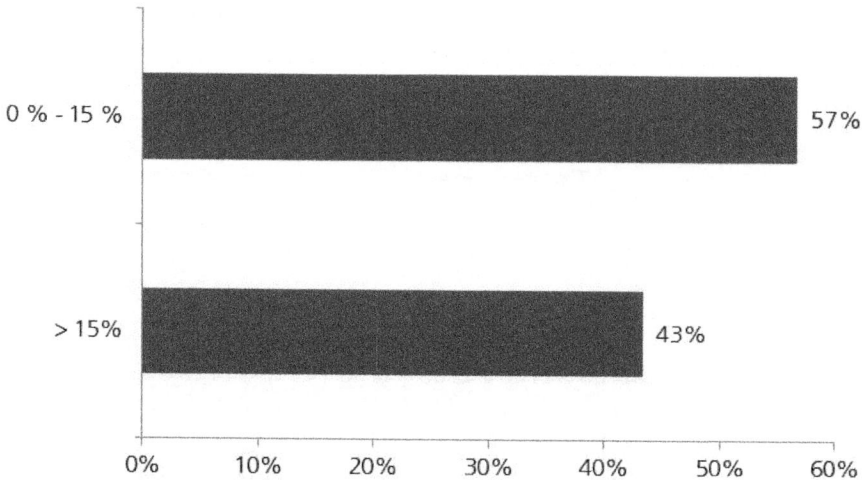

Fig. 10. Additional time required for corrective efforts and tasks

It seems to be especially worrisome that the effort invested into error correction can to a certain extent be avoided through early quality management approaches. This can be drawn from the fact that 43% of detected process errors are classified as 'avoidable'.

5.3   Assigned Responsibilities for Process Related Projects

The relatively low success rate of process related projects poses several questions, one of which concerns overall responsibility for these kinds of projects. In order to determine if the role or background of the project head was an influencing factor on the success or relative failure of the project, the survey tried to identify who led process related projects in enterprises.

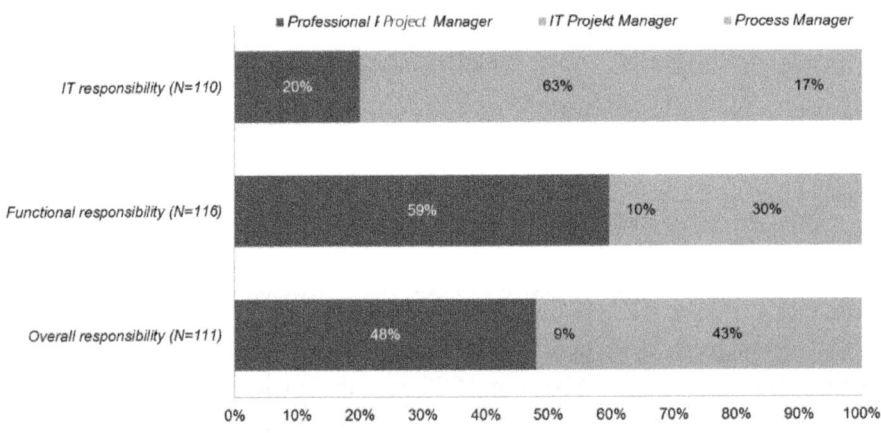

Fig. 11. Assignment of project responsibilities

The numbers generated through this question become particularly relevant when taken in conjunction with the scope and scale of the addition effort required to correct process defects.

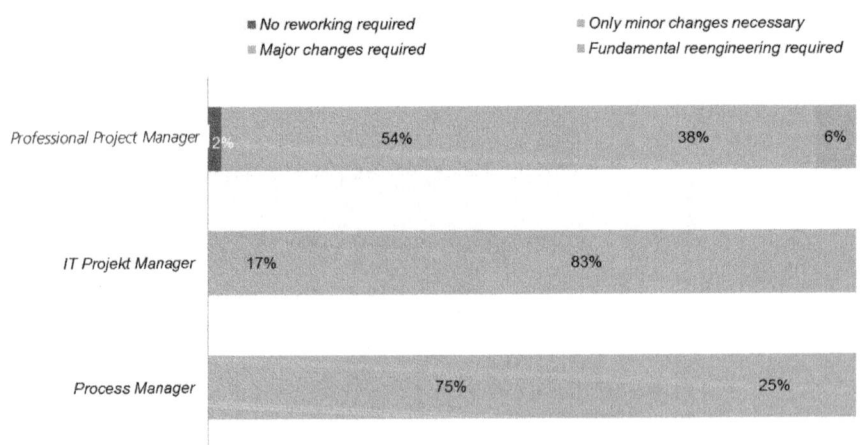

Fig. 12. Correlation of project responsibility with scope of error correction

As can be clearly seen from figure 12, process related projects run by process managers as opposed to IT or professional project managers seem to require far less changes in order to make defective processes operational.

5.4   Summary of Process Quality Observations

The responses from the questions described in the previous paragraphs seem to suggest that companies still enter into a great risk when attempting to design or change business processes. This can be inferred from the following results:

- Only 46% of projects deliver according to expectations
- 43% of companies need to invest an additional 15% of project time from post-project error correction
- 37% of processes delivered as project results require major or even fundamental changes prior to being made operational

6   Processes and Organization

Irrespective of the tools and methodologies used to create, design and implement processes, the human factor has often been overlooked. Suggested approaches from vendors and consultants focus heavily on technical creation and implementation of processes but only seldom on the organizational aspects and the integration of processes into the working environment. For that reason, the survey looked into organizational issues and tried to identify if the way to push processes into the organization poses risks to process performance or if companies have found or developed approaches for a smooth transition from the project to the operational phase. Furthermore, we tried to identify if, how and to what extent employees are informed and trained with regards to processes – as opposed to IT systems.

6.1   Duration of Process Life-Cycle Phases

While purely technical tasks such as coding, implementation and roll-out of BPMS may today require less effort with the advance of standards such as BPEL, BPMN etc., the authors of the study [1] had gained the impression in recent years that the overall length of time required until a new process was firmly embedded in the organization had not in fact profited from this development. Some cases even suggested that the average time required from design to operations may have risen in recent years. To test this hypothesis, we asked participants to imagine that their company had been subjected to radical market developments which required a reengineering of their processes. Against this scenario, we asked how long companies would take to complete different tasks which usually form part of the overall process life-cycle.

The response clearly shows that organizational factors have a far bigger influence on project time than is usually thought of. Figures 13a shows the proportion between organizational and technical asked in a typical process development situation. Whereas BPM still has a large IT label attached to it, the survey responses show that with an average duration of 36 months from situation analysis to completion of the process remedy, 27 of those months are spent on pre-dominantly organizational tasks and only 11 months are required for traditional IT-tasks.

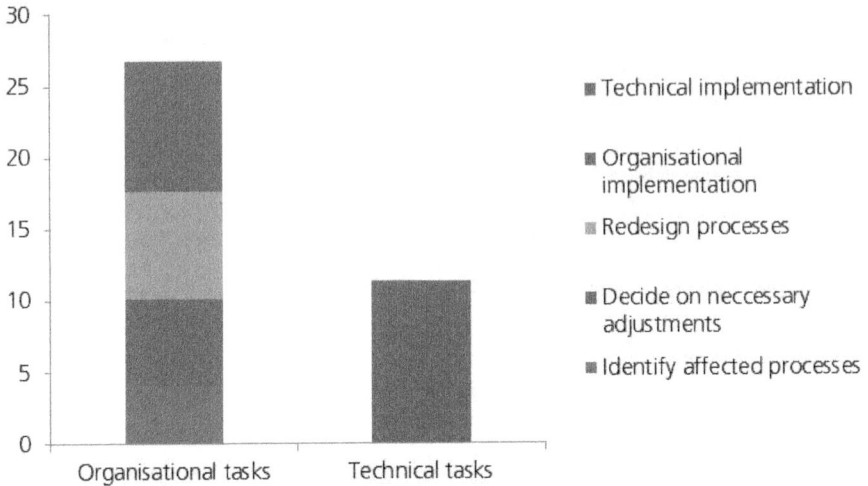

Fig. 13. Comparison of organizational vs. technical tasks in a radical reengineering scenario

Figure 14 allows us to take a more detailed look at how the different components have been weighted by the respondents. For a better understanding of the implications of figure 14, attention should be paid to the wording of the original question: "Imagine that the situation in your industry will change radically in the next six months (new business model, IT developments, radical changes in competitive environment etc.). From the point of noticing the changed situation, how long would your company need to ..."

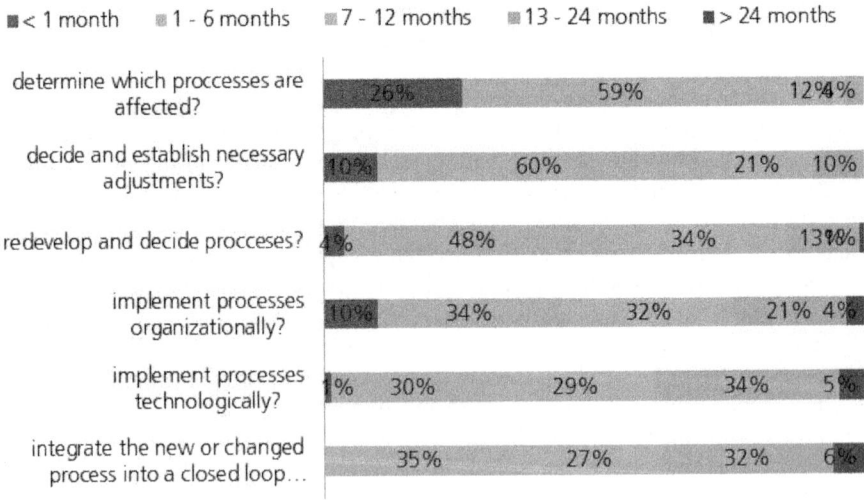

Fig. 14.

The data from figure 14 shows that

- 59% of companies need between 1 to 6 months to determine which processes may be affected by the changed market conditions
- 31% need more than 7 months to decide on what to do
- 57% of companies take longer than 7 months in organizationally implementing new processes

These numbers may lead to several conclusions which we formulate as hypothesis:

- Companies do not possess an up to date overview of their process landscape. While some sort of process architecture may well exist, it is more focused on structure than on content
- Companies are not aware of the influencing factors on processes
- Decision making processes on processes are not established and only have a low priority
- There are no procedures to cover the introduction of a changed or new process into an organization

The last mentioned hypothesis is of particular interest as it contains to two fundamental changes: the change from an isolated project situation into the integrated daily business as well as the handover from IT implementation to the business users.

A closer examination of how the introduction of a new process is handled provided some remarkable results. Figure 15 shows that while companies go to some length to do 'something' to facilitate the introduction of new processes, steps taken are mostly of a passive nature with information by email or via intranet leading the way. Active measures such as process training are more rarely used.

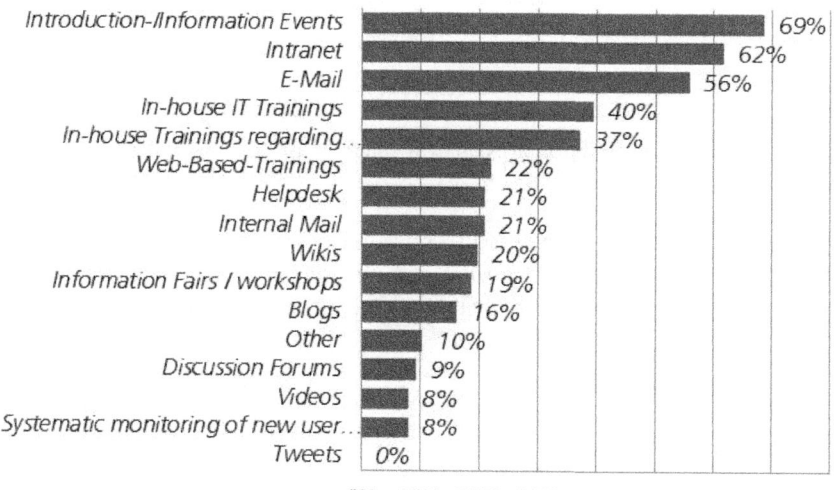

Fig. 15. Supporting measures for the introduction of new processes (multiple responses allowed)

It can be concluded that in many cases it is up to the employee to research available information on new or changed processes and that a comprehensive process introduction strategy is not yet state-of-the-art. The consequence of this is reflected in the high level of dissatisfaction of employees with their information basis with 46% claiming that they feel ill-prepared when faced with new processes.

6.2   Using Employee Experience to Improve Processes

When changes to existing processes need to occur, it has often been suggested that the concept of the learning and evolving organization offers the opportunity to use information sources for continuous process assessment and improvement. We therefor asked participants to assess the extent to which some of the available information sources are used in real life to improve process quality.

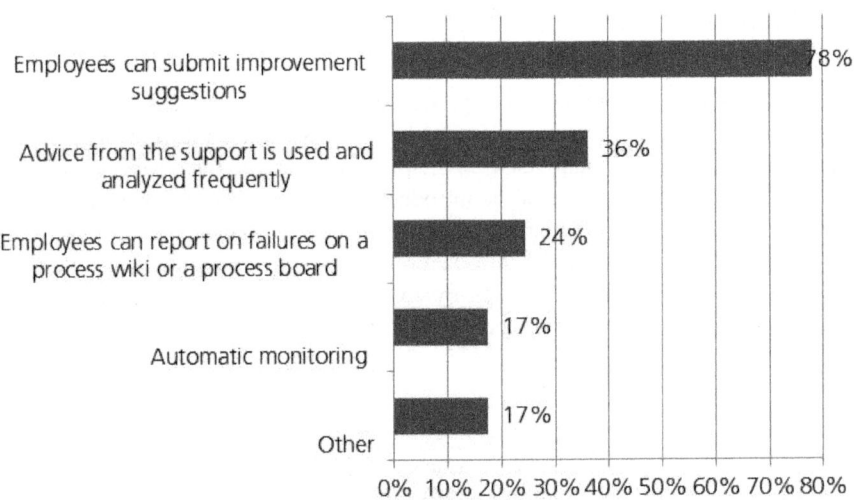

Fig. 16. Using available information sources to improve process quality (multiple answers allowed)

The results of this question may explain to some degree why companies find to difficult to continuously improve processes as they do not have an active policy of collecting and using information, even though it is freely available.

7   Processes and Agility

In the final part of the survey we took a closer look at the extent and frequency in which companies change their processes. This seemed to the authors to be of particular importance as the ability to change when circumstances demand it, is regarded as an indication of good process management practice. Surprisingly, 44% of companies responded by stating that they change their processes to a significant degree at least once a year.

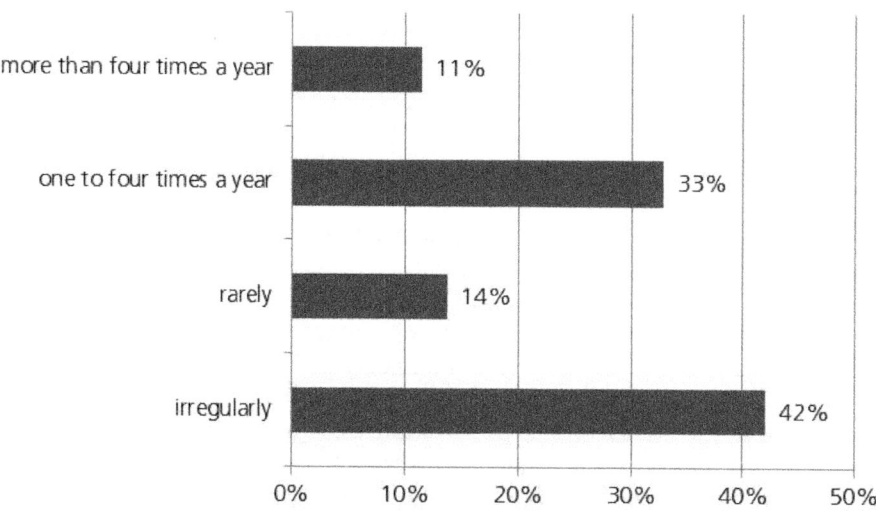

Fig. 17. Frequency of process changes

Of course, the frequency of processes changes does not indicate good process management practice per se. But it does show a general willingness and ability to adept. As such, it can be regarded as a strategic capability to be used when needed. Companies that possess this capability can be said to be on the winning side as can be seen from the relationship between change frequency and market success.

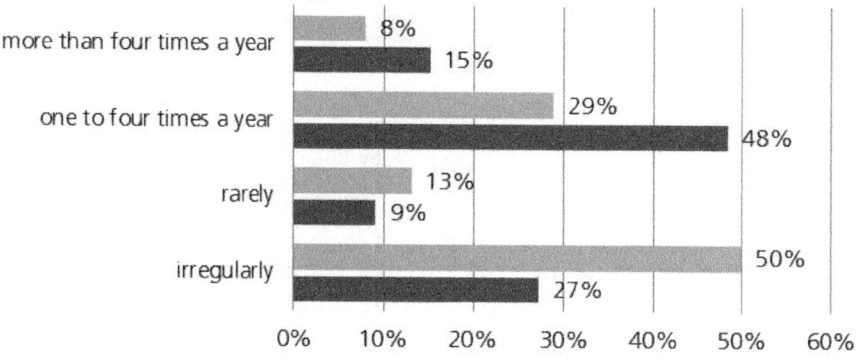

Fig. 18. Correlation between market success and process change frequency

The conclusion that may be drawn from this is that companies with the ability to change processes on demand run their processes along a continuous improvement strategy rather than on an isolated one-off project approach.

8   Preliminary Conclusions from the Survey Results

In this paper we have offered and discussed selected responses to the survey. Although evaluation is still on-going, the authors feel that a number of preliminary conclusions may be drawn from the results.

As a general observation we feel that the survey has shown that for BPM to be successful, companies must not only focus on finding the right BPMS suited to their IT requirements but should put a much stronger emphasis on issues such as process quality, organizational readiness and employee information. It seems improbable that successful technical implementation of a process will lead to an overall successful process performance if the employees and management do not understand the processes they should be working on or managing, if the step from implementation to operation is postponed because of necessary work to correct basic process design errors or because process responsibility in wrongly assigned.

In discussions about the survey results with some of the participants, we have found that the numbers generated have proved helpful in making more obvious some of the facts people involved in processes had until now only regarded as impressions gained from their daily work without putting them into context.

The survey also shows that for a large number of issues and risks, some of the more successful companies have used or developed appropriate approaches, some of which are:

- Operating a continuous process quality approach incl.
  - Testing of process designs pre-implementation to identify avoidable errors
  - Validating processes pre-operation
- Training and education of employees and management
  - Creation of the role of dedicated process manager in conjunction with appropriate training
  - More active participation and integration of employees into process development and process operations as well as heightening general process awareness levels

While it may take time to plan and implement these measures, the results show that the current state of BPM in many companies lacks quality, is regarded as a lengthy and risky undertaking and as such has given rise to a critical view on BPM. Indeed, a critical assessment of the approaches and methods connected with BPM is justified given the results of his survey as is the overall assessment of BPM as a 'risky business', when companies can only demonstrate a success rate of 46%.

On the other hand, the survey results also show that companies can do much to reduce risks and lower costs for developing and operating processes. However, to achieve this they need to look beyond the technical aspects of BPM and focus on creating an environment and mindset that allows them to make best use to the BPMS capabilities provided.

9   Addendum

In the course of the revision process for this paper, it has been suggested that the study might have profited from referring to existing definitions of the term 'quality'. It should be noted that this approach was discussed during the early planning stages of the survey but was dropped for the following reasons:

- Initial discussions during the face to face interview showed that interviewees tended to have difficulties with formal definitions of the term quality as applied to processes
- Definitions such as they do exist tend to have a background in individual disciplines that are part of BPM and cover only to a lesser extent the range of the BPM spectrum of disciplines. As such the authors wanted to avoid having to subject participants to a discipline-specific viewpoint.
- During discussions the authors also found that some companies had developed their own understanding of the quality term. Rather than forcing these companies to try to combine a given definition with their own before responding to the survey, it was decided to make it as easy as possible by not limiting the answers to a given understanding.

References

1. Komus, A., et al.: Quality in Business Process Management: Results and conclusions from the first international study into the quality of business process management, available through (2012), http://www.processtestlab.com
2. Fleischmann, A., Schmidt, W., Singer, R., Seese, D. (eds.): S-BPM ONE 2010. CCIS, vol. 138, pp. 209–215. Springer, Heidelberg (2011)

A Proposal for Modeling Standards for Subject-Oriented Modeling with PASS

A Paper for the Interactive Education Material Track for Modeling Principles Based on the Usage of the Metasonic Build PASS-Editor and Their PASS-Engine

Matthes Elstermann and Detlef Seese

Karlsruhe Institute of Technology (KIT)
Institute AIFB
Bldg. 05.20, KIT Campus South, 76128 Karlsruhe, Germany
(matthes.elstermann,detlef.seese)@kit.edu

Abstract. This paper discusses and proposes a few standard conventions or best practices in subject-oriented business process modeling with the Parallel Activity Specification Schema (PASS). It is derived from experiences gained at Metasonic as well as teaching experience for several seminar projects at an university. The ideas and concepts were derived as solutions for several minor or mayor problems or issues connected to the creation and handling processes of PASS-graphs. They are presented as a basis for discussion on the topic of practicability and usefulness of certain standards or paradigms. The ideas of this paper have been taught to students and applied in several successful S-BPM projects.

Keywords: process modeling, S-BPM, PASS, modeling standard.

1 Introduction: The Paper and Proposal of Conventions

The authors of this paper have been teaching process modeling with the subject-oriented method and the Parallel Activity Specification Schema (PASS) for the last two years in advanced courses at university level. The paper collects experience gained and concepts taught to the students that were necessary or deemed useful and practical in order to make project work easier.

Proposing standards or norms can be quite controversial. Since the different communities of S-BPM practice across the world probably have developed their own personal habits of modeling PASS diagrams fitted to their needs. There may be cases where those habits may simply be a traded down custom that do not actually come from certain needs or requirements and the only reason not to change to another way of doing things may be not to give up on old ideas even though another way may be better.

Since it is hard to distinguish between these two points of view this paper is intended as a proposal for what could be called good PASS modeling. The paper

S. Oppl and A. Fleischmann (Eds.): S-BPM ONE 2012, CCIS 284, pp. 16–32, 2012.

presents and examines practical ideas and conventions that seem promising in order to allow an easy and fast modeling-work-flow, and should reduce the perceived (optical) complexity of especially larger S-BPM Models. They are the result of the need to solve certain problems and issues encountered in modeling projects during the last two years in the seminar projects at our university.

Since there does not seem to have occurred any research on this topic up to now, this paper is intended to start the scientific discussion whether the herein presented concepts and solutions can be transferred and taught to new practitioners of S-BPM, as has been done in our classes and brought to moderate success. Many ideas presented here might already be considered standard practices, but have not been called this explicitly.

There are two major reasons why thoughts and efforts should be spent on this matter.

A united style can help S-BPM learners by not confusing them with optical differences between examples. Even if they may be only superficial, such optical differences can occupy and avert a person long before the actual differences are noticed and understood.

And secondly even more important, adhering to certain conventions should allow different users to gain faster and better understanding when being presented with models new to them, which in turn can help to ease communicating and knowledge sharing about S-BPM modeling in the community. Not in bounds and leaps, but in a small yet solid way – as another cornerstone to be built upon.

It is expected that the reader has a basic understanding about the Parallel Activity Specification Schema (PASS)[1] that is a cornerstone of S-BPM.

Since Metasonic Build is currently the only functional editor for such graphs, the paper, in parts, addresses issues derived from the work flow and that is determined by the powerful or less practical features that this editor[2] offers.

The paper is split up into two parts after a brief explanation of the terms that are being used.

The first part (section 2) is concerned with conventions and concepts meant for the general handling of models and modeling. The order the problems and their solutions are presented tries roughly to follow the idea more general aspects are covered first.

The second part (section 3) presents ideas concerned with the actual layout and graphical design of PASS Graphs. The ideas follow no particular order and all represent different ideas to make the diagrams better to handle and to understand.

1.1   Terms and Descriptions

The terms used in this document are:

Subject Interaction Diagram (SID): the 'upper' or first part of PASS diagram, representing all involved subjects in a process and the communication between them.
Internal Subjects: Boxes in SIDs that represent the actual subjects. Each Internal Subject is linked to its individual underlying Subject Behavior Diagram.

---

[1] PASS was introduced in [5] end elaborated in [6]. A short article introducing the method can be found in [4].
[2] We want thank Metasonic for allowing the free use of PASS for our educational purposes.

External Subject: subjects-symbols in an SID graph that are used to link to other model-files/SIDs, and are not associated with an SBD.

Message Connector Arrow (MCA): the directed path connecting subjects in an SID, that are annotated with a list of allowed messages.

Subject Behavior Diagrams (SBD): a diagram associated with an internal subject appearing in an SID describing its behavior. Composed of transitions between three possible states: Send, Receive and Function.

Process Overview Diagram: a diagram type that shows how certain process models are connected to each other (has not technical relevance at the moment in Metasonic)

2   General Handling and Design of PASS Diagrams

2.1   Reference Model vs. Implementation Model

When presented with the task to model a business process in PASS one of the first problems for the students to solve was to grasp the overall idea of what that model was going to be used for. The projects they were tasked with were of very different nature, ranging from finding and explaining the cause of problems to actually integrating a whole process system to support processes. There were many differences in the nature of the models they had to create – or at least on major distinction. In order to define and explain their task we had to define terms necessary to precisely describe on what to work and how.

Each model, PASS as well as others, is created with a purpose – be it to get a process engine working, be it to model the specification for technical systems, or also very often simply to capture tacit knowledge in an organization in order to make it explicit, and to use that knowledge afterwards for explanation and teaching purposes.

The basic differentiation we have encountered is between what we have come to call "reference models" of processes and "implementation models".

The former are models that are used to explain or even define standard process and to store, or keep knowledge about them in an organization – models that in the first place need to be understood by humans. "Reference models" may need to include modeling that is not compatible with existing interpreter engines (for example messages between two multi-subjects which do not work properly at all at the moment) and include other non-functional parts.

The latter are models that are meant to be used with actual machine interpreters or process engines in such a way that the applications behind those engines allow their users a smooth operation of the process while also giving the developers of the according system a model that is easy enough and allows simple solutions. Basically as focus "implementation models" may need to adhere more to technical requirements making model interpretation harder for humans.

The experience gained during the last years invites to the somewhat bold statement that is nearly impossible to create one single model for all purposes. We came to the conviction that it is most often necessary to conceive at least two separate models about the same domain and not try to use the same model for all purposes. To distinguish the models we came to use the herein presented terms in order to cope with this problem.

To give an example: the following process was modeled for an ordering process to be implemented into the portal that coordinates the orientation-week for the Department of Economics and Business Engineering's student council of our university.

During the orientation week the tutors offer the freshmen ('Ersties') goods that can be ordered during that week. Parts of that process are done completely on paper because it is much easier and faster for the student council to do the ordering and delivering in the old fashioned way. Yet since the tutors do change every year, it is necessary to have a reference of what to do. So for explanation reasons the freshmen are included in the reference model including a description when to give their orders and money to their tutors and what else needs to be considered.

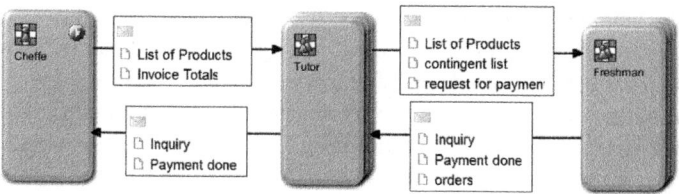

Fig. 1. Reference model for ordering process of student council including freshmen

The same process is also to be included into the planed process portal to help and automated at least parts of it. Since freshmen are not planned to have access to the system[3] the implementation model does lack a whole subject and the according interaction.

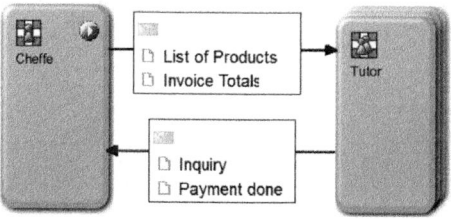

Fig. 2. Implementation model for ordering process of student council without freshmen who do not use the system since all interaction is done on personal interaction level

The distinction between 'reference model' and 'implementation model' was necessary for our projects and has helped us to prevent misunderstanding while talking about the models. Furthermore it is necessary to understand the difference of these two concepts for the following sections.

We propose to teach S-BPM beginners the awareness about the differences and were it will be relevant in order to give them a clear idea what kind of modeling they need to undertake.

---

[3] The effort needed to allow 500 students access for the one-week orientation phase was not deemed worth the cost.

And secondly we propose the name convention of 'reference model' and 'implementation mode' to differentiate such models especially where both types need to be developed in parallel – as it was the case with some of our projects.

As a side note: even though not part of the formal PASS standard, Metasonic Build allows two mechanisms to circumvent this issue in parts. On is the use of so called 'manual subjects' that allow users of the process engine to control actions modeled for subjects that have no actual access to the process system. The other is the use of dummy-subjects (using external subject with the 'instant interface' option) that always provide all messages expected from them.

In the example presented above both methods were considered but not optimal. As of Version 4.4 Build does not allow multi-manual-subjects and the feature is not widely documented. Dummy-subjects on the other hand do not allow for SBDs which may be necessary to describe what the non-system user is actually supposed to be doing. Furthermore the modeled interaction with the dummy-subject must still be executed by the other subjects, if not completely hidden/automated. This in turn may be confusing since it differs from the normal work flow and/or would require additional function states to represent the actual interaction. In the example above this could be the actual collecting of the payment.

2.2   Modeling of Machine Components and Systems

A similar problem that derives from the previous section, but is partly a stand-alone question, is the topic of how to model the interaction with IT-systems and machines that are part of almost every business process. Their representation in the model has often been a topic of discussion in our projects.

The first idea to model an IT-system, for example a database, is to use a separate subject, e.g. in the following figure.

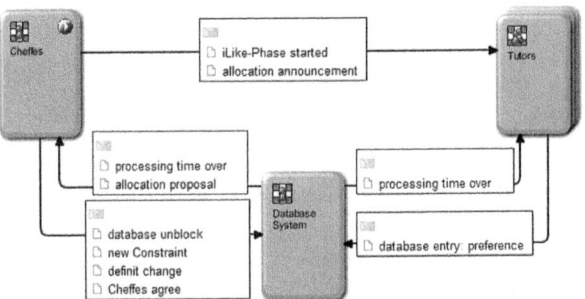

Fig. 3. Subject Interaction diagram of a simple group allocation process with a database-subject

For reference models, as they were modeled by us, this has proven to be recommendable in any case. The interaction between humans and IT infrastructure and in what order it occurs is essential for the grasping of complex processes. Especially to examine what kind of information will go from which source to what end. Therefore we found it to be advisable to always model out major systems and their interaction with other subjects if understanding is of importance for the model.

Of course the explicit modeling of system can be done for implementation models as well – as in the example that is actually meant for an implementation. In that case, though, a whole access protocol, regulating read- and write- accesses etc. needs to be modeled via the definition of message-types. Furthermore the subject representing the system needs to be programmed and automated to execute completely autonomous. In turn that may lead to a usually more extensive need for technical development (meaning: manual programming).

The other option a modeler has to represent such interaction into the model, and to integrate access to external systems, is to use function states that are refined to execute the required data transfer. In many cases that solution is quicker and requires less programming and modeling effort, on the short term.

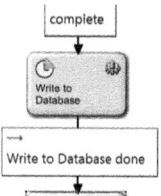

Fig. 4. Example for a refined function-state

But it hides the technical system in the depths of the SBDs of other subjects, a circumstance we have found to be misleading and confusing when trying to understand the model. Still that option was chosen frequently by the students for implementation models because it requires only one state instead of 3-6 states across at least two SBDs[4].

The question to be asked is when to choose which option?

As stated before our experience does make us believe that the first way is necessary to create good reference models if major IT-Systems (like SAP) or important databases are involved.

For implementation models it depends on the extent of interaction between systems and process engine/users. While the function-state-refinement seems to be the easier way, the explicit modeling of subjects and the involved extra modeling has the advantage that all accesses to the same system are in the same SBD in relative closeness to each other and not strewn around many SBDs, making maintenance on the according services easier.

From our experience a possible rule of thumb may be that in cases where the same or similar read or write access to systems in the process does occur more than 3 times, a separate implementation of an IT-system as a subject in the model could be advises. That way only one function state in the IT-System-subject needs to be refined instead of many function states that happen at different stages in the process.

But of course it is a topic for discussion here when exactly to choose which modeling option.

In any case should the general problematic be part of any advanced introduction to PASS modeling, since it has been a frequent question from our students.

---

[4] Special, automated, send and corresponding receive states, plus the actual function states.

2.3   Concerns of Separation of Process Model (Monolithic vs. Fragmented Models)

Metasonic allows splitting up of process models via the use of the so called external subjects in their PASS SID graphs. To connect two separate process models the communication between an internal and external subject in an SID of a process model needs to be mirrored in another process model with inversed roles of internal and external subjects. The according external subjects then need to refer to the according other process model file.

Fig. 5. Inversely mirroring communication patterns in two process models

The relation of process models connected in such a way does vary. The construct can be used to model sub-processes that support a main process, it can be meant as follow-up process on the same level that starts when the first process has finished, or it can simply be used to split up a larger process model in order to not overload the SID of one model with too many subject and using this way to outsource certain parts.

Technically there is no difference at the moment between these scenarios since the actual meaning is determined within the according SBDs of the connecting subjects. The nature therefor is on pure semantically basis[5].

The question is when to split up a model or if it should be done? The answer is, of course, it depends on the circumstances.

A major concern here is again the question whether a reference model or an implementation model is being constructed.

Formless interviews with stakeholder, who have been presented with fragmented and non-fragmented models, seem to indicate the following: For reference models that need to be viewed and understood by humans, splitting up the model should be kept to a minimum if possible. Too many process fragments, especially if they are cross linked tend to confuse viewers when confronted for the first time (especially if they are not familiar with PASS).

This has its limits though, since the human mind can roughly distinguish between seven to nine different items at the same time[6]. An SID with much more than this number of subjects involved will give the viewer at least a feeling of uneasiness when seeing it for the first time. Also with more than this number involved the chance for crossing paths of message-connectors is increased, and those will increase the chance

---

[5] As a small rule of thumb: since sub-process instances are often started more than once from a main process, the representation of the external subject as a multi-subject often indicates a master-sub-process constellation.

[6] The concept behind this "magic number seven" and other limitation of human cognition relevant for this paper can be found in [2].

for confusion, which is to be avoided if a model should be good source of knowledge (see later section).

Another drawback of monolithic structures we have found is that they rarely, or only with some effort, can be instantiated in a process engine. That is mainly due to the probability of errors that may have occurred in such a large model as well as the testability which is much easier with small manageable process-bits. And sometimes monolithic reference models simply violate the requirements of a functional PASS graph and the abilities of a process engine to process the model correctly in order. (See the previous sections on reference-models)

Consequently our observations indicate the following advice: For implementation models many smaller connected process model-modules were the choice of many of the seminar teams during the curse of several projects and have prevailed as good praxis. This should allow for easier and faster development and does matters less to the users who do not see the whole model in those case many times and have as their main goal the simple hope to run through the process as easy as possible (as long as it works there is no problem).

As a little excurse: The most extreme case to split up a PASS SID model would be to put only one single internal subject with an SBD into each process model[7] and use only external subjects as connectors to other subjects. The resulting overall model would probably be ideal for execution purposes, but with certainty not easy to understand, because of its fractured nature.

It could be argued that that kind of modeling would best fit the actual philosophy behind S-BPM by not trying to bind the individual behavior to a greater instance-context that spans more than the individual subject, and that itself is based on files, and not subjects. Just as a thought to keep in mind.

But for now and for the descried purposes that kind of modeling is not functional for now and other options may need to be chosen. So the rules of thumb for the splitting of process models we have developed are:

Prefer monolithic models for reference purposes if possible.

In SIDs try to fit subject so they can all be viewed at once on the medium of choice (monitor, paper etc.) if not split up.

In order to avoid crossing paths and not overload the model in general in a single process file there should be roughly 7-9 involved subjects at maximum.

If possible only split up a model at points where there is only one connection point (only to communication subject) in the communication between the two processes models.

Split up the model if there are clearly defined, repeatable sub-tasks.

The following figures should demonstrate the principle discussed before, give the reader a feeling for what is meant here, and what to decide on. It also demonstrates that it is merely rules of thumb and not set-in-stone laws.

The models describe a process of registering for university exams including the prior registering of the test itself in the according systems.

Even though probably not legible in the print version, the following facts about both models can be noted: There are 11 subjects in the monolithic version (Fig. 6), including 2 system-subjects. In Fig. 7 overall there are 21 Subjects, with four subjects appearing in more than one process.

---

[7] Meaning the SID that gives a context to the SBDs of the model.

Due to the special requirements of the Metasonic process engine the first model is technically not executable (it has for example two subjects that can start the process on their own – the student and the examiner). But it shows with one glance who or what is all involved in the overall process and the SBDs describe a complete process for one subject including all (modeled) possibilities and options. It also gives no illusions about the fact that there is no explicit information for the student to start registering. In reality it is up to the student to gain the necessary information and start the registering process for the test. This way an automatically generated description of that process can give a person a single united description of what to do when in this process - or more important in special cases.

The process in Fig. 7 is executable by the Metasonic process engine. It is split up and has been optimized for actual usage in the FLOW process portal to allow users an acceptable work flow. The split makes it necessary for a subject-carrier to know that his role/subject is involved in more than one sub processes that, in principle – but not technical, belong to the same overall instance. A singular description derived from the model for one person could only be generated if an option would allow for grouping by the underlying roles, instead of grouping by the separate process-models. Technically that should be no problem, but at the moment no such option does exit, making understanding a particular role in such split up models a relatively hard task.

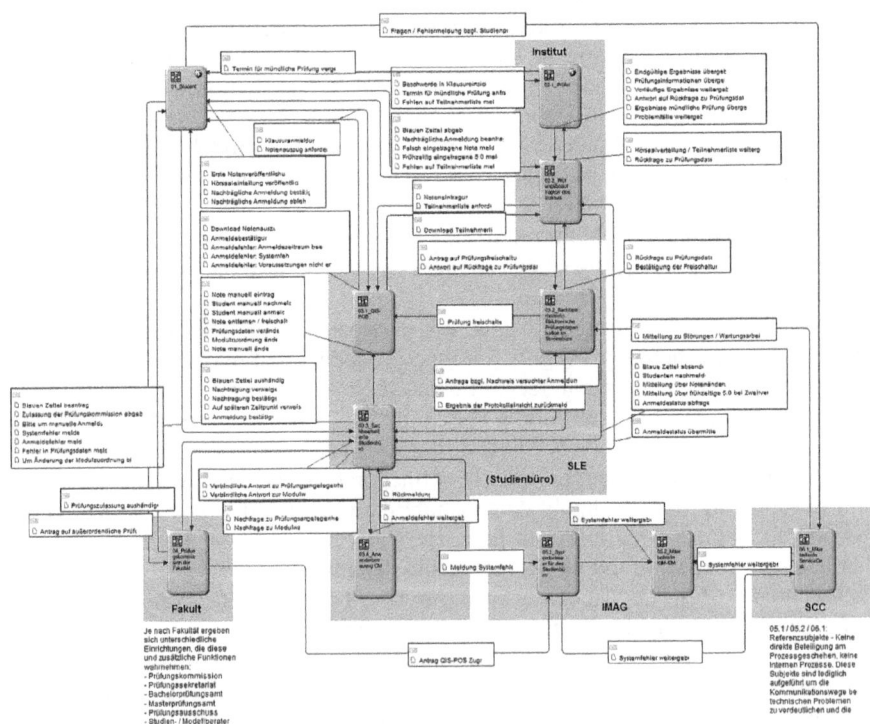

Fig. 6. Monolithic SID of a reference model for a university administration process (the details are of minor importance but the reader should be able to grasp the dimensions)

The same process as a split up model is depicted in the following Fig. 7.

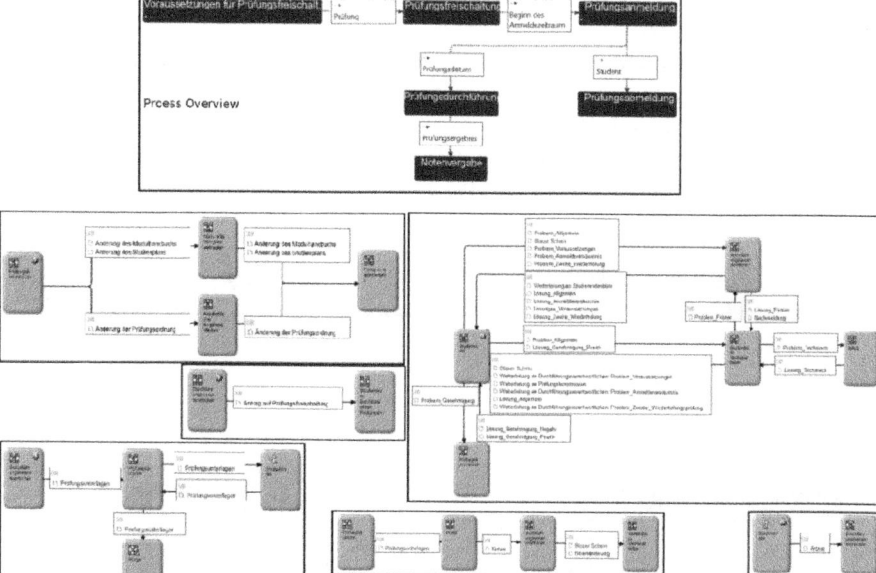

Fig. 7. The same process as in Fig. 6 as a fragmented model (optimized for execution)(again only the general dimensions of the process are of importance)

2.4   Naming of Processes and Messages

In larger and more complex processes the handling of messages can become hard due to the sheer number of messages that occur, especially if many separated processes are created and if, in consequence, more than a few so called global-messages exist.

Depending on the needs, the number of message-types can easily go up to over 50 to 70 different types – a non-unusual number encountered by us. The current message overview window of Metasonic Build is able to display about 10 messages in the overview – sortable if required. The larger this list becomes the harder it usually gets to keep an overview about what message does belong in which context and to rework and modify the whole model in consequence[8].

One possible solution we have developed and a proposal for a teaching standard for this issue is: In order to keep an easy overview, process-names should start with a double digit-numbers (as a default 10 for the center process model to start with). Sub-process-names should be numbered with three (or more digit numbers starting with the same digit as their origin process. Process on the same semantically hierarchy-tier (follow-up process e.g.) continue the in the two digit count, but increasing the decimal power.

---

[8] This can be an argument in favor of smaller, split up models (see previous section) since they allow for smaller context if the number of global message can be kept to a minimum.

In consequence the names of global messages should start with the number of the process they first originate from. For example the message send from a subject in a process that starts with 10 to initialize a sub-process should be named 10_Start_Sub_Process.

This simple convention can allow for much easier modeling work-flow, and is a simple way to gasp the context of messages in the overview window or when choosing message from a list to be applied to message connectors in SIDs, since messages can now easily be sorted and their context be grasped.

The following figures demonstrate the concept:

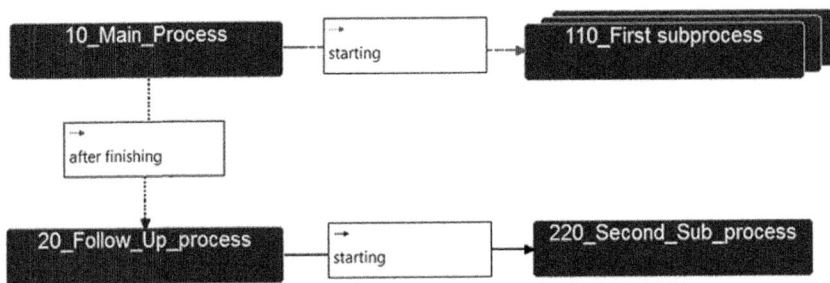

Fig. 8. Process Overview with numbered processes

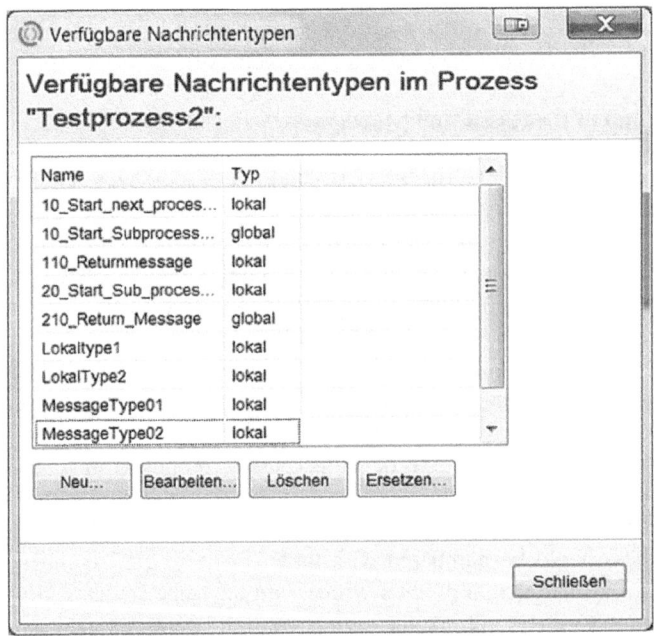

Fig. 9. Example for available message screen with sorted messages

This numbering schema is derived from old-school BASIC programming and allows to insert other process files in-between (e.g. 15 in between 10 and 20) if the need should arise during modeling. This idea is partly due to the problems that arose with renaming of process models in various versions of Metasonic Build– which at the moment cannot be advised to do.

Of course more complex numbering schemas can be used and applied where necessary as long as they fit a purpose. Which to choose is up to discussion. This solution may not be the most elegant one and the necessity of such naming conventions may be due to the editor it was used in, but it is quick, simple and has proven useful.

This concludes the first section of this paper that was mainly concerned general topics and process interaction. The following section now is concerned with the actual modeling of PASS graphs.

3   Composition and Layouts

3.1   Colored Grouping

One of the first and strongest advises is to use and teach the use of the extra elements that Metasonic Build offers – colored squares, markers, flags and text elements - to group states into functional blocks and describe them. Even though this has no effect on the functionality of the model it is a great help for other modelers. This can be compared to annotating program code with comments to explain what is going on.

Of course this is no original idea and part of pretty much any business process modeling tool and guideline (e.g. [1]) even to the extent that their usage is considered common sense and mentioning it here may seem unnecessary.

What makes it mention-worthy is the realization that this kind of model annotation is especially important for PASS-Graphs and their SBDs because of their fractured nature. Often a combinations of receive-, function- and send-states belong to a single conceptual process step. Underlying them with colored boxes makes their connection visible instantly. Furthermore if there is are follow-up steps in another SBD their connection can be shown by using the same color. Thus one aspect of criticism for PASS – the lack of an easy to understand depiction of the time-sequence of process-steps no matter by whom – can be reduced by enabling faster understanding of process flow across subjects.

As with annotating code, the main purpose of this convention proposal is to allow other modelers and viewers of the model (e.g. stake holders) to grasp the underlying concept much faster an easier transmission of ideas. It also allows to regain quicker re-insight into the model after longer periods of time where details may have been forgotten by the original modeler. Personal experience on that matter was gained during an assignment to understand an actual live process model without such annotations. It took over 3 days and a lot of feedback from the original creators that were available at the time – a luxury or a waste of resources that can and should be avoided.

The Following figure demonstrates the principle in an SBD.

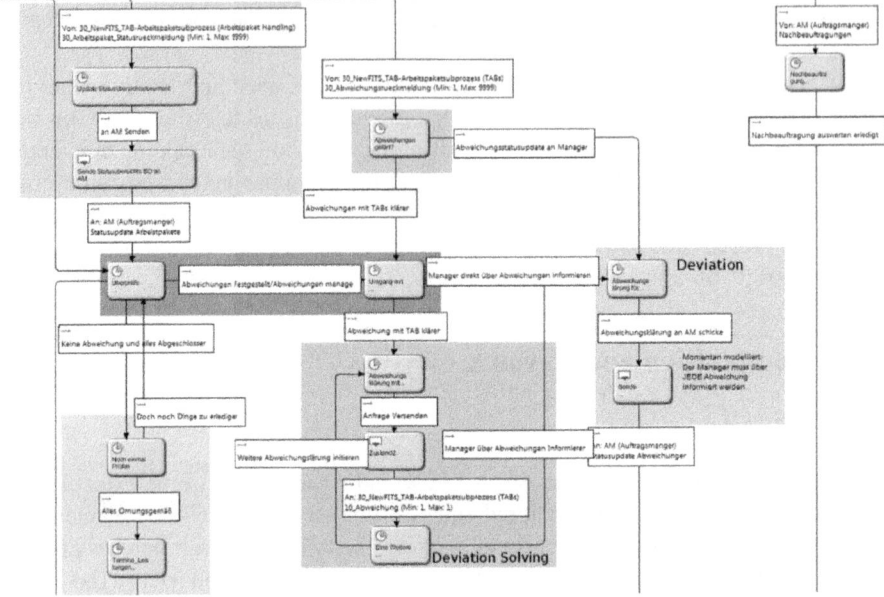

Fig. 10. Example for visual color coded grouping

As a practical side-note: it is recommended to only use muted colors, otherwise it simply would be a strain for the viewer instead of a help – imagine for example a neon-pink area in the graph above.

There is room for certain sub-conventions here: green colored were used for the "finish line" while red colors indicate really important or central states or hubs[9]. Groups with similar purpose should also be kept within the same tone-range. Except for the red- and green convention, a set-in-stone definition for color coding would be over-specification and is of no real value.

Within Metasonic Build the use of modeling-parameters allows to group states also on a functional level. Such groups can and should match the groups defined by the color highlights. A feature that would allow the combination of both should be possible and helpful.

3.2   A Convention for Vertical and Horizontal Layout

The following proposal for a standard to be applied is concerned with the flow-layout of process steps when modeling an SBD. It is rather simple:

---

[9] As another proposal for terms: Hub or Hub-state, refers to a function- or receive-state that is revisited by the subject many time over the course of a process and has many in- and outgoing transition options.

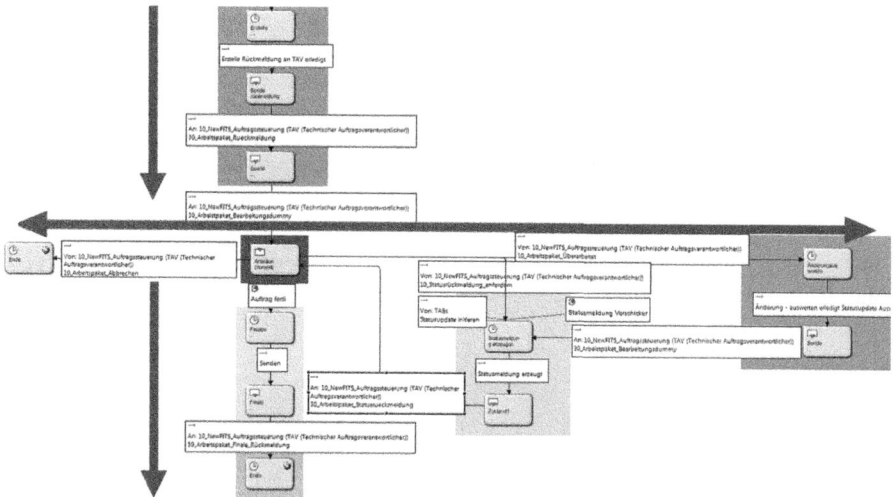

Fig. 11. Vertical timeline and horizontal alternative choice layout in an SBD

Go vertical down when modeling states that are in a timely sequence and follow after each other. For alternative choices model the states – or groups of states – horizontally, as demonstrated in Fig. 11. (As shown in the figure the concept can be combined with color grouping principle of the previous section)

Of course it can be argued that this choice is arbitrary and could also be defined the other way around since it may depend on the actual use case of the model. In other modeling languages like ARIS or BPMN examples for both options can be found[10]. Which to choose for S-BPM should be up to discussion, but a consensus should be found in the still small community of S-BPM modelers. At the most basic level for one model there should be either one way or the other, with a clear description of what was used and not deviation from that chosen convention should happen.

An argument against the here described way (vertical flow) would be that for smaller processes the model is much harder to fit to a PowerPoint Slide, since temporal sequences are often much more common than a wide selection of choices, and standard slide or monitor is wider than it's tall.

But in the large, real life process-models encountered by us the temporal sequences often became very long, spanning more than one or two pages and required scrolling in any case. The required scrolling does come much more familiar when done vertically (think for example mouse wheels for scrolling documents and texts) and the concept of a downward flow with optional choices to go left or right, is more natural than side-scrolling (waterfalls, hour glasses, pinball games etc.).

Combined with the right presentation tool[11] a good presentation of the model can be done, as was demonstrate with success to our stakeholders. Therefore we propose this convention and not the other way around. It has shown to be functional and effective, even though a final prove or investigation on the concept has not been undertaken, yet.

---

[10] See for example [1]

[11] E.g. Prezi (http://prezi.com/), or animated MS PowerPoint slides.

3.3   Avoidance of Unnecessary Crossing of Path

This proposal for a definition of how a good SBD-Diagram should look is rather obvious, but taking it into account can strongly be advised. It calls to allow modelers the extra effort and time to organize their SBDs in order to achieve better quality models.

If possible the crossing of paths should be avoided or kept to a minimum, since crossing paths always introduce an unnecessary increase in the perceived complexity.

The following figure demonstrates that with a simple example (from an implementation model). It shows the exactly same process part once with and without a crossing. It is up to the viewer to decide which layout does look better structured and may be more suitable.

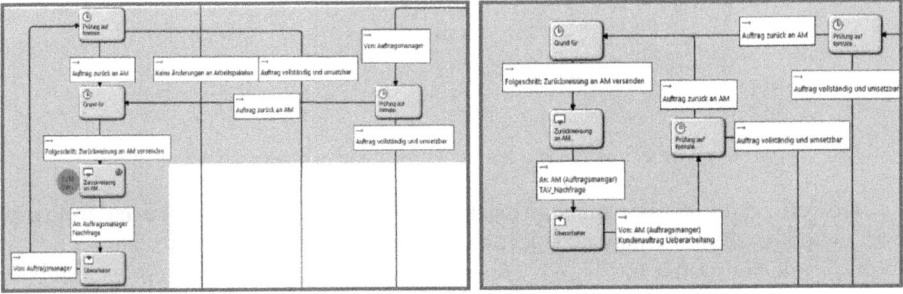

Fig. 12. Same SBD with (left) and without (right) crossing paths

Preventing crossings is of course no easy task. There do exist algorithms to prove or automate the process of arranging states and transitions. Within the Metasonic Build editor there is no such functionality and it is up to the experience of modelers to avoid this kind of construction.

The proposal here is again to add this concept to the teaching canon for good style in PASS graphs as yet another little but not unimportant step in order to improve model quality.

3.4   Joint Routing Back of Transition Arrows

Along the same notion is the following proposal for a modeling convention: In order to reduce the sheer count of visible elements in a graph it is recommended to route paths that have the same target state, together.

The perceived complexity for humans raises at the most elemental level simply with the number of objects to be perceived and understood at the same time[12]. Complex processes of course make it impossible to simply leave out bits, but reducing the number of elements without losing content of the model can help working with the model.

One way to achieve that is by routing transitions together – visual above each other – instead of parallel to each other if they destine in the same state. Under the condition, of course, that the individual transitions descriptors can still be distinguished together with the state they originate from.

---

[12] See for example [3] were the problem is described.

The following figure demonstrates the concept and readers should be able to agree that it simply looks better and simpler.

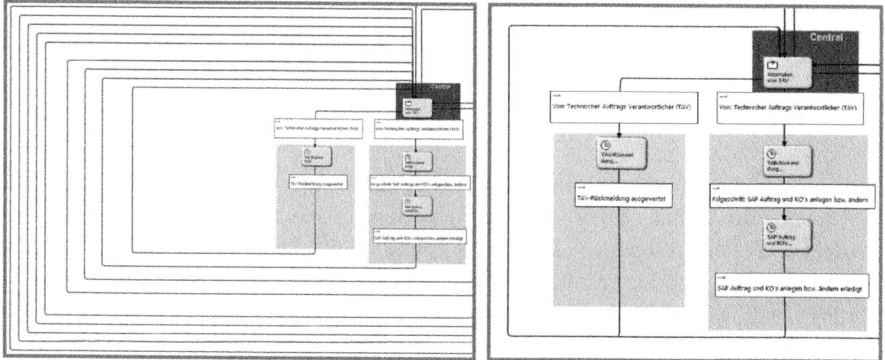

Fig. 13. SID without (left) and with (right) joint transitions to a same state

This has been taught as a convention to our students in order to achieve better models and so far no counter evidence for negative effects has been found.

As the previous proposal this one may seem rather obvious and common sense not worth to be mentioned, especially when taking one glance at Fig. 13. Yet the shown model on the left side did come from an actual live-process and was done by a rather experienced modeler at Metasonic. Thus it is not unlikely for such a style to reappear again if not mentioned. Therefore we think it is worthy to be proposed as another best-practice.

3.5 Principles for SIDs

Of course the same concepts introduced here for SBDs can and should also be applied for SIDs.

Taking the effort to invest a little time and diligence into a model can greatly improve the handling and usefulness of the model. Especially when understandability of the model is a major concern – and that should pretty much always be the case.

It took an experienced modeler roughly 50 minutes to rearrange the SID in the following diagram into the second version.

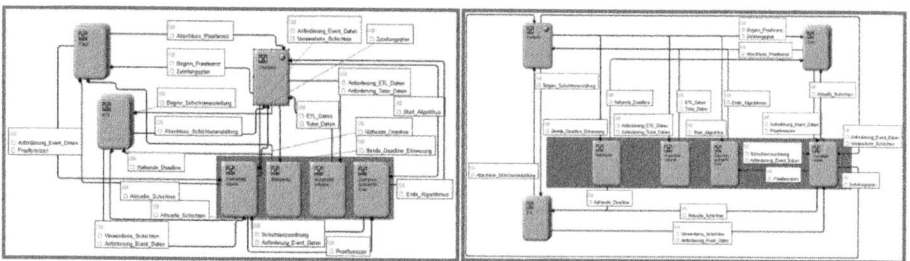

Fig. 14. Unordered (left) and ordered (right) SID of the same process

From personal experience and common sense it can be argued such that effort is worth it as long as more than one modeler is involved and a later reusage or remodeling of a model is probable. Thus caring for good modeling is what we teach our students and what we think should be taught in general, like it has been standard with program code for a long time.

4   Final Thoughts

As stated in the introduction the presented concepts and ideas are meant as proposals and up for discussion. They represent experiences and best practices and lack hard evidence. Yet no counter-evidence was found in the last years either, and the presented ideas incorporate results from different directions of research like human psychology, and, as well as simple common sense.

The main purpose is and was to do a first step in defining what a good S-BPM or PASS model may be – under the conditions that are currently possible and available.

The necessity of such definitions derives from the question of what and how to teach people that are new to S-BPM and PASS. And as argued, a unified standard (or at least a rough direction guide that different experts can agree on) will be more than helpful for that purpose.

Furthermore exchanging experiences about processes and how to model them can be greatly improved in the community if the actual matter of discussion is on the content level and not stopped, or at least hindered, by superficial optical arguments alienating modelers from one another.

For question, comments, and ideas please contact:
`matthes.elstermann@kit.edu`

References

1. Silver, B.: BPMN - method and style, Aptos. Cody-Cassidy Pr., Calif (2009)
2. Miller, G.: The Magical Number Seven, Plus or Minus Two - Some Limits on Our Capacity for Processing Information. Psychological Review 63, 343–355 (1956)
3. Dörner, D.: Die Logik des Misslingens: strategisches Denken in komplexen Situationen. Reinbek bei Hamburg, Rowohlt (2009)
4. Schmidt, W., Fleischmann, A., Gilbert, O.: Subject-Oriented Business Proces Management. HMD - Praxis der Wirtschafsinformatik (266), 52–62 (2009)
5. Fleischmann, A.: Distributed systems: software design and implementation. Springer, Heidelberg (1994)
6. Fleischmann, A.: Subjektorientiertes Prozessmanagement: Mitarbeiter einbinden, Motivation und Prozessakzeptanz steigern, Hanser, München (2011)

Designing a Public Management Process with S-BPM

Stefan Obermeier and Thomas Keller

Hamburger Fern-Hochschule
Alter Teichweg 21, 22081 Hamburg, Germany
{stefan.obermeier,thomas.keller}@stmas.bayern.de

Abstract. Business Process Management is becoming more and more important for the public sector. There are several initiatives to establish solid and secure communication between Government and citizen (G2C), business (G2B) or another Government (G2G). We describe the implementation of a process for the Bavarian Ministry for Social Affairs (StMAS). A dialogue between Government and institutes has to be designed and implemented. The process should be created with S-BPM.

We show the results and discuss the advantage of S-BPM in context of the complex organisation of a federal Government organisation. This shows that S-BPM may be a useful concept for E-Government.

Keywords: subject-oriented business process management (S-BPM), E-Government, G2B, federal proceeding, online request.

1 Introduction

1.1 Motivation for E-Government

The business process management is becoming more and more important for the public sector. Authorities have to exchange data and documents in order to work together. The future of Government is to manage communication between authorities and citizens (G2C), business (G2B) and other authorities (G2G) [1].

The most important use of E-Government is public information: Many portals are used to find an appropriate office for a concern or download documents for a request. These concepts may be helpful but don't use the technical potentials of today. Seamless online communication is not yet established in the public sector.

Business Process Management is a concept to improve processes in enterprises. Different efforts advise to manage Government processes in order to analyse business processes before implementing an IT-application [2]. So Business Process Management becomes more and more relevant for Government, too. A good example is the E-Government-law of Schleswig-Holstein 2009 [3]. It demands that Business Processes should connect Government offices and establish efficient communication.

But the reality falls behind the recommendation of the law. Several projects with complex process architecture failed, the last one was the project "ELENA", which

S. Oppl and A. Fleischmann (Eds.): S-BPM ONE 2012, CCIS 284, pp. 33–40, 2012.

was finally cancelled in December 2011 [4]. The aim had been to collect income data of nearly all citizens of Germany in a central data base and make them available in many processes where the data are needed. The implementation of the data base succeeded but not the implementation of the business processes. At last the project was cancelled and all data had to be deleted.

Therefore we are looking for a new approach. How to manage business processes in Government? The methods of S-BPM could be helpful. There are already attempts in Government to consider S-BPM [5].

In the context of E-Government we could call Business Process a *Public Process*. Nevertheless, in context of public management it is common to use the economic term.

2   Initial Position

The Ministry of Social Affairs (StMAS) in Munich has published a new regulation in 2011 called *"Verordnung zur Ausführung des Pflege- und Wohnqualitätsgesetzes (AVPfleWoqG) vom 27. Juli 2011"* (PfleWoqG [6]):

Since 2011 institutes that offer training and qualification in care of the elderly need federal recognition. An application called "CWA" (*Curriculum Weiterbildung in der Altenpflege*) has to be established to manage the requests and the proceedings. The application should consider a concept of the academy *Hans-Weinberger-Akademie* Munich. The academy describes training modules for different curricula in care of the elderly people. Institutes for qualification may request a certification that it is able to offer adequate training modules.

The IT house of the Ministry of Social Affairs (StMAS) in Munich was mandated to design and develop an application to support the process. Here is experience from other BPM-approaches in the past: comparable requirements were the implementation of an online request for parent subsidies or public-sector services for severely handicapped people. Together with the Ministry and the Hans-Weinberger-Akademie a concept has been developed.

3   Objectives

3.1   Dialogue between Institutes and Government

There are many E-Government-applications with a *"one way"*- communication: citizens send requests and a notification will be filed – the further communication of the operational agents will be handled offline. Figure 1 describes the communication:

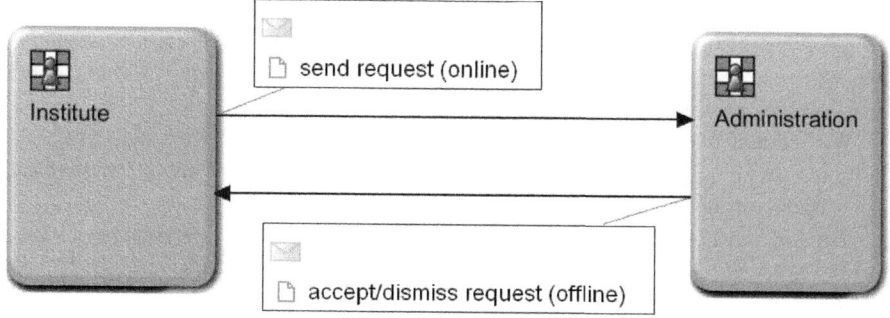

Fig. 1. Classical approach of a business process in E-Government

It is a demand for the project that a dialogue between institute and agent should be established. Questions on the request and problems should be solved easily. It should be considered that a request can not only be accepted or dismissed, but there may be other options as well, f.e. a withdrawal.

3.2   Handling a Distributed Organisation

Having the administrative office close by is an advantage for customers both in business and in Government. Electronic communication may help to bring services all over the world, but many people like to know that there is a service point nearby. Service organisation may be a mixture between face-to-face-service and online-application. As with customer management, Administration of Government should be located in each of the seven districts of Bavaria. Most offices are situated in the bigger towns, so most of the customers have a contact in the local area. Therefore we have a distributed organisation, which has to be managed.

3.3   Minimal Amount of Work

Recognising the overall shortage in staff, clerks have to manage more and more tasks, while there is no sign in the downward trend in headcount. There is the tendency that fewer and fewer people have to deal with more and more tasks. Furthermore: In many public offices decision processes take a long time. Citizens have to wait several months, because an elaborate processing of documents needs a long time. But in our case the decision process must not last longer than four month.

4   Designing and Implementation with S-BPM

The proceeding was designed with S-BPM. Would be S-BPM help to reach the goals? Would a subject-oriented process be simple and efficient enough for the public management process?

After the framework conditions had been determined the project was started with the analysis of the regulation for establishing the process. The process was analysed with the subject-predicate-object-model: We consider only two relevant subjects: *institute* and *administration*.

We learned that the major focus will be put on the communication between the subjects. A common internal behaviour among the administration in the seven districts could not be established.

Together with the Hans-Weinberger-Akademie the minimal information necessary for the proceeding was discussed and outlined. The information was designed as business object.

Each subject has two kinds of behaviour: communication and internal behaviour. They discuss with common objects, details for admission [7]. To keep the process simple office tools like *visio* where sufficient to describe a model which could be validated and implemented in only a few weeks.

Establishing a new law usually means al lot of political discussion and frequently changed drafts. The same happened with the regulation *PfleWoqG*. There were a lot of change requests but few for the communication. Most changes corresponded to documents or data of the business object.

The integrated S-BPM-cycle [7] is useful to repeat the analysis phase several times. The phases were quite short. In most of times the process and the application were robust and showed that they were well designed. Only in few cases the implementation had to be modified.

5   Results

5.1   Designing Dialogue – No "One Way" Data Transfer

Classical online-based communication between Government and citizen usually ends with forwarding the request. The citizen may fill in several data fields and press the button "send" at last. The administration gets a printed document and the further proceeding stays paper-bound and offline.

Several questions cannot be answered: What happens if the applicant withdraws his request before it is being processed? What to do with obviously wrong "joke" requests? How to build an application in a workgroup? Is it possible to send additional requests whose objectives are consistent with the first one?

We consider two subjects: "institute" and "administration" and examine the communication status on each side. The different status depends on the behaviour of the subject: an institute may withdraw its request and inform the office concerned. This may be handled in different ways: an early withdrawal may delete the request, the cancellation at a later time has to be confirmed. Figure 2 shows the communication based process in detail.

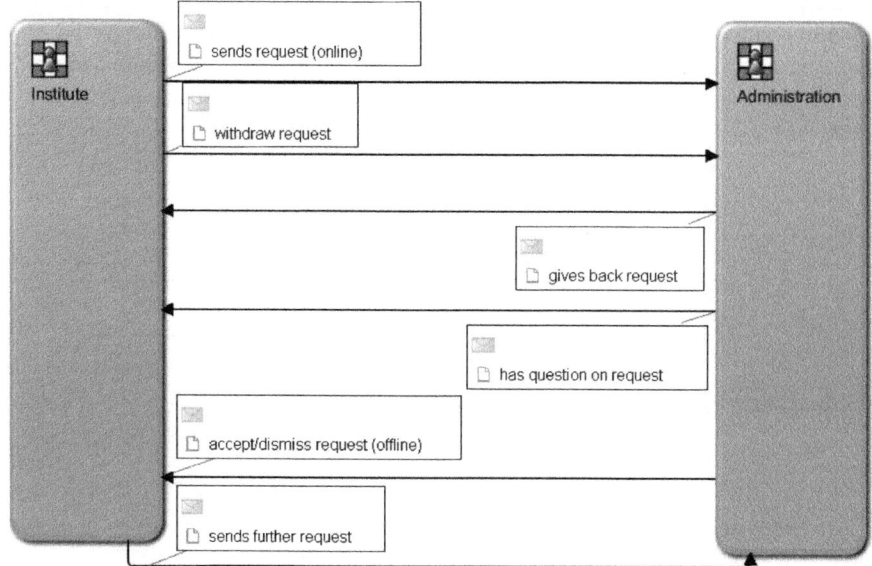

Fig. 2. New approach of the business process

Having set the focus on the communication between two subjects, we enable dialogue from institute to administration. Government is no longer a "black box" for the citizen. Is it possible to become a part of the business process.

5.2   Handle Heterogeneous Organisations

The proceeding is distributed to seven district head quarters of Bavaria: *Oberbayern, Niederbayern, Oberpfalz, Oberfranken, Mittelfranken, Unterfranken* and *Schwaben*. The head quarters are independent organizational units. They got the mandate for the proceeding of CWA. The Ministry only has the professional surveillance of this organisation. The districts, by contrast, operate independently. That means for the process management that it is not allowed to intervene in the internal behaviour of the district. It is up to the respective district administration how they manage their work.

S-BPM distinguishes between internal subject behaviour and communication behaviour [6]. A subject has to perform different activities, for example an agent will accept a request, he will inspect documents etc. On the other side the employee has to communicate with the institutes, at least he has to send the decision to the institute.

When designing the process with S-BPM it is allowed to reduce the process to communication behaviour only. This restriction simplifies business process at an acceptable level. Furthermore the workflow that has to be implemented is not very complex.

The seven districts not only operate independently and the internal behaviour of the subjects may differ. Furthermore there are districts which have to include the decision of additional subjects (Figure 3). For example the district *Oberpfalz* has to coordinate its decision with the administration of education. The additional subject would have to be integrated in the business process. Usually you would have to ignore certain characteristics of a single subject, otherwise you have a lot of particular functions to implement.

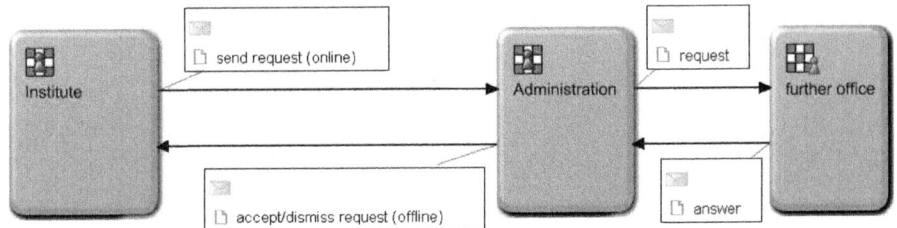

Fig. 3. Hidden communication with a third subject

In other situations each district may consult the ministry or another government unit. It would be very difficult to plan these exceptional processes and to model this business process with flow-orientated methods.

The same may happen with the subject institute: An institute may also have further communication with a third party: It may be compulsory to consult an advocate to discuss legal consequences. It seems to be impossible to integrate all aspects in a flow-orientated process. The realization would be too expensive and generate no significant benefit.

S-BPM enables a modelling method *"reduction to visible behaviour"* [7]. That means, further subjects may be involved in the business process, but their internal behaviour and even communication with further subjects need not be noted.

5.3   Working together with Shared Objects

The institutes need to prove that they are able to offer trainings in care of the elderly. That is possible in different ways: They could send in all reports about the certifications of the trainer, all information about the training facilities with size of the training rooms etc. The mass of information would overwhelm the administration. And worse: How to decide about two institutes where one has sent many details and another has sent less but nevertheless enough. And further: How to decide whether a single trainer is able to teach the curriculum?

The decision should be based on the following data:

• Information about institutes and offices
• Information about equipment
• Information about trainers and their qualification
• Information about the head of offices and their experience

These data are treated as a business object as suggested in S-BPM [7]. With this business object the institutes need to prove that they are able to offer trainings and otherwise the administration has to check whether the request could be approved.

With the defined business object, the amount of information is very limited. The institutes are enabled to send the obligatory information within a short time, the administration can check the request easily. Furthermore an automatic check helps the administration:

5.4   Automatic Check of the Business Object

The Business object will be evaluated by an automatic competence check. The competence check validates the object if it is plausible. If f.e. a certain qualification for a special curriculum is not provided, then the administration will be informed. In that case the administration should contact the institute and draw the attention to the fact that the request is not complete.

The competence check will not replace the clerk: some anomalies can only be detected by a human being: one institute got a successful competence check. But the clerk noticed that one trainer had incredibly many qualifications: a nearly completed law degree, he was qualified in psychology, care of the elderly and more. In this dubious case the clerk should require further documents to review the request.

The competence check about the business object shortens the processing time and helps the districts to manage their new task.

6   Conclusion

S-BPM can help establish business processes which are easy, efficient and manageable. The focus will be set on the subjects. Especially for Business Processes it is very helpful to change the view from flow-orientated representations towards communication-orientated models, like S-BPM.

S-BPM could even be a milestone for Open Data: In the example of CWA the citizen shares common data with the clerks in the administration. Both subjects have access to the same data and may communicate about it.

By far the larger share of work was the designing of the process. With the guideline described with S-BPM is has been possible to finish the implementation in only a few weeks. The product could be offered a long time before the regulation was passed in 2011. The communication model of CWA could easily be transferred to other online requests. Further proceedings with business and business processes may profit from S-BPM.

Shortcomings: We learned that a simply structured business object will makes a concise and quick decision possible. However it was noted, that another process – the recognition of equivalence – was more complex. This process has not been dealt yet but it is estimated that a similar approach may be not sufficient because the designing of the business object may be too complex.

References

1. Reinermann, H., von Lucke, J.: Speyerer Definition von Electronic Government, Forschungsinstitut für öffentliche Verwaltung, Speyer (2001)
2. Bayerische Richtlinien zur Softwareentwicklung, München (2012)
3. Gesetz zur elektronischen Verwaltung für Schleswig-Holstein vom 08 (EGovG) (July 2009)
4. Official website of ELENA, http://www.das-elena-verfahren.de/ (January 15, 2012)
5. Handy, B., Dirndorfer, M., Schneeberger, J., Fischer, H.: Methods of Process Modeling in the Context of Civil Services by the Example of German Notaries. In: Schmidt, W. (ed.) S-BPM ONE 2011. CCIS, vol. 213, pp. 281–295. Springer, Heidelberg (2011)
6. Verordung zur Ausführung des Pflege- und Wohnqualitätsgesetz, AVPfleWoqG vom (July 27, 2011)
7. Fleischmann, A., Schmidt, W., Stary, C., Obermeier, S., Börger, E.: Subjektorientiertes Prozessmanagement. Hanser-Verlag München (2011)

Development of an Integrated Procedure Model for Optimization of Distribution Processes within Industry

Uwe Brunner[1] and Katharina Schiefer[2]

[1] FH Joanneum GmbH
Industriewirtschaft/Industrial Management
Werk-VI-Strasse 46, 8605 Kapfenberg, Austria
uwe.brunner@fh-joanneum.at
[2] Verein Netzwerk Logistik, Region Süd
Wehrgrabenstraße 5, 4400 Steyr, Austria
katharina.schiefer@vnl.at

Abstract. The requirements placed on logistics increased in recent years due to highly dynamic and competitive markets. A high degree of flexibility with regard to the processes needed in order to fulfill customer needs and to stay competitive is paramount. Consequently the knowledge of one's processes and realistically achievable potential is vital in order to meet the challenges of the market. Whereas flow chart oriented methods allegorize conventional methods for modeling the actual processes, the subject-oriented business process management can be seen as a high potential alternative. Distribution logistics in particular offers many options and permeations to design optimal transport processes; from the choice of the distribution structure to miscellaneous inventory and transport concepts. In the course of optimization the logistical costs should be reduced but, simultaneously not fall below a defined service level.

The focus of the publication is to present an integrated procedure model, optimizing the processes for industrial distribution centers by minimizing the transport costs and striving for continuous improvement.

Keywords: distribution logistics, process procedure model, supply chain management, process optimization, subject-oriented business process management.

1 Introduction

A continuous improvement of logistics processes and a systematic cost reduction program in all sections of logistics department have become necessary due to heightened competition in increasingly dynamic markets. Especially a few support processes of a company, which generate added value, have to be tracked in order to keep the costs at a minimum. As the logistics costs account for between 5% and 15% of the sales volume, it is of utmost importance to control them continuously [1].

S. Oppl and A. Fleischmann (Eds.): S-BPM ONE 2012, CCIS 284, pp. 41–56, 2012.
© Springer-Verlag Berlin Heidelberg 2012

In industrial companies, distribution logistics belongs to the afore mentioned support processes, with a huge scope for optimization: beginning from the choice of the distribution structure to miscellaneous measurements in inventory and transport. The optimization and the associated requirements depend on the balance and structure of orders. It is characterized by quantity, inhomogeneity and disparity of orders [2]. The higher the order quantity, the easier advantages can be realized in terms of material and goods flow. The more different and inhomogeneous the order composition and the chronological appearance become, the more complex are the issues for distribution logistics to be optimized. In addition to that, it is important to minimize internal cost drivers which influence the company's processes and procedures: the number and amount of the applied load and transport units; the characteristics of the material transported; the number of transports and the handling frequency [1]. As a result, more organizational effort and higher transport costs are required for delivery items with a low weight. Hence, the following central scientific question arises: With which procedure model is it possible to reduce the transport costs in an industrial distribution center?

Many approaches for optimizing the internal processes of a company are available in the literature but they are not fitting for the special requirements which are demanded by the distribution logistics. Therefore – and as within the first step – it is necessary to define what a process is and in detail, what the process of distribution looks like. A *process* is defined by several authors in very different ways: **Davenport** describes a process as an amount of activities with a chronological and areal appearance, a beginning and an end as well as a defined input and output [2]. Related to the description of **Davenport**, **Osterloh/Frost** define a process as a bundle of activities with a structured order of cross-functional activities with a beginning and an end as well as a defined input and output [3]. **Hammer/Champy** sum up the companies processes as such activities, which generate a value for the customer. All in all it is important not only to define the several steps of a process, but the interfaces within the supply network as well [4].

This paper deals with the suggestion how to optimize the distribution logistics by developing a procedure model which tends to fulfill the requirements of industrial needs.

2   Basic Principles

To work on the optimization of distribution processes it is important to have a specific procedure model, which follows the detailed regulations of distribution. Therefore the basic principles are split into to the two parts in this chapter: the *Procedure Model* and *Distribution Logistics*.

The principles of process management were analyzed, because the change of a process/organization calls for a deep methodical knowledge of process management including its procedures. For this purpose, three different procedure models – by **Becker/Kugeler/Rosemann**, **Brunner** and **Füermann/Dammasch** – were described and compared to find a basis to develop a new procedure model. The model should meet the requirements of the distribution logistics in order to answer the scientific central question.

The principles of distribution logistics are defined to identify the duties, the objectives and the responsibilities involved in the processes to find out what is important and necessary for performance to be significantly improved. The principles comprise the distribution structure, the transport systems with their influencing variables, supply chains, transport and inventory indicators.

2.1   Procedure Models

In order to implement improvements within a process oriented organization, project management tools are commonly used methods. Whether the realization of each project is successful or not depends on a target-oriented coordination of several project phases. Initiated with brainstorming; set milestones for the implementation and a well-thought-out concept is indispensable [6]. Such concepts are frequently used in the course of project management and process management, as well as in the course of software engineering, thus making them widely accepted procedure models. They support organizational processes to reach the optimization target step by step respectively. Additionally, they manifest different characteristics reliant on the complexity of the project.

All in all a procedure model describes an approach, which helps to realize the project incrementally and which provides the order of the subtasks to find the appropriate solution for an optimized process [7].

Procedure Models for Business Process Management

The first model for business process management described is an integrated model by **Becker/Kugeler/Rosemann**, who were faced with the problem of having to reduce and control the high complexity regarding the modeling of information. Thereby the communication channels as well as the choice of the model types are relevant. They present a highly detailed concept for optimizing the business process with a logical design. For this reason the risk in terms of failure is reduced significantly. The level of modeling detail is left to the requirements of the company itself. However, when there are excessive levels of detail, a resource bottleneck occurs.

The realization of comprehensive organizational projects calls for knowledge of the company's targets, which go along with the targets of the process. Should targets diverge; a failure of the project would be the consequence. Besides the targets of the process, the individual goals and prerogatives of employees and the management, as well as those of a social nature must be considered. Fulfilling these targets ensures both the success of the project as well as attaining acceptance in the company [8].

The second model described is called "Accelerated Process Modeling (APM)" for a quick and effective modification of business processes according to economic circumstances, developed by **Brunner**. The model requires intrinsic knowledge of business process management so that the model can be applied without any difficulties. A carefully chosen process team is indispensable for all business process management projects. The moderate level of detail can make implementation more difficult for those companies which have no experience with process management [9,10].

The third model was created by **Füermann/Dammasch.** The model has a very high level of detail and presents an integrated procedure for process management implementation and execution. Step by step the model shows, what has to be done at each stage and which benefits (pitfalls and tips) are achievable. The procedure model is a complex sequence of issues, which requires a lot of human resources. This aspect is not necessarily a disadvantage. By incorporating of the employees, motivation rises and the process improvements where the employees collaborate actively are retained more often than top-down executed process improvements they were not involved in. In addition to this the assigned responsibility creates strong mutual trust and acceptance across the whole company is guaranteed. After implementing the improved process, companies will not be left unattended as advice for maintaining improvement is provided. In addition to the several steps provided by **Füermann/Dammasch,** proposals for various useful methods and tools are given and explained [11].

End-to-End Process Management Approach

An approach, which do not go along with the above mentioned, is the end-to-end process management approach and therefore mentioned separately [12]. While the others focus on the definition of sub-processes with their input-output-transformation and on the continuous improvement of all processes, the end-to-end process management approach is based on real end-to-end processes, beginning from the customer's requirements to the completed value performance. **Bergsmann** vitiates the aspects of the before mentioned authors and represent the established process management approaches as follows:

- Processes are not definable arbitrarily; they are not a simple input-output-transformation, but they are based on the requirements and on the performance of the customers.
- Company's functions and processes are no irreconcilable opposites. Both are necessary and complement each other in regard of the structure of a company.
- The organization of the process is not the aim and also not the consequence of process management. It is a very inefficient form of organization and because of that it does not appear often in practice.
- Process management is an element of the secondary organizational structure and supports together with others the integration function in a company.
- Real process management does not improve all processes continuously and does not aim for the highest level of maturity, but it concentrates on the important processes and develops them target-oriented.

Comparison of Procedure Models

Details are listed in the following table to able to compare the three different procedure models. It gives an overview of the main procedure steps; the applied methods and tools; advantages and disadvantages, as well as the required knowledge.

Table 1. Comparison of different procedure models for business process management

	Becker / Kugeler / Rosemann	Brunner	Füermann / Dammasch	Bergsmann
Name	Process oriented integrated organizational design	Accelerated Process Modelling	Integrated optimization of business processes	End-to-End process management approach
Requirements	• No	• Knowledge of process management	• No	• Customer's requirements • Target of the organizational structure • Knowledge of the business processes
Process Steps	• Arrange modeling • Strategic, organizational framework • Analysis, modeling of actual process • Target-process, process optimization • Process oriented structure • Restructuring • Continuous process management	• Definition and boundary • Organization framework • Methods for modeling • Modeling and Optimization	• Arrange process work • Describe processes • Structure processes • Control processes and continuous improvement • Stabilize processes	• Identify end-to-end business processes • Organization of the company • Process responsibility • Integration of sub-processes, organizational unit, IT-systems, products and services, resources, ... • Manage the process management • Manage the processes
Tools / Methods	• Value-added-chain-diagram • Technical-term-model • Trading-H-model • Reference-model • Cause-effect-diagram • ARIS	• Petri-Net • Flowchart • EPC • Procedure-chain-diagram • Value-added-chain-diagram • Data-flow-diagram • Function tree	• Process structuring • Brainstorming • Workshop • Flowchart • Process reengineering • Result-customer--matrix • Control plan • Plan-do-check-act-cycle • Trend-card • U-Layout • Cause-effect-diagram • Action-plan	• Interview • Workshops for collecting data • Document analysis • Survey • Process slip • Process inspection • Reference-model • Process Performance Monitoring • Process Mining

Table 1. *(continued)*

Advantage	• High level of detail	• Quick • Easy • Low human-resource allocation needed • Multifunctional applicable • Room for maneuver	• High level of detail • A lot of technics and alternatives	• Includes customer's requirements • Improve and develop only the most important processes
Disadvantage	• Time-consuming, cost-intensive • High human-resource allocation needed • IT driven	• Low level of detail (for companies without knowledge of process management)	• Time-consuming • Medium human-resource allocation needed	• Due to the new approach some processes could be missing
Usage	• Commonly used and widely accepted from experts	• New approach useful for consultants and university projects	• As strongly related to business and new, probably insertable henceforth	• Additional method to existing procedure models with a strong focus on customers needs

2.2 Distribution Logistics

Based on literature sources, the main tasks and general problems in the field of distribution logistics are [13]:

- Location of distribution warehouses
- Order management
- Consignment and packaging
- Transport
- Warehouse management
- Securing goods for transport

All these tasks must be taken into consideration, if distribution processes have to be improved or optimized. The location of distribution warehouses could be seen as the strategic part of the distribution tasks. Basically, various aspects of infrastructure will strongly influence the choice of the distribution warehouses. Based on that, the other tasks of distribution logistics especially transport costs, handling costs and warehouse costs would be significantly influenced. The huge potential benefits of optimization within the distribution processes could be divided into internal savings and savings concerning intercompany processes in the supply network. A supply network consists of the material, information and financial flow in the network. For the purposes of this paper, material flow is highlighted due to the fact, that they represent the main potential for cost reduction. The next chart (Fig. 1) shows in detail the composition of industrial logistics costs [14] and the following chart (Fig. 2) some important factors for the design of material flow networks within the supply network [15].

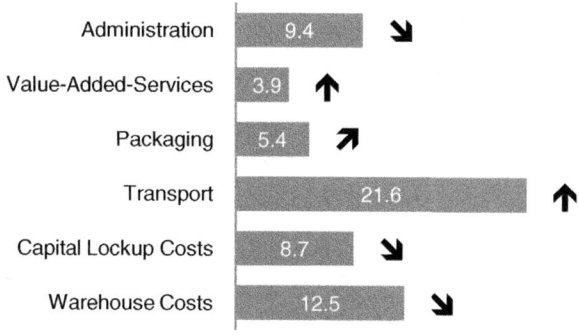

Fig. 1. Percentage of industrial total logistics costs and properties

The figures pointed out in the above chart (Fig. 1) focus on industrial logistics costs. As mentioned, transport costs are the largest factor of logistics costs (21,6%), followed by warehousing costs (12,5%), administrative costs (9,4%) respectively, as well as capital lockup costs (8,7%) which are strongly related to warehouse activities [16,17]. The arrow next to the bar shows the overall tendency for the different cost areas. Another study describes the composition of logistics costs similarly. Also transport costs and operational logistics costs, followed by capital lockup costs are the main cost components of the general logistics costs.

All in all the main cost areas within the logistics costs are strongly related to distribution activities. Products must be transported, stocked and handled through the material flow system when they are distributed. This is why the distribution system could be seen as a driver for all afore mentioned costs. Therefore, this article focuses on a procedure model to improve distribution processes. To know which cost drivers are responsible for the distribution costs – in detail transport (increasing tendency), warehousing (decreasing tendency), capital lockup costs (decreasing tendency) – some company-internal and external factors must be named. The chart below (adapted) shows the internal cost drivers for distribution processes in the small doughnut:

- Complexity of processes: Distribution processes are becoming more and more complex, an increase in orders. At the same time order volumes are decreasing which leads to the fact that changes in the order structure of companies are business trends in time and therefore responsible for new and cost-effective requirements for logistics systems.
- Capacities: Companies have to deal with the never ending story of target conflicts between the production needs and distribution needs or demand. Production departments are driven by the idea of constant demand and thus far constant production outputs; but distribution is driven by customer needs, especially to fulfill the varying demands of the market. The required production flexibility leads more or less to some nonproductive or cost efficient processes within manufacturing.

- Stocks: In the past many companies became aware of the importance to control and decrease stock. Companies meanwhile have realized a lot of potentials to lower stock, but were not always able to find a professional balance between availability and low inventory.
- Lead time on the one hand directly influences process costs yet on the other hand is very important for customer's satisfaction in terms of the order management processes of a company.

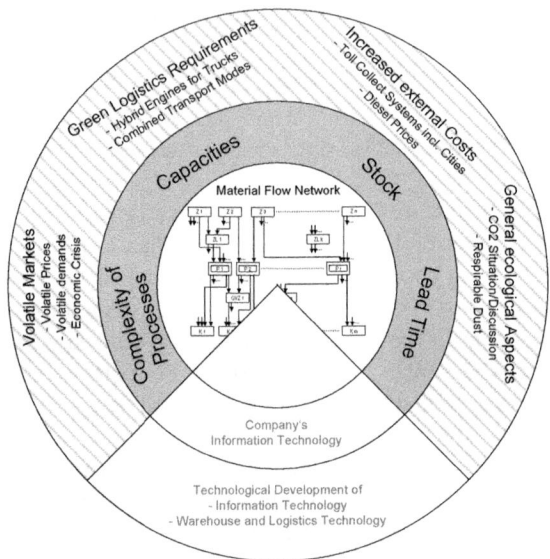

Fig. 2. Indications for the design of supply networks (adapted from Brunner/Seiner, 2005)

Of course the internal cost drivers mentioned above could be generally controlled by the management of a company. However, there are additional external drivers which are unswayable in most instances – shown in the bigger doughnut of the graph (Fig. 2) – to be discussed:

- Volatile markets: Volatile markets are responsible for certain variations in customer demands. Therefore production capacities must be very flexible because only availability can satisfy the customer; it is very easy to change suppliers due to strong market competition.
- Green logistics requirements: Forwarders and carriers are forced to offer their customer's added value based on the argument of acting sustainably and using natural resources efficiently. This leads to new and "green" technologies which are generally connected to higher TCO-costs. Using combined transport modes instead offers the opportunity to decrease transportation costs for longer distances.
- Increased external costs: There are two main aspects responsible for increasing freight rates in road and railway transportation. We have to pay tolls for trucks on motorways and then there is the issue of fuel prices rising – of course with fluctuations, but in long term – continuously.

- General ecological aspects: Transport and traffic are under public scrutiny, because the emissions are attributable to the enormous CO_2 problem of our planet. Furthermore, in some regions of Europe there is heightened public awareness and debate of emitted fine particular matter, which is said to represent a serious health risk. Based on that, further political measures in terms of traffic regulation are to be expected, which is why those aspects have to be taken into consideration within an optimization process in distribution.

3   Development of an Integrated Procedure Model for Optimization of Distribution Processes within Industry

Based on the existing procedure models in chapter two, a special procedure model is to be created to optimize distribution processes (Fig. 3). Therefore the model consists of two different gross phases. The first one "Logistics Process Management" provides the basis for the implementation of optimized distribution logistics processes. The procedure model of **Becker/Kugeler/Rosemann** was most adequate in terms of itemization and therefore chosen as a guideline for the developed procedure model.

The second was configured as a continuous procedure, because it is necessary not only to implement a new process, but also to improve it periodically. For this purpose, improvements in the material flow must be analyzed regularly thus requiring key accounts to be restructured. The activities focus on reducing transport costs and can be used for industrial distribution centers.

Phase four of *logistics process management* is simultaneously the first phase of *continuous process management*. The model hence adds up to seven phases shown below and described further. Regarding to the end-to-end business process management, there is on the one "end" the customer's requirement and on the other "end" the generated performance to the customer.

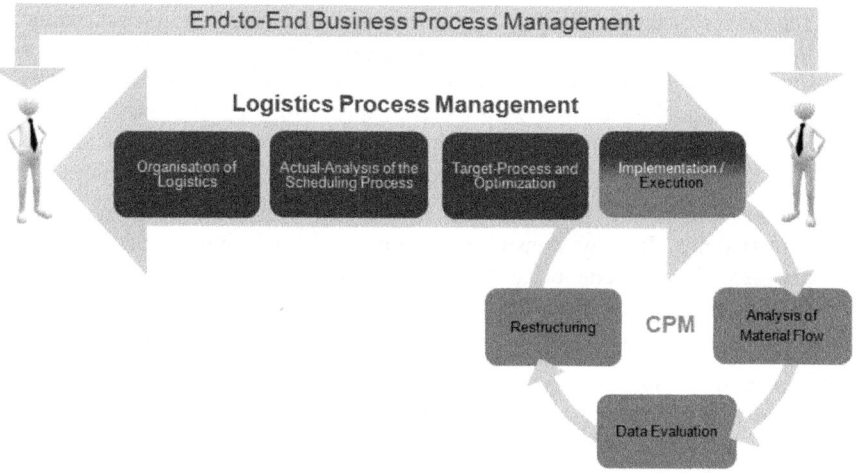

Fig. 3. Integrated procedure model for optimization of distribution processes within industry

The several phases of the model will be described in detail on the following pages.

Phase 1: Organization of Logistics
In the first step it is necessary to define the general framework. The framework includes, besides issues with project management, the definition of system boundaries as well as the adherence to the initial position of the company in relation to logistics organization.

(1) System Boundary

Distribution logistics deals with the transportation of goods from a source to a sink. In the case of a reduction in transport costs, it is important to differ whether the costs for the internal transport or the external transport are in the focus of the optimization. It makes an enormous difference if the costs for the transportation between the manufacturing and the storage facility or if the costs from the facility storage to the costumer are considered. Furthermore, it must be defined at which point in the process of the disposition starts and where it ends.

(2) Distribution Structure

The reason for warehousing in industry range from guaranteeing the delivery reliability over advantageous delivery conditions in the purchasing to protection against delivery failure. The position of a warehouse in the logistics process can be very different. They can exist as transshipment warehouses, as production or distribution warehouses, as warehouses near the production site or as retail warehouses. Furthermore, the modeling of an optimized distribution process depends on the distribution structure in terms of whether central or local. Transportation costs, as well as the effort involved, are much higher in the case of central warehousing than in local warehousing. The inventory on the other hand is subordinate resulting in a high quality delivery service [18].

Local solutions lead to shorter transport distances and, as a consequence to shorter delivery times. The big disadvantage is that the inventory of all warehouses in sum is much higher [19].

(3) Transport Systems

The means of transport which come into operation were chosen according to the requirements of the customer, to the transported goods and to the capacity of the source as well as of the sink. As a consequence not all means of transport come into consideration. It rests with the company, which criteria are more important and to determine on this basis, which means of transport will be used [20].

(4) Infrastructure

Another important point in the course of optimization is the prevailing infrastructure. It may constrain the choice of the means of transport. The commercial road vehicle has the biggest advantage with regard to loading and discharging stations, because it can independently go from point door to door, unlike ships, trains or planes.

(5) Transport provider

To provide the transport service and the transportation itself do not account to the core competence of an industrial distribution center. Therefore these issues are mostly outsourced to a third party. A special matrix model can be helpful if the decision either to make or buy is undetermined. On the one axis the company's own degree of competence compared to those of the provider is plotted. On the other axis the strategic meaning of the considered logistics function for the company were plotted. Depending on in which segment the point falls, the decision of whether to outsource should be taken [21].

(6) Transport orders
This point deals with the way transport orders are transmitted. A connection over an enterprise-resource-planning-system (ERP-System) in terms of supply chain management (SCM) shows high potential. By transmitting information of material which is ready for dispatch via electronic data interchange (EDI), the transport times can be reduced and all information for planning the routes is available for the transport provider immediately.

Phase 2: Actual Analysis of the Scheduling Process
The second phase of the procedure model tends to answer following question: "Does a documented scheduling process exist?

- If yes, what does it look like and where are the weaknesses?
- If yes, what does is look like and is it maybe still optimal? In this case phases three and four will be skipped and the cycle of continuous process management begins.
- If no, the modeling of an optimal scheduling process is necessary.

As the scheduling process is a support process of an industrial distribution center, a high level of detail is not necessary. However, all important information should be contained to identify the weaknesses and room for improvement. The following parameters in table 2 have to be considered:

Table 2. Parameters for a checklist in the course of actual-analysis [22]

CHECKLIST	
Strategic framework	• customers market • transport market • efficiency
Customers data and market data	• mass flow
Transport process	• transport capacity • criteria for choice of the mean of transport • definition of sources and sinks • collection of standard routes • transport time • transport costs
Handling process	• loading time per traffic carrier • handling costs
Storage process	• kinds of storage • storage capacity • analysis of loading and unloading zone • hauling means • loading staff • loading costs

A flow chart offers a simple method for modeling the actual process. It is filled with information, which can be searched for in different ways. The information search is important because only on the basis of relevant facts can the actual and prospective situation of a company be estimated. Within the scope of the actual analysis for the procedure model, the interview method is an easy way to receive the information needed. With this method, the information is exchanged verbally, directly and immediately. Depending on how interviews are conducted, the method combines flexible design and quick action. During the information search it is necessary to filter which information is important, what is unimportant and what is good to know. Furthermore, the data volume should be reduced (less is more) and the information should be obtained on several levels [23].

As a high potential alternative the subject-oriented business process management method can be consulted. While the flow chart deals with objects and events, the subject-oriented method focusses on the subject, which describes process roles, participants of processes or process actors. All these subjects have essential characteristics like the exercised communication, the exchanged information as well as the action itself. Subject-oriented processes define which tasks the participants of a process have to execute and which interaction to coordinate the tasks is necessary. Activity based charts were already implemented in the 90s, but they did not become accepted in practice, even though the processes are designed very precisely and the static aspects were considered as well as the dynamic aspects [24].

Phase 3: Target Process and Optimization
After modeling, the actual process and the target process have to be designed goal-oriented in order to solve the following problem in industrial distribution centers: a lot of different consignees were provided with a little amount of goods. This solution lies in the bundling of the flow of materials and a consequential reduction of individual trips. There is no general valid target process modeled in this phase because it depends on the logistics organization and is different from company to company. The focus of this phase lies on *how* the optimized process can be reached. The optimization includes the following steps shown in Fig. 4:

Fig. 4. Procedure to reach the optimized target process

By bundling the flow of material a consolidation transport is formed and the following distribution of the goods to the consignees arranged by a local logistics provider. In the case of an optimized scheduling process it is necessary to measure two parameters: the delivery service and the costs per transported quantity unit. By bundling, and through an adapted transport cycle, it is possible that the delivery service declines below a defined level. The costs per unit of quantity have to be collated before and after the implementation of the new process for comparison.

(1) Analysis of the Material Flow
    The material flow analysis has to find out what is transported, to whom and in which quantities in order to detect patterns in the transport process or in the orders of the customers respectively. **Stabauer** alludes in this case to the deduction of attributes

and their connection with the complexity of the process. The complexity of corporate sub-processes depends on the input (number of materials in the purchasing process, number of positions, ordered weight and the frequency of the orders) on the one hand and on the output (number of transports) on the other hand [25].

Figure 5 shows the several components which have to be regarded in the course of a current analysis. After collecting the current data, a planning phase, divided in gross and real planning can be started [26].

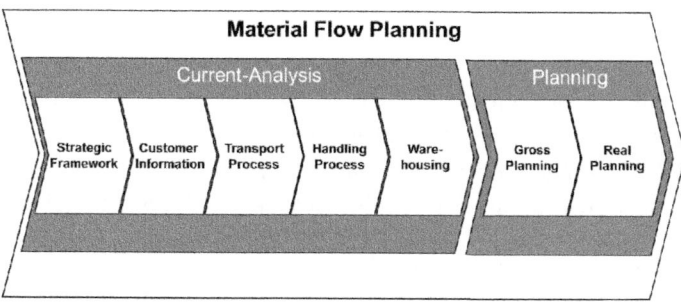

Fig. 5. Planning of the material flow (adapted from Noche/Druyen, 2004 and Arnold, 2003)

(2) ABC-Analysis

As the focus of the procedure model is on those customers, often received deliveries but in low quantities, an ABC-analysis is to be done twice. Once, in order to find out which quantities the customers received in relation to the whole delivered quantity. As the quantity is not meaningful on its own, the ABC-analysis is be done a second time related to the number of the delivery items. For classification the annually delivered quantity to the customer is opposed to the whole annual delivered quantity. Customers who received 10% of the whole delivered quantity are classified with "A", customers with 20% of the whole delivered quantity with "B" and the rest with "C". The classification for the delivery items is carried out in the same way.

After the operated analysis the results were transferred in the following matrix (Fig. 6):

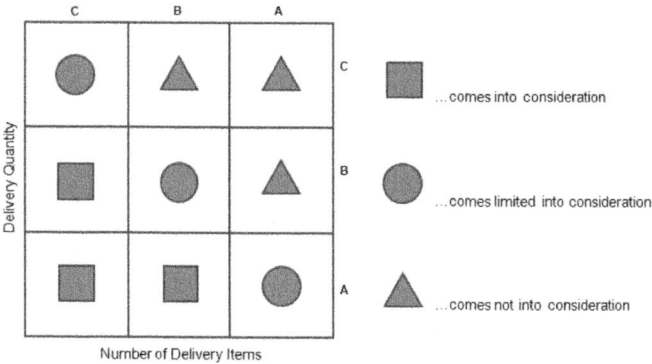

Fig. 6. Quantity-Position-Matrix

(3) Bundling of the Consignees

Based on the quantity-position-matrix those consignees are filtered, which come into consideration for a consolidation transport. They are summarized by areas, regions, cities or other meaningful criteria. After that a consolidation transport to an assembly point is arranged and finally the goods were distributed to each consignee.

(4) Logistics Provider

The transports from the assembly point are provided by a local logistics provider. Because of the proximity to the customers and the shorter transport ways respectively, it is much easier for the local logistics provider to plan routes. Furthermore, the delivery system as well as the planning, controlling and monitoring of the transports are guaranteed.

(5) Consolidation Transport to an Assembly Point

Because of the consolidation and the delivery to a shared assembly point, the costs for the main run should be now be lower, as the shipment from the warehouse to the assembly point is more extensive from the warehouse directly to the customer. The distance of the following transport from the assembly point to the customer is comparatively low. This should also have a positive effect on the transport costs.

Phase 4: Implementation / Execution

After evaluation the results of the flow of material and the ABC-analysis the new process can be implemented to any user-defined point in time in the course of a big-bang-strategy. The execution of the flow of material and the ABC-analysis has no influence on the organizational structure of the company. But the execution implicates some additional process steps, which have to be managed by human resources. The question arose if the analysis can be managed in the course of operational tasks or if the analysis can be done by the sales department in the course of sales activities.

Phase 5 to 7: Continuous Process Management

The last three phases of the model reflect procedure, which was already applied in phase 3 – the optimization of the target-process. These phases will be iterated in defined time intervals in the course of a continuous improvement of the process. The intervals have to be adapted not least to the economic circumstances. In case of significant deviations in overturn the analysis of the material flow has to be started by all means, otherwise every six months for example, to react with changes in order and customers structure accurately timed.

- Phase 5: Analysis of the material flow
- Phase 6: ABC-Analysis based on delivered quantity and number of delivered items
- Phase 7: Restructuring the costumers.

The last phase of the procedure model contains the new arrangement of those costumers, who come into consideration for a consolidation transport. If the costumers differ from the first survey, maybe a new assembly point has to be defined.

The cycle is complete with phase 1 of the continuous process management, respectively the execution phase 4 of process management.

4   Recommendations

To summarize the authors would like to give three main recommendations. First it is necessary to point out, that general procedure models are less useful for optimization tasks than procedure models for distribution logistics. However, the general models provide a sound basis for the development of a distribution logistics procedure model. The developed model for distribution processes was created by transferring and interpreting certain steps and aspects from the general model, thus providing the main idea and also motivation for this article. The problem which remains is that the translation process from *general* to *specific* requires a certain degree expertise of people working with and in logistics distribution processes, because only they can deal with the industrial needs and common methods or tools used in the procedure of optimization of distributional processes.

Secondly we could recommend this model for different tasks within distribution processes. To point out some of them could show the variety of opportunities for its usage. The model can generally be used for optimization in the supply chain with focus on distributional networks, but also for warehouse locations or questions like if a centralized or decentralized distribution structure is more efficient. The model could be used for across a broad range of industries, but it must be taken into consideration, that different sectors need different structures; of course the respective output from the procedure could differ greatly from case to case.

Third it must be mentioned that it is a simple method, also with some sub-procedures in it, but without any further investment calculation methods.

Further industrial research is seen in the development of special procedure models for other processes within the supply chain or the supply network, e.g. in cases of procurement or purchasing activities.

References

1. Gudehus, T.: Logistik. Springer, Berlin (2007)
2. Kummer, S., Grün, O., Jammernegg, W.: Grundzüge der Beschaffung, Produktion und Logistik. Pearson Studium, München (2010)
3. Davenport, T.H.: Process Innovation. Reengineering Work trough Information Technology, Boston (1993)
4. Osterloh, M., Frost, J.: Prozessmanagement als Kernkompetenz. Gabler Verlag, Wiesbaden (2006)
5. Hammer, M., Champy, J.: Business Reengineering. Die Radikalkur für das Unternehmen, München (1994)
6. Litke, H.-D.: Projektmanagement – Methoden, Techniken, Verhaltensweisen, evolutionäres Projektmanagement. Hanser Verlag, München (2007)
7. Jenny, B.: Projektmanagement in der Wirtschaftsinformatik, vdf Hochschul-Verlag, Zürich (2001)
8. Becker, J., Kugeler, M., Rosemann, M.: Prozessmanagement – Ein Leitfaden zur prozessorientierten Organisationsgestaltung. Springer, Heidelberg (2008)
9. Brunner, U.: The Need for Process Management in the Course of EU-Enlargement. Leykam Buchverlag, Graz (2005)

10. Tschandl, M., Pérez Alonso, A.: The challenge of EU-Enlargement. Leykam Buchverlag, Graz (2005)
11. Füermann, J., Dammasch, C.: Prozessmanagement – Anleitung zur ständigen Prozessverbesserung. Hanser Verlag, München (2008)
12. Bergsmann, S.: End-to-End-Geschäftsprozessmanagement. Organisations-element – Integrationsinstrument – Managementansatz. Springer, Wien (2011)
13. Schulte, C.: Logistik – Wege zur Optimierung der Supply Chain. Franz Vahlen Verlag, München (2009)
14. Straube, F., Pfohl, H.-C.: Trends und Strategien in der Logistik – Globale Netzwerke im Wandel. Deutscher Verkehrs-Verlag, Bremen (2008)
15. Brunner, U., Seiner, M.: Effizienzsteigerung und Kostenreduktion durch prozessorientiertes Redesign überbetrieblicher Materialflüsse in der Distribution. In: Wissenschaftliche Themenhefte zur Logistik, Otto von Guericke Universität Magdeburg, Magdeburg (2005)
16. Miebach Studie: Österreich in Europa – Chancen und Stärken in der inländischen Produktion und Logistik, Frankfurt am Main (2011)
17. Chopra, S., Meindl, P.: Supply Chain Management – Strategy, Planning, and Operation. Pearson Education, New Jersey (2010)
18. Küpper, H.-U., Hoffmann, H.: Ansätze und Entwicklungstendenzen des Logistik-Controlling in Unternehmen der Bundesrepublik Deutschland, Die Betriebswirtschaft-Verlag (1988); The objectives of warehousing as result of a survey in 1986, carried out by Küpper/Hoffmann
19. Alicke, K.: Planung und Betrieb von Logistiknetzwerken – Unternehmensübergreifendes Supply Chain Management. Springer, Berlin (2005)
20. Pfohl, H.-C.: Güterverkehr: Eine Integrationsaufgabe für die Logistik. Erich Schmidt Verlag, Berlin (2003)
21. Voigt, S.: So treffen sie die richtige Wahl. In: Logistik Inside, Heft (June 2007)
22. Fischer, D., Dittrich, L.: Materialfluß und Logistik: Potentiale vom Konzept bis zur Detailauslegung. Springer, Berlin (2004)
23. Andler, N.: Tools für Projektmanagement, Workshops und Consulting – Kompendium der wichtigsten Techniken und Methoden. Publicis Publishing Verlag, Erlangen (2009); He gives an overview over different methods for information search, how and when they can be applied
24. Fischer, H., Fleischmann, A., Obermeier, S.: Geschäftsprozesse realisieren – Ein praxisorientierte Leitfaden von der Strategie bis zur Implementierung. Friedr. Vieweg & Sohn Verlag/FWV Fachverlage GmbH, Wiesbaden (2006)
25. Stabauer, M.: Logistische Kennzahlensysteme unter besonderer Berücksichtigung von Nachhaltigkeit. Diplomica Verlag, Hamburg (2009)
26. Noche, B., Druyen, J.: Planung von Materialflusssystem. In: Koether, R., Arnold, D. (eds.) Materialfluß in Logistiksystemen. Springer, Berlin (2003-2004)

How to Learn to "Speak S-BPM" - Lessons from Language Learning

Edith Stary

VS Pantzergasse - Individualized Learning Support
Pantzergasse 25, 1190 Vienna, Austria
edith.stary@aon.at

Abstract. S-BPM promoters claim a stakeholder perspective for modeling processes and organizational development. By moving actors or active system components to the center of interest, functions and business objects are specified in the context of subjects and their behavior. Although the correspondence to natural language sentence semantics is evident, stakeholders in their routine tasks need to be trained to express their business processes in a subject-oriented way, in particular taking into account task-relevant communication with other stakeholders. Moreover, function-oriented developers need learning support, as S-BPM represents a novel BPM paradigm. Findings from language learning facilitate not only structuring information according to standard sentence semantics, but also designing learning environments through principled S-BPM learning support.

Keywords: language learning, modeling, standard sentence semantics, didactic guidelines.

1 Introduction

Recent articles on S-BPM reveal the orientation towards stakeholders and their capabilities constructing subject behavior specifications (cf. [10]). Empirical results stemming from S-BPM case studies and application designs indicate positive effects on organizational velocity (cf. [22]). The stakeholder orientation for organizational change processes is grounded on the short distance to natural language (representations). Not only can natural language sentences be generated from subject-oriented representations (cf. [32]), but also each bundle of activities of the BPM life cycle (cf. [11]) can be mapped to natural language representations, due to the continuous use of the (diagrammatic) S-BPM language. Various stakeholders could profit from such seamless support (cf. [25]):

- employees (assigned to functional roles in business processes), as they are fed back the same type of information they put in for organizational change
- change managers while negotiating and mediating contents of change
- requirements analysts, as natural language facilitates mutual understanding between stakeholders and various communities (share/stakeholders, IT specialists / organizational developers, controlling / operation etc.)

S. Oppl and A. Fleischmann (Eds.): S-BPM ONE 2012, CCIS 284, pp. 57–76, 2012.
© Springer-Verlag Berlin Heidelberg 2012

- managers, as they need not to spend effort on transformation processes while participating in or monitoring business development.

Either starting with process analysis and proceeding with modeling, validation, and execution, or exporting natural language from S-BPM models reflecting organizational change, guidelines or rules need to be enforced to ensure valid semantic representations und mutual understanding. The development of such guidelines might be a straightforward task once a formal representation scheme exists, but is even more challenging when natural language is the starting point of modeling activities, as it is the case for S-BPM. In general, human development of language skills is a learning challenge, due to the nature of natural language and its contexts of use ([3], [14]). However, expressing modeling-relevant information in terms of standard sentence semantics is crucial for effective S-BPM, otherwise modeling problems well known from other BPM developments, such as BPMN (cf. [24]), might occur.

Learning processes for constructing S-BPM models using standard sentence semantics of natural language have hardly been addressed explicitly. Even recently, only few authors have addressed learning processes and education material related to model construction, when we revisit the contributions of the latest S-BPM-ONE conference [30] to that respect. Consequently, a closer look to existing findings on language learning could reveal how learning processes should be designed for stakeholders to become informed members of organizational S-BPM change communities.

In section 2 some resources from language learning are introduced. In section 3 the role of natural language in S-BPM with respect to modeling activities is recaptured, revealing basic requirements for understanding the use of the S-BPM modeling language. Both inputs are required for informed model construction and respective learning designs. As the findings from language learning allow formulating principles, S-BPM language learning processes can be structured according to transfer-oriented guidelines. In section 4 the major principles are detailed and various S-BPM implementation proposals are introduced. Their exploration and evaluation is still subject to further studies, as sketched in the conclusion of the paper.

2   Language Learning and Development

The origin and complexity of natural language makes it exceedingly difficult to isolate factors responsible for language learning. For example, in natural language processing, semantics, syntax, and phonology operate in parallel [12]. Hence, language needs to be learned, built-in structure guided in early stages (cf. [4]), while structure that is available in experience is acquired later on [37]. Thus, both innate endowment and learning contribute to language acquisition, the result of which is still a sophisticated body of linguistic knowledge.

In education there is still a controversial debate to what extent standardized forms of language, such as the regular structure of sentences, should be trained to achieve language competence (cf. [8]). Although this issue is quite crucial to capture standard sentence semantics, it is only one aspect of successful mastery. Understanding in verbalized interaction requires four different categories of knowledge (cf. [16]):

(i) grammatical knowledge
(ii) lexical knowledge
(ii) 'world' knowledge
(iv) context knowledge

Grammatical knowledge consists of rules to express semantically valid content. Of particular importance are the mutual relationships of words in a sentence enabling sentence semantics, as they form the baseline of understanding (see below). Lexical knowledge allows recognizing the meaning of words, in contrast to expressions, sentences, and paragraphs. Knowledge about the 'world' subsumes experiences and cultural achievements including social roles, values, and conventions.

Finally, knowing the context of language content brings in situation-specific information. 'The context provides a pool of shared information on which both parties to a conversation can draw. The information, both contextual and general, that a speaker believes his listener shares with him constitutes the cognitive background of his utterance' ([20], p.125). This type of information also highly influences the dynamics of interaction, as it is self-referential to the system the speaker and the listener are part of.

The acquisition of a grammar is not only based on an analysis of the linguistic input but also depends on an innate structure that guides the process of language acquisition [17]. This dependency needs to be considered as inherent to language learning, even when a person learns different languages. The competence to use already acquired languages has to be attributed to an individual, being able to grasp innate structures (cf. [6]). The innate structure seems to be strongly influenced by the origin of languages. For instance, the subject as the agens in linguistic utterances has been strongly tied to the predicate, as Schneider [31] already indicated for the Greek language. The Greek term hypokeimenon for subject denotes the subject as subordinate to the predicate. This also holds for Latin sentence semantics (- see http://www.thg.hn.bw.schule.de/index.php?option=com_content&view=article&id=95& Itemid=120&limitstart=2), and can still be found in modern languages, such as Spanish.

Looking at educational practice language skills are acquired in several steps in institutional settings (cf. [4]): listening, drawing, imitating, and self-creating utterances up to second grade, reflective speaking, documenting, and writing in a grammatically structured way from the second grade on. Such stepwise acquisition corresponds to the evolving human capabilities in language acquisition (cf. [34]). Of particular interest for S-BPM is the initial identification of predicates, as it occurs through the 'I-lens', since in the beginning of standard sentence semantics production the person speaking is identical to the subject of an uttered sentence. The decoupling of activities from the self occurs in subsequent development steps. The decoupling seems to be a major milestone in language learning, eventually due to the historically tight structural coupling of predicates to subjects (see above).

Maria Montessori cared about the development of language in her concept of "Children's Houses", as she intended to replace the incorrect use of language and the subsequent correction procedures, and defect language through guided self-construction processes of learners. In her institutional setting she has provided various 'exercises for the corrections of language' ([21], p.325f):

(a) *'Exercises of Silence*, which prepare the nervous channels of language to receive new stimuli perfectly;
(b) *Lessons* which consist first of the distinct pronunciation by the teacher of *few words* (especially of nouns which must be associated with a concrete idea); by this means clear and perfect *auditory stimuli* of language are started, stimuli which are *repeated* by the teacher when the child has conceived the idea of the object represented by the word (recognition of the object); finally of the provocation of articulate language on the part of the child who must repeat *that word alone* aloud, pronouncing its separate sounds;
(c) *Exercises in Graphic Language*, which analyze the sounds of speech and cause them to be repeated separately in several ways: that is, when the child learns the separate letters of the alphabet and when he composes or writes words, repeating their sounds which he translates separately into composed or written speech;
(d) *Gymnastic Exercises*, which comprise, as we have seen, both *respiratory exercises* and those of *articulation.'*

Her approach to learn the correct use of a language is a multimodal approach, both, with respect to perception and language construction, and with respect to the use of material, as the exercises in Graphic Language show (see (c) above). The latter supports understanding of fundamental structures, and thus, syntax finally constituting meaning.

The acquisition of semantics is accompanied by mental model activation [20] *and* imagination through generating inner pictures [33], finally leading to picturing [26]. The latter competence allows generating a visual representation required to relate to individual 'world' knowledge [15]. It transforms perceived information into a conscious representation of the 'world' regardless of the symbols used for transmitting the information. Hence, mental models are figural mental representations of complex, while systemically structured information relationships, with sentence-based information as baseline (*ibid.*)

The visual correspondence of factual information to language symbols is particularly important in the early stages of language acquisition, as physically recognizable things can be drawn and allow an immediate mapping from 'world' entities to language items. Later on, such correspondences are not required anymore [38], as inner pictures can be generated by abstraction from perceived information. This capability allows creating and interpreting abstract models, such as S-BPM specifications.

Language learning processes should not only be guided by findings how language is acquired, they should also be supported by corresponding materials, arranged in a carefully prepared environment [21]. According to Tomlinson [35] so far, only few language learning materials are actually guided by learning principles or coherent content, although they rely on didactic fundamentals, such as clear presentation and active, relevant language practice. Language learning support reflected in materials should take into account:

i) theories of language acquisition and development;
ii) principles of teaching;

iii) our current knowledge of how the target language is actually used;

iv) the results of systematic observation and evaluation of materials in use.

Applying theories of language acquisition can contribute positively towards the principled development of learning support materials (cf. [19]). They facilitate the effective use of language when

- exposing learners to language in authentic use
- helping learners to pay attention to features of authentic input
- providing learners with opportunities to use the target language to achieve communicative purposes
- providing opportunities for outcome feedback
- achieving impact in the sense that they arouse and sustain the learners' curiosity and attention
- stimulating intellectual, aesthetic and emotional involvement [35]

So-called grammar consciousness-raising tasks can be used for learning fundamental structures and recognizing problematic grammatical features with the provision for meaning-focused use of a target language [13]. Since task performance equals grammar teaching in promoting gains in knowledge of a language structure, standard sentence semantics should be introduced as a concept to represent meaning in itself rather than being a syntax construct.

In this context, the role of communication frameworks seems to be essential. One way to achieve successful conveyance of meaning is to consider regular communicative tasks as opportunities for communicative language exchange. Results from investigating consciousness-raising tasks dealing with sentence structures indicate that the tasks successfully promoted both proficiency gains and target language negotiated interaction in the participants (cf. [7]). Interestingly, the negotiation quantity has been determined by the combination of task features present rather than by the nature of the task content. Thus, grammar consciousness-raising tasks can be recommended as one way to train standard sentence semantics, promoting communicative language exchange.

Communicative settings facilitate generating and conveying meaningful information through natural language structures, such as sentences. However, the efficiency of information transmission requires the conscious distinction between syntax (sentence form) and the type semantics (sentence meaning) (cf. [9]). The effective distinction form the basis for efficiency in information transmission ([5], [23]).

Finally, the developmental transition from an initial universal state of language processing to one that is language-specific also requires social interaction. According to Kuhl [18], relating human language learning to a broader set of neurobiological cases of communicative development, the social brain 'gates' the computational mechanisms involved in language learning. Social interaction has to be considered essential for language learning, since it affects motivation and content handling.

Motivational factors are the attention and arousal which in social interaction induces learning. The handling of content addresses the information content of natural settings – the relations between auditory labels, objects, and speakers' intentions that are available during language-based interaction. Hence, live situations provide specific information that fosters learning. Social signals enhance learning because they provide enriched information, such as the referential information. However, so far it is not clear, whether the underlying mechanism is the increased motivation or the enriched information that social settings provide, or both.

While contingency and interactivity matters, it seems that a richer social environment extends the duration of the sensitive period for learning (cf. [21]). Amato [1], in his study combining artificial grammar and sentence comprehension methods investigated the learning and online use of probabilistic, nonadjacent combinatorial constraints. Participants learned a small artificial language describing cartoon monsters acting on objects. Self-paced reading of sentences in the artificial language revealed comprehenders' sensitivity to nonadjacent combinatorial constraints, without explicit awareness of the probabilities embedded in the language. These results show that even newly-learned constraints have an identifiable effect on sentence processing. The rapidity of learning reveals the role of interactivity in language learning.

Further inputs to resolve interaction issues stem from recent studies, such as exploring CLIL - Content and Language Integrated Learning [7]. They bring up the crucial role of preparing learning support by revisiting content-subject methodologies. CLIL as a fusion of subject didactics, features emerging content in an explorative social setting, which brings us back to the initial reflection on the role of material. Encoding didactic knowledge learning material could serve as cognitive anchor point and social baseline reference to interactive learning processes - as already proposed and out to practice for fundamental skill development by Montessori [21] - see also www.youtube.com/watch?v=yTYCMHiKI18 and www.virtualmontessori.com.

3   Modeling in S-BPM

Subject-oriented business process models aim to bridge the gap between describing, documenting, and processing collaborative work processes. When expressing their understanding of work behavior they have to meet several challenges (cf. [10], [11]):

- They need to able handling *standard sentence semantics* - which they are able once they have acquired natural language skills.
- They have to understand communication as the process of *exchanging messages between actors and systems* - which they are capable once they collaborate and use mail, in particular e-mail.

Then they can reflect what they have expressed in terms of standard sentence semantics and communication behavior, due to the precise control flow that results from the specified communication patterns.

In S-BPM stakeholders start using standard sentence semantics when representing business processes. They use subjects, predicates and objects. The S-BPM language comprises these constituent elements of natural language sentences [11], termed essential model elements as they lay ground for model understanding [10]. These elements capture communication qualities and behavioral patterns, focusing on the interaction of subjects occurring in the technical and/or organizational environment.

While models formulated in natural language terms allow for universal use, due to the standard semantics for sentences (comprising subject, predicate and object), in S-BPM a certain quality of information needs to be captured using this structure, namely level 2 of sentence semantics ([28] in [10]). It addresses agency, predication and theme as semantic roles. It can be based on level 1 structures. For instance, 'Mary is an accountant' is located on level 1, whereas 'Mary writes an inquiry request' is located on level 2. The latter embodies the activities related to a certain situation in its predicate part. This requirement might be a challenge for stakeholders when they need to express their daily business or organizational change proposals in proper S-BPM language format. It requires the following understanding of modeling (cf. [10]):

- Giving a *subject* is the starting point for describing a situation or events.
- Activities are described by *predicates*.
- An *object* is the target of an activity (predicate).

A crucial implication when using subject-predicate-object sentence semantics concerns passive voice that is often used in natural language communication. Humans use passive sentences in case they do not reflect, or want to ignore who acts or triggers an action in a certain situation. In S-BPM, modelers are forced to use active voice (=complete standard semantics) for sentences, in order to provide coherent model descriptions.

Finally, current tradition in BPM is to specify business processes primarily based on functional descriptions, e.g., using function trees as starting point for modeling (cf. [27]). Hence, existing modeling approaches tend to focus on predicates or objects, and adding the subject for natural language explanations of the represented information. It might require some effort to shift from such an understanding to role-specific interactions, as communication is considered essential when persons or systems in specific roles (inter)act according to S-BPM.

Models play a crucial role in S-BPM. They are generated or processed, respectively, along a chain of various activities [11]:

- *eliciting* and representing knowledge about work and its organization
- *analyzing* process description with respect to specifity, accuracy, and completeness
- *validating* models whether they could be executed in a stringent way
- *executing* models allowing hands-on experience of specifications
- *embodying* processes in organizational and technological settings of organizations
- *monitoring* with respect to expected achievements
- *simulating* in order to explore alternative or novel ways of task accomplishment

Looking at these bundles of activities which represent development phases of organizational development, the benefit of natural language specifications that can be used throughout becomes evident. Once in each phase of development all stakeholders can participate due to their natural language capabilities, the transparency and traceability of organizational development processes can be ensured or even increased.

4   Towards Principled Development of S-BPM Learning Support

S-BPM language learning concern acquisition activities in the context of work activities subjects are engaged in, namely in terms of level 2 standard sentence semantics (behavior orientation - see section 3). Learning support can be considered from a process and material perspective (see section 2), with material as reference point for didactically relevant activities. They follow specific learning principles facilitating learning support development and finally, coherent skill development.

In the following we apply and adapt several principles and guidelines, proposed by Arnold [2], McGrath [19], and Tomlinson ([35], [36]), in order to support capacity building in S-BPM language learning. While focusing on theories of language acquisition and elaboration particularities for S-BPM modeling language learning can be recognized. Hereby, we take into account category i) and iii) for development as given in section 2, namely theories of language acquisition and development, and our current knowledge of how the target language is used. Each of the principles is introduced initially from the language learning perspective, and then exemplified for learning how to 'speak S-BPM'.

4.1   Provide Meaningful and Comprehensible Input of the S-BPM Language

In order to acquire the ability to use a (target) language effectively learners should be provided with opportunities to build up experience of the language being used. This could be done in a variety of ways for modeling purposes, e.g., by providing mutual reflection for stakeholders performing identical tasks. Learners need to be able to understand enough of this input to gain positive access to it, and it needs to be meaningful to them.

Learners also need to experience particular language items and features several times in meaningful and comprehensible input in order to acquire them. Each encounter helps to elaborate and deepen awareness, and facilitates the development of hypotheses needed for acquisition and required for building behavior capacities in work situations.

For material development in language learning spoken and written text should be provided. They allow direct experience of how the language is used. Such an endeavor supports achieving outcomes in intended text types and genres related to domain topics, themes, events, locations etc., as they are likely to be meaningful to the learners.

For learning to 'speak S-BPM' meaningful and comprehensible inputs concern

(i) relevant *language constructs*
(ii) *structure* of the language constructs,
(iii) their *context of use*.

The constructs are primarily subjects, predicates, and objects. Additional items, such as properties of subjects, could be used to illustrate the application of these core elements. The structure of the language constructs concerns standard sentence semantics. The context of use is the business and work environment at hand.

A typical example that could be provided is the application for vacancy in an organizational setting (cf. [10]). Of particular importance for the understanding in this case is to focus on the exclusive use of standard sentence semantics. It might require corrective interventions animating persons to reconstruct the meaning in terms of standard sentence semantics. A traditional or initial reflection of the vacation application process could start with: 'When I want to go on holidays, our group decides. It includes informing my co-workers and the department. In some cases my request is propagated to the management.'

Besides containing passive voice (last sentence), the start sentence is unspecific to the interaction sequence and details of subject behavior. S-BPM compatible elements to be used in that context could be: 'I need to inform my co-workers before sending the official request to the head of the department.', and 'The head of the department passes the request on to the line manager, in case more than 2 persons in the same position are absent.' The first sentence clarifies the start of the behavior sequence with respect to who needs to be informed first. The second sentence not only reveals the required active form of describing (inter)actions, but also details the constraints under which the request (i.e. the (business) object) is passed on to another actor in the process.

Consequently, providing meaningful and intelligible input of the S-BPM language needs to be implemented from a structure and behavior perspective. Besides the standard sentence semantics (structure) all relevant communication items (behavior), such as passing on the vacation request to the manager, needs to be represented for building up S-BPM language capacity.

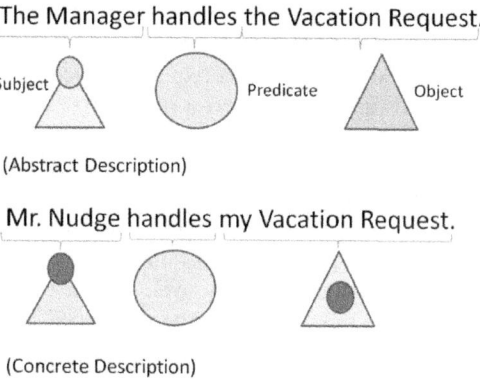

Fig. 1. Enforcing Intelligibility of Structured Sentence Semantics

Figure 1 shows an application of providing meaningful and comprehensive input of standard sentence semantics to acquire S-BPM language understanding. The learners are provided with sentences both, on an abstract and a concrete level of work abstraction. 'The Manager handles the Vacation Request.' is an abstract representation of a work task. It contains a functional role description ('Manager') representing the subject, an activity ('handles') representing the predicate, and a general object identifier ('Vacation Request'). The used symbol set contains respective elements, indicating the level of concreteness. The symbols are placed below the relevant part of each sentence, such as the circle below 'handles'.

'Mr. Nudge' handles my Vacation Request.' is a representation on a concrete level for an employee. His/Her manager is Mr. Nudge, and it is his/her Vacation Request. Accordingly, the symbols can be adapted through intensifying parts of the general representation. The dark dot indicates the level of concrete description for the subject and the object; the predicate's layout does not need to be adapted (in this case). In this way, patterns of intensity can be used to recognize the level of concreteness when describing work situations.

Of particular importance are mixed occurrences, i.e. different levels of abstraction for subject and object within a single sentence, as they need to be clarified when proceeding with further S-BPM activities. Concrete subjects and objects are required for organizational and technical embodiment according to the S-BPM life cycle [11]. Abstract representations are traditionally used in the course of process analysis and design.

4.2   Language Exposures Should Be Authentic and Contextualized

Learning should occur in situations revealing how the language is typically used. If the language is used in that authentic way it allows exemplifying particular language features which in turn allows learners to use language constructs effectively. Although it might be useful to focus attention on a feature of a language by removing distracting difficulties and complexities from sample texts, since a contrived focus helps learners to focus on salient features, prior and subsequent exposure to those features in authentic use is essential.

S-BPM modeling language exposures should refer to work situations that can be experienced in organizations. They should be scoped to be experienced as self-contained units, such as handling a vacation request. Typically, event-driven scenarios trigger communication and functional behavior in organizations. These scenarios need to comprise actors or information systems, activities to be set, and business objects that are manipulated and exchanged in the course of task accomplishment.

Typical authentic exposures are role-specific behavior descriptions, as shown in Figure 1. We assume an employee applying for holidays in a traditional way: He/She starts by sending a vacation request to his/her manager. It can be expressed by the sentences provided in the figure on both layers of abstraction, according to the employee's capabilities. Such description can be developed for different settings and work situations employees are part of. Employees might receive sample descriptions, such as the ones in Figure 1, before starting to describe their own work. Routine tasks should be described before tackling complex work situations.

Language use is determined and interpreted in relation to its context of use. Decontextualised examples do not contain sufficient information about the user, the addressee(s), the relationships between the interactants, the setting, the intentions or the outcomes for them to be of value to the language learner. We can, for example, think of at least three different interpretations of, "Send her the request. Let her handle it." But we might not know what it really means nor why the speaker has used the imperative until we know who is saying it, to whom it is said, what the relationship between speaker and receiver is, where both are, what has happened before, and what the objectives of the interaction are.

Only samples of language capturing context of use can provide learners with the information they need to develop awareness of how a target language is actually used. Hence, for S-BPM scenarios the set of events required to trigger actor- or system-specific behavior should be identified. In addition, the outcome of the activities should be transparent, in order to understand the rationale for acting, including the handling of business objects.

Once language exposures are authentic and contextual, learners might re-cycle existing language items and features. However, they are likely to follow different styles of perception and acquisition. To ensure effective learning a variety of authentic use case can help. For S-BPM these cases have to be related to work situations embodying actor- or system-specific activities.

As already indicated with respect to the traditional use of language for the vacation application the difference between model-specific descriptions focusing on standard sentence semantics and the traditional way of describing situations needs to become evident when studying S-BPM language material. Although learners use identical language constructs and follow the same grammar, they need to experience the different qualities on the level of descriptive representations. As such, simple re-cycling of language items and features might not be sufficient for effective S-BPM language acquisition.

It could also help to demonstrate the difference by showing validated diagrammatic models and their translation to natural language. This leads to the following learning support steps:

1. Make use of *established, however personalized scenarios* of task accomplishment
2. Develop a sequence of sentences representing the *scenarios' semantics*
3. Identify *re-cycled language constructs* and features
4. Discuss the *shift in quality*
5. Provide *additional information on that shift*, e.g., through validated and executable S-BPM models

Such a structured development of authentic and contextualized learning environment preserves individually perceived information on work situations, as stakeholders can develop personalized engagement for the scenario. Their vocabulary capturing situational semantics can be used for description, which in turn allows grasping possible shifts in representation, if not meaning when using S-BPM language constructs.

4.3   Provide Affective and Cognitive Engagement in the Learning Experience

If the learners do not think *and* feel whilst experiencing the language they are unlikely to build up respective capacity [2]. Thinking whilst experiencing language in use helps to achieve the deep processing required for effective and sustainable learning. Moreover, it helps learners to transfer high level (cognitive) skills such as predicting, connecting, interpreting and evaluating to language use.

Feeling enjoyment, pleasure, empathy, or being amused, excited and stimulated are most likely to influence (language) acquisition positively, whereas feeling annoyance, anger, fear, opposition and sadness is more useful than feeling nothing at all. Ideally, learners should be experiencing positive affect in the sense of being confident, motivated and willingly engaged even when experiencing 'negative' emotions. The following guidelines should be followed with respect to affectively and cognitively challenging learning support:

- *Prioritize the potential for engagement* by, for example, basing a unit on a text or a task which is likely to achieve affective and cognitive engagement rather than basing a learning unit on a topic selected from a training course syllabus or prefabricated occupational learning environment
- Make use of activities which *get the learners to think about what they perceive, and to respond to it personally.*
- Make use of activities which get learners to think and feel *before, during* and *after* using the target language.

S-BPM learning support could comprise stories or scenarios in which the starting point for developing each learning task is a potentially engaging spoken or written text, eventually accompanied by a video illustrating work scenarios and/or explaining relations to S-BPM modeling. Readiness activities help learners to activate their minds prior to experiencing the (text) information, giving learners an holistic focus to think about when experiencing the content and encouraging them to articulate their personal responses to the input before going on to use it to stimulate their own language production, e.g., applying S-BPM language constructs.

Once affective and cognitive engagement in the learning process occurs, learners can benefit from using those mental resources which they typically utilize when using the language they are familiar with. It not only facilitates building up new capacities, but also allows intervening in an appealing way, e.g., correcting misunderstandings when using passive voice, when practicing the S-BPM language.

When using the initially acquired language learners typically make use of mental imaging (e.g., generating pictures in their mind), of inner speech, of emotional responses, of connections with their own lives, of evaluations, of predictions, of personal interpretations. When learning and using another language than the initially learnt learners typically focus narrowly on linguistic decoding and encoding, 'constructing' standard sentences in the sense of composing according to structure rather than meaning.

Multi-dimensional representations of languages experienced and used can enrich the learning process in ways which promote sustainable capacity, the transfer from learning activities to real life use, and the development of the ability to use the language effectively in a variety of situations. They also help to increase the self-esteem which derives from performing complex language communication tasks.

In the originally learnt language individuals use an 'inner voice' to give their own voice to what they hear, read, and speak. They also need an own voice to make plans or decisions, to solve problems, to evaluate, to understand and 'control' the environment and to prepare outer voice utterances before saying or writing them.

When persons 'talk' to themselves they use a restricted code which consists of short elliptical utterances expressed in simple tenses with the focus on the comment rather than the topic, on the predicate rather than the subject (cf. original binding of subjects to predicates discussed previously). Introspection is content and context dependent, implicit, partial, vague, novel and salient to individuals.

However, learners acquiring a new language rarely use an inner voice for the language to be learnt until they reach an advanced level – though there is evidence that the use of an inner voice of the language to be learnt at lower levels can enhance performance in the new language and can be facilitated by coaches and materials, e.g., providing elements compatible to inner images or patterns.

As visual imaging in language use and acquisition plays a very important role in original language learning and use, it also can be beneficial for learners acquiring another language. These learners can even be trained to use visual imaging to improve their learning and make practical use of the new language. Consequently, the acquisition of a language with respect to inner imaging and voicing can be facilitated in various ways:

- Make use of activities which get learners to visualize and/or use inner speech before during and after *experiencing* a written or spoken text.
- Make use of activities which get learners to visualize and/or use inner speech before during and after *using* language themselves.
- Make use of activities which help the learners to *reflect* on their mental activity during a task and then to try to make more use of mental strategies in a similar task.

S-BPM materials should lead to activities which encourage and help the learners to visualize content, to talk to themselves in inner speech, and to make connections with their work situation. For example, before asking learners to study work situations they should be asked to visualize their interpretation of relevant items characterizing a situation, and then to talk about how they felt about it. For the sake of seamless learning support they already might use diagrammatic S-BPM elements or symbols supporting the acquisition of standard sentence semantics.

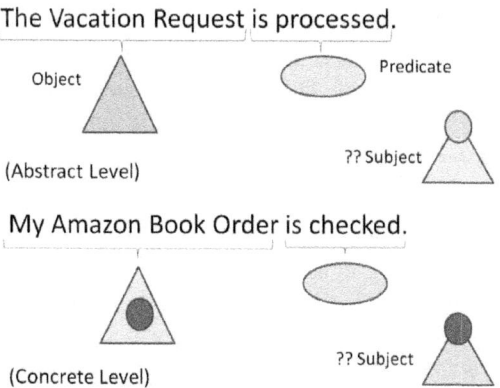

Fig. 2. Recognizing Patterns for Standard Sentence Semantic Completeness - a Grammar Consciousness-raising Task

In Figure 2 a crucial case for S-BPM is shown. Many languages, such as German allow skipping the subject when describing processes. For instance, the abstract description 'The Vacation Request is processed.' does not contain the subject performing the operation. The same holds for the example on the concrete level 'My Amazon Book

Order is checked.' Consequently, learner might be used to express themselves in such an indirect way, in conformance with their inner voice or mental model.

The language symbols can help to recognize patterns from original language utterances as incomplete, both on the concrete, and the abstract level of description. In a corresponding grammar consciousness-raising task the provided elements by a learner, e.g., 'The Vacation Request is processed', are marked according to their occurrence, e.g., with an object and predicate symbol. Then, the missing symbols are presented to the learner from the entire set of language learning symbols, e.g., 'subject', preceded with question marks, as shown in Figure 2.

After the learner might have recognized how standard sentences need to be completed semantically, he/she should provide the missing elements and information. In this way, experiencing and reflecting are intertwined, leading to cognitive and emotionally appealing action learning.

Finally, in addition to recognizing incompleteness with respect to standard sentence semantics, learners could be guided to switch from passive voice to active voice when using language. Again, the language learning symbols can be used. In case a passive voice is spotted this S-BPM-'defect' can be visualized deforming the predicate symbol, as shown in Figure 2 through the ellipse for 'is processed' and 'is checked'. It might either be set by the learner or be provided in language learning material.

4.4   Learners Can Benefit from Noticing Salient Features of the Input

In case learners notice for themselves how a particular language construct is used, they are more likely to develop their language awareness, and they are also more likely to achieve readiness for acquisition. Such noticing is most salient when a learner has been engaged in a text affectively and cognitively and then returns to it to investigate its language use. This is likely to lead to learners paying more attention to similar uses of that construct or feature in subsequent inputs, and to increase its potential for eventual acquisition. Noticing salient features of input can be supported through two strands of activities:

- Use an *experiential approach* in which learners are first of all provided with an experience which engages them holistically. From this experience they learn implicitly without focusing conscious attention on any particular features of the experience. Later they re-visit and reflect on the experience and pay conscious attention to features of it in order to achieve explicit learning. Such an approach enables learners *apprehending before comprehending*, and *intuiting before exploring*. It also means that when they focus on a specific feature of a text they are able to develop their discoveries in relation to their awareness of the full context of use.
- Rather than drawing the learners' attention to a particular construct of a language, and then providing explicit information about its use, it is much more powerful to help learners (preferably in collaboration) to make *discoveries for themselves*.

Hence S-BPM language learners should be exposed to material in which they can experience a potentially engaging situation, respond to it personally, and then focus on a particular construct or feature, such as standard sentence semantics, of the text, in order to make discoveries about it.

For instance, learners could read about a unit employee who was asked to start modeling a critical incident work case within a BPM project in an organization. They then discussed the reasons why the modeling process had been initiated and the reasons he was reluctant to start it. Then the unit manager's use of the interrogative and the employee's use of the imperative have to be analyzed. Learners should come together in groups to share their discoveries and then they should write a version of the story or scenario in which the manager helps the employee to start modeling, since he has been engaged in the objective and convinced of the endeavor from the very beginning. Such kind of self-referential settings are likely to provide semantic contiguousness triggering affective and cognitive learning processes.

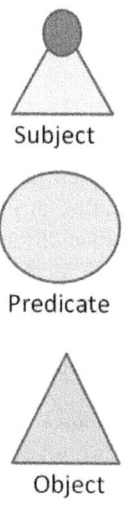

During my second month of nursing school, our professor gave us a pop quiz. I was a conscientious student and had breezed through the questions, until I read the last one: 'What is the first name of the woman who cleans the school?" Surely this was some kind of joke. I had seen the cleaning woman several times. She was tall, dark-haired and in her 50s, but how would I know her name? I handed in my paper, leaving the last question blank. Before class ended, one student asked if the last question would count toward our quiz grade. Absolutely, said the professor. "In your careers you will meet many people. All are significant. They deserve your attention and care, even if all you do is smile and say hello". I've never forgotten that lesson. I also learned her name was Dorothy.

Subject

Predicate

Object

Fig. 3. Subject-Predicate-Object Marking (Story entitled 'Most Important Question' taken from http://www.rogerknapp.com/inspire/most_important_question.htm)

In Figure 3 another experiential approach to text input is shown. It is also a metaphorical approach, as actors should be recognized. Taking a closer look with respect to learn how to 'speak S-BPM' several salient features of the input pop up:

- sentence semantics in context through the story
- the explicit and implicit use of subjects
- explicit and implicit subject involvements in situation-specific activities
- explicit use of standard semantics
- stringent line of activity context leading to a scattered pattern of subject involvement
- indirect messaging - communication without explicit communication

Each of the items contributes to raising consciousness to standard sentence semantics. In order to notice salient features of the input learners can be asked to mark all subjects (using language learning symbols as shown in Figure 3) to start grasping the variety of use (e.g., subjects can also be objects), and then explore and visualize their scattered occurrence throughout this self-contained piece of information. In Figure 3 different shapes of subject symbols are used to recognize different subjects.

For each sentence its completeness with respect to standard sentence semantics can be determined using the subject-predicate-object set of language learning symbols. Learners should start with a complete example (as indicated in the Figure 3 - 'I had seen the cleaning woman several times.') before identifying incomplete sentences and communication-relevant information.

4.5   Opening Up Opportunities to Achieve Communicative Purposes

For S-BPM explicit communication among subjects is of crucial importance. Hence, besides direct interaction indirect messaging among subjects should be recognized by S-BPM language learners in text representations, in order to model task accomplishment accordingly.

When using language in this way learners are gaining feedbacks on the hypotheses they have developed as a result of generalizing on the language in their intake and on their ability to make use of them effectively. If they are participating in interaction, they are also being pushed to clarify and elaborate content items. In addition, they are likely to elicit meaningful and comprehensible input from their interlocutors - a precondition for both, successful information transfer, and accurate modeling.

Striving for communicative purposes, in particular through noticing salient language features, can be implemented through several activities:

- Provide many opportunities for the learners to *produce language* in order to *achieve intended outcomes.*
- Make sure that these output activities are designed in a way that learners are *using language* rather than just practicing specified features of it, such as constructing standard sentences for the sake of practicing the required structure to express semantics.
- Design output activities so that they help learners to develop their ability to *communicate fluently, accurately, appropriately and effectively.* It is the storyline that matters, not only a sequence of operations describing a work scenario or task.
- Make sure that the output activities are fully contextualized in that the learners are *responding to an authentic stimulus* (e.g. a text, a need, a viewpoint, an event), that they have specific addressees and that *they have a clear intended outcome in mind.* Typically, critical incidents leading either to success or failures in operation provide constructive stimuli.
- Try to ensure that opportunities for *feedback* are built into output activities and are provided for the learners afterwards.

Corresponding S-BPM material should allow learners to construct representations as a development from ones they have just experienced. For example, in one learning unit the learners have to tell a circle story about part two of a story about customers which they act out from a current business case. In another learning unit, they have to re-locate the story set from their own work unit to another one. In another learning unit they have to design an improved version of a service mentioned in their story in a visual social media appearance and then set up a customer knowledge relationship management environment for that service based on the developed social media appearance.

As a consequence, emotionally appealing (affective) learning experience can be coupled with social and cognitive learning.

Language learners who achieve positive affect are much more likely to achieve communicative competence than those who do not. Language learners need to be positive about the target language, about their learning environment, about their coaches or mentors, about their fellow learners and about their learning materials [2].

They also need to achieve positive self-esteem and to feel that they are achieving something worthwhile. Above all, they need to be emotionally involved in the learning process and to respond by laughing, getting angry, feeling sympathy, feeling happy, feeling sad etc. Positive emotions seem to be the most useful in relation to language acquisition, as to learning in general.

Becoming aware about the emotional processes of learning requires integrating social and cognitive learning support in learning spaces. Starting point could be emotionally appealing designs, followed by tagged content and focused social interaction features.

1. Make sure the *content and tasks are as interesting, relevant and enjoyable* as possible so as to exert a positive influence on the learners' attitudes to the language and to the process of learning it.
2. Set *achievable challenges* which help to raise the learners' self esteem when success is accomplished.
3. Provide *tagged content elements*, such as examples, background information, definitions, and explanations, and use them to prepare both, language constructs, and their context of use.
4. Stimulate *emotive responses* through the use of video, music, song, literature, art etc., through making use of controversial and provocative content, through personalization and through inviting learners to articulate their feelings about a scenario before asking them to work with it.
5. Provide *social media* to enrich face-to-face settings with documented discussions and discourse.
6. *Link* social media entries to content items *directly*, allowing to trace learning intertwined affective, cognitive, and social learning processes.

S-BPM material could offer learners choices of content and of tasks in an emotionally appealing learning setting. It should consist of engaging (hedonist) interaction features and material, and allow for immediate personalization and social interaction.

The S-BPM learning platform provided by the Institute for Innovative Process Management (www.i2pm.net) can be considered a first step to that direction. It provides a variety of material, stemming from textbooks, case studies, and events. On the same level a forum is provided where topics of learners' choice can be selected and further addressed.

The filter function allows browsing of learning material according to selected didactic tags, such as example, case study, or explanation. Content can be annotated, both, in terms marking and highlighting, and in terms of linking content elements to other content elements or forum entries. All annotations become part of individual views that can be shared with other learners.

In this way, cognitive, affective, and social interaction is enabled according to individual preferences and needs. Information observers and knowledge consumers can be served in the traditional way, while information explorers and knowledge producers are rewarded through sharing and engaging.

5   Conclusion

As already has been stated by Schmidt et al. [29], setting up an informed S-BPM community requires substantial effort, in particular when model representations are crucial for a variety of S-BPM activities, ranging from process analysis to simulation [11]. Following a language learning approach requires

- *Meeting language capabilities* of modelers, i.e. stakeholders involved in business processes, in particular when learning to describe organizations as communicating subjects using 'merely' standard sentence semantics.
- *Flexible access to material*: The way support material needs to be developed is in a way that stakeholders and facilitators can make use of it as a baseline resource. Hence, it requires semantic annotations, and support for non-linear learning paths when being used in learning tasks.
- *Socially rewarding engagement*: Affective, social, and cognitive learning processes need to be supported in an intertwined while open and transparent way.

After reviewing some literature on language learning various principles could be identified and applied for developing S-BPM language learning support material and tasks. They support active skill acquisition rather than reproduction of language learning content with respect to standard sentence semantics. Some scenarios have been exemplified to demonstrate possible benefits of principled education and training. Facilitators and educators could directly utilize them for S-BPM trainings and constructive learning space developments.

The work being presented is only a first step towards achieving the objectives listed above. Although we could develop some applications of principled, language learning-based S-BPM education, and refer to an existing implementation of an integrated cognitive and social learning space, field studies still need to be set up to validate the results empirically in the context of S-BPM projects.

References

1. Amato, M.S., MacDonald, M.C.: Sentence Processing in an Artificial Language: Learning and Using Combinatorial Constraints. Cognition 116, 143–148 (2010)
2. Arnold, J. (ed.): Affect in Language Learning. Cambridge University Press, Cambridge (1999)
3. Bruner, J.: Wie das Kind sprechen lernt. Huber, Bern (2008)
4. Bundesministerium für Unterricht, Kunst und Kultur: Lehrplan der Volksschule, BGBl. II Nr. 368/2005 (2005)
5. Cancho, R., Ferrer, I.: When Language breaks into Pieces. A Conflict between Communication through isolated Signals and Language. Biosystems, 242–253 (2006)
6. Chomsky, N.: Knowledge of Language. Praeger, New York (1986)
7. Coyle, D., Hood, P., Marsh, D.: CLIL: Content and Language Integrated Learning. Cambridge University Press (2010)
8. Criblez, L., Oelkers, J., Reusser, K., Berner, E., Halbheer, U., Huber, C.: Bildungsstandards. Klett und Balmer, Zug (2009)
9. Dapretto, M., Bookheimer, S.Y.: Form and Content: Dissociating Syntax and Semantics in Sentence Comprehension. Neuron 24, 427–432 (1999)
10. Fleischmann, A., Stary, C.: Whom to Talk to? A Stakeholder Perspective on Business Process Development. Universal Access in the Information Society (2011), doi: 10.1007/s10209-011-0236-x
11. Fleischmann, A., Schmidt, W., Stary, C., Obermeier, S., Börger, E.: Subject-oriented Business Process Management, Hanser, Munich (2011) (in German)
12. Folia, V., Uddén, J., de Vries, M., Forkstam, M., Petersson, K.M.: Artificial Language Learning in Adults and Children. Language Learning 60(suppl. 2), 188–220 (2010)
13. Fotos, A.S.: Integrating Grammar Instruction and Communicative Language Use through Grammar Consciousness-Raising Tasks. TESOL Quarterly 28(2), 323–346 (1994)
14. Greene, H.A., Petty, W.T.: Developing Language Skills in the Elementary Schools, 5th edn. Allyn and Bacon, Boston (1975)
15. Grzesik, J.: Texte verstehen lernen. Waxmann, Münster (2005)
16. Heringer, H.J.: Lesen - Lehren - Lernen. Eine rezeptive Grammatik des Deutschen. Niemeyer, Tübingen (2001)
17. Jackendoff, R.: Foundations of Language: Brain, Meaning, Grammar, Evolution. Oxford University Press, Oxford (2002)
18. Kuhl, P.K.: Is Speech Learning 'gated' by the Social Brain? Developmental Science 10(1), 110–120 (2007), doi:10.1111/j.1467-7687.2007.00572.x
19. McGrath, I.: Materials Evaluation and Design for Language Teaching. Edinburgh University Press, Edinburgh (2002)
20. Miller, G.A., Johnson-Laird, P.N.: Language and Perception. Belknap Press, Cambridge (1976)
21. Montessori, M.: The Montessori Method. Frederick A. Stokes, New York (1912)
22. Nakamura, S., Tan, T., Hirayama, T., Kawai, H., Komiyama, S., Hosaka, S., Nakamura, M., Yuki, K.: CGAA/EES at NEC Corporation, Powered by S-BPM: The Subject-Oriented BPM Development Technique Using Top-Down Approach. In: Schmidt, W. (ed.) S-BPM ONE 2011. CCIS, vol. 213, pp. 215–231. Springer, Heidelberg (2011), doi:10.1007/978-3-642-23471-2_15
23. Piantadosi, S.T., Tily, H., Gibson, E.: Word lengths are optimized for efficient communication. Proc. Natl. Acad. Sci. USA 108(9), 3526–3529 (2011)

24. Recker, J.: Opportunities and Constraints: The Current Struggle with BPMN. Business Process Management Journal 16(1), 181–201 (2010)
25. Reusser, K., Reusser-Weyeneth, M. (eds.): Verstehen: Psychologischer Prozess und didaktische Aufgabe. Huber, Bern (1994)
26. Sachs-Hombach, K., Rehkämper, K. (eds.): Was ist Bildkompetenz? Deutscher Universitätsverlag, Wiesbaden (2003)
27. Scheer, A.W.: ARIS - Business Process Modeling. Springer, Berlin (2000)
28. Schmidt, J.E., Rabanus, S., Vilmos, A.: Syntax, download from (2005), http://www.web.uni-marburg.de/dsa//Direktor/Rabanus/SS2005/Grundlagen.pdf
29. Schmidt, W., Stary, C.: Establishing an Informed S-BPM Community. In: Buchwald, H., Fleischmann, A., Seese, D., Stary, C. (eds.) S-BPM ONE 2009. CCIS, vol. 85, pp. 34–47. Springer, Heidelberg (2010)
30. Schmidt, W. (ed.): S-BPM ONE - Learning by Doing - Doing by Learning. CCIS, vol. 213. Springer, Heidelberg (2011)
31. Schneider, C.E.C.: Akademische Vorlesungen über griechische Grammatik. Verlag von A. Gosohrsky, Breslau (1837)
32. Sneed, S.H.: Exporting Natural Language: Generating NL Sentences Out of S-BPM Process Models. In: Fleischmann, A., Schmidt, W., Singer, R., Seese, D. (eds.) S-BPM ONE 2010, Part II. CCIS, vol. 138, pp. 163–179. Springer, Heidelberg (2011), doi:10.1007/978-3-642-23135-3_9
33. Stücke, U.: Das Verstehen und Behalten von Texten mit Hilfe von Vorstellungsbildern. Shaker, Aachen (2001)
34. Szagun, G.: Sprachentwicklung beim Kind. Beltz, Weinheim (1996)
35. Tomlinson, B. (ed.): Materials Development in Language Teaching. Cambridge University Press, Cambridge (1998)
36. Tomlinson, B.: Principles and Procedures of Materials Development. In: Harwood, N. (ed.) Materials in ELT: Theory and Practice. Cambridge University Press, Cambridge (2010)
37. Yang, C.D.: Universal Grammar, Statistics or Both? Trends in Cognitive Sciences 8, 451–456 (2004)
38. Vygotskij, L.S.: Denken und Sprechen. Beltz, Weinheim (2002)

In or Out?
A Student Project on the Enrollment Process
Developing a Reference Model for a Service-Oriented Portal through S-BPM Process Exploration

Norbert Graef, Nils Tölle, Oliver Schöll, and Detlef Seese*

Karlsruhe Institute of Technology (KIT)
Institute of Applied Informatics and Formal Description Methods (AIFB)
Kaiserstrasse 89, 76133 Karlsruhe, Germany
{norbert.graef,nils.toelle}@student.kit.edu,
{oliver.schoell,detlef.seese}@kit.edu

Abstract. This paper describes a project realized by university students at a university administration. It shows which results are achievable through subject-oriented business process modeling by (in this subject area) unexperienced students. The explored process is the enrollment process which, was intransparent to the applicants and not well documented, although it is a central process and represents the first contact of students with university. After process exploration a subject-oriented model of the enrollment process portal was developed as a reference model for the implementation of this portal.

Keywords: process management, service quality, S-BPM, public administration, student project.

1 Introduction

This paper is intended to share some experiences in working with students in BPM projects involving the S-BPM methdod. Business Process Management (BPM), in general, 'includes concepts, methods, and techniques to support the design, administration, configuration, enactment, and analysis of business processes' (see [5], p. 6). The project on the enrollment portal was conducted in three main phases. The first phase is process exploration through the S-BPM method. It was conducted by students, who were all new to process management and worked on the project in small weekly junks. As an evaluation of the first phase an interview contrasting the S-BPM-method and results with other experiences in process management.

The second phase is the developement of the subject 'monitor' as a reference model for the implementation of the new enrollment portal. In the third phase the impact of the tranparency provided by the new monitor is checked.

---

* Special thanks go to Michael Kurth for his interview and his support.

S. Oppl and A. Fleischmann (Eds.): S-BPM ONE 2012, CCIS 284, pp. 77–90, 2012.
© Springer-Verlag Berlin Heidelberg 2012

2   Context of the Projects

The project was triggered by experiences with the university start of first year students. For some of the students starting their student life was difficult because of administrative problems. Some of them lack a full enrollment and therefore access to university systems, too. The resulting problem is that they are unable to register for the obligatory tutorials, e.g. for the foundation course in programming. This causes a lot of inconveniences not only for the students but for teaching staff, too. After a first analysis two reasons, which were unidentified before, were discovered:

- The process of enrollment stopped at some point without giving notice to the students.
- The process of enrollment was too time-consuming and had not finished before the lectures started.

Further research it found that there were several organization units involved and none of them could actually give reasons for the delay. This was the starting point of the project 'Enrollment Process', because the delay did not only cause the supervisors a lot of work, but also gave the new students a negative impression.

3   Student Project 'Enrollment Process'

A first look at university's administration processes was that quite some organizational units work together, which had different cultures, problems, and goals. Furthermore, a university has a very hierarchical structure, where different functions are srictly separated, even in the same process. An organizational structure like this, needs an approach enabling the process team to find out the behavior bit by bit, subject by subject, unit by unit. S-BPM is an adequate method in such a situation.

The following project started as a seminar with two teams of three students each. The students had some prior knowledge in general organisation management and programming but none in process management or any kind of BPM Tools as Fig. 1 shows.

As you can see, all of them had to learn (business) process management from scratch with the side effect of being open towards the new paradigm of Subjectoriented BPM (S-BPM). For an introduction to S-BPM see [2] (in German) or [1].

3.1   Project Goals

The goals of this seminar-project were to:

- find out who is involved in the process (one assumed group has nothing to do with the process and some unexpected were found)
- give a first process model to be able to discover the key problems
- give some improvement sugestions (esp. easy and cheap ones)
- give hints for duration(s) and variance(s) of the process including possible reasons

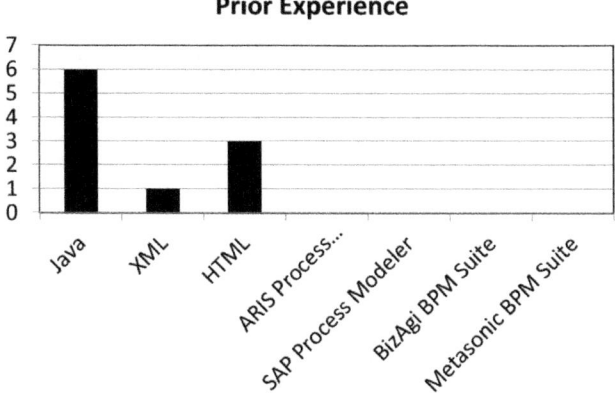

Fig. 1. Prior (BPM-)Experience of the Project Team

3.2 Project Structure and Method

As this was the fifth S-BPM project seminar we had quite some experience in how to use S-BPM in student projects with external partners. The S-BPM method, as we learned to use it, has the advantages of loose coupling between subjects which helps to distribute the work over time and people. This is useful because, although it is a one-semester project, students are unable to work on a project full-time and the priority to talk to students is often not the highest in organizations. Nonetheless, we intend to teach process management in practice and S-BPM is clear and easy enough to keep track of the process models.

To come to models we first determine the process borders by looking at it from the customer's perspective. The result is then a service, like completed immatriculation, offered to the customer through some task execution. But we prefer not to start by following the tasks, but by following the agents or subjects involved in the process. Therefore, the next result are the subjects and their interaction or communication. So we come to the draft of the subject-interaction diagram. The main goal in the first round of interviews is to find all (or most of) the interaction and messages interchanged starting with the drain of the process (the customer) back to the initiator (often the same customer) which is then the end-to-end-process.

Only after that, in a second round we focus mainly on the specific tasks of the subjects and try to validate process execution.

3.3 Assessment of the Project

The project evaluation is given in the form of an interview with the director of the administrational unit. In the following you find his personal opinion about benefits, the S-BPM method, and the general cooperation with student teams:

Question: Please describe your role and function in the administration:
In June 2010, I took over the director's position of the student administration unit at a renowned university at short notice. Summer is the peak time for the 15 members of staff in this unit since the application for the next year has to be processed.

Starting Points

1. Question: Which goals and which concern did you have in conducting this project?
   Handling the application is a high-volume business. The days before the deadline we receive about 1000 applications daily. In total the volume of applications is about cubic meter. The main project goal was to analyse the existing processes and identify the bottle necks in advance.
2. Question: Which doubts did you have beforehead?
   The team had done a general, descriptive process analysis in another project before. The challenge was: Is a team of students really able to maintain a detailed analysis of such a mass process in a short seminar project? And this with the side condition of high responsibility for all future applicants and students?.
3. Question: Which expectations did you have?
   The project should maintain the process steps in detail, give empirical numbers for durations, uncover internal dependencies and - last but not least - improve the whole process flow.

Initial Situation

1. Question: In which form was the knowledge about the processes available (e.g. implicit vs. explicit, in systems/heads/paper)?
   We had a global process analysis. The detailed knowledge about the processes was - as so often in businesses and public administrations - only in the brains of the staff. Inevitably, this causes differences in the way the work is done.
2. Question: Did you have any experience in process modeling and/or process management? If so, also with S-BPM?
   I had some experience in process modeling especially in value analysis. S-BPM was new to me.
3. Question: Did you have preferences concerning the methodology (in process projects)?
   I was sceptical about the approach of two competing student teams because of the overhead. So I insisted on them to act as one team when exploring processes and data.

Cooperation with the Student Teams during the Project

1. Question: Did the student consultants disturbed administrations work?
   Quite the contrary!

2. Question: How do you think your employees felt about that?
   They especially appreciated, that the project members were able to switch from their customer role as a student to the role of staff in the administration.
3. Question: Do you think the students had the ability to ask the right questions?
   Yes, without any doubt.
4. Question: Were the process models understandable to you and your staff?
   Certainly, to understand the process models you have to study a new language. An open question for us is if the models are useful as a basis for training new staff.
5. Question: Do you think your employees recognized themselves again in the process model?
   Yes, they did. Although some of the bottlenecks were known, the consequences of, say, the breakdown of a particular station for some days, wasn't known before.
6. Question: Do you think, the process analysis covers the current situation in the administration sufficiently?
   Yes, it does.
7. Question: Which positive/negative influence had the applied S-BPM method from your point of view?
   The follow-up project was the developement of a process monitor.

Results

1. Question: Did you get new insights in the administration by this project? Which are the most relevant to you?
   New and particularly important is the continuous information of the applicants about the state of the application. The admission (or rejection) is very important for every applicant's life. On the other hand, hundreds of phone calls daily are critical for the administration if callers just want to know their application has arrived or how likely admission is.
2. Question: Do you think these results could have been reached with another method and comparable time and effort?
   The effort was easily manageable. Conduction this analysis on our own would have meant much more preparatory work, like choosing appropriate tools, and evaluation of the results.

What Would You Tell Other Managers in a Comparable Situation Concerning ...

1. ...obstacles, that have to be overcome in process projects in general or S-BPM projects?
   The biggest obstacle is, in many cases, the attidude of: Yet another project - I've some work to do!
2. ...possible successes to be reached with the (S-)BPM method?
   See above
3. Would you recommend S-BPM? Why/Why not?
   Yes, definitely.

3.4 Main Results

An important result in most projects analysing processes is: We now see our own process for the first time. This was the effect when presenting the process model to managers and employees also in this case. The second result was that the students can give them the lower bound of the duration of the happy path. And this turned out to be much longer than expected. The third result was a set of reasons for delays where many of them were due to the fact that the applicants don't receive their current status during the process. Consequently, applicants aren't aware of incorrect forms, payment, missing data and the like. This observation was the starting point to the project to improve the transperancy of the process through a portal with information about the status and problems in the individual process instance. This project is described in the next chapter in some detail.

4   S-BPM Analysis as Monitor's Basis

This chapter describes the usage of the process model as a reference model to improve the value for the applicant/customer. Although the aim of the project was to improve process transparency, it wasn't intended (and possible) to launch a new (S-)BPM software system. Therefore, the solution was implemented in the existing portal based on the knowledge of the process obtained by the S-BPM model. Hence, the resulting serviceoriented architecture is independent of any BPM engine and the IT environment. With the process knowledge behind the actual states are deduced from very selective read accesses to the underlying databases of the IT environment without any change in the environment.

4.1 Project Initialization Phase

Development of the Project Goals for the Monitor. The results described above had been the starting point of the following implementation project. Some of the potential in the process would have involved deep changes in the organization or organizational culture or even legal obstacles. Therefore, the project concentrated on these issues:

- generating (well-grounded) data about the process, like durations and variances
- reducing the detection time of failures through transparency of process states and details
- reducing the duration and variance by giving status information to the applicants to increase reaction speed to problems and failures and reduce communication overhead with the administration

The Project Environment. All this should be reached without additional costs in the administration neither during the project nor in their daily work. In addition, the monitor should be modular and flexible since there was a change in the underlying administration software planned. Therefore, the monitor had to be platform independent.

4.2 Process Model Matching and Detailing

The first target was to identify the most important milestones from an applicant's point of view in this application and enrollment process. Therefore, the first step was to obtain a deep understanding of the process not from scratch but from the two existing models. The two process models turned out to have a mature structure but considerable discrepancies in the details. These were found especially in the granularity of the models and in aspects of data synchronization of the involved legacy systems. The next step was then to consolidate the two models systematically since both had their strengths and weaknesses. By the way, this fact points to an advantage of working with two independent models: You've a much better chance to capture all of the important information and you get two perspectives on the same case often stimulating discussion about key issues of an organization.

Manual Model Matching. The model consolidation was done manually. The list of all activities of both process models was the initial step which were listed side-by-side ease comparability. Part of the resulting comparison is shown in figure 2. Additionally, for sending and receiving states the corresponding subject were documented.

In figure 2 a part of the subject 'administration employee' in the subprocess 'payment and immatriculation'is shown. In this example the first model includes a step 'rejection' ('Absage') and 'exceeding deadline' ('Fristüberschreitung'). Whereas it only includes a payment confirmation but no signed immatriculation form which is mandatory for immatriculation. As you can see, it is the combination and consolidation that describes the real process best.

		model team 1				model team 2		
	from	involved subject	to	description	from	involved subject	to	description
payment and enrollment		applicant	→	admission documents	→	ZUL		application accepted
	→	applicant		rejection of application		applicant	→	application accepted
	→	ZUL		confirmation of transaction	→	applicant		enrollment
	→	ZUL		manual matching	→	ZUL		payment incorrect
		ZUL	→	manual matching incorrect		internal function		checking for sibling rule
		applicant	→	matching incomplete		applicant	→	payment request (Loop)
		ZUL	→	manual matching OK		ZUL	→	add payment manually
		applicant	→	manually matched				
		ZUL	→	transfer from ZUL to SOS	→	ZUL		data transfer to SOS

Fig. 2. Matching the two Model Variants (Example)

The Consistent Process Model. This method of matching the models manually allowed to analyze the discrepancies isolated and especially independent of other subjects (parties) in the process. After this isolation step, the next step was to ask the particulat subject (one of the employees that perform the process step) for the correct procedure. This resulted in a refined process model.

In figure 3 you find a part of this consolidated model where, for example, an applicant is immatriculated after the administration received a signed immatriculation form and the correct payment.

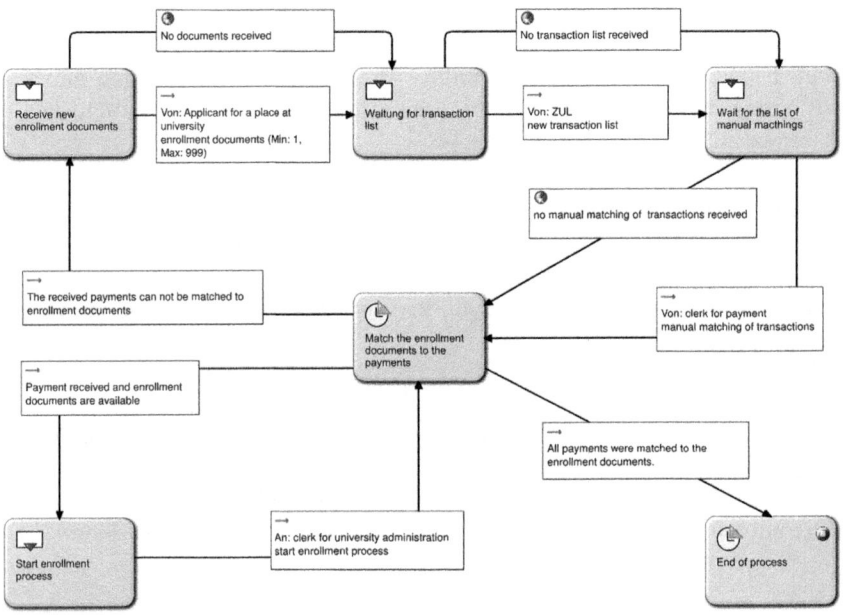

Fig. 3. Subject Diagram of the Subject 'Aministration Employee'

4.3 Defining Milestones from an Enrollee's Point of View

As mentioned, one of the requirements was that no BPM engine could be used. So why was this process model useful after all? It proved its usefulness in defining the milestones. These milestones were the key steps from an enrollee's point of view, so the most important steps from a customer's perspective. These steps included:

- completeness of application forms
- payment problem
- waiting list
- rejection
- admission
- student ID card
- ...

The result was a consolidated process model with coarse-grained process steps from milestone to milestone because they were identified as the most interesting ones to communicate to applicants. Furthermore, these steps provided the basis of the search for the relevant data in the IT systems (the technical subjects) as is shown in the next part.

4.4   Implementation of the Monitor

Identifying Available Data to Feed the Milestones. Due to the project condition to prevent additional workload for the administration, the milestones had to be derived from dataset changes of the given it-infrastructure. The focus has been set on the resources identified in the consolidated process. Based on these information, the databases had been analyzed in detail to extract the relevant datasets and data tables, which reflect the occurrence of specific milestones or interdependencies between those. For the analysis interviews with IT-experts within the administration and documentations of the software systems were essential for the successful tracking. Milestones which weren't trackable by dataset changes in the local IT-environment had to be handled exceptionally. To track these conditions we specified project specific web services to register external dataset changes which represented the thread in of a millstone or its interdependency. Milestones which were not trackable within the global it-environment are triggered by a predefined time. The duration of these time triggers have been defined on basis of empirical values and experiences from decision makers within the administration. By this data mining process in combination with the process exploration the organizational monitor process has been mapped on its technical representation in the surrounding IT-infrastructure.

The Process Model as a Reference Model. After checking the interdependencies between the different milestones, their technical implementation had to be realized. An abstract, technical process model had been developed as a fundamental communication instrument using the subjection oriented modeling notation. Due to this communication instrument we achieved to realize the technological concept with a minimum of failures and in a short amount of time. Figure XX shows a technical sub-process of the enrollment process regarding the verification of the transferred amount of money. In this sub-process the preconditions in the database are being checked with SQL-Statements for the purpose of firing the outgoing transition of the actual StatusID. Transition 222241 has two preconditions to fire. First, a money transfer has to be registered in the Database. Second, the amount of money registered in the Database has to be sufficient. If these conditions are met, Transition 222241 will fire. If it only complies with the first requirement, transition 222233 is fired, because it shares precondition one and the negation of precondition two. With a triggered transition the Monitor Database is being informed to update the persisted StatusID. The Status

Id references to information shown in the context of each process step and will be enriched with a visual process which also represents the history of each process instance.

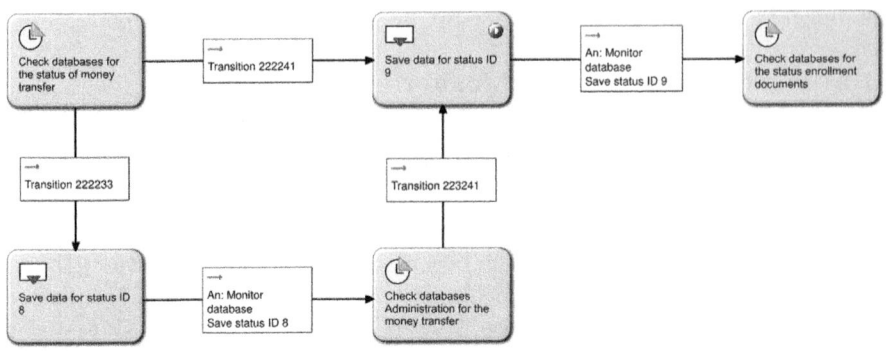

Fig. 4. Part of the Subject 'Monitor'

4.5   The Monitor

Our main target was to give every student the ability to track his own application-and-enrollment process (AEP) in real time in an intuitive web interface, which is enriched by context specific information and contact options regarding the individual process status. Due to the strict project conditions, we had to develop a new software system to generate transparency in the application-and-enrollment process while avoiding extra workload for the administration. At the same time, the system had to be highly independent from the IT-environment, but integrated in a heterogeneous IT-infrastructure. To balance these opposing conditions a software system based on web services has been developed, which has a highly modular architecture. Each 'data connector' has been encapsulated in a single web service, which can be substituted with the replacement of the underlying Infrastructure in an affordable development time. The presentation layer, application logic and persistency layer of the monitor itself is decoupled from the underlying IT-infrastructure by restricting the communication with the IT-environment on web services via SOAP (see [3], p. 120). The presentation layer has been implemented with Java Server Pages, while the application logic itself is written on Java to run on an Apache Tomcat (see [4] and http://tomcat.apache.org/) application server. For the persistency layer a relational Postgresql Database has been used and its access is managed by the object-relational mapper Hibernate. The Monitor Database has the task to store every relevant information regarding the process status, history as well as information regarding the history. The application logic is designed to handle two types of web services. On the one hand update services, which are necessary to

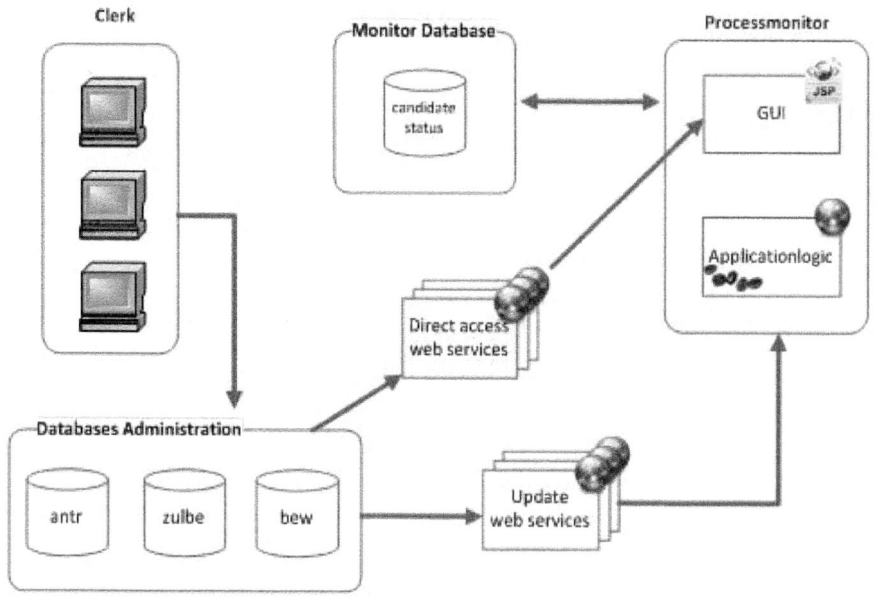

Fig. 5. Monitor's Architecture

check process conditions and to fetch all registered candidates from the Administration Database in predefined time cycles. On the other hand direct access web services, which are fetching context specific information for predefined process steps in real time.

Fig. 6 shows the graphical user interface, which has been designed to give the user an intuitive view of their individual process status enriched by context specific information. Therefore a traffic light has been used to represent the process health. When it shows a red light, the process stops and if the candidate does not act as advised in the status information the process will not continue. If it shows yellow, the process will continue, but has been compromised for example by missing documents. If the traffic light shows green, the process will be in optimal "shape". No interaction is needed. The upper right side shows candidate specific information regarding the subject and a unified number to identify himself, when contacting the administration. The contact information is shown below and can be defined context specific for every process step individually. The last row shows a help text to bring up additional information to the traffic light and process semantic, the overall process progress and the appliance status. The process diagram below shows the currently active process part including a graphical representation of its progress and the individual process path of the candidate. The two swim lanes are assigning the subject to each process activity, while the green pin shows the currently active task. The bottom of the monitor documents the process history of each candidate.

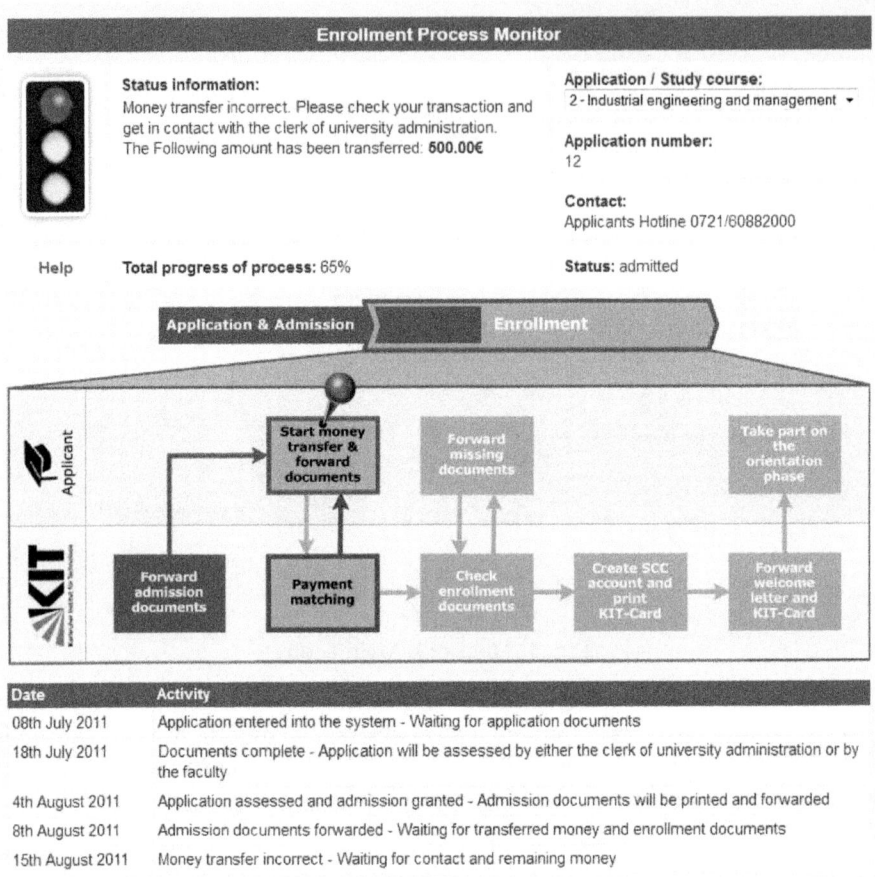

Fig. 6. Screenshot of the 'Monitor'

5 User Experience and Outcome

In this last chapter we want to give some data which illustrate, in our opinion, the work was worth doing it.

5.1 Acceptance of the Monitor

After intensive tests on old datasets the enrollee monitor was introduced for the application process of the pilot courses:

– Industrial Engineering and Management
– Mechanical Engineering
– Electrical and information engineering

Luckily, in this year there was another new service for the applicants: a telephone hotline. Luckily, because this turned out to be the fastest feedback channel about the monitor failures or drawbacks. In table 1 you find some usage data. The monitor was highly accepted since nearly all of the applicants used it at least once. As you can see in the last line there were also some 'power users' although their intentions must be left unknown. Nevertheless, the average number of requests per user indicates that such a tool is highly accepted.

Table 1. User Acceptance

number of user	3061
number of requests	43706
average number of requests per user	14.2
requests of top 3 requester	478 / 396 / 385

5.2   Higher Fault Tolerance of the Process

One of the goals has been to give information earlier to the applicants to speed up the process in case of disturbances. By chance the monitor happen to prove its contribution to fault tolerance of the proces in just another way. Due to a bug in the software that generates the ranking of applicants this ranking was incorrect. The consequence was that many applicants with a lower ranking position were accepted whereas some higher ranked applicants weren't. These wrongly refused applicants found themselves on the waiting list. A fact they were informed by the monitor so they called the administration and the problem was eliminated in a very short time and avoided the same faults in the admission process of other courses.

5.3   A First Analysis of Service Quality

Although, an analysis of service quality had not been planned for this project we obtained some information by asking how long some step may take. In one

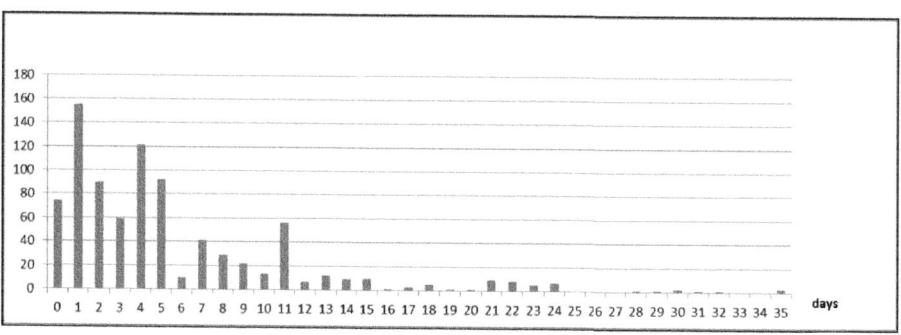

Fig. 7. How much time do they need for confirmation?

particular step the manager told to use a time trigger of 6 days because it won't take longer. In figure 7 the real distribution of durations is shown. It took up to 35 days and the average was 5.44 days. For this step we get a sigma-level of about two with 29% instances that took longer than 6 days.

6 Outlook

The next step is to improve process transparency without policing the employees of the administration. This should be reached by providing data about which variables are most important to be improved for higher customer satisfaction. Therefore, an evaluation of the effects of the monitor will be launched based on a system dynamics model concerning the satisfaction with administration services. The aim of this evaluation is to find the best starting points and control points for a continous improvement process.

The general objective are fixed service level agreements, e.g. deadlines and durations, and the development of a service quality index for the administration based on these agreements for the most important milestones in administration processes.

References

1. Fleischmann, A.: What is S-BPM? In: Buchwald, H., Fleischmann, A., Seese, D., Stary, C. (eds.) S-BPM ONE 2009. CCIS, vol. 85, pp. 85–106. Springer, Heidelberg (2010)
2. Fleischmann, A.: Subjektorientiertes Prozessmanagement: Mitarbeiter einbinden, Motivation und Prozessakzeptanz steigern. Hanser, München (2011)
3. Papazoglou, M.: Web services: Principles and technology. Pearson Education Limited, Harlow (2008)
4. Vukotic, A., Goodwill, J.: Apache Tomcat 7. Apress and Distributed by Springer Science+Business Media, Berkeley and CA and New York (2011)
5. Weske, M.: Business process management: Concepts, methods, technology. Springer, Heidelberg (2007)

Mapping Possibilities of S-BPM and BPMN 2.0

Implementing a BPM Interface

Stephan Sneed

Metasonic AG
Münchner Straße 29, Hettenshausen, 85276 Pfaffenhofen, Germany
stephan.sneed@metasonic.de

Abstract. BPMN 2.0 is well on the way to becoming an international process modeling standard and will soon become the modeling method used for many process execution engines such as BPEL. Since it also provides the possibility to model distributed systems, a major concept of S-BPM, its usage is a natural step toward analyzing S-BPM and BPMN mapping possibilities. As will be demonstrated here, conformance to the BPMN 2.0 semantics as a sub class of modeling conformance can be achieved almost completely by the mapping method proposed by this paper. Those conformance deviations and losses that do occur on both sides are due solely to methodological differences discussed at the end of the paper or to be the issue of future work. The achievement of common execution conformance will not be discussed in detail here. The execution of BPMN models requires far more information than what is currently contained in most user models, as recent research has shown.

Keywords: S-BPM, BPMN, mapping, interface, model interchange.

1 Motivation for This Work

The basic motivation for this work is to avoid a vendor lock-in for S-BPM customers and to show that S-BPM models can be readily transferred into a subset of the BPMN 2.0 notation ('BPMN' is used as an abbreviation for BPMN 2.0 from now on). BPMN is, in spite of some weaknesses, about to become an industry standard and will soon serve as a common standard for business process model interchange in practice, even if other approaches for business process meta models exist, e.g. POP*, proposed by Ziemann et al. [1]. Accepting the fact that BPMN will inevitably become a worldwide standard, the purpose of this paper is to introduce a bidirectional mapping between subsets of both modeling languages. The goal is to reduce the loss of information by language translation and to translate as many entities of both specifications as possible. BPMN defines some classes and subclasses of conformance at the beginning of the BPMN specification [2]. For the purpose of the interface proposed here, the BPMN descriptive modeling conformance (a subclass of modeling conformance) has been chosen as the proper point of reference on the BPMN side. Regarding S-BPM, the point of reference is the basic paper of Albert

S. Oppl and A. Fleischmann (Eds.): S-BPM ONE 2012, CCIS 284, pp. 91–105, 2012.
© Springer-Verlag Berlin Heidelberg 2012

Fleischmann which introduces the S-BPM method and its basic modeling concepts [3] as well as his recent book on that subject [4].

To introduce the S-BPM language to the reader, it is to be noted here that, as opposed to BPMN, the S-BPM model entities are defined bottom up. S-BPM process models can be reduced to abstract state machines and hence to executable code. Furthermore, the entities defined within S-BPM are derived from nature in order to support our natural way of thinking. Subjects within S-BPM can represent real world entities, which may be machines, human actors, systems, and so on. All of these subjects have certain abilities, can perform certain tasks and can communicate through predefined communication channels. They are abstract state machines, that can be called in a given state and which will return a response or delegate information for further processing to subordinate subjects after their own processing steps (states) have been closed. For more detailed information on S-BPM and its modeling entities, the reader should refer to [3], [4] and the initial work of Fleischmann, Distributed Systems [5].

2   Mapping Definitions

As stated above, the mapping proposed here is a notational one and will not support the transformation of executable models. That would go beyond the scope of this paper and would, on the other hand, fail because of semantic weaknesses within the BPMN specification. Börger [6] has pointed out that process models with the BPMN notation are not specified deeply enough to allow any kind of interpretation or execution and that there is a tremendous gap between notated and executable models within BPMN. Hence, an interchange of executable models would require a BPMN reference implementation which is not yet available at this point in time. The following sections introduce mappings of atomic and complex structures following a straight bottom up approach.

2.1   Atomic Mappings

The term "atomic mappings" is understood here as the opposite of complex mappings which are handled in the next section. An atomic mapping does not necessarily mean a 1-1 mapping relation, since single entities and relationships in BPMN might be expressed by multiple entities and relationships in S-BPM and vice versa. Atomic entities are basic modeling constructs, that are not aggregations of other, more detailed modeling constructs, while complex constructs are such aggregations. As previously stated, all mappings should be bidirectional and will be explained here based on the following figures (BPMN is always displayed on the left, S-BPM on the right side).

The carrier of functionality in the modeling language S-BPM is always the subject.

One or more subjects compose a S-BPM process in terms of a distributed system (as opposed to BPMN, where a process is something that is attached to a single actor). This functionality is represented by states and the control flow which orchestrates that functionality is represented by state transitions. In BPMN, the owner of functionality is a process entity, but processes can be owned by a participant within a collaboration entity. Here, the carrier of functionality, the process, consists of tasks, activities or in the most general expression flow nodes, while the orchestration of these flow nodes is expressed by sequence flows. Bearing this in mind, it seems logical to map the atomic functionality entities of BPMN (tasks) to the atomic functionality entities in S-BPM (states).

As shown above, BPMN makes intensive use of inheritance. For instance, a task entity in BPMN is a specialization of the "activity" entity (a specialization of the flow node entity), while certain types of tasks are specializations of the task entity.[1] For example, a state in S-BPM is always mapped to a task in BPMN, but this is an abstract definition. In fact, only instances of states occur in S-BPM, either as a "send", a "receive" or as an "action state" ([3], p. 14). While activities in BPMN can be either atomic or compound ([2], p. 151), the specialization "task" is always an atomic activity within BPMN ([2], p. 156) just as a "state" in S-BPM is atomic too.[2] Hence, a given type of BPMN task is mapped to a corresponding type of state in S-BPM:

Fig. 1. Bidirectional mapping of Manual Task to Action State

Subjects within S-BPM consist of states and transitions. As already mentioned, there are three types of states, "send", "receive" and "action". A state of the type "action" in S-BPM defines any internal operation of a subject ([3], p. 15). If the action state contains any refinements, it is said to be "automated" and hence not manual. Therefore the manual task in BPMN ([2], p. 163) is represented by an action state without refinements in S-BPM and vice versa.

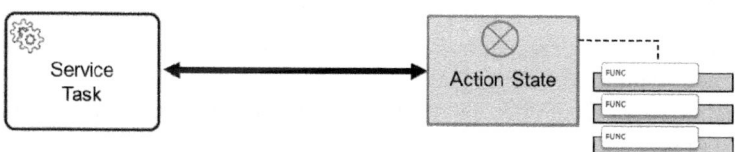

Fig. 2. Bidirectional mapping of Service Task to Action State with Refinements

In BPMN, any task that is performed by a web service or any other automated application is a service task ([2], p. 158). In S-BPM, internal actions that are automated contain a set of sub actions, i.e. refinements of that action as defined by Fleischmann in his book "Distributed Systems" ([5], p. 263). A service task in BPMN is represented by an action state with refinements in S-BPM and vice versa.

---

[1] The BPMN specification [1] contains various class diagrams with aggregation and inheritance structures of the described entities. For example, the class diagram of a task is shown on page 159 within figure 10.10.

[2] States and tasks do not consist of entities of other types nor do they consist of other states and tasks on a lower level of granularity.

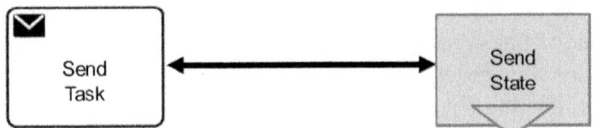

Fig. 3. Bidirectional mapping of Send Task to Send State

In BPMN, any task whose purpose it is to send a message to another participant is a send task ([2], p. 159). Since send and receive tasks go beyond the scope of a single participant (or subject) there must also be a relation between two participants or subjects. In BPMN this is represented by message flows while S-BPM calls are referred to as messages. In any case, they are triples of a sender, a receiver and message content. At this point it is enough to state that each send task in BPMN is represented by a send state in S-BPM and vice versa.

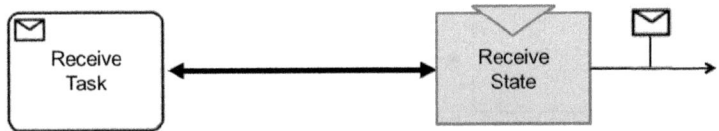

Fig. 4. Bidirectional mapping of a Receive Task to single message Receive State

Within BPMN, a receive task is designed to wait for a certain message from another participant ([2], p. 161) and is completed once the message has been received. The relation between participants has already been briefly mentioned above, but message constructs will be explained in full detail later. In contrast to the simple 1-1 mapping of send tasks and states, there comes up a transformation problem here, caused by the different treatment of receiving multiple messages. Figure 4 shows the simple case of a state (or task) that waits for exactly one message from one participant. While each receive task in BPMN can only be associated to exactly one message and sending participant ([2], p.161, Table 10.10), S-BPM allows for multiple incoming messages from different sending subjects for any one receive state. This is discussed in the following section (see Figure 5).

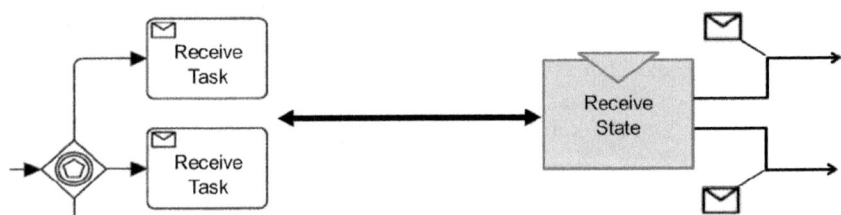

Fig. 5. Bidirectional mapping of multiple Receive Tasks to a Receive State

In S-BPM a single receive state is capable of receiving multiple messages. As already stated, this is not possible in BPMN. There each message needs to be consumed explicitly by a single receive task, i.e. there is a 1-1 relationship between messages and receive tasks. Each outgoing transition in S-BPM is executed if and only if the connected message has been received ([3], p. 14). In BPMN the messages are not connected to the outgoing transitions but to the receive tasks. In order to define a multi message control flow in BPMN, a gateway needs to be placed in front of each receive task to split up the control flow properly ([2], p. 287). There are multiple types of gateways in BPMN, but the right one for this situation is the event based gateway since the decision is triggered by a message from an external participant ([2], p. 297). Due to semantic redundancies, gateways are discussed separately within this paper in section 3, but are mentioned here to form the basic required mapping construct.

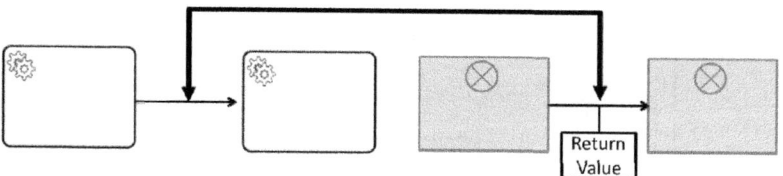

Fig. 6. Bidirectional mapping of a Sequence Flow to a Transition

The behavioral structure of a process (participant) in BPMN and of a subject in S-BPM consists of nodes and edges. So far, only the different types of nodes have been discussed. In both cases, nodes are connected via edges, called sequence flows in BPMN and transitions in S-BPM. In both cases they are binary relations, connecting two flow nodes (BPMN [2], p. 97) or two states (S-BPM). In S-BPM, transitions also have a certain type, depending on the type of the source state. Such transitions in S-BPM are always conditional. Function transitions are executed only if the source function state returns the value defined on that transition, receive transitions only when the defined message is received, and send transitions when the defined message is sent. There is a possibility of conditional sequence flows in BPMN ([2], p. 97), but conditions can also be expressed by using a combination of exclusive gateways and tasks (as shown in Figure 5). That is the solution proposed here.

The following figure shows the mapping situation of a function with the evaluation of multiple return values (2) while case (1) has been already demonstrated within section 2.1 below Figure 5. Thus, a S-BPM action with multiple outgoing transitions - depending on the return value - is mapped to a task with a following exclusive gateway and vice versa.

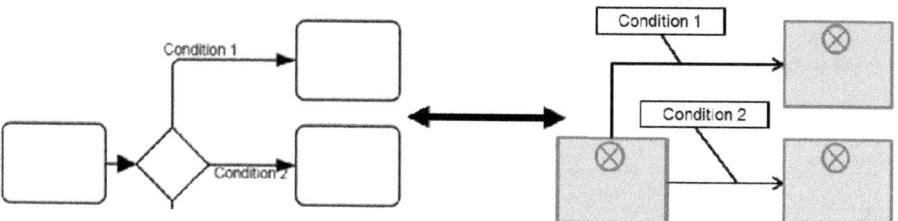

Fig. 7. Bidirectional mapping of conditional forks

2.2   Complex Mappings

The mappings in the section above have been considered atomic because neither of the mapping constructs (BPMN or S-BPM) contained other atomic entities. This section will now discuss complex mappings, where the entities being mapped are aggregations of these atomic entities.

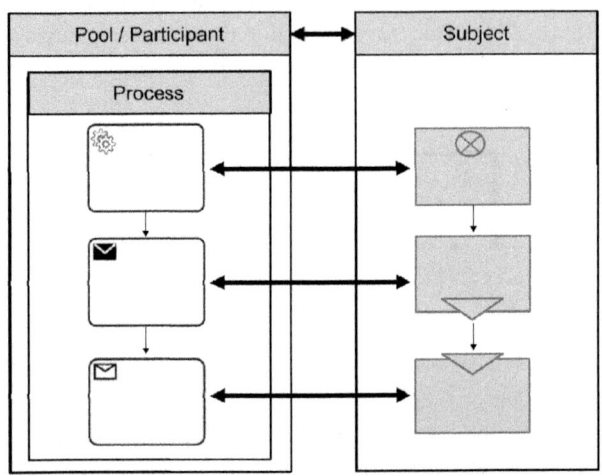

Fig. 8. Bidirectional mapping of a Participant with a Process to a Subject

The carrier of functionality in S-BPM is, as pointed out before, the subject. Within BPMN, it is the process ([2], p. 145). But a process is actually a standalone work flow. The ability of interacting with other actors in BPMN (which is a major issue in S-BPM) is provided by the pool or participant as a member of a collaboration set ([2], p. 109). However, a BPMN pool or participant need not contain a process ([2], p. 112) but can also be a single black box. The mapping proposed here will make no use of this option at this point. It requires that the BPMN participant always be a process. Hence, a S-BPM subject can be mapped on to a BPMN participant with a process and vice versa.

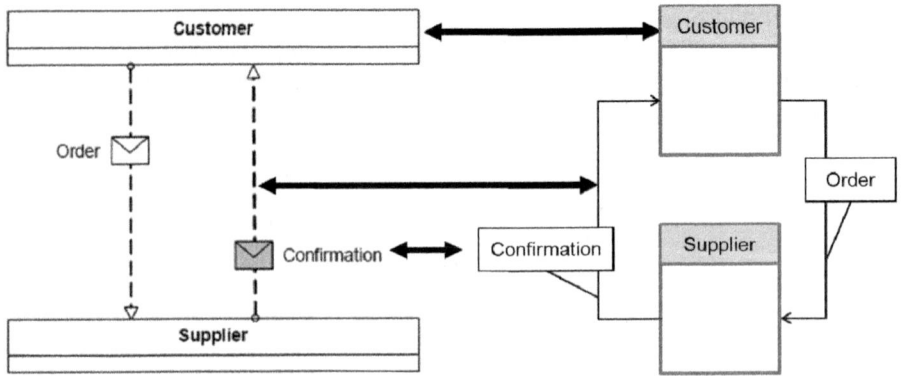

Fig. 9. Bidirectional mapping of a Participant with a Process to a Subject

The BPMN participants and the corresponding S-BPM subjects that are shown in Figure 9 may imply that they are black boxes but this is not necessarily the case. Entities below these high level ones are being mapped as proposed above. As explained in [3] there are two views in S-BPM: The internal view showing the behavior of a subject and the communication view, showing the interaction of a subject with others. In Figure 9 the internal behavior of the two participants is also hidden on the BPMN side. As already mentioned, participants can be black boxes with message flows connecting them to their environment ([2], p. 112). This might serve well for the figure, but the mapping proposed here will not allow or generate a black box participant.[3] As shown above, the participants are mapped to subjects and vice versa. In addition, the message flows of BPMN (dashed lines) are mapped to the messages in S-BPM and vice versa. In BPMN, a message can be associated to a message flow (order, conformation) ([2], p. 120) in the same way that any message in S-BPM is associated to a message type. The message in BPMN is mapped to a message type within S-BPM and vice versa. Thus the collaboration concept of BPMN fits well together with the distributed systems approach in S-BPM and can be mapped bidirectional without any loss of information.

In S-BPM, each subject has a message input pool where all incoming messages are stored and then evaluated when the subject takes on the receive state associated to a certain message. In BPMN it is possible to draw a message flow to the environment of a participant or to a certain receive task. So it would appear that the execution semantics of S-BPM are meant to behave like those of S-BPM, although there is no explicit chapter about messages within the BPMN execution semantics chapter ([2], p. 425).

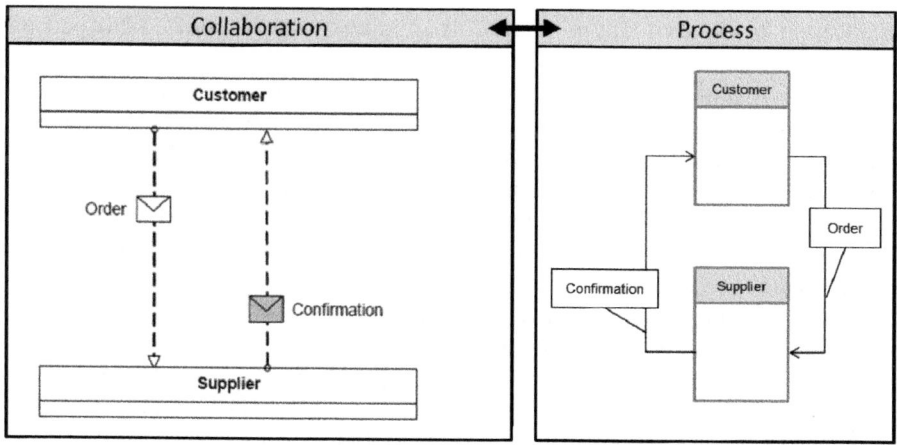

Fig. 10. Bidirectional mapping of a Collaboration to a Process

---

[3] There might be a possibility of using this option within the concept of information hiding within the S-BPM JCPEX approach ([7], p. 11).

The last (and highest level) mapping of the proposed interface is the one from a BPMN collaboration to a S-BPM process. Whereas in BPMN collaborations contain participants which contain processes with tasks, S-BPM processes subjects which directly contain states. This is more of a naming issue and does not cause any significant problems since another layer serving as a container (like the process entity in BPMN) can be collapsed or generated when translating models. It should be mentioned that the proper source of reference for BPMN entity relations (like references, aggregations and so on) are the BPMN class diagrams. There are figures with detailed UML class diagrams for each BPMN entity all over the BPMN specification [2]. In order to complete the proposed mapping the last mapping relation is the following: A BPMN collaboration entity is mapped to a S-BPM process entity and vice versa. The next section discusses some specific mapping issues that are for some reasons not part of pure syntactical relations that have been shown in this section.

3   Dealing with BPMN Events

As mentioned already in section 2 (see Figure 5) there is a problem with BPMN events that does not exist in S-BPM. BPMN defines numerous types of events. There are start-events, end-events, message-start-events, message-end-events, timer-start-events and terminate-end-events defined to achieve BPMN descriptive modeling conformance. All of these do not exist as syntactic constructs within S-BPM. But on a semantic level, they actually do exist.

For instance, there is a pure BPMN start event in front of an activity (super class of a task) as part of the semantic definition so that the activity will be executed when the start event is triggered ([2], p. 238). This is the case, when a process (as part of a participant) is started by an action triggered internally. This semantic construct is present in S-BPM as well. Any S-BPM subject that starts with an action or a send state is also triggered by itself, thus giving it an active role within the process. Let's consider the opposite case of a passive participant or subject. BPMN would put a message-start-event ([2], p. 240) in front of the initial tasks within a process to express that this participant is naturally passive and waiting for requests from another one to start its operations. In S-BPM, this would be expressed by a subject whose initial state is a receive state.

In any case, there is a start and end attribute for each state in S-BPM, indicated by the dark bold line of the S-BPM states in Figure 11.

It is, of course, always possible to introduce a mapping that is not based on syntax but on semantics. Any send, action and service task with a pure start-event in front of it in BPMN becomes an active start state in S-BPM (action or send state) while any message-start-event becomes a passive receive state or start state. The problem is that this mapping is not bidirectional in a true sense. It seems that BPMN has some semantic redundancies at this point. In BPMN, process initiating messages can be consumed either by a message-start-event ([2], p. 242) or by a pure start-event with a following receive task ([2], p. 161). In the first case the token is instantiated by the

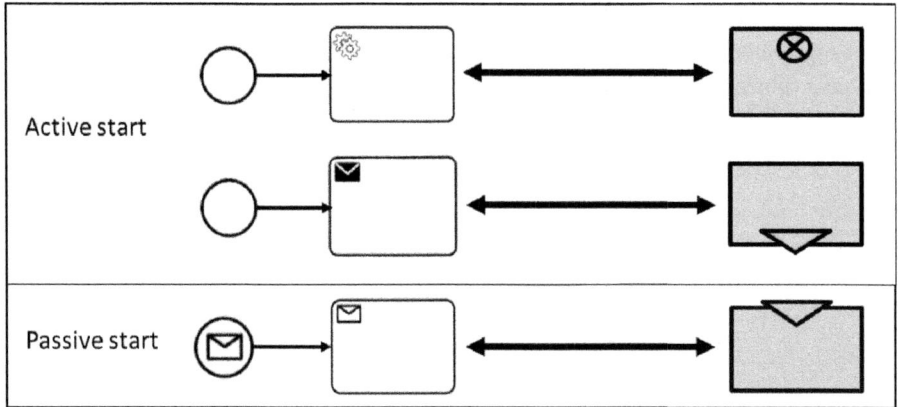

Fig. 11. Bidirectional mapping of start situations within BPMN processes and subjects

incoming message within the event and then moves on. In the second situation, the token is instantiated without a trigger ([2], p. 240) and then moves on to the next receive task to wait for the incoming message before moving on. Hence there are two valid notations for the same semantic situation.[4]

This applies also to end events but in an opposite way: Here a participant terminates its life cycle on its own (active) or by sending a message to the calling or another participant (passive).

4   BPMN Export Prototype and Sample Output

To fulfill the goals set forth by this paper an interface prototype has been developed, which is based on the interface specification given above. At this point, it has the restriction of not being bidirectional but it could be extended to do so at any time. By now, it is only unidirectional, i.e. it is capable of deriving a BPMN model from a S-BMN model. Let's assume a conference. The author writes a paper, sends it to the reviewer and gets either an "Accepted" or a "Rejected" as feedback. In S-PBM the communication view would look like this:

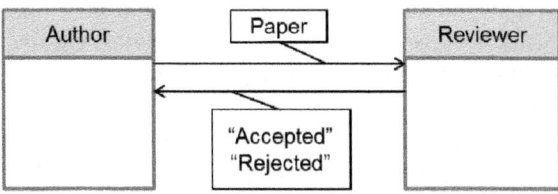

Fig. 12. S-BPM Communication view

---

[4] The token concept is not part of the BPMN design but it is still used often to demonstrate the semantic behavior of entities and modeling concepts so as it is here.

While the communication view shows the two subjects and the messages they exchange, the internal behavior shows the states and transitions that are defined within a subject. Both subjects are depicted in Figure 13.

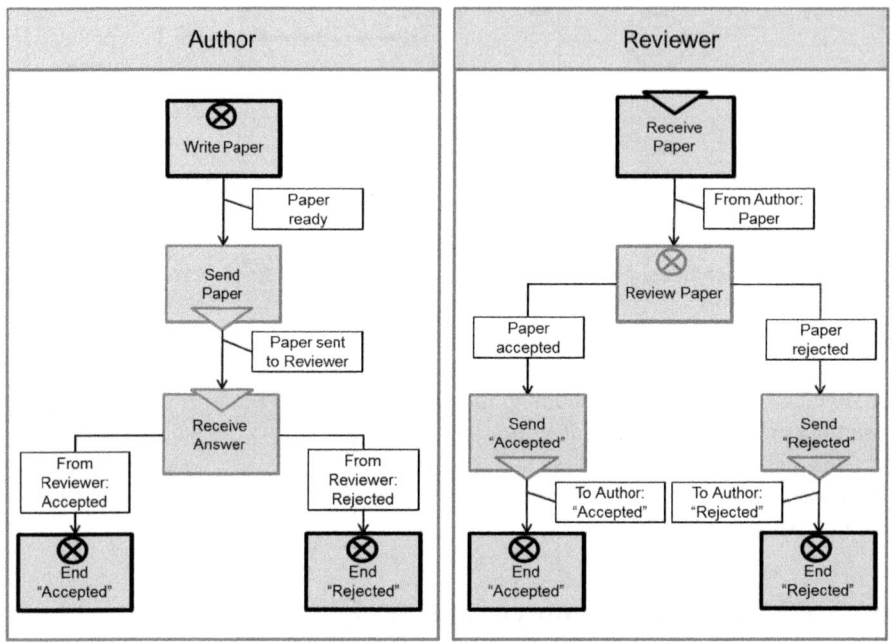

Fig. 13. S-BPM : Internal behavior of the subjects "Author" and "Reviewer"

These separate views in S-BPM are joined by the export interface to generate a single BPMN collaboration diagram. All of the discussed mappings are necessary to translate this basic S-BPM process model into a valid BPMN representation as shown in Figure 14.

Within this example almost all of the formal S-BPM constructs have been used except for the business objects (refer to the next section). Of course, not all of the existing BPMN entities (regarding modeling conformance) are being used by the import. Thus, it is also just generating a subset of BPMN from a subset of S-BPM. The java based implementation of the prototype is built upon an eclipse plugin for the Metasonic suite and using standard eclipse components like EMF (eclipse modeling frame work) , Graphiti and the BPMN editor for eclipse.

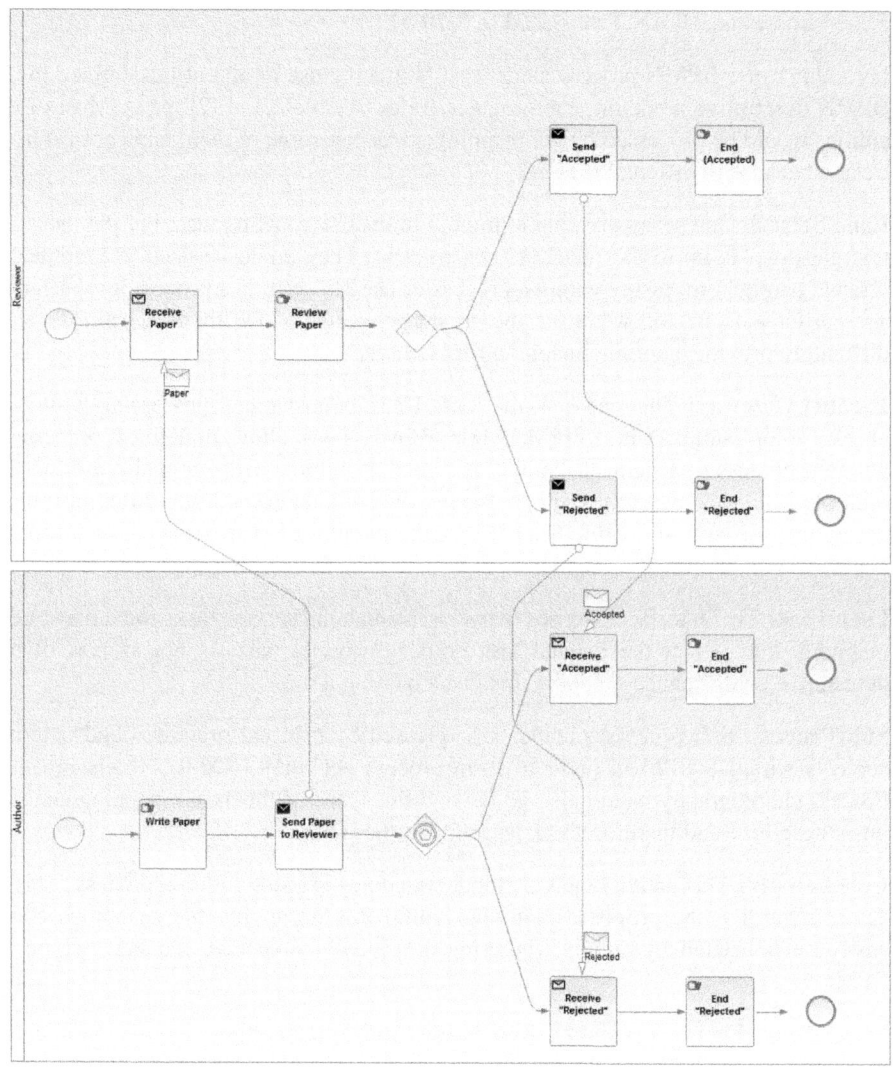

Fig. 14. BPMN output generated by the prototype interface

5   Losses That Come along with the Interface

This section now discusses the losses that come along with the proposed interface. Mappings may be either too complex for this early approach, would require a missing BPMN reference implementation or would go beyond the scope of this paper.

5.1   Losses of BPMN Translated to S-BPM

Let's think of a BPMN process model that is making use of all entities defined in the BPMN descriptive modeling conformance (refer to table 2.1 at [2], p. 3). Most of the entities would be processed by the mapping so far but some of them have not yet been treated because of different reasons:

Lane Sets: A lane set is dividing a process in different swim lanes, but the usage of this construct is up to the modeler ([2], p. 305). They could be used to graphically arrange parallel processing within a process or used to split up a process into different sub-participants or for whatever the modeler wants to use them. Therefore it is difficult to provide a definite mapping for lane sets.

Parallel Gateway: This one is a true loss. There is no parallel processing within an atomic actor (subject) in S-BPM, while BPMN does allow undefined processing within a process / participant. Parallel processing within S-BPM is realized either by multiple instances of a subject or by having different subjects doing different things, but no token is split up within S-BPM. So, the parallel gateway needs a work around that somehow expresses its semantics. This is left for further investigation.

User Task: This interface chooses between manual and service tasks to be part of the mapping, but in fact the manual task could always be taken - not as part of the descriptive conformance - making this just a naming issue.

Sub Process: Sub processes could be expressed by external processes and external subjects within S-BPM in order to form process networks [XX Ref: Fleischmann]. Process choreography would also go beyond the scope of this basic mapping concept introduced here and therefore is an issue for further research.

Call Activity: This activity calls a global (standard) process within a process. This is a loss regarding the proposed mapping within this paper, but the semantics could easily be translated by simply triggering a "global" subject by message within S-BPM.

Timer-Start-Event, Terminate-End-Event and Intermediate Events: While the other specific event types for BPMN descriptive modeling conformance have been shown to be feasible in section 3.1, intermediate events and two special types remain. A timer start event ([2], p. 240) could be expressed by a starting action state within a subject that returns the time constantly while any outgoing transition is only executed when the return time value equals the time labeled on that edge. The terminate end event has currently no expression in S-BPM. Intermediate events could be easily expressed using the transition labels between states within S-BPM.

Group, Documentation and Text Annotation: These items are just additional information based on text or graphics, but, like lanes, do not define any semantics and hence represent no losses regarding the expressiveness of the model itself.

5.2   Losses of S-BPM Translated to BPMN

In this section, we consider the same problem from the other direction - the translation of an S-BPM process model to a BPMN descriptive model. As the prototype demonstrates, most of the S-BPM core features can be easily translated into BPMN. But here too there are some losses.

Business Objects: The major issue regarding this is the detailed modeling possibility of business objects provided by S-BPM. Of course there is a modeling entity within BPMN that represents a business or data object ([2], p. 206) but as will be demonstrated, the BPMN concept is much weaker in this respect because some information can't be mapped to the BPMN model.

As Peter Kesch states in his paper "Business Objects as a Mediator between Process and Data" [8] there are some standard operations that are common for data base accesses and hence related to business (data) objects: create, read, update and delete. These functions have become part of the S-BPM business objects specification. Besides this, S-BPM business objects can also be nested and combined, referring even to different data storages [8].

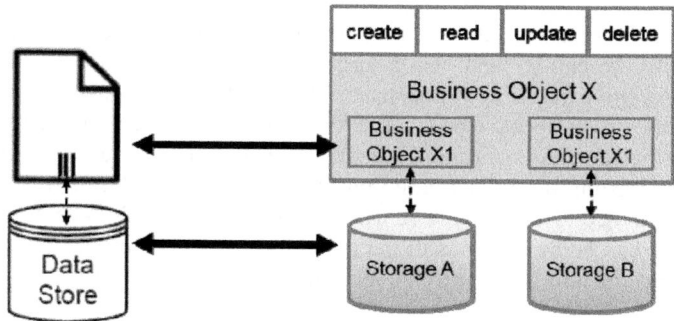

Fig. 15. Bidirectional mapping of business objects

Business objects in BPMN do not provide these two features. Although BPMN provides a data object and a data object collection entity as well as a data store (see Figure 15), it is not possible to access build in standard database operations. Probably there could be a combination of single data objects of different data storages within collections in BPMN, but these structures would not be part of the model anymore. The business objects, which have not been part of the prototype so far, could be implemented at any time, however with the mentioned losses.

Multi Subjects: Within S-BPM there is the possibility to have multiple instances of a subject in order to express situations like a bunch of vendors with the same behavior. They give offers and the process continues with the best offer, thus with this specific instance of the multi-subject vendor. Instantiation is a complex issue that would also go beyond the scope of this model based mapping. There might be constructs within BPMN that could be used to express a situation like this, but probably the specification document would not be sufficient. As stated by Börger, instantiation is semantically underspecified by the BPMN document [6]. Hence this is a topic of further investigation in regard to the mapping but also as regard to BPMN on its own merit.

Roles: Within S-BPM there is the possibility to assign resource roles (resources, performers, potential owners) to activities. There might be another semantic problem at this point within BPMN. This mapping interprets the name or id of the swim lane (participant) as the name or id of the subject. Roles (or resources) within S-BPM are assigned to the subjects. But assigning resources to single tasks within BPMN, resource assignment could either be redundant or even create conflicts with this interpretation. Anyhow, when mapping from S-BPM to BPMN, all tasks could be assigned with the resource that has been assigned to the S-BPM subject, but the problem occurs when mapping BPMN to S-BPM: There could be tasks with different resources assigned within a process / participant which is corrupting the concept of this mapping: The interpretation of a BPMN participant as the performer of all tasks within its process definition.

6   Conclusion

In this paper it was shown that the proposed mapping serves well to translate most of the S-BPM core entities and also a large portion of the entities demanded for the BPMN descriptive modeling conformance on a notational translation.

Also some proposals have been made as to how even more BPMN entities could be mapped using semantic interpretations like a timer subject for a timer start event and so on. The existing prototype, based on the mappings introduced within this paper, could be extended to cover these remaining constructs as well as to be bidirectional. Hence there can be no doubt as to the possibility of a bidirectional S-BPM / BPMN interface that converts an S-BPM model to BPMN and vice versa.

In order to translate executable models, further research is required and some prerequisites have to be fulfilled as well. Redundant or underspecified semantics within BPMN are a problem that would have to be solved first, probably by some kind of reference implementation. As stated by Börger [6], there is a huge gap between drawn and executable models within BPMN. In order to execute BPMN models a significant amount of engine dependent information is still needed. Thus, the interchange of executable models would require a specific BPMN reference implementation as well as a commitment to a specific BPMN engine. But these problems would also apply to an interchange of executable BPMN models form one BPMN engine to another. Thus, the problem of vendor lock-in as recognized by Hohwiller and Schlegel ([9], p. 81) seems to be solved as concerns non executable model interchange.

References

1. Ziemann, J., Ohren, O., Jaekel, F.-W., Kahl, T., Knothe, T.: Achieving Enterprise Interoperability Applying a Common Enterprise Metamodel. In: Doumeingts, G., et al. (eds.) Enterprise Interoperability. Springer, London (2007)

2. OMG: The BPMN specification, http://www.omg.org/spec/BPMN/2.0/PDF/
3. Fleischmann, A.: What Is S-BPM? In: Buchwald, H., Fleischmann, A., Seese, D., Stary, C. (eds.) S-BPM ONE 2009. CCIS, vol. 85, pp. 85–106. Springer, Heidelberg (2010)
4. Fleischmann, A., et al.: Subjektorientiertes Prozessmanagement. Carl Hanser Verlag, München (2011)
5. Fleischmann, A.: Distributed Systems. Springer, Heidelberg (1994)
6. Börger, E.: Approaches to Modeling Business Processes - A Critical Analysis of BPMN, Workflow Patterns and YAWL. To appear in J. Software & Systems Modeling (2011)
7. Meyer, N., Feiner, T., Radmayr, M., Blei, D., Fleischmann, A.: Dynamic Catenation and Execution of Cross Organisational Business Processes - The jCPEX! Approach. In: Fleischmann, A., Schmidt, W., Singer, R., Seese, D. (eds.) S-BPM ONE 2010. CCIS, vol. 138, pp. 84–105. Springer, Heidelberg (2011)
8. Kesch, P.: Business Objects as a Mediator between Processes and Data. In: Fleischmann, A., Schmidt, W., Singer, R., Seese, D. (eds.) S-BPM ONE 2010. CCIS, vol. 138, pp. 180–191. Springer, Heidelberg (2011)
9. Hohwiller, J., Schlegel, D.: Funktionale BPM Produktauswahl – Erfolgreiche BPM-Projekte durch ganzheitliche Betrachtung in OBJECTSpectrum 6/2011, SIGS DATACOM, Troisdorf (2011)

Mapping the Integrated Care Pathway into BPM for Health Case Management

Hessah AlSalamah[1], Alex Gray[1], and David Morrey[2]

[1] School of Computer Science & Informatics, Cardiff University, Queen's Buildings,
5 The Parade, Roath, Cardiff CF24 3AA, UK
{h.alsalamah,w.a.gray}@cs.cf.ac.uk
[2] Clinical Information Unit, Velindre NHS Trust, Velindre Road, Whitchurch,
Cardiff, CF14 2TL, UK
dave.morrey@wales.nhs.uk

Abstract. Teamwork, collaboration and coordination are key aspects of the patient-centric approach taken by modern healthcare. Although many projects have been and are currently being undertaken to improve support for health care professionals, adequate support for teamwork, communication and coordination has yet to be achieved. The delivery of the healthcare service is very challenging as it involves heterogeneous distributed systems, multi-professionals and dependent tasks among each. In addition, the treatment journey of each patient is unique as a decision is usually made according to several constraints related to the patient, medical condition, patient's choice, available resources and/or doctor's consultation decision. We believe that, in order to provide the required support, it is necessary to explicitly acknowledge the patient's medical state within their treatment journey. This project proposes the use of a Business Process Management (BPM) system that uses associations between patients, health care professionals, and the Integrated Care Pathway (ICP) to provide improved support for healthcare professionals as individuals and members of integrated care teams. Moreover, mapping the ICP into the BPM system will help support the implementation of best practice according to the national guidelines. By leveraging the information contained in these associations, and understanding the patient progress along the dynamic care pathway, this proposal provides tailored context-based actions. This includes automated notifications, alerts, scheduling and timers, as well as supporting treatment continuity and tracking as the patient progresses through their treatment journey. Clinicians' and developers' feedback on this proposal has been very positive.

Keywords: business process management (BPM), case management, context-based actions, integrated care pathway (ICP), workflow technology.

1 Background

Modern healthcare has seen an ongoing move towards a patient-centric approach. This approach emphasises teamwork and collaboration as key aspects of the

S. Oppl and A. Fleischmann (Eds.): S-BPM ONE 2012, CCIS 284, pp. 106–120, 2012.
© Springer-Verlag Berlin Heidelberg 2012

healthcare process. Patients within such a collaborative model follow an Integrated Care Pathway (ICP) which is a structured multidisciplinary care plan, which details essential steps in the care of patients with a specific clinical problem [1]. The treatment journey followed by patients within the patient-centric model usually involves multi-professional care team members providing different healthcare services at distributed sites. This process requires an effective mechanism to support the interaction and collaboration among the care team members as well as management of potential interactions between complex care pathways being followed by a single patient with more than one disease, e.g. cancer and diabetes. Current Hospital Information Systems (HIS) used at different healthcare organisations were originally designed to support the traditional disease-centred delivery model. The challenges imposed by political influence and dealing with legacy systems, add to the challenge of the complex nature of the domain with its many conflicting requirements and confounding factors. It has been a priority to support the implementation of modern healthcare, however it is not yet adequately supported by HISs [2]. Many proposals have been made and followed to address different aspects of this problem, but there are still many challenges which have not yet been addressed, such as: teamwork collaboration with respect to the roles, actual care progress and case specific needs. In recent years, there has been wide exploitation of Information Communication Technologies (ICT) in the healthcare domain. Recent informatics projects emphasise the implementation of standards and the need to provide access to knowledge resources and patient data. Examples of these ICT projects include: Electronic Patient Records (EPR) (e.g. [3]), knowledge management systems (e.g. [4]), triage systems (e.g. [5]), assessment systems, prescribing systems (e.g. [6]), test ordering and result delivery systems [7]. Within the National Health Service (NHS) in the UK, notable projects in this domain include: developing and making available guidelines and standards through the National Institute for Health and Clinical Excellence (NICE) [8] and the Map of Medicine (MoM) [4], the Scottish emergency care record [9] and proposals for a shared, unified patient record accessible at any location, as required [10,6]. We believe that, while these projects are an important first step in improving healthcare support systems, there is still more work to be done. For example, shared patient records support the treatment process in terms of provision of patient information and medications prescribed. However, they do not actively indicate to practitioners that relevant information is available, nor do they consider the individual information requirements of practitioners with different specialties or the dynamic communication requirements beyond pure provision of information. Similarly, decision support and knowledge management systems support coordination between different tasks or processes by managing their sequence. This is suitable for patients following the anticipated treatment pathway; however a patient's state is dynamic, and often a patient's needs evolve and they follow a non-predicted care pathway. As each patient is unique, changes to the treatment plan can happen at any time and in many ways. This requires support for dynamic team allocation and the management of changes along the care pathway to support this extremely dynamic process.

2   Proposal

This project considers the dynamic requirements of health and care practitioners which are beyond the traditional decision support and knowledge management systems provisions. We believe that, in order to address this problem fully, it is necessary to take account of the activities of practitioners as members of a dynamic team handling the treatment of a patient. Moreover, it is important to have this linked to the flow of a patient's treatment(s) and the dynamic processes involved, and to do this in a patient-centric way. This includes associating the patient record with the involved care providers and connecting both back to the patient's ICP. The work described includes tracking care teams and individual team members dynamically as the patient progresses along the dynamic care pathway. It proposes the integration of a BPM[1] system's interface into the HIS's interface as it will better support both the individual work of health and care practitioners as well as improve support for team communication, and care coordination throughout the patient's care. The innovation is on the use of ICP to be the common goal/subject among the healthcare providers while keeping the information system adaptive, flexible, and pro-active. This is supported among the individual users representing the healthcare providers of a shared patient.

This paper is based on a joint project between Cardiff School of Computer Science and Informatics at Cardiff University and Velindre NHS Trust cancer centre in Wales, UK. A proof of concept prototype was developed to test our assumptions and investigate the capabilities of the BPM based system and how much support it could give in the treatment process. Moreover, the prototype will be used to demonstrate the proposed system in an evaluation by multi-professional care team members and HIS developers.

3   Approach

This is not a proposal for a completely new system but for a tool to evolve existing HISs and improve their support functionalities. This can be done by mapping the clinical guidelines into a BPM system engine and having this operate as an invisible intermediate layer between users and the HISs currently used by them (see Figure 1(a)). This aims to make the support for care teams more proactive by taking appropriate actions with regard to the support needed at the treatment stage, while utilising the information and facilities of existing HISs. It follows the best clinical practice guidelines available to healthcare professionals through NICE and other reported clinical guidelines, such as MoM. These guidelines aim to enforce quality standards to achieve: clinical effectiveness, patient safety and improved patient experience [11]. As can be seen in Figure 1(a), the WFMS layer

---

[1] BPM and WFMS are used interchangeably throughout this research. This is because we refer to WFMS as Business WFMSs that satisfy the specifications listed in section 3. This is also based on the studies stating that WFMS is part of BPM. Conversely, BPM is a superset of WFMS with more control over processes, integration and optimisation

is an upper layer which is independent of the structure of the HISs underneath it. Moreover, the WFMS can act with any number of HISs and is a hub connecting to these systems (see Figure 1(b)). The strength of the BPM system is in its ability to invoke existing systems at any stage during the process flow in a way which overcomes the system heterogeneity challenges. WFMSs and BPMs can be adjusted to enforce a specific sequence and/or enable an extremely flexible order of processes. In the breast cancer scenario, some stages of the treatment journey are pre-structured examples, for instance single tasks performed in sub-processes, such as tests. While other stages are dynamic in that the process flow cannot be predicted in advance. This is common among patients with multiple diseases. In order to achieve maximum flexibility, the system should be driven by the patient's condition yet fully controlled by the multi-professional care team members. The proposed system can provide suggestions and support the process according to best practice guidelines, however the final decision is controlled by members of the medical team using it. This is to ensure and emphasise the fact that this proposal is for a tool to support the treatment process which is not meant to takeover the decision maker's control on the treatment flow decisions.

By looking at an ICP we can see that it resembles a workflow with all its elements, such as: process, paths, routing decisions and roles. In an ICP, processes are represented by diagnosis and treatments, paths by flow of treatments, routing decisions by clinical decisions on treatment and diagnosis and, finally, the multi-disciplinary care team represent the different roles interacting with the system. This led to WFMS and BPM systems being chosen as the approach investigated to support the implementation of the ICP. This is based on our belief that the system needs to take account of the treatment flow and sequence of tasks in addition to a patient's condition in order to perform accurate and related actions

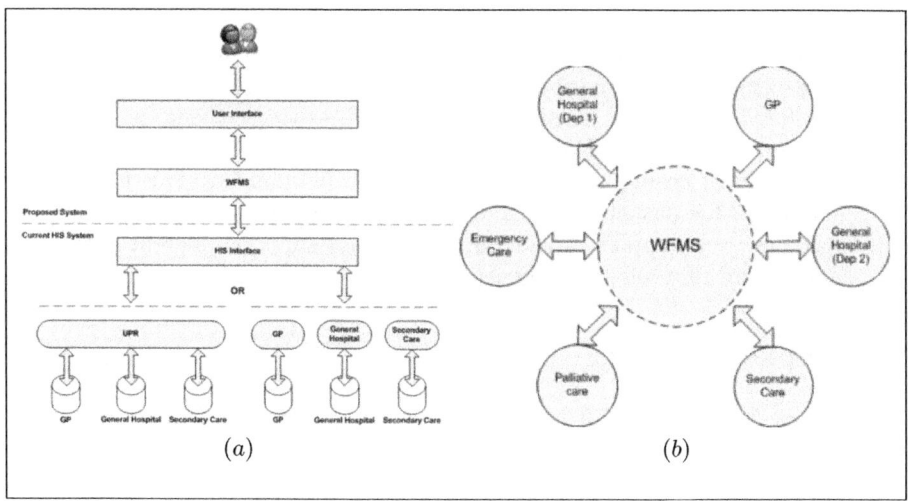

Fig. 1. System's Architecture

that improve healthcare provision. Different WFMSs were investigated in order to determine the most appropriate engine to address collaboration problems in the healthcare domain. These different WFMSs were tested and compared taking account of aspects such as: availability, portability, functionality, operation, behaviour, information and organisation [12], and also the characteristics of the WFMSs engine that had been identified as needed for the approach. These were:

- **Business Workflow:** This is required to model the huge number of processes interacting in a healthcare system. Business workflows support human interaction with the system. This is necessary in healthcare systems, where different care team professionals interact with the system and support the decision making process and therefore the routing of the flow. Moreover, the ability to set security and privacy controls is extremely important in such a domain, as is assigning activities to different roles or associating a role with a special member. Human interaction is a major element that must be considered in a healthcare system to support security and privacy. Another benefit from using business workflows is the ability to set timers that are capable of starting activities and alerts, as this can add enormous benefits to a HISs support.
- **Activity-based Workflow:** This is needed as the heart of the process is the activities. Activities represent all the treatment and diagnosis options a patient can follow. These options should be modelled in the WFMS and form the main part of the system.
- **Support Control Flow:** This can be coupled with activity-based workflow systems. It is the controller of the routing process along the flow. In the healthcare scenario and for our proposal, the system should be state-driven. This means that a patient's medical condition is the main driver along the treatment journey. Using other drivers could interfere in the routing process, by affecting the available resources and the decision of multi-professional care team members.
- **Support Data Flow:** This option is also extremely important in a healthcare scenario as information referencing the patient should also be sent along the flow to relate the running process/activities to a patient.
- **Support Workflow Patterns:** The variety of patterns supported by the WFMS must ensure that multiple cases can be mapped. This is extremely important for patients with multiple conditions as the treatment journey becomes very complex. If the system does not support different patterns, it should provide tools to implement them.

4   Implementation

Stateframe BPM system [13] from Alia Systems Ltd. was selected to implement the prototype. It was chosen because: it fulfils the required characteristics explained (in section 3); it supports Rapid Application Development (RAD); and the developers will provide technical support. The diagnostic breast cancer clinical guidelines were selected as the trial scenario to be used in the proof of concept prototype, since there is extensive information about cancer and its clinical guidelines online which made searching and understanding the treatment process easier; the process is complex enough to show the challenges involved in the treatment delivery, as it involves interaction among different systems, organisations and care team professionals; and our co-operation with the Velindre NHS cancer unit is of long standing. The guidelines of the diagnostic breast cancer clinic and the treatment choices used in the implementation of the prototype are taken from the MoM diagnostic for breast cancer [14] and advanced treatment [15]. These guidelines show the different stages of the treatment process and have an attached document explaining the details of the organisations involved, information required, roles involved, flow logic and any constraints. In using this information, a good sense and understanding of the treatment process was achieved. The scenario represented in Figure 2, which is based on a combination of [14] and [15], starts with a GP suspecting a patient has cancer and therefore referring the patient to a Surgeon Oncologist. The Surgeon Oncologist checks the patient's history and requests assessments such as examinations, imaging, fine needle aspiration, and core biopsy. The results of these tests will then be reviewed at an MDT meeting to decide whether there are no abnormalities, if more tests are needed, or if there are positive findings. In the case of no abnormalities, the patient will be reassured and then will be discharged to primary care. In the case of more tests being needed, the MDT will decide whether a surgical or core biopsy is needed before the patient is reviewed again in an MDT meeting. In the case of a positive finding, the reviewers will decide whether it is benign or if cancer is confirmed. If a benign disease is confirmed, the patient will be educated on the principles of management and then will be discharged to primary care. If Breast cancer is confirmed, the GP will be informed. This will be followed by a number of stages until the care reaches a point where a decision is made on the treatment options for this patient, which could be a surgical or non-surgical option, such as radiotherapy or chemotherapy. By looking at the flow in the MoM guidelines, its associated document, and the literature, we can identify the treatment stages where there is a need for communication and care coordination among the different care professionals involved in this flow. Figure 2 highlights the different critical stages of the treatment flow, which are:

- *referral* from the GP to the surgeon oncologist. This is initiated by the GP, activated by the primary care nurse and sent by the administration at the GP surgery. The referral is picked-up by the administration at the secondary unit scheduled on the secondary care system and picked up by the breast cancer nurse to be processed by the appropriate surgeon oncologist.
- *notification* of MDT reviewers about the triple assessment results and clinical examination notes; these have to be gathered and made available before the MDT meeting. The notes will be forwarded by the breast cancer nurse to the haematologist, radiologist, and pathologist from the stored information in the secondary care records, (haematology laboratory system, radiology system and pathology system). The results are gathered by the MDT coordinator so that they can be discussed at the MDT team meeting involving a surgeon oncologist, radiologist, pathologist, clinical and medical oncologist, and a nurse.

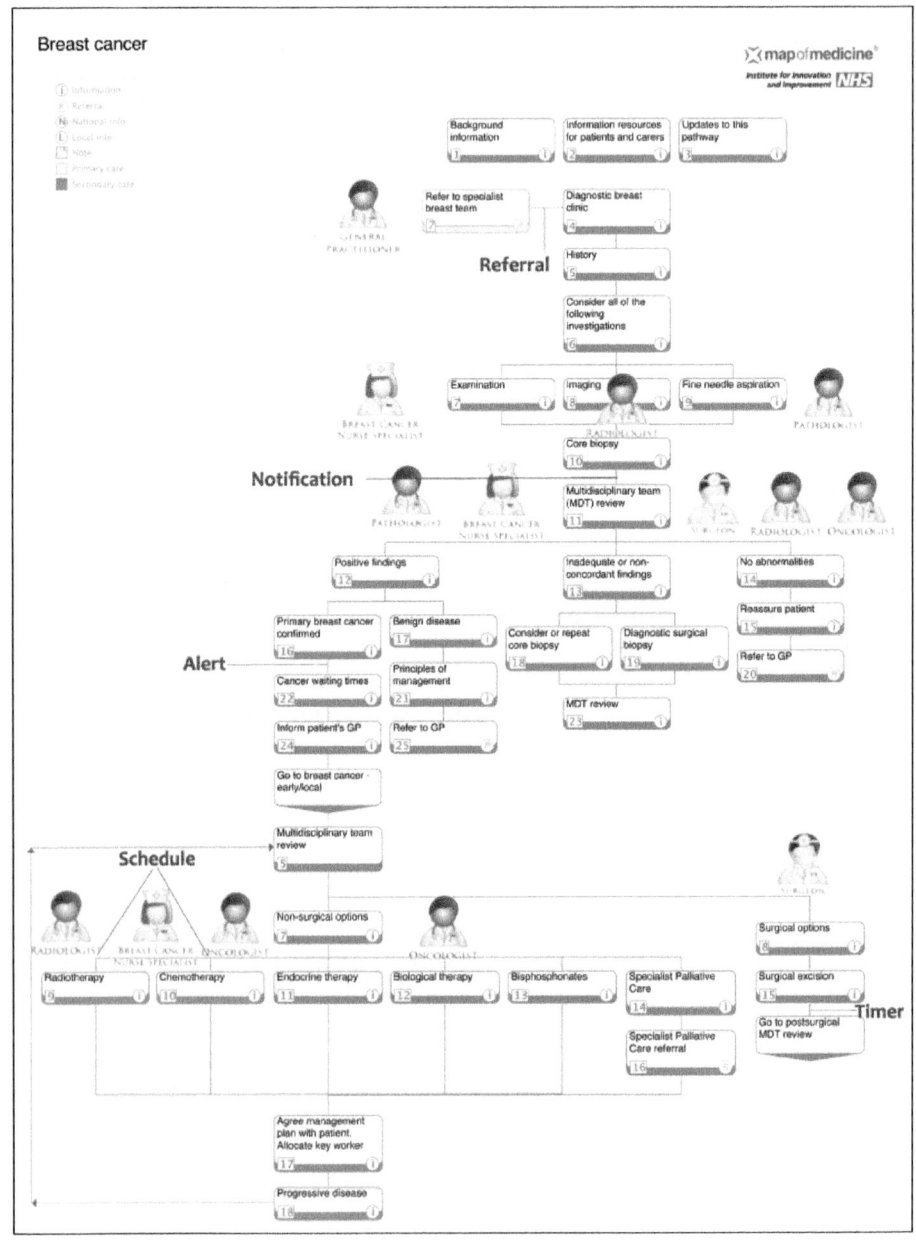

Fig. 2. ICP of Breast Cancer Treatment

- *alert* for a patient diagnosed with breast cancer, this informs the patient's GP. It is initiated by the surgeon oncologist, performed by the breast cancer nurse and sent by the administrator at the secondary care unit. The message is picked-up by the administrator at the GP surgery, scheduled by the primary care nurse to inform the GP and update the patient's record in the GP surgery system. This alerts the GP, that a patient is undertaking chemotherapy or radiotherapy. It is used to avoid any conflict. It is usually managed and controlled by the clinical oncologist using the available information about the patient's medical and treatment history and the medical information revealed by the patient.

- *scheduling* required if the patient is under both chemotherapy and radiotherapy; a minimum of two weeks must occur between these two treatments. This sequence is managed and controlled by the clinical oncologist using the available information.
- *timing* required to refer patients to their oncologist after recovering from a surgical operation. This is usually a specified waiting time after surgery to allow recovery. The patient's condition is reviewed at a post-surgical MDT to agree on the treatment plan after surgery. This will be requested by the surgeon oncologist, performed by the nurse and picked up by the MDT.

Figure 2 shows a simple flow with no complications which is not the usual case. Patients do not usually follow the anticipated care pathway and each patient's flow is unique as many elements interact and affect its progress.

After selecting the scenario it is mapped into our chosen WFMS (Stateframe). The Stateframe process designer tool is used. This mapper uses Microsoft Visio with a customised template. The map designed by the mapper is linked dynamically to the system's engine. The data about the flow logic and the cases processed is stored in the process server database and organised as a User Data Properties (UDP) file, which is used at runtime to manage the process. The process map consists of of the following elements:

- **A Process:** this is the actual workflow map of the clinical guidelines. Each process could be a representation of a specific task within the guidelines or the whole disease treatment. Sub-processes representing specific tasks within a treatment can be internally (within the map) linked to the task. Tasks repeated along the treatment pathway can be mapped in separate processes which will be called when required. For this project, the whole treatment journey represented in Figure 2 was mapped into a single process. The scale of the project is small and therefore it did not require splitting the treatment guidelines into multiple processes. However, to improve the visibility of the processes and for a more organised manageable mapping, the map is divided into separate sheets, each representing a different role or location the patient is referred to. Figure 3 is a sample of a process map showing an MDT's sheet. It shows a small portion of the whole process map represented in Figure 2, however the different steps are linked with anchors to sustain the flow of the treatment according to clinical guidelines.
- **An Activity:** these are the steps of the clinical guidelines. Activities represent tasks which provide productivity gains throughout the process flow. An activity can be: a prompt for manual decisions, an automated referral,

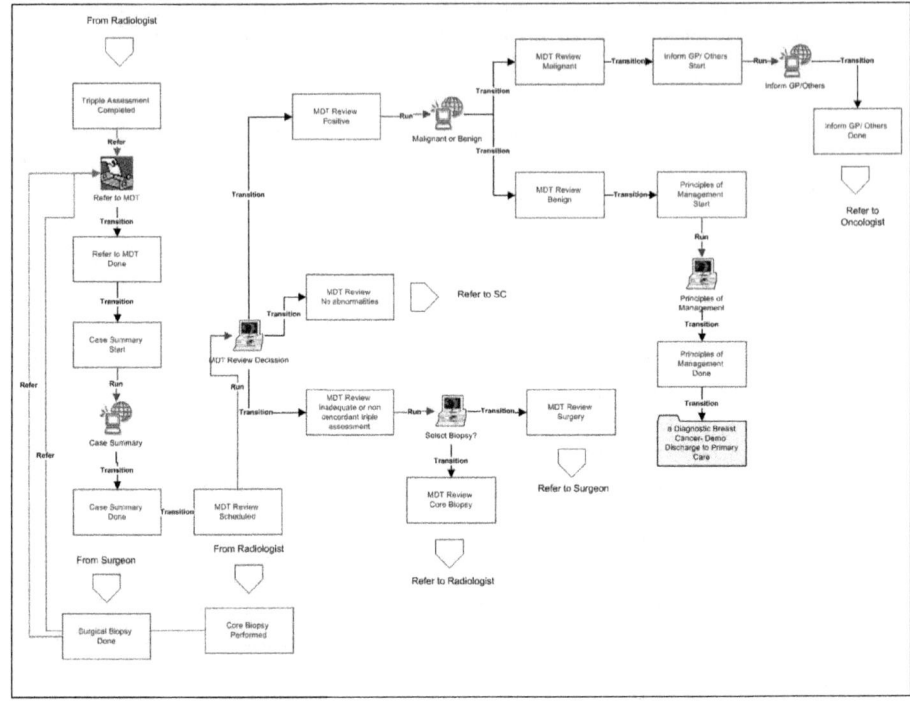

Fig. 3. Process Map of MDT's Actions

an automated step where no user interaction is required, or a decision support tool (ASP activity) where relevant information is displayed to the user and their decision is expected. Activities along the map will be associated with the actioning roles of care team members (if any) which will be then linked to the patient as he/she progresses along the treatment journey. In this project, each stage within the treatment flow of the breast cancer diagnosis and treatment was represented by at least one activity. The choice of type depends on the nature of the task. These activities can be coded to add constraints to the logic and access related data when additional information is required.

– **A Process object:** this provides control or audit to the case according to its state. As a state-driven engine, the actual driver of the flow is the case process object state representing the patient's status or condition at certain points of the treatment. Process objects can change the state of another object, initiate an activity or just state a condition. Activities, on the other hand, change the state of the process object that initiated them. Process object states identify the state of the case. This is usually defined before and after each activity by showing the initial state and the resulting state after processing the task. For this project, process object states are a representation of either the treatment flow progress or the patient condition.

In most of the cases, treatment flow progress is used. Examples include: examination start or examination completed (see Figure 3). When the object state initiates an activity, it should identify its state before and after it is processed. The patient condition state is used at some stages in the process map, such as MDT review decision of malignant, benign or no abnormality (see Figure 3).

– **A case:** this is the scenario in progress. Each case represents a single patient treatment flow. For each patient, the treatment pathway is unique and is processed by considering a patient's health condition and the available resources. The case hierarchy at run time usually shows treatment history, the progress, the state in each and the roles or users involved in different stages.

At runtime, as the patient's case progresses along the process, the reference to the patient's record will be passed through. The driver of the case progress will be the process object state. When an activity gets activated, if a role is associated with the activity, the role will be associated with the case. Moreover, if a rule is associated with the activity, the rule will be processed considering the different roles involved with the patient.

5 Implication of Proposed System

The proof of concept prototype showed that the application of Workflow Technology in the healthcare domain is very promising. It can be used to evolve and utilise the functionalities of existing HIS, so that they can be used to support the implementation in the ICP and associated treatment flow for a patient. It is believed that these functionalities are important as they result in safer more effective and efficient care and treatment. Functionalities of the prototype system include: providing a pro-active system, routing and information filtering. These functionalities are:

– **Pro-active System:** this is the primary advantage of using Workflow Technology in the healthcare domain. It is the difference between having a reactive or a proactive system. In the case of a reactive system, which most traditional HISs are, reactions are a response to requests made by users while proactive systems are capable of identifying the need to take an action and activating it. The workflow engine within the workflow management system can be coded to fetch triggers, understand which of the users or roles are affected by this trigger, how they are affected and finally, take appropriate actions to inform them. These pro-active functionalities can be used to execute many different actions, such as: alert, notify, refer, schedule and set timers.

  • **Alert:** is fired when urgent or immediate action is required, or when specific information about a patient's condition needs to be noticed (e.g. a patient under chemotherapy).

- **Notify:** this is gathering the information required at a certain stage of the process flow (e.g. gathering all requested test results before a clinic patient's visits).
- **Refer:** this is done automatically and targeted not at the organisation but to the exact administrator or even to the specific role. This is done by delivering the referral letter to a targeted user and making it available in their in-tray/inbox (e.g. GP referring a patient to an Oncologist when new symptoms appear).
- **Schedule:** is needed to formalise a process. This involves maintaining prerequisites or a sequence of steps which are essential and required in the care process (e.g. a patient stops taking aspirin two weeks before scheduled surgery, or maintaining two weeks waiting time between chemotherapy and radiotherapy sessions for a patient).
- **Set timers:** these are required when a certain action needs to be processed at a specific time. This is important in ensuring continuity of care and that patients do not get lost in the process. This functionality is carried out by making sure that information is delivered to a targeted user before the time it is needed. This can involve: sending letters to a user's in-tray, executing alerts, sending notification, and/or doing referrals (e.g. at end of two weeks recovery period following surgery, a patient needs to be scheduled for a clinical visit, and reminders of requests after a certain waiting time).

- **Routing:** this is based on the ICP to help the system use the sequence of processes and the consequences of any decision made. This is either by suggesting the next stage or automating a set of processes. While routing is a tool that WFMSs provide, routing is only made with a user's approval or suggestion. This is done by providing a message to the user showing the different alternatives according to the ICPs' logic and the user can approve any or simply skip it (e.g. MDT referral after a set of examinations for a patient is performed, and the system suggests an imaging test according to age (mammogram for older than X or an ultrasound otherwise)).
- **Task automation:** is performed when a number of tasks need to be processed as a set. In this context, it includes tasks that do not require user interaction.
- **Information extraction and filtering:** to ensure a summary of important information is visible to healthcare professionals when viewing a patient's records. This aims to facilitate tracking a patient and improving the decision-making process by making healthcare professionals aware of the development of the care process and therefore making better use of their time. This includes improved visibility of: a treatment history, milestones, order and time, and acting healthcare professionals.

6 Evaluation

Evaluation of this prototype was aimed at examining its technical aspects and usefulness. The technical evaluation was conducted by implementing a proof of concept prototype and interviewing members of the Clinical Information Unit (CIU) at the Velindre Trust to evaluate the possibility of adopting the proposed ideas. The usefulness evaluation is conducted through a literature survey and brainstorming sessions and also through one-to one interviews with actual users of the current HIS (CaNISC)[16] used at the Trust. The proof of concept prototype showed that mapping the ICP into the workflow technology could provide many functionalities (as detailed in section 5). These include providing a more pro-active system capable of performing the following actions: alert, notify, refer, schedule, and set timers. It also provides a flexible system that handles dynamic changes happening during a patient's treatment. This includes routing the flow and performing automatic tasks. Moreover, the workflow system provides a tool to track patients and ensure continuity of the flow by filtering and extracting important information. The treatment information extracted includes: history, milestones, order and time and involved care team professionals. We will have an evaluation session with developers at the CIU at Velindre to evaluate the possibility of getting this proposal implemented in practice. This will include the technicalities involved in mapping, integrating, and interacting with the system. However, we have had several sessions with technical experts in BPM and HIS, who agree on the possibility of these ideas being implemented in reality. BPM experts are the developers and founders of Alia systems, and they assured us that it is technically possible to implement this proposal using current systems. The coordination problem was originally brought to our attention by the team at the CIU at Velindre Trust. They pointed out their need for a more intelligent proactive system. They highlighted that there is a need for a system that facilitates following patients up and providing interaction. In discussion sessions about our proposal, they confirmed that the functionalities that workflow technology can provide are already in their agenda for the current system's improvements. Members of the CIU approved the general ideas and confirmed their need for a more proactive system to help support the current system in use. Finally, five one-to-one semi-structured interviews with care team professionals with different specialities in cancer treatment were conducted. These one hour interviews aimed to evaluate the opinions of the multi-professional care team members on this proposal in terms of its usefulness, advantages, disadvantages and to identify their concerns. All five care team members interviewed agreed on the potential benefits that could be gained from having such a system. They agreed that there is need for a more proactive system that facilitates care coordination among care team members. The majority provided examples where they had been unable to make a decision due to inappropriate or unavailable information at a clinical visit. They also highlighted some of the difficulties they face in using the existing system to search for certain information and that it would be very useful to have highlights of the case visible in one place. They all agreed that it would not reduce their current work load, as this is mainly spent with patients, however it could save them some time searching for medical information in a patient's records. A physiotherapist interviewed highlighted that she can see the benefits of having this proposal implemented for care team members other than physiotherapists, as she believes that the physiotherapist's role in cancer care rarely requires urgent reaction unless they are in-patients and that she finds manual communication tools to be effective and so there is no need for a change. An oncologist interviewed discussed his concerns that it would lead to information overload and being over-alerted about his cases. He suggested giving the users an option to turn the private alert messages off and having a patient's information visible only when viewing the patient's case. However, he stated that having important information highlighted in a patient's records would be beneficial. He also highlighted that we need to measure the benefits gained by implementing this system against the effort and cost required for implementation. The oncologist later explained that the information gathering process for his cases is conducted by a general oncologist before cases are transferred to him, which explains why he did not experience similar challenges to his colleagues.

7 Discussion

This paper considers ways to improve current healthcare information systems when they are supporting a collaborative patient-centric approach. The main focus is supporting the healthcare provider's interactions who act on common clinical guidelines as the shared processes. This links it directly to the aspects of Subject-Oriented BPM (S-BPM) as proposed by [17]. We have not proposed a new system to replace the existing HISs, but present an approach which evolves and extends the functionalities of current systems. This is by integrating the proposed system's interface to HIS's. The proposed system forms an invisible layer between a user's interface and the underlying HISs used. This intermediate layer consists of a Workflow engine to support a care team member's communication and care coordination as the patient progresses along one or more ICPs. This is based on our belief that the system cannot take intelligent meaningful action unless it takes account of the treatment flow. Moreover, the main driver of the flow should be the patient's medical condition. Accordingly, the system will provide a suggestion to the user who controls these suggestions of: accepting, rejecting or deciding a different route. Having a system that is adaptive to the condition and completely controlled by the user increases its flexibility and so makes it better able to support a situation where the user may decide to choose an unexpected way forward. There are many potential benefits from the proposed system. The system allows explicit support of team working in a dynamic, distributed environment, including communication, coordination, and collaboration. The approach supports patient-specific care automation which is managed by a workflow management system and the embedded actions at critical stages for tailored messaging. This includes performing actions, treatment flow routing and information filtering as the patient progresses along the dynamic care pathway. Moreover, automation is combined with intelligent tools that read events and deliver tailored alerts to appropriate care team members at the time of an event. To support communication, the system provides users with highlights of the medical case and treatment. This is done through the information filtering and extraction techniques supported by the workflow engine. Moreover, the routing and automation of the processes covers the interaction part of the communication. Finally, context-based actions are supported though the inclusion of rules. Possible rule actions include sending notifications about treatment and medications, sending alerts when immediate attention is required, managing change along the care pathway of a patient and supporting referrals. To support coordination, the approach manages the progress of the care flow. This includes identifying change triggers, affected roles, and the appropriate actions/rule associated with each. The coordination process also involves different organisations, systems, team members, tasks, actions, and processes, as well as considering the different care pathways followed by a patient. Coordination actions include setting timers, follow-ups and scheduling/rescheduling. This will ensure that care is coordinated between care teams and team members as a patient progresses along the ICP, taking into account timing and sequence. A proof-of-concept prototype has been implemented which shows how the range of functionality identified by this proposal can be achieved in a WFMS. Initial evaluation of the usability of the prototype involved clinicians at a cancer care trust. One-to-one, structured interviews with clinicians were conducted where the proposal, requirements, functionalities, and prototype were presented and discussed. Feedback was very positive; clinicians felt that patient care could be improved if this proposal were implemented effectively. Further evaluation will include evaluation by HIS developers and will assess the practicality of the system and whether it is technically possible to integrate it with current systems. Also barriers to its implementation and whether it requires re-engineering will be investigated. Although the current proposal has been demonstrated to show promise, there are still several areas requiring further investigation. Although an interface integration should require minimal training, further research needs to be conducted on assessing the impact of alerts on working practice and interface usability and the workload for users. Future work will also identify the needs of the different roles to be extracted from the patient record, the information requirements of each and how they would like to receive it. The focus of this research was on a Breast Cancer scenario and its requirements. Future plans include specifying a generic pattern flexible enough to accommodate other medical scenarios. This will ensure that the system is capable of accommodating any national or local ICP and that it has maximum flexibility. Currently, automation within the system is done according to treatment history and current treatment stage. Future work will include considering the anticipated care pathway in the automation process. This will improve care efficiency and reduce cost by avoiding redundancy and future complications. It will allow the system to inform practitioners whether a complication is likely to affect upcoming patient appointments, and to schedule tests to fulfil not only current requirements but also those likely to occur in the near future and therefore improve planning and scheduling of patient treatment. This paper proposes a model for providing support to healthcare teams working patient-centrically and considers the entire care process. While there are many potential benefits to this approach, there are also still many challenges to be addressed. However, research and feedback achieved so far has been positive and has shown that the proposal is worth pursuing further.

Acknowledgments. The authors would like to acknowledge Hazel Bailey, Principal Information Analyst in Business Analysis Team at Velindre Hospital, for her support and feedback. The first author would also like to acknowledge her sponsor; College of Computer & Information Sciences at King Saud University, Riyadh, Saudi Arabia.

References

1. Campbell, H., Hotchkiss, R., Bradshaw, N., Porteous, M.: Integrated care pathways. BMJ 316, 133–137 (1998)
2. NHS Wales Informatics Service: NHS wales informatics service - an official NHS wales website, http://www.wales.nhs.uk/sitesplus/956/home
3. NHS Wales Informatics Service: NHS wales informatics service - informing healthcare strategy - summary, http://www.wales.nhs.uk/nwis/
4. Map of Medicine: Welcome to the map of medicine - england, http://eng.mapofmedicine.com/
5. NHS Direct: NHS direct - we're here, http://www.nhsdirect.nhs.uk/
6. Connecting for Health: National library for health - NHS connecting for health, http://www.connectingforhealth.nhs.uk/resources/systserv/national
7. Mitchell, N., Randell, R., Foster, R., Dowding, D., Lattimer, V., Thompson, C., Cullum, N., Summers, R.: A national survey of computerized decision support systems available to nurses in england. Journal of Nursing Management 17, 772–780 (2009)
8. NICE: Welcome to the national institute for health and clinical excellence, http://www.nice.org.uk/
9. St. Andrew's House Scottish Government: Your emergency care summary: What does it mean for you? (2006)
10. NHS Wales Informatics Service: NHS wales informatics service - welsh clinical portal, http://www.wales.nhs.uk/nwis/
11. NICE: NICE quality standards, http://www.nice.org.uk/
12. Al-Salamah, H., Gray, A., Allam, O., Morrey, D.: Change management along the integrated care pathway (icp). In: Proceeding of the 14th International Symposium for Health Information Management Research, ISHIMR 2009 (2009)
13. Alia Systems Limited: Stateframe - innovators in business process management (bpm), http://www.stateframe.com/
14. Map of Medicine: Secondary care - triple assessment clinic (2011)
15. Map of Medicine: Advanced breast cancer - management (2011)
16. NHS Wales Informatics Service: NHS wales informatics service - canisc, http://www.wales.nhs.uk/nwis/
17. Fleischmann, A.: What Is S-BPM? In: Buchwald, H., Fleischmann, A., Seese, D., Stary, C. (eds.) S-BPM ONE 2009. CCIS, vol. 85, pp. 85–106. Springer, Heidelberg (2010)

New Modeling Concepts in S-BPM: The First Implementation of the "Message Guard" and "Macro" Behavior Extensions

Florian Strecker

Metasonic AG
Münchner Strasse 29, Hettenshausen, 85276 Pfaffenhofen, Germany
florian.strecker@metasonic.de

Abstract. Until 2011, S-BPM has been lacking the possibility to model special issues like reacting to events at any time. This paper gives an overview over two new modeling constructs ("message guard" & "macro") proposed by Fleischmann et al. It further connects these constructs to the well-known workflow patterns and offers the first (technical) implementation of the behavior extensions within an S-BPM modeling- and workflow-tool. At the end, two examples for real-world processes making use of the new extension are given.

Keywords: behavior extension, macro, message guard, workflow patterns, implementation, modeling convention.

1 Introduction

When Fleischmann initially described his parallel activities synchronization scheme (PASS) [2] and applied it later on for description of business processes [3], there started a bit-by-bit-growth of the need of some more elaborate modeling constructs in S-BPM. Driven by practitioners, it became evident that the overall concept of subjects who simply react to messages at certain steps of their internal behavior needs some more refining:

Business processes must be able to react to certain (sometimes external) events[1], like it is possible in BPMN 2.0 [10]. These requirements are also reflected in some of the well-known workflow patterns[2] ([13], [12]). Even if there seems to arise a discussion about the suitability of the workflow patterns "for comparing and evaluating different business process modeling systems" [1], the workflow patterns reflect a number of modeling issues which arise in real-world processes.

Kurz & Fleischmann define (among other criteria) the quick & easy "rearranging [of] the activity sequence of processes" [4] as a driver for flexibility of business

---

[1] An „event" or better: „an event's output" in S-BPM is always a message.
[2] Especially these with „cancel" or „trigger" in their title.

S. Oppl and A. Fleischmann (Eds.): S-BPM ONE 2012, CCIS 284, pp. 121–134, 2012.

processes. The jCPEX! Approach of Meyer et al. [9] also requires flexibility and the possibility to react to events because of its cross-company focus.

Finally, Fleischmann et al. introduced behavior extensions like exception handling and macros for subject-oriented processes ([5], chapters 5.7.2 & 5.7.6). These concepts offer a solution for the modeling issues and requirements mentioned above.

The main goal of this paper is to provide the BPM community with the first technical implementation of the S-BPM behavior extensions.

Therefore paper gives a short overview of the concept of behavior extensions and discusses a few details the author proposes to change in contrast to the definition of Fleischmann et al. Afterwards it is shown how the behavior extensions link to certain workflow patterns. Then, this paper describes a first implementation of the behavior extensions based on an S-BPM modeling- and workflow-system. To point up the need for these extensions, two simple real-world examples based on the implementation are described.

2   S-BPM Behavior Extensions

In 2011, Fleischmann et al. introduced extensions of the S-BPM modeling language. Amongst them are "behavior macros" ([5], chapter 5.7.2) and "exception handling" (or "message guard", chapter 5.7.6).

2.1   Behavior Macros

Behavior macros offer the possibility to model recurring sequences[3] only one time and then "calling" it at different points in a subject's behavior. In analogy to macros in computer programming languages, a behavior macro has one or more entry points (like functions) and can have one or more return values (also alike).

Figure 1 shows a simple example of an order processing[4]. The macro has two entry points, "order" ("Best." in figure) and "delivery" ("Ausl." in figure). The entries are marked at the left upper corner. The end of the macro is marked with a black or greyed bar.

The behavior of a subject can call a macro. The calling of a macro is represented by a box, indicating the possible entry points in the first third, the macro's name in the second third and possible returns in the last third. The incoming transition should point to the desired entry, whereas each outgoing transition starts at the return, in which case the transition should be followed.

In figure 2, our order processing macro (in German: "Auftragsabwicklung") can be called at two different points. In the left sequence it is called with entry "Best.", in the right sequence with entry "Ausl.". In both cases the (in this example one-and-only possible) return is "Lieferstatus aktualisiert" (delivery status refreshed).

---

[3] Better: „behavior parts".
[4] Figures 1 – 5 show original graphics from [5] and are therefore in German language.

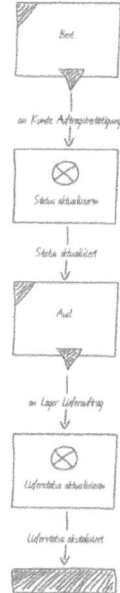

Fig. 1. A behavior macro ([5], p. 139)

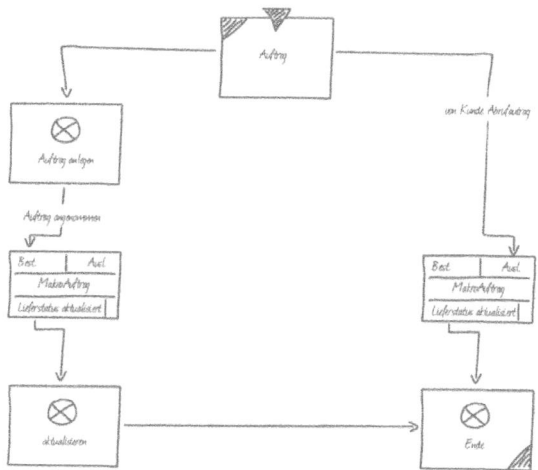

Fig. 2. Subject behavior with macro calls ([5], p. 140)

In their description of behavior macros, Fleischmann et al. propose implicitly, that a macro cannot have an end-state, but must return ([5], p. 138: "The end of a macro is a grey bar, which represents the subsequent steps of the original behavior" [author's translation from German]). In the author's opinion, a macro does not have to have a return, but can also terminate (= having an end state). A macro is essentially a subordinate behavior, which therefore should have all possibilities a standard behavior has.

124   F. Strecker

2.2   Message Guard

The message guard pattern enables a subject, to react to certain messages which arrive
in its inputpool without the need of being in a suitable receive state at that time. This
concept enables subjects to react to exceptions which can occur at any time and have
to be handled immediately (like a cancelling of an order).

Figure 3 shows a service processing with the standard behavior as the left sequence
and the message guard behavior on the right. The message guard behavior starts with
a box indicating all states from the normal behavior, from which the message guard
sequence can be reached. Additionally, all relevant states must be marked with a grey
triangle on their right side.

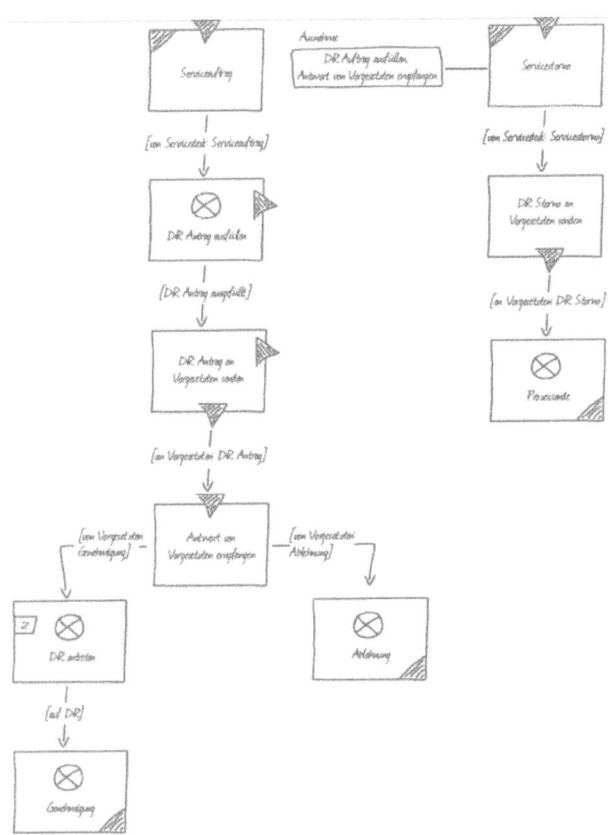

Fig. 3. Subject behavior with message guard behavior ([5], p. 150)

In the author's view, the message guard is an extension to the behavior macros,
because it is also a separate behavior sequence within a subject. The difference is, that
it is not called via a (modeled) certain point within the subject's behavior, but due to
an event (= a message).

Fleischmann et al. define, that the starting state of a message guard behavior can be a receive state or a function state ([5], p. 151). From the author's point of view, the starting state must be of type receive: A message guard behavior models a reaction to high-priority events or triggers. In S-BPM, an event or trigger is a message – therefore the reaction to it has to start with receiving (of the message).

3   Relevance for S-BPM Modeling of Workflow Patterns

As already mentioned in the introduction (chapter 1), the workflow patterns of van der Aalst, ter Hofstede et al. ([13], [12]) are currently well-accepted even if there seems to arise a discussion about their suitability for comparing different BPM languages ([1]). Therefore, the above mentioned S-BPM extensions should be reflected against their ability to cover different patterns which could not be covered with the "extension-less" S-BPM. As proposed by Rodenhagen & Strecker ([11]) in 2010, S-BPM should be checked with extensions to react on events against the workflow patterns.

The S-BPM language, employing standard subject behaviors and multi-subjects, can model all workflow-patterns, which don't employ "exceptions" or "triggers". The reason for this is that exceptions or triggers come from the outside (like external systems or other events) and have to be handled immediately. That is not possible with a standard subject behavior, because a subject can only react to an event (= message in S-BPM terms) if it is currently in a receive state.

With the introduction of a message guard, subjects are enabled to react to events immediately. Therefore, the S-BPM coverage of workflow patterns extends to the following patterns:

- *Cancel Task* (Pattern 19, [14]): An enabled task is withdrawn prior to it commencing execution. If the task has started, it is disabled and, where possible, the currently running instance is halted and removed.
- *Cancel Case* (Pattern 20, [15]): A complete process instance is removed. This includes currently executing tasks, those which may execute at some future time and all sub-processes. The process instance is recorded as having completed unsuccessfully.
- *Transient Trigger* (Pattern 23, [16]): The ability for a task instance to be triggered by a signal from another part of the process or from the external environment. These triggers are transient in nature and are lost if not acted on immediately by the receiving task. A trigger can only be utilized if there is a task instance waiting for it at the time it is received.
- *Persistent Trigger* (Pattern 24, [17]): The ability for a task to be triggered by a signal from another part of the process or from the external environment. These triggers are persistent in form and are retained by the process until they can be acted on by the receiving task.
- *Cancel Region* (Pattern 25, [18]): The ability to disable a set of tasks in a process instance. If any of the tasks are already executing (or are currently enabled), then they are withdrawn. The tasks need not be a connected subset of the overall process model.

- *Cancel Multiple Instance Task* (Pattern 26, [19]): Within a given process instance, multiple instances of a task can be created. The required number of instances is known at design time. These instances are independent of each other and run concurrently. At any time, the multiple instance task can be cancelled and any instances which have not completed are withdrawn. Task instances that have already completed are unaffected.
- *Complete Multiple Instance Task* (Pattern 27, [20]): Within a given process instance, multiple instances of a task can be created. The required number of instances is known at design time. These instances are independent of each other and run concurrently. It is necessary to synchronize the instances at completion before any subsequent tasks can be triggered. During the course of execution, it is possible that the task needs to be forcibly completed such that any remaining instances are withdrawn and the thread of control is passed to subsequent tasks.
- *Cancelling Discriminator* (Pattern 29, [21]): The convergence of two or more branches into a single subsequent branch following one or more corresponding divergences earlier in the process model. The thread of control is passed to the subsequent branch when the first active incoming branch has been enabled. Triggering the *Cancelling Discriminator* also cancels the execution of all of the other incoming branches and resets the construct.
- *Cancelling Partial Join* (Pattern 32, [22]): The convergence of two or more branches (say m) into a single subsequent branch following one or more corresponding divergences earlier in the process model. The thread of control is passed to the subsequent branch when n of the incoming branches have been enabled where n is less than m. Triggering the join also cancels the execution of all of the other incoming branches and resets the construct.
- *Cancelling Partial Join for Multiple Instances* (Pattern 35, [23]): Within a given process instance, multiple concurrent instances of a task (say m) can be created. The required number of instances is known when the first task instance commences. Once n of the task instances have completed (where n is less than m), the next task in the process is triggered and the remaining m-n instances are cancelled.

Thus, the S-BPM language can increase its coverage of the workflow-patterns and – at the same time – can offer existing tools, which can execute process models reflected by the aforementioned patterns.

Example models of the aforementioned workflow patterns can be found at the author's homepage [24].

4   Technical Implementation

The above chapters demonstrate the importance of the behavior extensions, especially of the message guard, for solving real-world process problems using S-BPM. Therefore, an implementation of these "new features" should be provided within a tool suite as soon as possible.

The author was able to do the first implementation of macros and message guard, using the "Metasonic Suite 4.4" ([6]) as a base.

4.1   Extension of the Process Engine (Runtime Environment)

The runtime environment ("process engine") of Metasonic Suite offers the possibility to create custom extensions ("engine add-ons", [7]). These extensions can react to certain, well-defined events, and are implemented using the observer-pattern (for events and point of execution, see [8]). Such an observer has the possibility to switch the state of a subject in execution-time, therefore, it can switch between "different" behaviors. Metasonic Suite offers also the possibility to create custom "modeling parameters" while creating process models. The custom observer can therefore check the process model for defined modeling parameters and react accordingly.

Thus, it is possible to implement additional behaviors for runtime usage.

4.2   Extension at Modeling Time

Metasonic's modeling environment "Metasonic Build" is Eclipse-based and can therefore easily being adapted or extended. On the other hand, an implementation of totally new modeling elements, like the symbols for usage with macros and message guard (as proposed by Fleischmann et al., [5]) would get to the very core of the modeling implementation.

Therefore, to get to a quick and easy implementation of the extensions, the modeling tool Metasonic Build has not been altered. Instead, out-of-the-box possibilities like drawing different, multi-colored symbols and adding custom modeling-parameters, were used. The author developed modeling recommendations which differ from the new symbols proposed by Fleischmann et al. (see next chapters).

4.3   Implementation of Behavior Macros

Figure 4 shows a subject's behavior employing a macro: The macro is simply placed as a separate behavior sequence on the same canvas to the right of the standard behavior. To distinguish the macro from the standard behavior, it follows some conventions:

- The macro has to be placed to the right of the standard behavior
- The complete macro has to be shimmed with a light-green box
- All entry-points have to be named
- An entry point has to be shimmed with a darker green
- An entry point has a text box with the entry point's name to its right
- The returns are marked with "MACRO RETURN", followed by the return value

With these 6 rules, macros can be modeled using out-of-the-box functions of an existing S-BPM modeling tool.

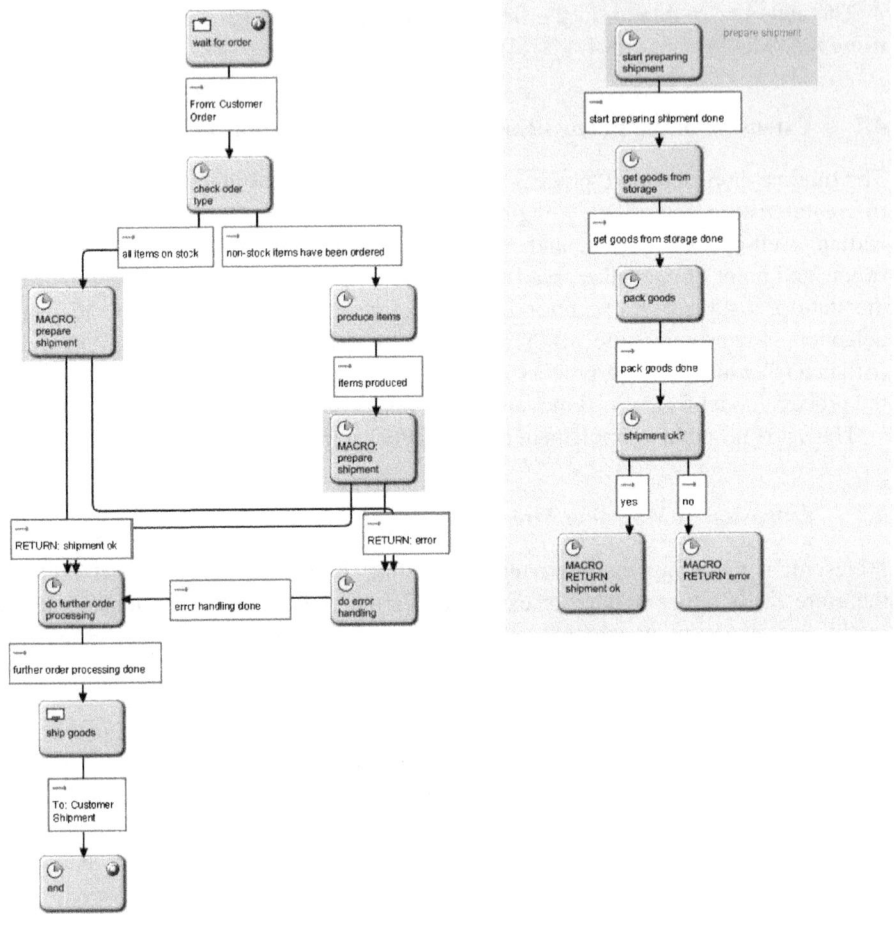

Fig. 4. A subject behavior employing a macro

The "calling" of the macro follows basically the same conventions:

- A macro-calling state has to be shimmed light-green
- A macro-calling state has to be named "MACRO: ", followed by the name of the entry point
- The macro-returns are modeled using the transitions outgoing of the macro-calling state; each transition is named "RETURN: ", followed by the return value

To prepare the process model for working technically (currently, we have just drawn a picture), a few modeling-parameters have to be added:

- *behaviour.extension.macro.entry* marks an entry point of a macro – the value is the name of the entry point.

- *behaviour.extension.macro.return* marks a macro return – the value is the name of the return value.
- *behaviour.extension.macro.react* is set on a state in the standard behaviour, where a macro should be called. The value is the name of the entry point.
- *behaviour.extension.macro.return* also marks a transition outgoing of a macro-calling state. The value is the name of the return value.

Employing these 4 modeling-parameters, an engine add-on has been implemented, using Metasonic Suite's StateChangeObserver, which is called when a subject changes its state at runtime. The runtime implementation employs a simple algorithm:

```
(A1) StateChangeObserverA: check if new state is marked
as "behaviour.extension.macro.react"; if no: return.
(A2) find state marked "behaviour.extension.macro.entry"
with behaviour.extension.macro.entry.value ==
behaviour.extension.macro.react.value; if no state found:
return.
(A3) save current state of the subject; set subject to
state found in (A2).
(A4) end StateChangeObserverA.


(B1) StateChangeObserverB: check if new state is marked
as "behaviour.extension.macro.return"; if no: return.
(B2) get previously saved state (see A3)
(B3) check this state for outgoing transitions marked
"behaviour.extension.macro.return".
(B4) set subject back to the saved state
(B5) follow the transition where
behaviour.extension.macro.return.value (on the
transition) == behaviour.extension.macro.return.value (on
the macro's state where the observer has been called).
(B6) end StateChangeObserverB.
```

This is the first implementation of behavior macros in an S-BPM tool suite. The implementation including some examples can be downloaded at [24].

4.4   Implementation of Message Guard

Following the implementation of macros (see chapter 4.3), the implementation and modeling of message guards can be done using similar engine add-on implementations and similar modeling conventions.

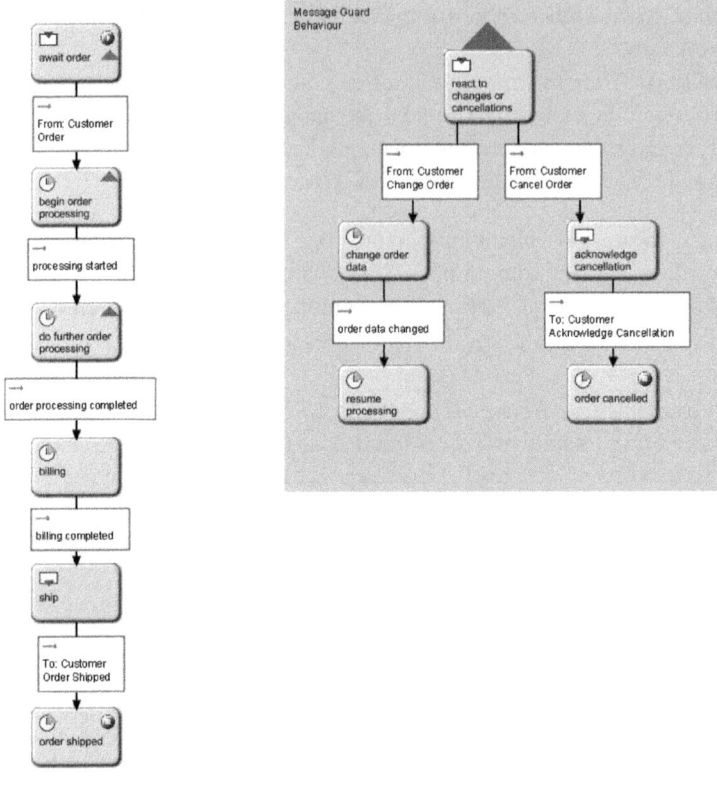

Fig. 5. A subject behavior employing a message guard behavior

As shown in Figure 5, a message guard behavior is modeled like this:

- The message guard behavior has to be placed to the right of the standard behavior.
- The complete message guard behavior has to be shimmed with a light-blue box and marked as "message guard behavior" with a text box.
- The start of the message guard behavior is a receive state; therefore, it is possible to distinguish different messages there.
- The start of the message guard behavior is marked with a dark-blue triangle on its top.
- In the standard behavior, all states which can be left to access the messages guard behavior, are marked with a dark-blue triangle on their upper right corner.

Like in macro modeling, the process model has to be enhanced by using modeling-parameters:

- *behaviour.extension.messageguard.entry = true* marks the entry point of the message guard behavior.

- *behaviour.extension.messageguard.return = true* marks a return from a message guard behavior.
- *behaviour.extension.messageguard.react = true* is set on all states in the standard behavior, where the message guard behavior can be reached.

Again, there exists an engine add-on employing these 3 modeling parameters. For message guard, we need an InputpoolObserver, which can react to incoming messages in the subject's inputpool. Additionally, a StateChangeObserver is used to handle the return from the message guard behavior (compare steps B1, B2, B4, B6 in chapter 4.3). The InputpoolObserver reacts like follows:

```
(C1) Message has been added to inputpool
(C2) check if current state is marked as
"behaviour.extension.messageguard.react"; if no: return.
(C3) search state marked as
"behaviour.extension.messageguard.entry".
(C4) check if state from (C3) has an outgoing transition
suitable for the message from (C1); if no: return.
(C5) save current state of the subject.
(C6) set subject to state found in (C2).
```

This is the first implementation of message guard behaviors in an S-BPM tool suite. The implementation including some examples can be downloaded at [24].

5   Working Examples

To illustrate the practical benefit of both aforementioned extensions to the S-BPM language, two simple[5] real-world processes should be shortly described. The processes reflect the same subject behaviors which were used in chapter 4 to illustrate the implementation & modeling of the behavior extensions.

5.1   Delivery (Macro)

Given is a simple delivery process (Figure 6): A customer sends his order to an order processor. After processing, the order processor sends the shipment back to the customer.

When we have a closer look on the behavior of the order processor (Figure 4), we discover that the order processor has two possibilities: If the ordered items are all on stock, the shipment can be immediately prepared. If some items have to be produced first, then the preparation of the shipment must wait until the items are produced. Because preparing the shipment consists of different steps, which would be the same on both sequences described above, we can employ a macro to simplify the internal

---

[5] Or better: simplified.

behavior of the order processor. Therefore, the preparation of the shipment is handled via macro, simplifying the subject's standard behavior.

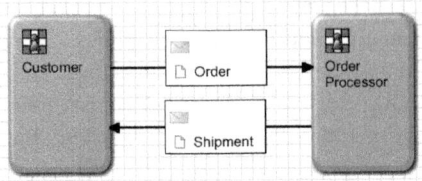

Fig. 6. Communication view of a simple delivery process

5.2   Order Cancellation (Message Guard)

In real-world order processes, a customer can not only place his order (send a suitable message to the order processor), but can also change or cancel the order – until the order is already shipped (Figure 7).

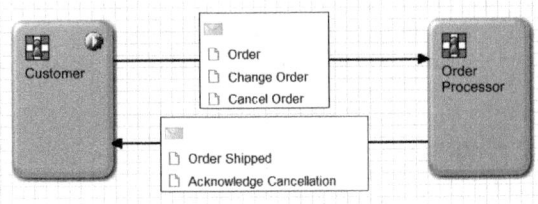

Fig. 7. Communication view of an order process with change- and cancellation-option

In this case, a message guard behavior can be added for the order processor, in order to enable him or her to react to changes or cancellations immediately. Figure 5 shows such a behavior: As long as the order is in processing states, the order processor can react to cancel or changes messages. In case of a change, the subject changes the order data and then resumes to the states where it came from when the change-message came. In case of a cancellation, the order processor acknowledges the cancellation to the customers, then performs no resume, but simply ends (because of the cancellation, no further processing is necessary).

If a cancellation or change arrives, when the order processor is already in the billing state, then he cannot react anymore: The message came too late. For this case, check the customer's behavior (Figure 8) in the state "wait for acknowledgement": It can happen, that the customer simply gets the shipment if the cancellation message has not been received in due course by the order processor.

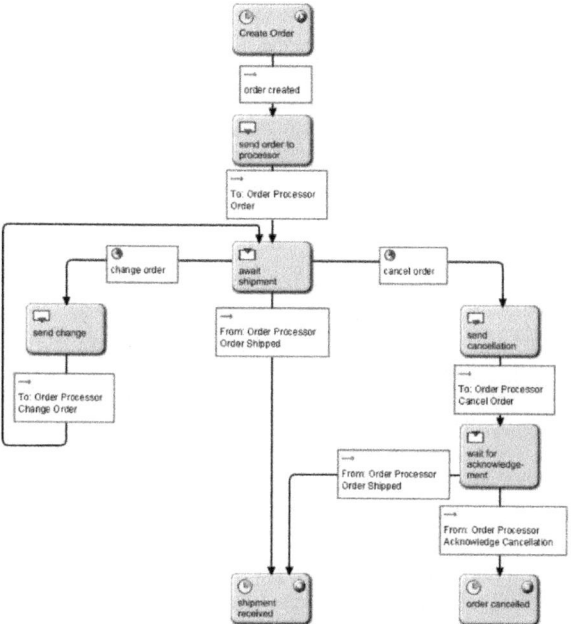

Fig. 8. Behavior of the customer in an order process with change- and cancellation-option

6   Conclusion

This paper shows the importance of the S-BPM behavior extensions proposed by Fleischmann et al. These extensions offer not only a wide coverage of the well-known workflow patterns, but can also being applied to real-word business processes.

With a simple, easy implementation of adding engine add-ons ([24]) to an existing S-BPM suite and following a few modeling conventions, it is possible to use these new extensions at once in S-BPM-based workflow systems.

References

1. Börger, E.: Approaches to Modeling Business Processes. A Critical Analysis of BPMN, Workflow Patterns and YAWL. To appear in J. Software & Systems Modeling (2011), http://www.di.unipi.it/~boerger/main.html
2. Fleischmann, A.: Distributed Systems: Software design and Implementation. Springer, Berlin (1994)
3. Fleischmann, A.: What Is S-BPM? In: Buchwald, H., Fleischmann, A., Seese, D., Stary, C. (eds.) S-BPM ONE 2009. CCIS, vol. 85, pp. 85–106. Springer, Heidelberg (2010)
4. Kurz, M., Fleischmann, A.: BPM 2.0: Business Process Management Meets Empowerment. In: Fleischmann, A., Schmidt, W., Singer, R., Seese, D. (eds.) S-BPM ONE 2010. CCIS, vol. 138, pp. 54–83. Springer, Heidelberg (2011)

5. Fleischmann, A., Schmidt, W., Stary, C., Obermeier, S., Börger, E.: Subjektorientiertes Prozessmanagement: Mitarbeiter einbinden, Motivation und Prozessakzeptanz steigern. Hanser, München (2011)
6. Metasonic, A.G.: Metasonic Suite 4.4. Pfaffenhofen (2011), http://www.metasonic.de
7. Metasonic, A.G.: Metasonic Suite Developer Documentation 4.4. Pfaffenhofen (2011), http://www.metasonic.de
8. Metasonic, A.G.: Execution Order Within Refinements And Observers (com.jcom1.documentation.refinements. Execution Order Within Refinements And Observers). In: Metasonic AG: Metasonic Suite Developer Documentation 4.4. Pfaffenhofen (2011), http://www.metasonic.de
9. Meyer, N., Feiner, T., Radmayr, M., Blei, D., Fleischmann, A.: Dynamic Catenation and Execution of Cross Organisational Business Processes - The jCPEX! Approach. In: Fleischmann, A., Schmidt, W., Singer, R., Seese, D. (eds.) S-BPM ONE 2010. CCIS, vol. 138, pp. 84–105. Springer, Heidelberg (2011)
10. Object Management Group (OMG): Business Process Model and Notation (BPMN): Version 2.0 (2011), http://www.omg.org/spec/BPMN/2.0/PDF
11. Rodenhagen, J., Strecker, F.: Using Multi-subjects for Process Synchronization on Different Abstraction Levels. In: Fleischmann, A., Schmidt, W., Singer, R., Seese, D. (eds.) S-BPM ONE 2010. CCIS, vol. 138, pp. 134–162. Springer, Heidelberg (2011)
12. Russell, N., ter Hofstede, A.H.M., van der Aalst, W.M.P., Mulyar, N.: Workflow Control-Flow Patterns: A Revised View. BPM Center Report BPM-06-22, BPMcenter.org (2006)
13. van der Aalst, W.M.P., ter Hofstede, A.H.M., Kiepuszewski, B., Barros, A.P.: Workflow Patterns. Distributed and Parallel Databases 14(3), 5–51 (2003)
14. van der Aalst, W.M.P.: http://www.workflowpatterns.com/patterns/control/cancellation/wcp19.php
15. van der Aalst, W.M.P.: http://www.workflowpatterns.com/patterns/control/cancellation/wcp20.php
16. van der Aalst, W.M.P.: http://www.workflowpatterns.com/patterns/control/new/wcp23.php
17. van der Aalst, W.M.P.: http://www.workflowpatterns.com/patterns/control/new/wcp24.php
18. van der Aalst, W.M.P.: http://www.workflowpatterns.com/patterns/control/new/wcp25.php
19. van der Aalst, W.M.P.: http://www.workflowpatterns.com/patterns/control/new/wcp26.php
20. van der Aalst, W.M.P.: http://www.workflowpatterns.com/patterns/control/new/wcp27.php
21. van der Aalst, W.M.P.: http://www.workflowpatterns.com/patterns/control/new/wcp29.php
22. van der Aalst, W.M.P.: http://www.workflowpatterns.com/patterns/control/new/wcp32.php
23. van der Aalst, W.M.P.: http://www.workflowpatterns.com/patterns/control/new/wcp35.php
24. Strecker, F.: http://www.floooooo.de/s-bpm/#sbpmone2012

Process Algebra and the Subject-Oriented Business Process Management Approach

Robert Singer* and Matthias Teller

FH JOANNEUM - University of Applied Sciences
Alte Poststrasse 147, 8020 Graz, Austria
robert.singer@fh-joanneum.at

Abstract. Recently there have been some discussion about possible revolutions in business process management. It is evident, that business process management up to now misses a solid scientific foundation. This has led to misinterpretations during implementation of business process management in organizations on one side, and uncoordinated research directions and results on the other side. It can be shown, that actual concepts, such as BPMN 2.0 or scientific community driven concepts such as Petri-nets do not fit business and organizational needs. We discuss one possible step forward to come up with a solid scientific definition of business process management, *id est* process calculi such as CCS and π-calculus. Based on these algebras, we can define and study business processes on a formal basis. Further on, we demonstrate that such calculi are not only theoretical concepts, but can be used for daily business process modeling and enactment in the from of the subject-oriented business process management (S-BPM) methodology.

Keywords: business process, business process management, process calculi, CCS, pi-calculus, theory, S-BPM, communication, agents, process execution.

1 Introduction

During last years more and more critical statements about the availability and state of the art of methodologies and technologies of business process management from business and IT practitioner arose. Sometimes the frustration is articulated, but more often it is implicitly evident. We do not want to repeat a discussion already done, but want to refer to a discussion thread starting with an article of Olbrich [20].

The main conclusion from past discussions is, that we need a stringent and commonly agreed definition of the terms business process and business process management – based on scientific foundations [27]. In this work we want to show, that process calculi fulfill actual needs and commercially available tools based on formal methods can be used to realize a "modern" understanding of business processes. Not all aspects of such a wide field can be discussed in one paper, so

---

* Corresponding author.

S. Oppl and A. Fleischmann (Eds.): S-BPM ONE 2012, CCIS 284, pp. 135–150, 2012.
© Springer-Verlag Berlin Heidelberg 2012

we will restrict our self to certain facets: modeling and direct execution of the model.

Business processes are not an entity of computer science alone, but we have to consider the social and human aspects on one side and business targets on the other side. Therefore, we think that we need a theory of socio-technical and socio-economic system views and one of the main concepts in social sciences is "communication" which is also a fundamental concept in computer science and thus could be the link between these different domains. The purpose of this paper is to show, that we can model processes based on communication between so called agents and based on formal methods with the option for direct execution. Formally defined processes are a prerequisite for executable versions of the designed process models. The lack of rigorous semantics is the main reason, why executable BPMN 2.0 still fails, as we will discuss later.

We propose to re-frame thinking from control to message oriented concepts, what we will explain in detail. Afterwards we will present the so called subject-oriented (S-BPM) approach as one of the possible concepts to realize such a new thinking.

2   Process Calculi and BPM

Recently there has been a discussion about a possible revolution in business process management, starting with a paper from Smith & Fingar titled "Workflow is just a Pi process" [28]. The paper was inspired by the π-Calculus developed around 1990 by R. Milner, J. Parrow and D. Walker [18,19]. This formalism belongs to the family of process algebras (or process calculi) and can be seen as an enhancement of the *Calculus for Communicating Systems* (CCS). While CCS could be used to describe concurrent communicating processes, the π-Calculus allows the formal description of mobile processes. We will shortly discuss both calculi in the following two sections.

2.1   Calculus of Communicating Systems

The Calculus of Communicating Systems was introduced by Robin Milner in 1980 [16]. Other process algebras developed around the same time are CSP (*Communicating Sequential Processes* published by Hoare in 1985 [12]) and ASP (*Algebra of Communicating Processes*), published by Bergstra and Klop in 1984 [6].

The main objective of CCS was to provide a mathematical framework to describe communicating systems in a formal way. This formalization allows for verification of properties like checking for two processes being equivalent (see checking observation equivalence using bisimulation [17]). *Observation* and *synchronized communication* are the two central ideas of the CCS [16]. Observation aims to describe a concurrent system accurate enough to determine the behavior seen by an external observer. If two systems are indistinguishable from the observer's point of view, they show the property of *observation equivalence*. Milner further states that every interesting concurrent system is built from independent agents which communicate in a synchronized way. So the objects whose behaviors are modeled are called agents. An agent can be seen as a term for a locus of activity, a process, or a computational unit [13]. The agent's behavior is defined by the action it can perform and represented using algebraic expressions.

The basic capabilities of an agent are sending a message, receiving a message and performing an unobservable action $Act = N \cup \overline{N} \cup \tau$. N represents a set of names, $\overline{N}$ the set of corresponding co-names, and τ stands for an unobservable or so called silent action. The ability to receive a message is denoted by using lowercase letters like $a, b, c, \ldots$ (names) whereas overlined lowercase letters like $\bar{a}, \bar{b}, \bar{c}, \ldots$ (co-names) are used to denote the ability to send a message. A simple example of an employee asking his boss for a few days off could be described as follows:

$$E = \overline{request}.date.\overline{answer}.(accept.E + deny.E) \tag{1}$$

An employee E sends an $\overline{request}$ for leave, get questioned about the *date*, gives $\overline{answer}$ and finally he receives an *accept* or *deny*. Afterwards the process is reset by invoking E again (recursion) in order to make the process runnable again. The semantics of the CCS is defined by a so called *labeled transition system* (LTS). A LTS is a triple $(\mathsf{Proc}, \mathsf{Act}, \{\xrightarrow{\alpha} \mid \alpha \in \mathsf{Act}\})$, where Proc is a set of states or processes, Act is a set of actions or labels, and $\xrightarrow{\alpha} \subseteq \mathsf{Proc} \times \mathsf{Proc}$ is a transition relation for every $\alpha \in \mathsf{Act}$. A LTS is finite if its sets of states and actions are both finite. For every action, *transition relation* is defined, which looks like the following:

$$P \xrightarrow{\alpha} P' \tag{2}$$

This means P evolves to P' by performing the action α. A further explanation of the CCS is beyond the scope of this paper but the interested reader is referred to [16,17,4].

To sum up the CCS was developed to represent all relevant concepts of concurrent communication and computation with a minimum set of expressions. This basic set should be used to realize more complex constructs. The CCS should facilitate the understanding, reasoning and development of formal tools supporting concurrency and was intended to play a similar role for concurrent computation like the λ-Calculus does for sequential computation.

2.2   π-Calculus

The π-Calculus was introduced by R. Milner, J. Parrow and D. Walker in "A calculus of mobile processes, Parts 1 and 2" [19]. The π-Calculus is a process algebra, like the CCS. It is designed to model systems with dynamically changing structures in which the links between different components vary during the evolution.

The π-Calculus can be understood as CCS enhanced with the so called link passing mobility [17,22]. The basic elements of the π-Calculus are, like in the CCS, names and agents. Agents perform actions (sending, receiving, execution of an unobservable action, performing a match between two names), and names are a collective term for concepts like links, pointers, references, identifiers, channels etc [23]. As a consequence of the concept names can act as both transmission medium and as transmitted data [28]. Agents (which can be seen as processes) interact with other agents by sending and receiving messages identified by a name. As contents of messages are also channels, at the end of a communication the recipient is capable of using the received channel for further communication (see link passing mobility).

For example: A process S uses the link a to send the value x to W (as can be seen in Figure 1). Now assume that instead of sending the value x directly, S delegates this action to C. To achieve this S sends the name of the link (a) and the value (x) to C via b. Now C can communicate via the link a and assuming that there is no further communication from S to W, the system has evolved to the state shown in Figure 2. The π-Calculus offers the possibility to model this mobile behavior. This is achieved by the combination of concepts like channel names, values, and variables to one single syntactic class called *names*.

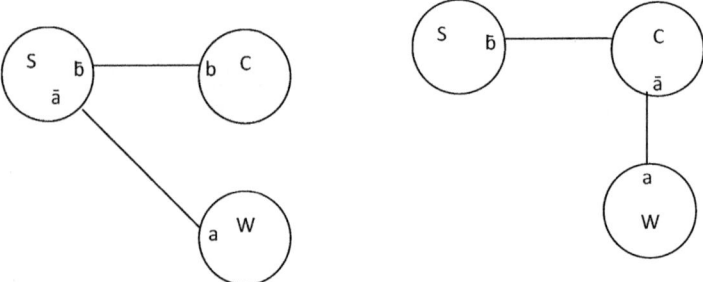

Fig. 1. Initial   **Fig. 2.** After change

A more practical example to show this unification: Suppose the DNS-server S holds the address to a website W that client C wants to visit. In the initial state only the server has access to the website represented by the communication link a (see Figure 3). Now the client asks the DNS-Server for the IP-address of www.pi-calculus.org in order to be able to visit it. After an interaction among the link b the possibility to access has transferred (see Figure 4). In terms of the π-Calculus this would be expressed as follows: the server that sends a via b would be denoted as[1] $\bar{b}\langle a\rangle.S$; the client that receives a link via b and then uses it to send data (e.g. the HTTP GET request d) would be expressed as $b(c).\bar{c}\langle d\rangle.C$.

The interaction would be denoted as:

$$\bar{b}\langle a\rangle.S \mid b(c).\bar{c}\langle d\rangle.C \xrightarrow{\tau} S \mid a\langle d\rangle.C \qquad (3)$$

As can be seen a has two different roles. First, in the interaction between DNS-Server and Client, a is an object (the communication link, represented by an

---

[1] Note that there is also an notation without angle brackets $\langle\rangle$ for outputs. So $\bar{b}\langle a\rangle.S$ can also be expressed as $\bar{b}a.S$

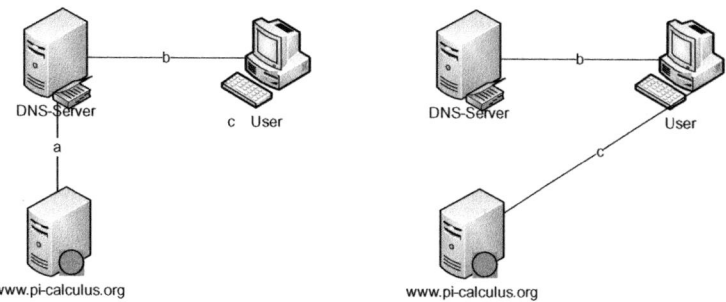

Fig. 3. Initial   **Fig. 4.** After change

IP-address) which is transferred. In further communication between the Client and the web-server a is the name of the communication link. This idea of that both objects transferred and names of links belong to the same concept called *names* is one of the corner stones of the π-Calculus according to [21] and one characteristic that distinguishes it from other process algebras. A more detailed discussion about the syntax and different variants like the Polyadic π-Calculus can be found in [21,17].

On this basis Robin Milner proved mathematically that computation and communication can be modeled and understood in a uniform way. In the world of the π-Calculus *everything is just a process.*

2.3 Process Calculi vs. Petri-nets

Smith & Fingar stated in "Workflow is just a Pi process" [28] that the power of the π-Calculus as mentioned above, can be used to realize Business Process Management Systems (BPMS) to overcome the problems of "traditional" Workflow Management Systems (WfMS). They argue that workflow engines hard-code a distinct process meta-model (dependent on their application area, design and vendor), which limits their ability to model certain processes. In contrast, a BPMS should be able to serve as universal engine for processes, allowing the expression of every possible process. It should enable the comprehensive management of end-to-end processes, while leveraging all existing investments in legacy systems.

The principles of π-calculus can be also discussed with the help of the well known concept of email. Consider electronic mail as a process. We can send an email to another person, this one, for example, forwards the email to a third party, and this one is then able to communicate and collaborate with me as initiator of the email. How does this happen? By receiving email, or more specifically by receiving an email address, directly or indirectly, interchange the capability to communicate with others linked to that email address. This is what makes email work. We give a name, in the form of an email address, to others, and this gives them the ability to communicate with yet other participants in the thread of the conversation - continuously extending the conversation over time, involving new participants that contribute value to the process. Through this simple model, a dynamic way of conversation becomes possible – a new business process. Another advantage in informal business processes is the possibility to send any type of business object (data) without the need to define a rigorous data model in advance (agent 1 sends a spread sheet to agent 2, agent 2 adds a column and forwards to agent 3 etc.).

As a reaction to the hypothesizes of Smith & Fingar Wil M. P. van der Aalst published a short note titled "Why workflow is NOT just a π-process" [1]. In it he states that, although he thinks the π-Calculus could be a solid foundation for modeling and analyzing processes, he is not convinced that the features of the π-Calculus are vital for Business Process Management Systems. He argues that the feature of mobility has little relevance for BPM and that anything that can be expressed in the π-Calculus can also be expressed in other models, like high-level Petri-nets. This is right, but still we complain that Petri-nets are not the tool of choice for all situations and ease of use, for example, is a key factor for application outside research in computer science.

In another paper [3] van der Aalst continues the discussion about π-calculus versus Petri-nets, listing pros and cons and stating seven challenges for those advocating the π-calculus. The paper is related to *Web Service Composition Languages* (WSCLs) and he names three reasons for using Petri-nets as a basis for WSCLs. First he mentions that Petri-nets allow graphical modeling, but also ensure formal semantics. The second reason is that Petri-nets are state-based instead of event-based, allowing states to be modeled explicitly. Third he states the availability of many analysis techniques to determine the correctness of process designs as an advantage of Petri-nets. Although Petri nets have their advantages they also exhibit several weaknesses [3]. We think that such technological aspects (web services) are not part of the main concept of business process management and will not help business to define and manage end-to-end processes.

A discussion about the applicability of the π-calculus as a formal foundation for business process management can be found in "Why do we actually need the π-Calculus for Business Process Management?" written by Frank Puhlmann [22]. He puts emphasis on an emerging shift in business process managements and formulates requirements BPM has to meet in order to follow this development. The shifts he proposes are as follows:

 - BPM shifts from state to message-based systems as the later supports intra- and inter-organizational workflows without a paradigm break between formalism and practical implementation.
 - BPM shifts from central engines to distributed systems as integration becomes a core BPM activity.
 - BPM shifts from closed to open environments as the application area is extended from internal office workflows to agile collaborations in open networks like the Internet.

These lead to the following requirements:

 - A formalism representing the first shift of BPM should be based on messages, or events, rather than states.

- A formalism supporting the second shift of BPM should support advanced composition and visibility of its parts.
- A formalism taking the third shift into account should support dynamic process structures that can support change.

Taking these shifts into consideration, Puhlmann argues that the π-Calculus is well suited to meet the new requirements in Business Process Management. The interested reader is also referred to [23] which delivers a comprehensive approach and discussion on how the π-Calculus can be used for BPM. A critical discussion about notions, tools and methodologies – i.e. BPMN 2.0, Workflow Patterns, YAWL and Petri-Nets – for the use of business process modeling and enactment can be found in [8]. Boerger concludes that all of them have serious weak points and are not suited for the tasks they are proposed for. He states for example:

> Process modeling languages tend to lack the concepts to be able to deal with the broad range of requirements one may encounter when trying to precisely capture business scenarios.

Nevertheless, Petri-nets are an excellent method to analyze, model and enact business processes [2]; but we doubt, that Petri-nets are a useful tool to be used in an industry environment for daily use for all employees. Many business processes are knowledge processes and not strictly defined workflows, or in other words, real world processes are no algorithms. That means, we do not know all possible states and transactions in advance, and this has to be considered. Without no doubt, CCS and other process calculi cannot directly be used for process modeling by same argumentation, but the concept of communication seems to be a much more natural way of modeling organizations, as the corner stone of societies is communication. We will show, how the CCS calculus can be used to model business processes in a more natural way and to get executable code without any further translation step.

3   Execution of Business Processes

The first step in a typical business process life cycle (see for example [32]) is to model the processes. That means we create a model of reality, but in many situations it is not useful to include all aspects of reality as long as people are the agents. The situation is quite different, if we consider systems workflows, i.e. fully automated business processes. In this work we focus on human interaction workflows driven by knowledge workers. Nowadays many processes typically are supported by IT. Therefore, specific technologies (BPMS) support the enactment, execution and management of business processes (workflows).

3.1   Validation of Process Models

After modeling a business process, its initial design has to be validated if the model reflects the actual process. A common instrument to validate a process model is a workshop where the people involved check whether all valid business process instances are reflected by the business process model. Also, simulation techniques can be used to support validation. These allow step-by-step execution of processes to check their behavior. Another powerful method is the analysis of the different properties a process can exhibit. Those can be undesired properties like deadlock or livelock, but also structural properties like the different soundness criteria (e.g. soundness criteria or observation equivalence). Reasoning these properties is enabled by a formal model of business processes like Petrinets or Workflow-nets respectively and process algebras like the CCS and the π-Calculus.

3.2   BPMN 2.0 and Execution of Business Processes

Implementation can either be realized by applying policies, procedures and guidelines which employees have to follow, or by utilizing a dedicated software system. In case of the latter, the conceptional process model has to be mapped to an executable model. Today BPMN 2.0 (*Business Process Model and Notation*) is a *de-facto* standard maintained by the Object Management Group[2] (OMG) to model business processes.

The BPMN process model has to be enhanced with technical information in order to enable execution in a specific software system. The problem arising is that the tasks of modeling and mapping are often executed by different people with different interests, skills, experience and educational background. For example at the beginning of the design phase the affected process is only documented in textual form or not documented at all. Now a business process designer designs the process model in BPMN and validates its correctness together with the involved people. Then the model is handed over to a system architect and her developers who are responsible for configuration and enactment. They are now challenged to transform the model into executable code like, for example, BPEL or BPEL4WS.

It is a matter of fact, that direct transformation of BPMN 1.x into BPEL code is not possible without exceptional handling, transformations or other work arounds as reported by many authors, for example [33][24][31][9]. The new major version 2.0 of BPMN is available since beginning of 2011. Among the new BPMN 2.0 features there are, according to [30], two particularly interesting ones. The first is a standardized metamodel and serialization model which allows the exchange of process models between tools of different vendors (similar to XPDL). The second one is the standardized execution semantics for BPMN. These semantics could be used by tool vendors to develop an execution environment for process models. Despite this BPMN 2.0 should also make the transformation from BPMN to BPEL easier, which is a very important issue due to the

---

[2] http://www.omg.org

fact that BPEL has become a *de-facto* standard for execution. This simplification should be achieved by allowing the use of special visual elements specifying BPEL-handlers within the BPMN model [14].

As a result, BPMN contains a visual language for BPEL that can be executed by BPEL engines. The drawbacks are that these notation elements are only a subset of BPMN, so not all constructs can be transformed and the complexity of BPMN is further increased. Bruce Silver explains in his book [26] what is needed to get executable BPMN 2.0; in his blog he concludes that no execution conformant tools are available yet: "It's been over a year since publication of the final spec, and it seems that executable BPMN 2.0 tools don't really exist yet."[3]; or even the more pessimistic conclusion "... but I think he means that the abstract nature of the BPMN 2.0 metamodel is in conflict with the requirements for any language that an engine can reliably execute. And I completely agree with that."[4] as the answer to a comment on his blog "Executable BPMN 2.0".

Beside the problems mentioned above the transformation is also very time- and therefore cost-intensive. The implementation is often one step behind the actual business needs in a changing environment, due to this fact. Also, the implemented processes may differ from the *real* processes. These problems are often referred to as the Business-IT Gap. In order to bridge this gap many different approaches have been proposed, but the final solution has yet to be found.

4   A Communication Based Approach

There is no industry implementation of the π-calculus beside some prototypes. For example Puhlmann [23] used a tool chain to convert BPMN to π-calculus agents in order to use it for bisimulation with the *Advanced Bisimulation Checker*[5]; not available anymore) and *The Mobility Workbench*[6]. Also Bog [7] developed a software called *PiVizTool*[7] which allows the simulation of business processes expressed in the π-calculus. While it only allows textual input it does provide a graphical output of the simulation. While these approaches provide a helpful basis for an academic discussion they are not intended for practical utilization in a company.

An interesting application, not of the π-Calculus, but of the CCS, is provided by Metasonic[8]. The company offers BPM software based on a methodology which is named *Subject-oriented Business Process Management* (S-BPM). According to [25] it is based on the CCS and enhanced with a graphical notation and aspects of object orientation. The focus of the S-BPM approach is on modeling the behavior of actors (which are called *subjects*) participating in a process and

---

[3] http://www.brsilver.com/2011/11/07/executable-bpmn-2-0/
[4] http://www.brsilver.com/2011/11/14/more-on-executable-bpmn-2-0/
[5] http://lampwww.epfl.ch/~sbriais/abc/abc.html
[6] http://www.it.uu.se/research/group/mobility/mwb
[7] http://bpt.hpi.uni-potsdam.de/Piworkflow/Simulator
[8] http://www.metasonic.de/

their interaction with each other. The modeling is divided into two layers. On the first layer there are the different subjects and the message flow between them. A second layer exists inside every subject where its behavior is modeled. The S-BPM methodology has been identified as "hype-technology" by Gartner in 2011.

The approach only contains five graphical symbols which are sufficient to model all possible business process, while in contrast BPMN has many more. Processes can be modeled based on natural language in mind, using the subject - predicate - object construction. When it comes to enactment the approach has the advantage of allowing models to be executed without providing additional information, due to the formal foundation of the approach. So no extra work has to be done. The focus on natural language is an interesting approach, but not convincing in our opinion. Language is linear and sequential in its nature and thus not appropriate to describe non-linearity and simultaneousness. Language is not complex enough for the real complexity of systems [15]. On the other side, as we have a formal model we can export it into formal natural language in principle, as demonstrated by Sneed [29].

In terms of expressiveness of modeling approaches and their implementations the workflow-patterns are often used as a criterion. The majority of these patterns can also be expressed in terms of the S-BPMN approach. Graef and Tölle [10], for example, transferred the control-flow patterns into the S-BPMN notation. It is remarkable that the authors achieved a reduction of the number of workflow-patterns (control-flow) from 43 to 25 choreography-patterns within the S-BPMN approach while still providing the same expressiveness as the original patterns. Van der Aalst requests, for example, to see implementations of the workflow patterns *Deferred Choice* (WP16) and *Milestone* (WP18) in the context of the discussion about "State-based instead of event-based" [3]. Both patterns [10, pp113 and pp119] can be presented in S-BPM, which is based on CCS as discussed.

5   Proof of Concept

Until now we have seen a lot of discussion about business process management, different process modeling notations with their pros and cons and their underlying concepts. We have presented process algebras like the CCS and the π-Calculus as formal foundations for process modeling and introduced a message based approach inspired by the CCS. The goal of this section is to examine how these concepts can be used in practice and whether they are suitable to meet the new shifts and requirements which were proposed, for example, by Puhlmann. As the basis for the examination we take the BPM-Suite from Metasonic – as it implements the CCS and allows a practical demonstration. Aitenbichler et al. [5] have proven that all language constructs used in jPASS (now renamed into *Metasonic Build*), the modeling part of the Suite, can be transformed into pure CCS.

5.1   Shift and Requirement 1

A formalism representing the first shift of BPM should be based on messages, or events, rather than states.

In figure 5 a simple version of an order process can be seen. It consists of two subjects which interact with each other using messages. This view was referred to layer one in section 4 . On this layer only the interacting subjects and messages can be seen.

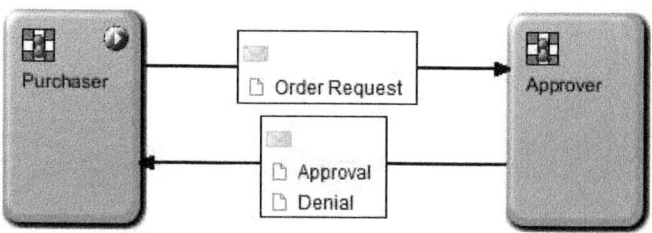

Fig. 5. A simple ordering process with two interacting subjects (*Purchaser* and *Approver*) sending messages (*Order Request, Approval* and *Denial*)

In layer two the actual behavior of the subjects is modeled. The internal behavior of the purchaser is shown in Figure 6.

As can be seen, the model of the internal behavior only uses three symbols: *send, receive* and *function.* They are equivalent to send, receive, and internal function actions of the CCS (the internal function may be implemented by a software service or may require user interaction). So, subjects are the same as agents in terms of the CCS (or interacting automata [17]). Also, the whole approach is based on sending and receiving of messages which fits well with the first requirement of Puhlmann. In the first BPM shift corresponding with requirement one Puhlmann [22] also states need to support *intra- and inter-organizational workflows without a paradigm break between formalism and practical implementation* (which is fulfilled by a message based approach). Intra-organizational processes can be modeled using so called *external subjects* which are used to link different processes. For external subjects no internal behavior is modeled. Figure 7 shows an advanced version of an ordering process with an external subject named *Supplier*. This subject acts as a link to an external process which is called *Supply* and shown in Figure 8.

The external subject in the process *Supply*, which is linked to the advanced ordering process, is called *Warehouse*. The actual behavior is modeled inside the subject *Supplier*. Another *subject* type is called *interface*. It is also used as a link to an external process (*inter-organizational*) but which is not specified (yet). The behavior modeled inside the *interface* only reflects how it interacts with the other subjects in the process, but does not necessarily look like the actual process which could, for example, be hosted by a business partner of the company.

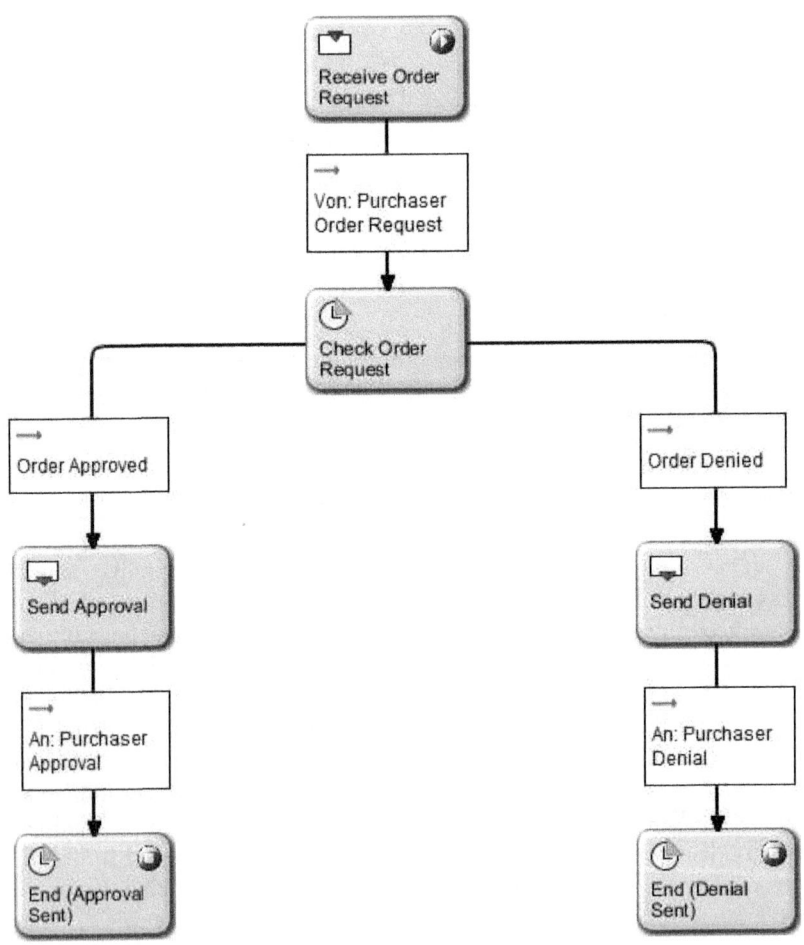

Fig. 6. The internal behavior of the approver

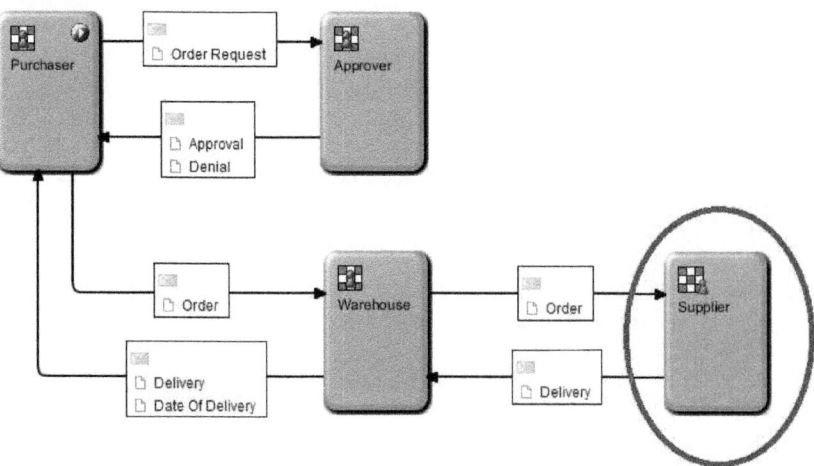

Fig. 7. A more advanced ordering process: The process *Ordering* interacts via the external subject *Supplier* with the external process *Supply*

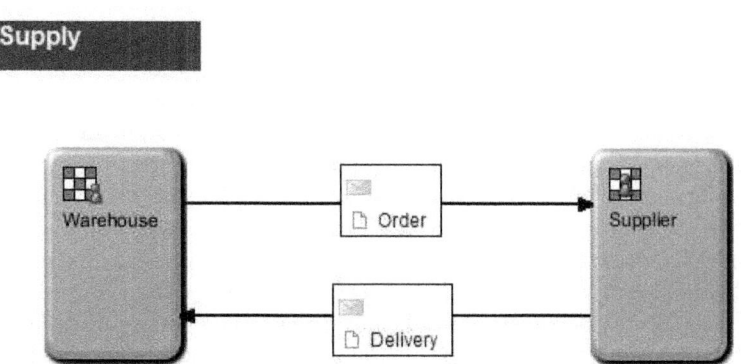

Fig. 8. The process *Supply* interacts via the external subject *Warehouse* with the process *Ordering*

5.2   Shift and Requirement 2

A formalism supporting the second shift of BPM should support advanced composition and visibility of its parts.

The capability of the S-BPM approach of distributed modeling and execution was proven by Aitenbicher et al. [5]. They showed how process models can be split up along its subject and executed in a distributed manner on different process engines running on different servers or even on mobile devices having no permanent connection to the Internet. Additionally the distributed modeling of processes was investigated, showing the ability of the subject oriented approach to model *subjects* in different cooperating businesses without full disclosure of their internal processes. This is realized with the use of the CCS restriction operator, which allows the hiding of internal behavior and disclosing of external interactions of the *subject*. While hiding internal behavior, it is still possible to perform the same model checks if the overall choreography is modeled as a single, centralized process.

5.3   Shift and Requirement 3

A formalism taking the third shift into account should support dynamic process structures that can support change.

While the S-BPM approach supports the first two shifts and requirements very well, it is actually not suited to express dynamic process structures. The lack of support is caused by its CCS foundation. In order to support the claimed process mobility the software suite would have to implement the π-Calculus instead of the CCS.

6   Conclusion

The goal of this paper was to investigate how formal methods like process algebras can be used for business process management. We have presented a discussion and different opinions about them and introduced their purpose, syntax and semantics using examples. Furthermore, we described arising problems during the transformation of process models into executable workflows using BPMN and BPEL. In comparison we introduced the *subject oriented* approach which is based on the *Calculus of Communicating Systems*. It emphasizes the modeling of internal behavior of *subjects* and their interactions rather than control-flows and allows the automated transformation into executable code for fast deployment and validation. In the last section we dealt with the suitability of the *subject oriented* approach to meet the requirements stated in section 2.3. While it could be proven that it fulfills the claim of message orientation, distributed modeling and execution, the modeling of mobility is not possible yet.

In conclusion, algebras and their implementations are an interesting and promising way of modeling business processes. Their greatest strength lies in their formalization allowing an unambiguous and automated transformation from the model to an execution environment, validation and verification in respect to properties like different soundness criteria.

Despite that CCS and S-BPM are rather mathematical and technical concepts, during the course of this paper the question arose whether a message based approach could be a more suitable paradigm to describe processes. This could be especially interesting when concerning how people actually work in companies in respect to their communication and interaction behavior. So, a message based approach might better fit to describe the processes and work flows of a company. Nevertheless, a message based approach fits remarkably well with some core entities studied in social sciences: agents, communication and collaboration which will be presented elsewhere [11].

References

1. van der Aalst, W.M.P.: Why workflow is NOT just a Pi-process. BPTrends (2004)
2. van der Aalst, W., Stahl, C.: Modeling Business Processes. The MIT Press (2011)
3. van der Aalst, W.: Pi calculus versus petri nets: Let us eat "humble pie" rather than further inflate the "pi hype". BPTrends (2005)
4. Aceto, L., Ingólfsdóttir, A., Larsen, K.G., Srba, J.: Reactive Systems: Modelling, Specification and Verification. Cambridge University Press (2007)
5. Aitenbichler, E., Borgert, S., Mühlhäuser, M.: Distributed Execution of S-BPM Business Processes. In: Fleischmann, A., Schmidt, W., Singer, R., Seese, D. (eds.) S-BPM ONE 2010. CCIS, vol. 138, pp. 19–35. Springer, Heidelberg (2011)
6. Bergstra, J.A., Klop, J.W.: Process Algebra for Synchronous Communication. Information and Control 60, 109–137 (1984)
7. Bog, A.: A Visual Environment for the Simulation of Business Processes based on the Pi-Calculus. Ph.D. thesis, University of Potsdam (2006)
8. Börger, E.: Approaches to modeling business processes: a critical analysis of BPMN, workflow patterns and YAWL. Software and Systems Modeling, pp. 1–14, http://dx.doi.org/10.1007/s10270-011-0214-z
9. Chun, O., van der Aalst, W.M., Dumas, M., ter Hofstede, A.H.: From Business Process Models to Process-oriented Software Systems: The BPMN to BPEL Way. ACM Transactions on Software Engineering and Methodology 19(1), Articel Nr. 2 (2009)
10. Graef, N., Tölle, N.: Evaluation, Mapping und quantitative Reduktion von Workflow Pattern (Control-Flow). Bachelor Thesis, University of Karlsruhe (2009) (in German)
11. Grossgasteiger, S., Singer, R.: Process Calculi and the Notion of Communication in Social Sciences (to be published, 2012)
12. Hoare, C.A.R.: Communicating Sequential Processes. Prentice Hall (1985)
13. Koomen, C.J.: The Design of Communicating Systems: a System Engineering Approach. Springer (1991)
14. Leymann, F.: BPEL vs. BPMN 2.0: Should You Care? In: Mendling, J., Weidlich, M., Weske, M. (eds.) BPMN 2010. LNBIP, vol. 67, pp. 8–13. Springer, Heidelberg (2010)
15. Malik, F.: Strategie – Navigieren in der Komplexität der Neuen Welt. Management: Komplexität meistern, vol. 3, campus (2011) (in German)
16. Milner, R.: A Calculus of Communication Systems. LNCS, vol. 92. Springer, Heidelberg (1980)
17. Milner, R.: Communicating and mobile systems: The pi-calculus. Cambridge University Press (1999)
18. Milner, R., Parrow, J., Walker, D.: A calculus of mobile processes, part i. Information and Computation 100 (1989)
19. Milner, R., Parrow, J., Walker, D.: A calculus of mobile processes, part ii. Information and Computation 100(1), 41–77 (1992)

20. Olbrich, T.J.: Why We Need to Re-think Current BPM Research Issues. In: Fleischmann, A., Schmidt, W., Singer, R., Seese, D. (eds.) S-BPM ONE 2010. CCIS, vol. 138, pp. 209–215. Springer, Heidelberg (2011)
21. Parrow, J.: An introduction to the π-calculus, ch.8, pp. 479–544. Elsevier Science (2001)
22. Puhlmann, F.: Why do we actually need the Pi-Calculus for Business Process Management? Business Informations Systems, 77–89 (2006)
23. Puhlmann, F.: On the Application of a Theory for Mobile Systems to Business Process Management. Ph.D. thesis, University of Potsdam (2007)
24. Recker, J., Mendling, J.: On the Translation between BPMN and BPEL: Conceptual Mismatch between Process Modeling Languages, pp. 521–532 (2006)
25. Schmidt, W., Fleischmann, A., Gilbert, O.: Subject-Oriented Business Process Management. Praxis der Wirtschaftsinformatik (266), 52–62 (2009)
26. Silver, B.: BPMN Method & Style, 2nd edn. Cody-Cassidy Press (2011)
27. Singer, R., Zinser, E.: Business Process Management – Do We Need a New Research Agenda? In: Fleischmann, A., Schmidt, W., Singer, R., Seese, D. (eds.) S-BPM ONE 2010. CCIS, vol. 138, pp. 220–226. Springer, Heidelberg (2011)
28. Smith, H., Fingar, P.: Workflow is just a Pi process. BPTrends (2004)
29. Sneed, S.H.: Exporting Natural Language: Generating NL Sentences Out of S-BPM Process Models. In: Fleischmann, A., Schmidt, W., Singer, R., Seese, D. (eds.) S-BPM ONE 2010. CCIS, vol. 138, pp. 163–179. Springer, Heidelberg (2011)
30. Voelzer, H.: An Overview of BPMN 2.0 and Its Potential Use. Business Process Modeling Notation 67(1), 14–15 (2011)
31. Weidlich, M., Decker, G., Großkopf, A., Weske, M.: BPEL to BPMN: The Myth of a Straight-Forward Mapping. In: Meersman, R., Tari, Z. (eds.) OTM 2008, Part I. LNCS, vol. 5331, pp. 265–282. Springer, Heidelberg (2008)
32. Weske, M.: Business Process Management: Concepts, Languages, Architectures. Springer (2007)
33. Wohed, P., van der Aalst, W.M.P., Dumas, M., ter Hofstede, A.H.M., Russell, N.: On the Suitability of BPMN for Business Process Modelling. In: Dustdar, S., Fiadeiro, J.L., Sheth, A.P. (eds.) BPM 2006. LNCS, vol. 4102, pp. 161–176. Springer, Heidelberg (2006)

ProcessWiki: A Contribution for Bridging the Last Mile Problem in Automotive Retail

Matthias Kurz[1], Sebastian Huber[1], and Bernd Hilgarth[2]

[1] Wirtschaftsinformatik II, University of Erlangen-Nuremberg, Lange Gasse 20,
90403 Nuremberg, Germany
{matthias.kurz,sebastian.huber}@wiso.uni-erlangen.de
[2] Department of Computer Science & Information Systems, University of Jyväskylä,
P.O. Box 35 (Agora), Jyväskylä, Finland
bernd.hilgarth@jyu.fi

Abstract. In many real-world business process management (BPM) installments, the benefit of BPM is diminished by an insufficient implementation of the to-be business processes. One of the key reasons for this problem is the complexity of classical process modeling representations that exceed the BPM knowledge of many target groups.

This contribution introduces the ProcessWiki method, which adapts the BPM 2.0 and adaptive case management (ACM) approaches. The ProcessWiki method has two primary objectives: (1) Providing a method that allows communicating business process models in a way that is easily understood by employees with little or no BPM knowledge and (2) enabling these employees to improve "their" business processes by using collaborative tools. The method was developed during a joint project with the BMW Group and is illustrated using a corresponding software solution.

Keywords: BPM, BPM 2.0, ACM, last-mile problem, collaboration.

1 Introduction

The *last mile problem* is a wide spread challenge in the business process management (BPM) discipline. This term depicts the insufficient implementation of well-defined business processes in the operative daily routine of today's organizations. This is rooted in the gap between the actual business processes and those which are described by sophisticated process models stored in the enterprises' reference process houses [1]. In the German speaking BPM community this observation is also known as "Schrankware" [2]. The problem gets worse when the complexity of the modeling notation exceeds the understanding of the target group. This becomes especially apparent in scenarios when employees with little formal BPM education are confronted with the complexity of widely used notations like event-driven process chains (EPC) or the business process modeling notation (BPMN). The dilemma in those situations is two-folded:

S. Oppl and A. Fleischmann (Eds.): S-BPM ONE 2012, CCIS 284, pp. 151–167, 2012.
© Springer-Verlag Berlin Heidelberg 2012

1. The process knowledge (e.g. process model or text) is difficult to adapt to the target groups' needs, because of the highly individual requirements. Rejecting its use in daily operations is the consequence.
2. Traditional BPM methods and software tools are less aware about the needed features that allow adapting process knowledge by the target groups (e.g., by providing collaborative BPM design and decision methods and features).

In order to overcome these challenges, the BMW Group currently conducts a pilot project which has the objective to provide a method as well as a software solution for standardizing and continuously improving the global aftersales retail processes. The outcome is a method and a software solution which shows collaborative design, decision, and publishing features.

This contribution introduces the ProcessWiki method that adapts the BPM 2.0 [4, 5] and adaptive case management (ACM) [6, 8] approaches. By providing carefully aligned modeling levels along with substantially simplified notations, it can be ensured that the respective target group of each modeling level can intuitively understand the process models. The method is not a one way street: Besides communicating business processes in a way that matches the BPM knowledge of the respective target groups, the members of these target groups are empowered to participate in the continuous improvement and adaptation of "their" processes without requiring explicit BPM expertise. A SharePoint-based prototype of a corresponding software solution shows how this method could be implemented and applied within the BMW Group. This software solution meets the requirements of BPM design, decision, and publishing processes in a collaborative character.

2   Status Quo of BMW Aftersales Retail Process Management

To understand the above described issues regarding BPM in the context of highly distributed workforces, this chapter introduces the situation that is currently apparent in BMW Group aftersales retail processes. The BMW Group shows the typical functional structure of large multinationally acting organizations. In general, BPM reaches various maturity levels within the organizational units. The aftersales retail processes exist within the aftersales organization which comprises four major levels: (1) Headquarter departments (HQ), (2) its dedicated sales regions (Regions), (3) the national sales companies (NSC), and the approximately 3.400 retail stores (Retail) which are mainly independent legal entities. The following two sub sections describe the current BPM approach that exists at the BMW Group and its observable effects as well as the challenges that have to be overcome for improving the implementation degree of BPM within the aftersales organization.

2.1   Current Approach

Currently, the BMW Group relies primarily on traditional BPM methods and software tools for designing and approving the aftersales retail processes. As Fig. 1 shows, process knowledge is documented using both *value chains* and *extended event-driven process chains* (eEPC), which are edited and stored in *ARIS Business Designer*. These notations focus on a formal and comprehensive documentation of the process architecture and strive to capture the existing complexity of the business processes.

Access to this process knowledge is restricted to a few persons working in the headquarter aftersales departments as well as in several sales regions. These graphical process models are the basis for a simplified documentation of the aftersales processes. This kind of documentation relies on a text- and media-driven description of process knowledge, which neglects formal methods like *value chains* or *eEPC*. The concept aims at spreading the process knowledge in the retail stores worldwide. Its distribution via DVDs takes place in the responsibility of the sales regions and their dedicated national sales companies.

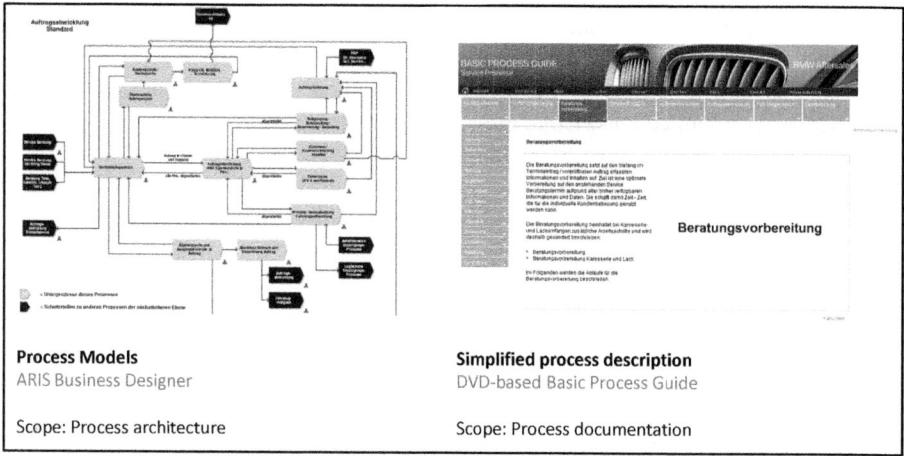

Fig. 1. Process models and simplified textual descriptions as current approach for BPM

Obviously, the implementation of the processes in this organization does not show the expected results. Observable reasons for this are:

1. **Critical divergences between the documented and the needed or expected process knowledge** exist. Centrally designed process knowledge (models and documentation) is not adapted enough to meet real existing situations.
2. **Process actors in retail shops are not directly reachable**. There is a lack of methods and tools which allow the fast and reliable distribution of and access to process knowledge. Collaboration and feedback mechanisms are not sufficiently implemented within the organizational units.
3. Reaching the process actors at retail level proves to be difficult, as the **process knowledge either is too complex or too unstructured in its modeling notation**. It seems to be hard to determine the sufficient level of complexity of notation.
4. **The current representation of process knowledge is decoupled from real existing context.** The process models as well as the textual descriptions that are provided by a BMW Group headquarter department are not integrated in daily incident management of retail store employees. This separation of abstract process knowledge from daily operations leads to inefficiencies for the process actors.

The next section treats the challenges that arise from this situation.

2.2   Challenges

Improving BPM in this heterogeneously and highly distributed workforce effectively goes along with following challenges for the BMW Group:

1. The creation of process knowledge cannot be a one-way approach. The collaboration between the different roles in this process community has to be improved by the use of clear responsibilities, rules, and the supplementing IT tools.
2. Simply accessible IT tools might also support the transfer of process knowledge (distribution) in a reliable and bidirectional way.
3. Process representation and modeling notation should be reduced to their needed and understandable level (symbols, texts, and logical connectors). Modeling of complex situations should be possible as well as simple adaptations by retail experts with limited knowledge of process modeling notations.
4. The process models have to be implemented in the daily operations of the retail store employees. A respective environment should be offered in which the retail staff can execute those models (e.g. by automated user-centric workflows).

Summarizing this, the challenge for BMW Group aftersales retail is to establish a dynamic process management community, which operates on a common process knowledge basis that allows a collaborative and bidirectional exchange of heterogeneous process experiences by using state-of-the-art IT tools.

3   Related Work

The ProcessWiki method is influenced by a large number of related BPM research domains. Fig. 2 depicts these fields and visualizes their relationship.

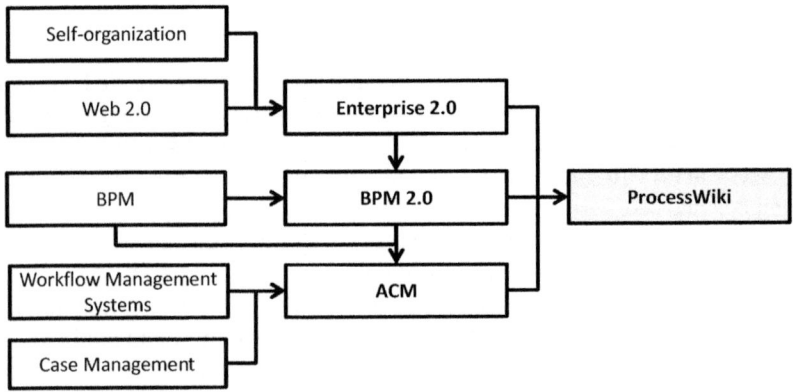

Fig. 2. Related research domains (cf. [3])

The widely known term *Enterprise 2.0* refers both to the idea of *self-organization* (i.e. transferring more decision power to employees) as well as the corresponding *Web 2.0* instruments that are used in a business environment. Especially the wiki idea promises to support the vision of empowered employees. E.g., [14] suggests using wikis for representing business processes and creating easy-to-navigate links between the processes and their artifacts like documents or glossaries. However, its focus is on supporting the process participants during the execution of the processes utilizing task lists and document libraries. Therefore, it provides little support for continuous process improvement by the employees executing this process.

BPM 2.0 picks up the idea of Enterprise 2.0 and adapts it for the field of *BPM*. The suffix *2.0* indicates that integrating employees who execute business processes as part of their day-to-day tasks into the design of business processes is the core idea of BPM 2.0 [4]. [4, 5] define BPM 2.0 as follows:

> "BPM 2.0 is a business process management approach, which encourages employees to improve "their" business processes. Web 2.0 technologies are utilized to enable contributions from employees with little BPM expertise."
> [4, 5]

Workflow management systems (WFMS) are well-established instruments that improve businesses' productivity by automating business processes [12]. As WFMS require that technical workflow models are derived from business-driven process models before process execution, workflow management is only suitable for repeatable and predictable routine processes [6].

Knowledge work is of increasing importance to BPM but it is difficult to support by WFMS, as the processes may change during execution and therefore cannot be sufficiently prepared [6]. Although approaches like *Adaptive Workflow* [15] or *DECLARE* [16] suggest solutions for incorporating changes to running workflow instances, they introduce new complexity by requiring formal instruments like temporal logic. This substantially limits the ability of business users without sufficient formal knowledge to make such changes.

In order to overcome this challenge, the *adaptive case management* (ACM) idea is proposed by [7]. It extends the classical case management approach and introduces a process-centric perspective. In contrast to WFMS, business processes can be adapted to new requirements during their runtime. This ACM variant described in [6, 8] refines the ACM idea from [7] by introducing a concrete procedure model and role concept that is derived from the BPM 2.0 approach. As another major extension, the refined ACM approach suggests a way how for integrating automated workflow fragments within the otherwise non-automated case process. A prototype illustrates this refined approach.

The ProcessWiki method is predominantly an extension of the BPM 2.0 approach. Besides BPM 2.0, it integrates ideas from Enterprise 2.0 and ACM.

In subject oriented business process management (S-BPM), a technique known as "modeling through restriction" [13] allows defining knowledge intensive business processes in a way that leaves the process participants sufficient room for responding to requirements and / or challenges that did not exist at the time of the definition of the process model. This allows the participants to develop new solutions to new challenges and / or requirements.

With leveraging feedback for the continuous improvement of business processes being one of the key objectives of ProcessWiki as well, ProcessWiki takes a similar path as S-BPM: Processes are not exactly predefined sequences of activities but recommendations how to achieve an objective. The key difference to S-BPM is the notation: Due to the insufficient BPM knowledge, ProcessWiki deliberately uses a simple hierarchy of activities instead of a graphical notation. Therefore, modeling the communication between the actors is detailed in the description of each activity rather than using explicit modeling elements.

4   ProcessWiki Project

Motivated by the existing challenges for BPM at BMW Group and the beforehand mentioned methodological ideas of the BPM 2.0 and ACM approaches, a pilot project in the aftersales retail department was initiated and implemented. In the following, the project goals and the big picture for the ProcessWiki project are the focus of this chapter.

4.1   Project Objectives

Derived from the challenges discussed in chapter 2.2, the project objective is to develop a methodology as well as a corresponding prototypical collaboration platform which allows the process community to...

1. develop, document and publish easily understandable process knowledge (graphical as well as text-based),
2. discuss, align, and adapt the process knowledge in a collaborative manner,
3. provide feedback to existing process knowledge, and
4. immediately and intuitively apply the process knowledge in the daily business.

In order to achieve these objectives, first the big picture consisting the target groups and platform solution elements was developed within the project. The following section introduces this big picture.

4.2   Big Picture

Fig. 3 depicts the main elements of the ProcessWiki idea. In the first dimension it illustrates the target groups of the ProcessWiki, which are aligned with the involved

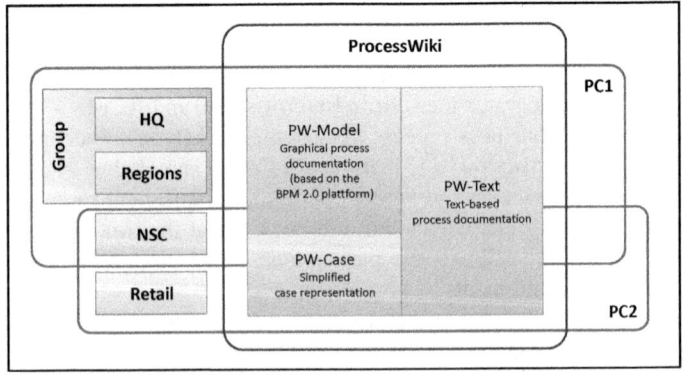

Fig. 3. ProcessWiki@BMW group big picture

sub organizations of the BMW Group aftersales business area. The second dimension is represented by the ProcessWiki solution elements. Combining both dimensions, two *process communities* are planned that will be focused on different content types and functionalities. *Process community 1* (PC1) comprises the HQ, Regions and NSC departments. It is focused on editing, designing, discussing, and adapting graphical (PW-Model) and text-based (PW-Text) process knowledge. This community is less involved (with exception the NSC and its hotline and support tasks for aftersales products) in the operational management of cases (PW-Case). PC1 aims at a steady aligned, quality approved process architecture and knowledge basis through collaboration across the vertical units in the aftersales channel organization. *Process community 2* (PC2) is composed of the NSC and the retail units. It focuses on the usage and commenting (in sense of providing feedback and customizing process knowledge to individual situations) of the text-based (PW-Text) and graphical (PW-Model) process knowledge that is provided in the ProcessWiki. Actors in the retail stores will use the PW-Case tools and instruments of ProcessWiki for assistance in the daily incident management (e.g. the management for service consultant processes).

This big picture helped to identify that the ProcessWiki is a coherent and comprehensive idea for tackling the challenges that exist in BMW Group aftersales retail BPM. The next chapter focuses on the methodological concept of the ProcessWiki.

5   ProcessWiki Method

The ProcessWiki method has the objective to (1) provide a means to globally communicate business process models to the retail employees involved in the retail aftersales services and (2) to allow and encourage these employees to improve these processes and adapt them to new challenges. (3) Therefore, the method has to consider the lack of BPM knowledge within the target group. (4) Furthermore, it serves as the theoretical foundation of the ProcessWiki software solution.

In order to achieve these goals, the method comprises the following major components:

- A *process structure* defines the objectives and target groups for each process level. It ensures that the processes are both available in the native languages and customized according to their cultural and legal context.
- The *interaction types* explain which tools are used for communicating and improving the aftersales service processes.
- The *procedure model* explains how the managers and employees cooperate in improving the business processes.

5.1   Process Structure

The process structure consists of four modeling levels (cf. Fig. 4). The top-most level is the *process architecture* (PA). The PA contains all major processes as well as their relationships. By enriching the processes from the PA with greater detail, the *template processes* (TP) are derived from the PA. Both the PA and the TP are reference processes defined by a policy unit of the BMW group. Due to the global nature of these processes, both the PA and the TP are documented in English.

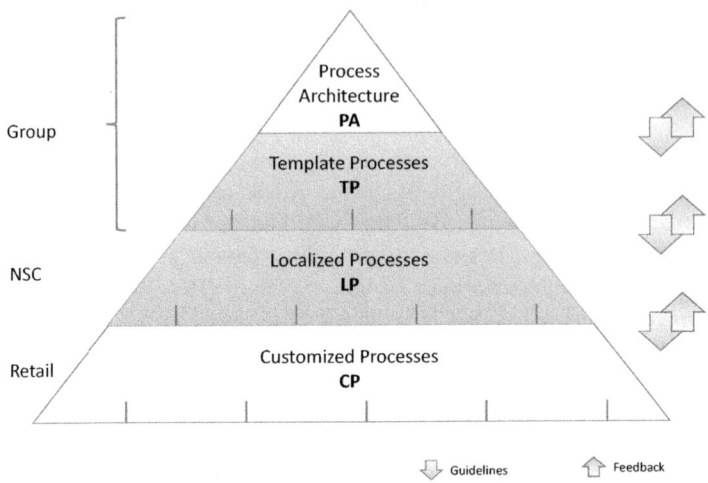

Fig. 4. Process structure

On the *localized processes* (LP) level, the generic TP are customized to the specifics of each national sales company (NSC). This includes adding or removing activities that are mandated by the lawmaker (e.g. creating a written contract for sold services) or implied by cultural differences (e.g. not mentioning the way of payment during the sales process).

In some cases, the individual retail stores need to customize the LP according to their needs. This is especially true for larger retail entities that comprise multiple stores. In this case, the LP processes can be adapted and made available to single retail stores or chains of retail stores as *customized processes* (CP).

The focus of the ProcessWiki methodology is on the TP and LP levels. Most process innovations are expected to occur here, as the PA has to be sufficiently abstract in order to remain mostly static and customizations on the retail level are only likely in the few cases, where single stores have an urgent need for customization. Otherwise, the effort for creating and maintaining customized processes is not economical.

5.2   Interaction Types

The method offers two basic process representations. The *graphical representation* utilizes a simplified subset of the widely used business process modeling notation (BPMN). It is used exclusively for the PA.

For all other process levels, a *text-based representation* is used. This representation is a simple list of sequential activities. Each activity is associated with a corresponding text-based wiki page. This simple representation is easy to understand and thereby achieves the objective of providing a simplified means of communicating the business processes to employees with little modeling expertise. On the other hand, it is a compromise between simplicity and expressiveness, as some of the information that is contained in the graphical process models of the PA is lost in the corresponding textual representation on the TP, LP and CP levels. For complex cases, the simple activity list can be optionally extended to be a hierarchy of activities. This allows for an improved structure of complex processes.

In the case of the graphical representation, a sophisticated graphical editor allows modifying the process models and creating hyperlinks to text-based wiki pages. For the text-based representation, the SharePoint wiki functionality has been substantially extended in order to not only allow editing the textual descriptions in a what-you-see-is-what-you-get (WYSIWYG) manner but to also provide an intuitive drag-and-drop mechanism for creating, rearranging, and deleting new process activities.

Both editors provide convenient undo and redo functionality in order to easily recover from unintended changes of the process models like accidental deletions. Discussion boards support identifying problems and developing new ideas without having to modify the process models.

The screenshots in section 6 give a visual impression of the software solution that is currently under development.

5.3   Procedure Model

The procedure model defines how the stakeholders of a process interact during process improvements. The procedure model has to ensure a compromise between the primary objective of enabling bottom-up feedback and a global harmonization of the business processes. Fig. 5 gives an overview of the procedure model.

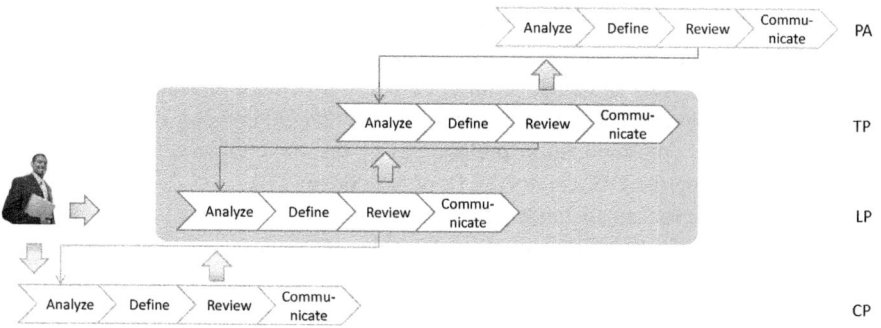

Fig. 5. ProcessWiki procedure model

The focus of the process improvements is on the LP and TP levels, as most retail stores will not customize processes and therefore have to provide their input directly to the LP level. These changes have to be propagated to the TP. The PA is not expected to change, as its processes are sufficiently abstract and only outline the basic structure of the TP.

The procedure model defines the tasks and responsibilities of each stakeholder in great detail. For demonstration purposes, Fig. 6 shows an excerpt of the procedure model on the LP level.

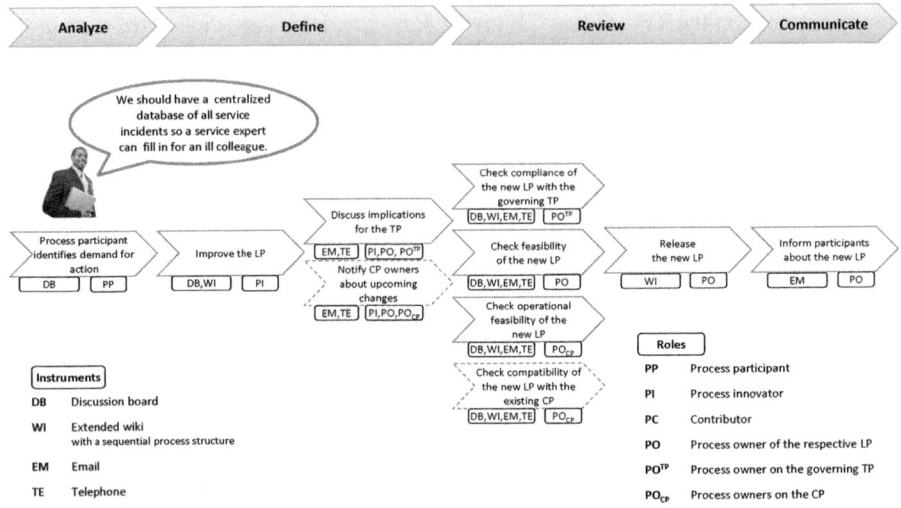

Fig. 6. Excerpt from the procedure model on the LP level

During the *analyze* phase, a *process participant* (PP) (e.g. a sales representative) suggests an improvement with the help of the *discussion board* (DB) of a LP.

In the *define* phase, a new process innovation workspace is created. Within this workspace, the suggestion is formalized by *process innovators* (PI) using the DB and the *extended wiki* (WI) which supports modeling activity list based processes. In most cases, the PP who triggered the innovation will become a PI driving "his" or "her" innovation. The *improved process is discussed* between the PI and the process owners of the LP (PO) as well as the governing TP (PO^{TP}). If there are customizations, the respective CP owners (PO$_{CP}$) are *notified about the upcoming changes* as well. Depending on the communication preferences of the stakeholders, these discussions are conducted using the DB, emails (EM), or telephone (TE).

The *review* phase has to ensure that the improved LP meets its objectives and conforms to the governing TP. Therefore, the self-organization, which is the prevalent principle in the "analyze" and "define" phases, is superseded by a classical hierarchical confirmation that legitimates the outcome of the self-organization within the organization [9, 10].

The review phase starts with the PO of the respective LP *checking whether the proposed LP is feasible* at all. In the next step, the PO^{TP} has to *check whether the new LP is compliant with the governing TP*. As integrating bottom-up feedback is encouraged, the PO^{TP} has to consider whether the changes proposed by the new LP should be generalized on the TP level as well. The PO$_{CP}$ of the affected CP (i.e. all PO$_{CP}$ within a NSC) have to *examine whether the new LP is operationally feasible* within the respective retail stores. For all stores that have introduced CP, *the compatibility with those CP has to be considered* as well.

Once the reviews by the process owners have been successfully completed, the process is formally *released*. Technically, the process model is copied from the innovation workspace to the original workspace.

Finally, during the *communicate* phase, the process participants are *informed about the new LP*. As some retail stores may have minor customizations which are not extensive enough in order to constitute a CP, an email is sent to the PO_{CP}. Thereby, the PO has the opportunity to modify this mail and introduce store-specific modifications if necessary.

Thus, each store has to appoint a PO_{CP} although it has no CP of its own. With on-site BPM expertise being a major success factor for the implementation of BPM, a similar role already exists anyway.

5.4   Validation

As the objective of the ProcessWiki project is to develop both a method and a software solution, the method has to be validated prior to commencing the major part of the software development effort.

Therefore, a semi structured qualitative expert interviews with two stakeholders and BPM experts within BMW have been conducted. In accordance with [11], these interviews were conducted according to an interview guideline. The questions of this guideline on the one hand had to ensure that the answers are comparable. On the other hand, the questions had to avoid limiting the answers too much as this would have caused the experts to omit potentially relevant information. [11] describes the resulting compromise as "closed openness".

The experts were selected according to their knowledge about the aftersales service processes. While two members were involved with the management of the global process framework, the third member had extensive first-hand experience in the aftersales processes. While a larger number of interviewees would have substantiates the findings of the interviews, the extensive time burden (each interview took between 90 and 120 minutes) for the managers and experts limited the number of interviews that could be conducted. As the ProcessWiki method is an extension of the extensively tested and validated [9] BPM 2.0 method, this effort seemed not to be economical.

Each of the three interviews started with a presentation of the objectives, the method itself, and an illustration of the applied method using a mock-up of the software solution. The following questions were asked:

1. Are the objectives of the method relevant?
2. Provides the method a substantial contribution towards reaching these goals?
3. Provides the sketched prototype a substantial contribution towards reaching these goals?
4. Can this method be implemented successfully?
5. Which major areas of improvement do you see in the method or the prototype?

All in all, the method and the outlined prototype were considered to be a valid and valuable solution for the problem at hand. Besides some rather minor changes due to suggestions of the experts, the method had been formally confirmed to be the methodical foundation of the software development project. The critique focused on two areas: (1) The description of the procedure model was too abstract. This was addressed by examples which made the procedure model easier to grasp. (2) The experts criticized that it was too time-consuming for retail stores to introduce minor customizations to the processes. By making the notification about changed processes the responsibility of the PO_{CP} instead of the PO, the PO_{CP} can easily add information or customizations like, for example, checklists.

The changes to the method following the expert interviews primarily focused on a more intuitive representation of the procedure model and a reworked navigation structure within the prototype.

6   ProcessWiki Prototype

After the theoretical framework has been iteratively improved, validated, and finally approved as the base for the software solution, the goal of this chapter is to show how this method is implemented and applied within the organization of the BMW Group. The first step is to develop an intuitive navigation considering the complex process structure (cf. chapter 5.1). Afterwards, the conception of the different interaction components (cf. chapter 5.2) is explained in detail.

6.1   Navigation Structure

As Microsoft SharePoint (SP) is set as the standard portal solution within the BMW Group, the navigation concept has to be compatible with the SP function set. Basically SP is differentiating two concepts for navigation:

- Site: A site is a collection of pages, lists and libraries. A site may contain sub-sites, and those sites may contain further sub-sites. To make maintenance easier, a site can inherit site-level settings from their parent site like for instance permission settings. Typically, sites are created from scratch but it is also possible to use pre-defined templates that provide packaged functionality.
- Pages: Fundamentally, there are two types of pages. In a standard *web-part page* zones are predefined, where additional components (web parts) like lists etc. could be added. Per default, pages are from type *wiki page* which enables free-form editing.

To meet the requirements in terms of internationalization and to reduce complexity, the portal solution will use the concept of sites. The basic navigation structure is shown in Fig. 7.

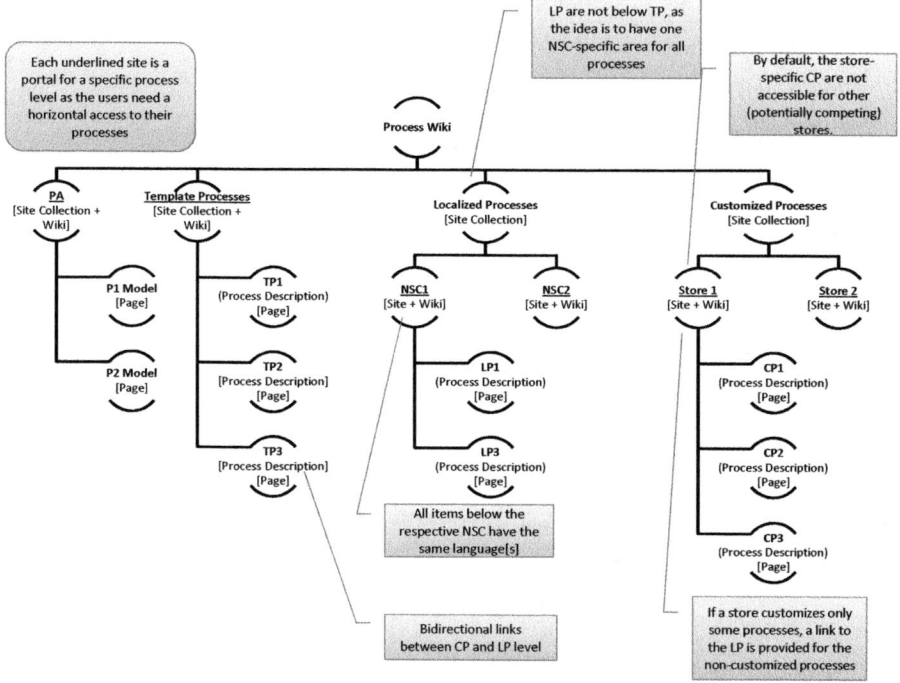

Fig. 7. ProcessWiki navigation structure

Root of the page is the site collection *ProcessWiki*. It serves as the main entry point to the portal solution. Below, a site collection is created for every level of the process structure. In the *Process Architecture* site collection (PA) all graphical models and collaboration tools (e.g., discussion board) are stored. The *Template Processes* site collection (TP) contains the derived process description pages in wiki format. PA and TP levels will remain English, as the operational employees (which may have little knowledge in English) on the retail level are not expected to interact on the PA and TP level directly. Linked to the TP process descriptions every NSC has its own localized process descriptions (LP). If it is necessary, even a specific retail store or a store chain may derivate its own customized processes (CP).

The component *Process Description* supports two different views. It consists of a process innovation page, where processes can be improved collaboratively with the extended wiki functionality described above or discussion boards. Each version is stored and accessible by an intuitive undo/redo function. A specific version can be also approved and published on the release page.

6.2   Process Architecture

Fig. 8 shows the main screen of the portal solution. Its purpose is to give a compact overview of the described core processes. On the top navigation one could directly go to the respective process. Another option is to directly click on the process phase on the image. With the hyperlink on the right hand side it is possible to change the current work mode from graphical modeling (PA) to wiki based process descriptions (TP).

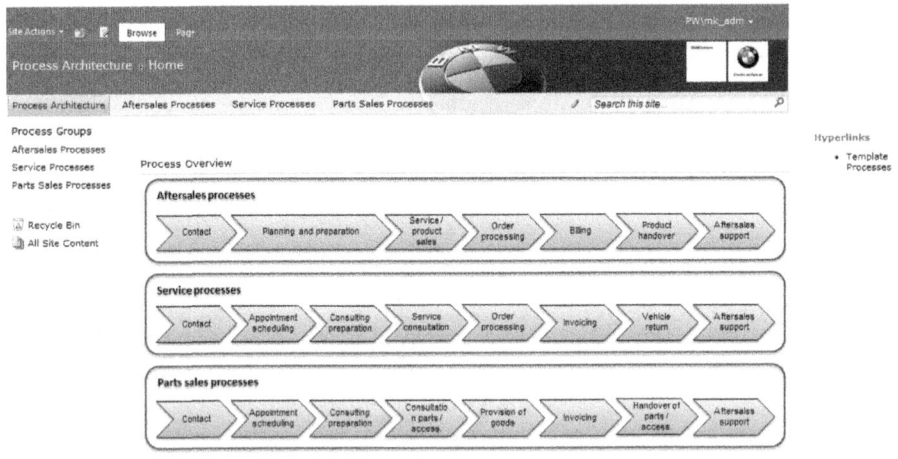

Fig. 8. Process overview

Assuming the PA mode, a click on a process will display the next screen (Fig. 9).

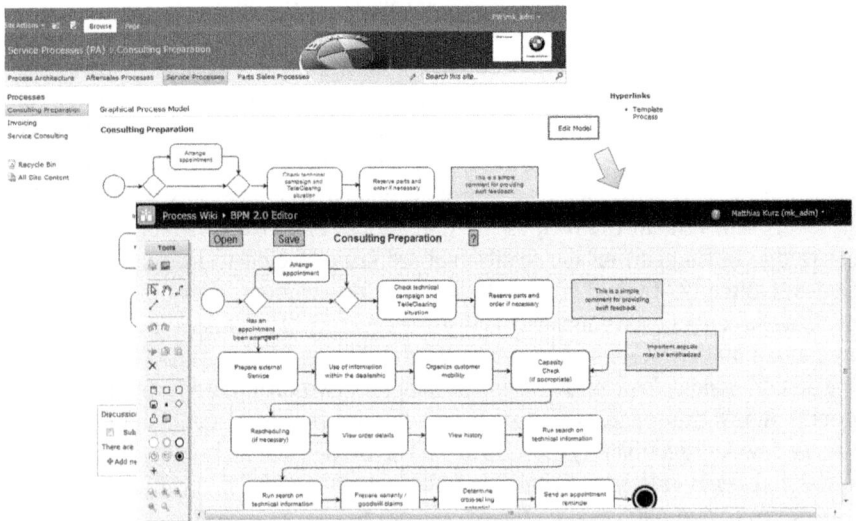

Fig. 9. Editor of the graphical process notation for the PA

In the background of Fig. 9 an image of the respective BPMN model is embedded into the portal. Here, the user can contribute his or her opinion by using the discussion board or click on *Edit Model* to get into the modeling workspace which is shown in the foreground. In this environment all features of the BPM 2.0 [4] platform are incorporated. The BPMN light subset reduces complexity and – with yellow "post it" comments – the process models can be collaboratively improved. A bold red border around an activity indicates changes to the model that needs to be further discussed. The system always tracks the different user changes and offers the option to revert back to an older model or to only accept certain changes on a model.

6.3   Process Documentation

After the process models have been created using the tools available for the process architecture, the next step is to transform those models into easily understandable rich-media process descriptions. The main idea of the following component is to represent the BPMN models with a sequential and optionally hierarchical list of process steps. This step has to be done manually because the tool cannot solve circular dependencies from the graphical models. Each process step is associated with a wiki page, which describes the respective activities in further detail. Fig. 10 shows the innovation mode of that component.

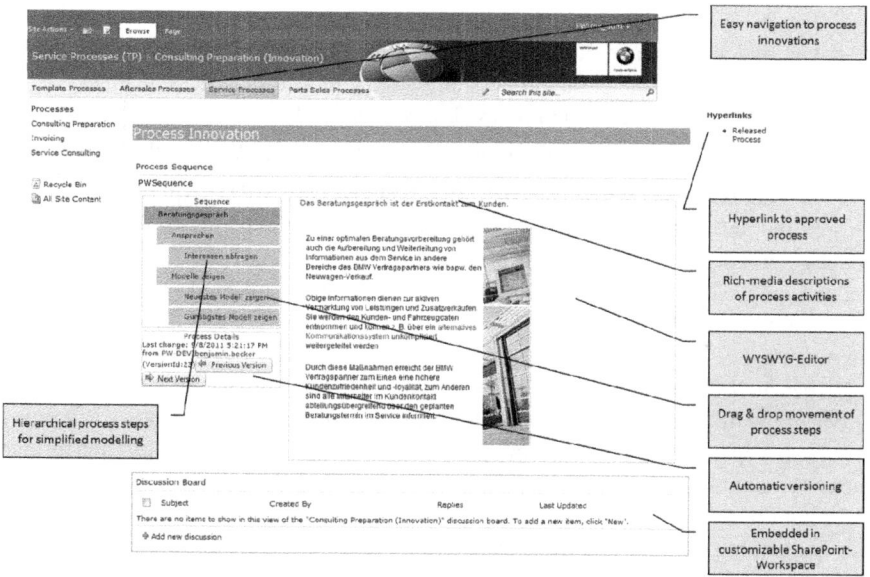

Fig. 10. Process innovation workspace

The hierarchical process steps are displayed on the left. In the innovation mode new steps can be created and existing ones can be modified, deleted, or rearranged easily via drag and drop. Below the process steps versioning information is shown. On each change a new version will be automatically generated. For the first (selected) step the according wiki page is displayed. The contents are modified by an intuitive WYSIWYG editor that also supports the insertion of video clips, pictures, or hyperlinks to other process steps or portal content. Being a WebPart, this component seamlessly fits into the SharePoint context. This enables the use of built-in collaborative tools, like the discussion board displayed below. Thereby the process owners of the different process levels can share feedback and improve those descriptions collaboratively. It is also possible to take advantage of document libraries to offer the end users document templates and checklists to directly support them fulfilling those processes.

7   Conclusion

The BPM implementation of the BMW aftersales services shows the typical symptoms many large companies face when trying to design, approve, distribute, and adapt process knowledge across complex organizational structures to the employees who execute these processes in their daily operations (this is known as the last mile problem). Therefore, in a first step the current maturity level of BPM in BMW Group Aftersales is analyzed and the key challenges are identified. To provide a solution the ProcessWiki methodology comprises a comprehensive framework that enables the process communities to…

1. develop, document and publish easily understandable process knowledge,
2. discuss, align, and adapt the process knowledge in a collaborative manner,
3. provide feedback to existing process knowledge, and
4. immediately and intuitively apply the process knowledge in the daily business.

This theoretical framework is tested and validated by BPM experts of the BMW Group and serves as foundation for the presented prototype. With this solution the process knowledge is effectively communicated to the retail stores. By enabling and encouraging their participation, feedback can be collected more easily and incorporated in the existing process models for further improvement. The involvement of the retail stores results in a higher acceptance and satisfaction.

It has to be remarked, that the solution still lacks of an automatic connection between the different layers. This could result in synchronization issues, difficulties to enforce proper process execution, and the inability to do process performance measurement. In future the method should be extended to offer tools for an easier information exchange and decision making within each layer and a notification mechanism to communicate the changes to a higher level. However, with localization and customization intentionally leading to derivations from the PA and TP, software cannot automatically synchronize the processes between the four levels but still requires human intervention.

To finally convince and actually support the retail store managers in their daily operations, the PW-Case module remains to be implemented. The main idea of PW-Case is to enable the users to instantiate and execute the process models. In contrast to a typical process execution with workflow management systems, the ProcessWiki framework aims at providing a collaborative workspace to support the participants in self-organizing their process instances at runtime as suggested by the ACM [6] approach.

References

1. Hilgarth, B., Purucker, J., Mayer, H., Göldner, F.: ProcessSharePoint® – ein Praxisbericht zur Lösung des Last-Mile-Problems in der Prozessimplementierung. In: HMD - Praxis der Wirtschaftsinformatik, pp. 90–99 (2009)
2. Freund, J., Götzer, K.: Vom Geschäftsprozess zum Workflow. Ein Leitfaden für die Praxis Hanser, München (2008)
3. Kurz, M., Herrmann, C.: Adaptive Case Management. Anwendung des Business Process Management 2.0-Konzepts auf wissensintensive schwach strukturierte Geschäftsprozesse
4. Kurz, M., Fleischmann, A.: BPM 2.0: Business Process Management Meets Empowerment. In: Fleischmann, A., Schmidt, W., Singer, R., Seese, D. (eds.) S-BPM ONE 2010. CCIS, vol. 138, pp. 54–83. Springer, Heidelberg (2011)
5. Billing, G., Kurz, M., Hettling, K., von Jouanne-Diedrich, H.: Applying BPM 2.0 in IT centric environments. In: Rosemann, M. (ed.) Case Studies in Business Process Management. Springer, Heidelberg (2011) (accepted paper)
6. Herrmann, C., Kurz, M.: Adaptive Case Management: Supporting Knowledge Intensive Processes with IT Systems. In: Schmidt, W. (ed.) S-BPM ONE 2011. CCIS, vol. 213, pp. 80–97. Springer, Heidelberg (2011)
7. Swenson, K.D. (ed.): Mastering the Unpredictable. How Adaptive Case Management Will Revolutionize The Way That Knowledge Workers Get Things Done. Meghan-Kiffer Press, Tampa (2010)
8. Kurz, M., Hermann, C.: Adaptive Case Management. Anwendung des BPM 2.0-Konzepts auf schwach strukturierte Geschäftsprozesse. In: Bartmann, D., Bodendorf, F., Ferstl, O.K., Sinz, E.J. (eds.) Dienstorientierte IT-Systeme für hochflexible Geschäftsprozesse, pp. 241–266. University of Bamberg Press, Bamberg (2011)
9. Kurz, M.: BPM 2.0. Selbstorganisation im Geschäftsprozessmanagement, http://www.forflex.de/uploads/AB/forflex-2011-005.pdf
10. Kurz, M.: BPM 2.0. Selbstorganisation im Geschäftsprozessmanagement. In: Bartmann, D., Bodendorf, F., Ferstl, O.K., Sinz, E.J. (eds.) Dienstorientierte IT-Systeme für hochflexible Geschäftsprozesse, pp. 193–216. University of Bamberg Press, Bamberg (2011)
11. Liebold, R., Trinczek, R.: Experteninterview. In: Kühl, S. (ed.) Handbuch Methoden der Organisationsforschung. Quantitative und qualitative Methoden, pp. 32–56. VSVerl. für Sozialwiss., Wiesbaden (2009)
12. Jablonski, S.: Workflow-Management-Systeme. Modellierung und Architektur. Internat. Thomson Publ., Bonn (1995)
13. Fleischmann, A., Stary, C.: Whom to talk to? A stakeholder perspective on business process development. In: Stephanidis, C. (ed.) Universal Access in the Information Society. Springer, Heidelberg (2011)
14. Djordjevic, D., Ghani, R., Fullarton, D.: Process-centric enterprise workspace based on semantic wiki. In: International Conference on Knowledge Management and Information Sharing, KMIS 2011, pp. 224-233 (2010)
15. van der Aalst, W.M.P., et al.: Adaptive Workflow-On the Interplay between Flexibility and Support. In: ICEIS 1999, pp. 353–360 (1999)
16. Pesic, M., Schonenberg, H., van der Aalst, W.M.P.: DECLARE: Full Support for Loosely-Structured Processes. In: 11th IEEE International Enterprise Distributed Object Computing Conference EDOC 2007, p. 287 (2007)

Requirements for Business Process Management Systems Supporting Business Process Agility

Richard Heininger*

Metasonic AG
Münchner Straße 29, Hettenshausen, 85276 Pfaffenhofen, Germany
richard.heininger@metasonic.de

Abstract. Organizational agility (OA) has emerged as a mission critical success factor in order to cope with the fast changing economic environment. Companies are forced to anticipate future developments and react to threats and opportunities in a timely manner. This concept has primarily managerial aspects, though science has evinced that information technology and systems are facilitators of OA. Moreover, Gartner Research Group identifies the business process management systems (BPMS) industry as one of fastest developing and growing markets for the near future. This raises one particular question, addressing the link between BPMS and a sort of OA, namely business process agility (BPA). Consequently, this contribution provides a theoretical base for the examination of BPMS regarding BPA, reviewing the scientific literature on OA and BPA, confronting it with the business process management lifecycle and finally deriving requirements for BPMS facilitating BPA.

Keywords: business process agility, business process management systems, organizational agility.

1 Introduction

Contemporary organizations have to cope with dynamic environments, where opportunities and threats arise suddenly. Right decisions at the right time are a critical success factor and *the* competitive advantage. Therefore, decision makers have to sense the environment for changes and have to react appropriately, which basically means that they have to make the right decision at the right time. Managers have to consider that usual planning cycles may not be the right administrative instrument.

As a result of this thoughts, scholars have developed the concept of organizational agility (OA). OA has yet to be defined in order to address all relevant issues and be accepted interdisciplinary by scholars. Nevertheless, processes may play an important role within OA [20,23], whereas business process management systems (BPMS) are usually implemented to administer and coordinate an organization's processes. The relation between OA and informations systems is being researched, though OA in respect of BPMS remains under-researched.

---

* The author wants to thank Markus Radmayr and Nils Meyer for their help and contributions.

S. Oppl and A. Fleischmann (Eds.): S-BPM ONE 2012, CCIS 284, pp. 168–180, 2012.

This contribution takes up the latter and examines the relation between OA and business processes. It has been stated that OA lies within business processes [26]. It might also be found as part of a corporation's information function, considering controlling and administering purposes within the corporation [14].

These deliberations delineate the structure of this article. Firstly, the idea of organizational agility is examined in more detail. The goal is to determine a definition and common understanding for organizational agility concerning business processes and BPMS. Secondly, OA and the business process management lifecycle are examined in particular. Finally, a set of requirements for BPMS is constituted to support OA.

1.1   Motivation

Our dynamic environment and advanced possibilities have aroused practitioners' and scholars' interest in the concept of *organizational agility* (e.g., [18,24]). For instance, Sambamurthy et al. [24] show a significant relation between OA and sustainable competitive advantage, whereas Meyer et al. [18,19] discuss a specific solution to the agility issue, addressing cross-organizational, loose coupled business processes. The latter approach focuses on OA in a way that business processes can be connected cross-organizational and can be altered flexibly, which may be a crucial factor of entrepreneurial success in dynamic industries. Thus, the influence to OA by business processes and business process management systems were examined practically as a first step. This contribution is designed to take this approach to the next level. It is motivated by creating a scientific-deduced, theoretical base for the verification of the impact of business process management systems on a sort of OA, called *business process agility*.

2   Agility

2.1   Organizational Agility

Organizational agility (OA) has been initially introduced by scholars at the Iacocca Institute, Lehigh University in the year 1991 [15], describing a concept for key aspects of the fabrication process. Since then, several different definitions of OA have been developed as Table 1 on page 170 depicts. The listed definitions do not always refer to *OA*, they do define at least a facet of *agility* though. Further definitions can be found in the literature, e.g., see [14] or [10]. The main aspect concerning these citations is to constitute an appropriate definition for business process agility, whereas the term *process* is often used within the provided definitions.

It has already been noted that the concept OA has stemmed from literature on manufacturing flexibility [10,15,5]. However, the development of this concept now spans several scientific domains [26], which includes the business process management community [26,22]. This development was inevitable, since OA "applies to sensing and responding capabilities for the entire firm" [20, p. 122]. As mentioned earlier in this chapter, the main focus is to define and further examine business process agility, which will be covered in the next chapter.

Table 1. Definitions of OA

Reference	Definition
Iacocca/Lehigh (1991)	A system that shifts quickly among product models/lines, ideally in real time in order to respond to customer needs [15]
Dove (1999)	"Ability to manage and apply knowledge effectively" [5]
Sambamurthy et al. (2003)	Ability of a firm to redesign their existing processes rapidly and create new processes in a timely fashion in order to be able to take advantage and thrive of the unpredictable and highly dynamic market conditions [23]
Raschke and David (2005)	"Ability of a firm to dynamically modify and/or reconfigure individual business processes to accommodate required and potential needs of the firm" [22]
Overby et al. (2006)	"Ability of firms to sense environmental change and respond readily" [20]
Sambamurthy et al. (2007)	*Entrepreneurial agility* denotes the ability "to anticipate environmental changes and conduct strategic experiments with new business approaches and models", whereas *adaptive agility* means the ability "to be resilient and adaptive to environmental change in order to maintain competitive parity and competitive leadership" [24]
Fink and Neumann (2007)	"Ability to respond operationally and strategically to changes in the external environment through IT, whereas this has to be quick and effective" [7]
Seo and La Paz (2008)	"A set of processes that allows an organization to sense changes in the internal and external environment, respond efficiently and effectively in a timely and cost-effective manner, and learn from the experience to improve the competencies of the organization" [27]
Seethamraju and Seethamraju (2009)	"Ability to dynamically modify, reconfigure and/or deploy a business process (and its various components) to accommodate required and potential needs of the firm" [26]
Hobbs (2010)	"Recognition of a business environment that fluctuates quicker than conventional planning cycles, the need to sense environmental fluctuations, the need to respond using existing information systems, and organizational readiness to effect the sensing and response" ([17] as cited in [14])
Tallon and Pinsonneault (2011)	"Ability to detect and respond to opportunities and threats with ease, speed, and dexterity" [28]
Trinh et al. (2011)	"OA refers to the business performance of an organization that excels in utilising its resources in order to quickly sense changes from its business environment and respond to those changes appropriately" [29]

2.2   Business Process Agility

The construct of business process agility (BPA) has been initially developed by Raschke and David (2005) [22], followed by an empirical study to verify the significant correlation between OA and business processes [21]. Consequently, the author adopts the definition of BPA ("Process-level Agility") by Raschke (2007), defining it as "the ability to add and/or reconfigure a business process by quickly adding new capabilities to the set of business process capabilities to accommodate the potential needs of the firm" [21, p. 12]. Figure 1 draws the derived components, namely reconfigurability, responsiveness, flexibility, employee adaptability, and process-centric view.

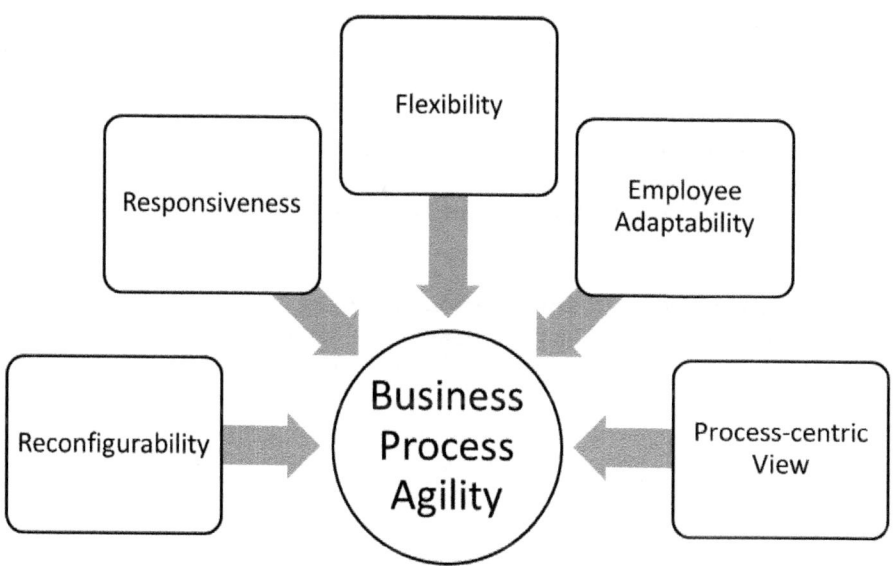

Fig. 1. Business Process Agility [21, p. 19]

In order to lead to the contribution's main goal, following terms have to be declared, which will be taken up in the following.

1. Business process
2. Components of BPA:
   (a) Reconfigurability
   (b) Responsiveness
   (c) Flexibility
   (d) Employee adaptability
   (e) Process-centric view

Business Process. This section covers a very short definition of business processes and considered types of business processes. Business processes are defined as "bundles of activities for the creation of a product or a service for a particular customer or market, or rather a suitable representation of cooperative workflows" ([12] as cited in [13], [4]).

Prior to further examine BPA, it has to be mentioned that the definition of a business process does not explicitly include any term considering management, leadership or administration. However, the more complex a bundle of activities becomes, the more effort is required to coordinate and lead the activities. This requirement has directed several scholars to examine OA supported by the management's or executives' business processes (e.g., [23,28,26]). The approach of this contribution is to figure out elements of OA in every business process.

Literature review has revealed many types of business processes [8], whereas the examination of these types was not part of the actual research. It has to be noted though, that the author briefly determined two types of business processes: a *specific* business process with an in input and an output; and a *governing* business process, which controls, administers and leads other business processes. The latter is of specific importance, since the link between strategic information technology alignment and OA has been identified as a corporates success factor [28]. However, this contribution is focused on the more abstract type, the specific process.

Business Processes and Information Systems. The definition of business processes does not include information systems (IS) per se; however, it has been shown that management of business processes is very well supported by IS – namely *business process management systems* (BPMS) [1,25,9,8]. Furthermore, Barua et al. (1995) pointed out that a considerable proportion of an IT's business value "stems from its complementarities with business processes ([2] as cited in [20, p. 126]). It gets even more specific and clearer, considering the findings by Sambamurthy et al. (2003), who identified the OA-benefiting opportunities generated through digitized platforms of business processes and knowledge ([23,24]). Besides, those scholars did not mention BPMS as such a platform. All these studies indicate a significant influence and support of IS on business processes and vice versa. On the contrary, scholars have identified possible misleads and problems, asserting the existence of a "dark side of IS in achieving OA" [27].

Components of Business Process Agility. Raschke (2007) points out that BPA consists of the following components [21], whereas these components do not refer to business processes represented in IS in particular.

Reconfigurability. This component depicts the ability to develop novel and altered functionalities/activities in order to build more adequate business processes.

Responsiveness. This aspect adds the timely dimension to reconfigurability. All modifications/innovations have to be implemented without any delays.

Flexibility. According to Raschke (2007), flexibility refers to the ability to instantly change the order of activities within a business process. As has been noted, business processes are bundles of activities, which may become quite complex. In such complex scenarios individuals have to be able to modify the order of these activities.

Flexibility may be mistaken as agility itself, though the sensing component is missing. Nevertheless, several contributions regarding the improvement of flexibility of BPMS have been published [8]. For instance, the integration of the service-oriented architecture [6] within BPMS may be considered as milestone.

Employee Adaptability. This facet determines the employees ability to adapt their working behaviours, as well as an attitude to do so, if the environment is changing. Thus, employee adaptability may be left out for this contribution's confrontation.

Process-centric View. This refers to the view of the management on the organization of business processes, i.e. the organizational structure. A functional view would lead to a worse understanding of business processes than a process-centric view. This implies that this aspect will not be considered further within the actual work.

Business Process Management Lifecycle. As has been noted, IS significantly facilitate the management of business processes (*business process management*, BPM). Due to that fact, the author chooses the widely accepted business process management lifecycle (BPM lifecycle, see Fig. 2 on page 174) provided by van der Aalst et al. (2003) [1, p. 5] to determine management aspects. There are four management aspects – *stages* by the means of the lifecycle – of BPM to be considered: process design, system configuration, process enactment and diagnosis. A short introduction to each of the phases will ease the confrontation with BPA.

Process Design. Business processes are initially designed within this stage of BPM and with further iterations changes and rearrangements might lead to a redesign.

System Configuration. The depicted business process has to be implemented on a "process aware information system" to be able to literally execute it.

Process Enactment. The actual execution delineates this phase.

Diagnosis. Collected data has to be diagnosed, errors and misleads should be taken into account for a possible changed or new business process.

Despite the choice of of the actual BPM lifecycle, scientific research has led to numerous different approaches in this domain. The author specifically refers to the approach by Fleischmann et al. (2011) [8, p. 48] considering the actual

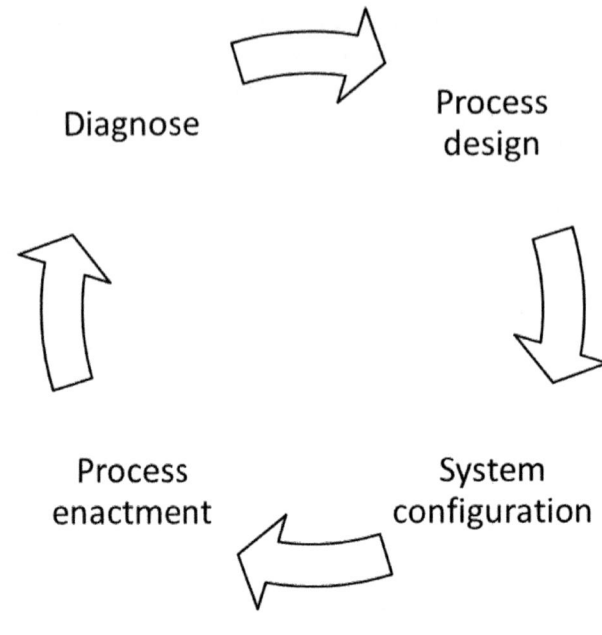

Fig. 2. BPM lifecycle [1]

research's subject matter. The "open/flexible control loop" features equal attributes to the chosen lifecycle, which are represented in Fig. 3. In brief, process design is determined by the tasks analysing, modelling, validating and optimizing, system configuration is depicted by corporate-specific implementation and IT-implementation, whereas process enactment and diagnosis are taken together as one task called action and monitoring.

2.3   Business Process Agility and the BPM Lifecycle

Figure 4 shows a rough draft of the BPM lifecycle enhanced by elements of business process agility, respectively its definition. Therefore, the lifecycle is surrounded by the environment, which basically stands for the possible threats and opportunities of the organization. It is by definition crucial that these threats and opportunities has to be sensed and/or anticipated by organizations. In order to deal with this requirement, the author has pointed out that business process agility addresses this issue. Consequently, Fig. 4 shows the BPM lifecycle within the dynamic environment to align stages of the BPM lifecycle and components of BPA construct.

Figure 4 draws possible reactions within the lifecycle's phases, which are presented in the boxes next to the particular phase. Moreover, Fig. 4 illustrates only reactions deduced by the chosen definition of business process agility, which might not be complete and clearly have to be further examined in future work. For instance, the findings by Sambamurthy et al. (2007) [24] have to be

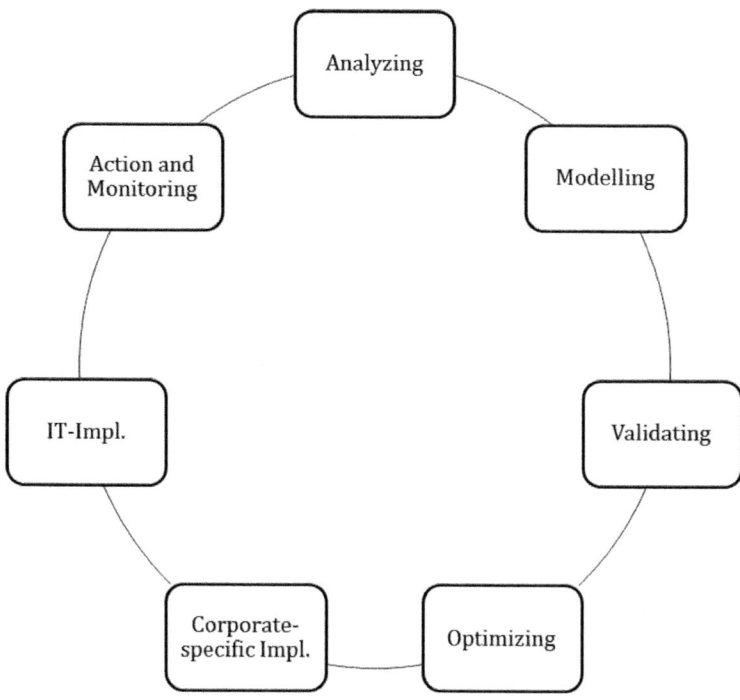

Fig. 3. S-BPM open control loop [8]

considered within business process agility, including anticipating and *experimenting* with future needs as well as sensing environmental changes with the ability to react in a timely manner.

Summing up, the BPA components have been confronted with the BPM life-cycle. This illustration leads to requirements for BPMS, whereas BPMS might be the sort of information systems achieving business process agility. The latter mentioned possibility is discussed in the following chapter.

2.4 Business Process Agility and BPMS

As has been noted earlier in this contribution, information systems and information technology facilitate OA (e.g., [26,29,24]). It has also been stated that business processes facilitate OA [26,22]. Therefore, it seems obvious that BPMS (i.e., information systems) might support OA.

Despite the scientific studies concerning the supporting link between information systems and OA, the author has not found any specific approach dedicated to BPMS achieving business process agility during preparation of the actual contribution. Due to this lack of evidence, the author has to prove that BPMS support/facilitate BPA as a first step. In order to address this proof, a list of requirements for BPMS supporting business process agility is provided. This is covered by Sec. 3.

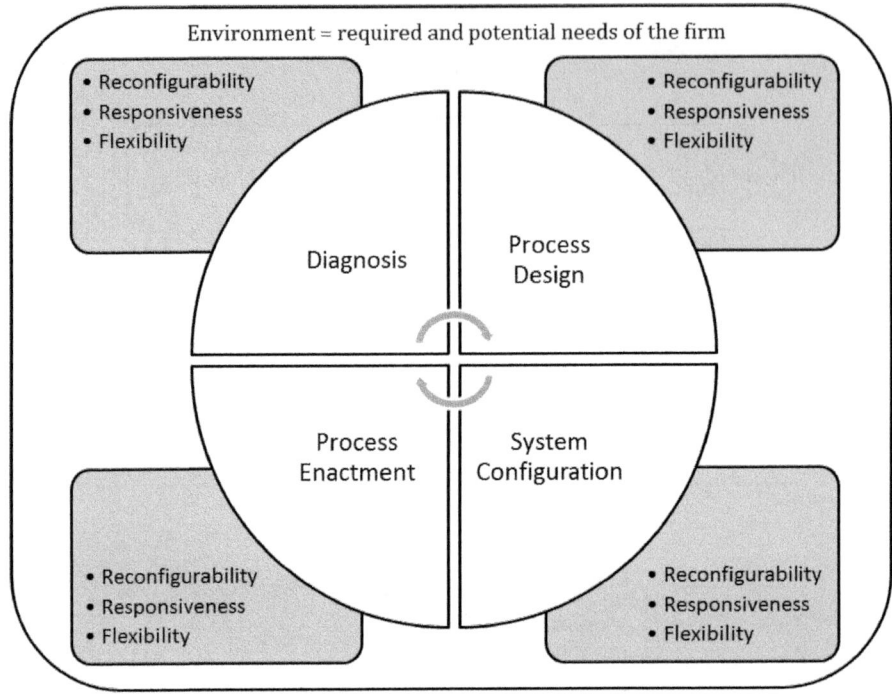

Fig. 4. Business process agility and BPM lifecycle

3   Requirements for BPMS Supporting Business Process Agility

The key aspect of BPMS supporting business process agility is to handle environmental influences in a timely manner. BPMS have to be designed "to accommodate required and potential needs of the firm" [26]. Regarding BPMS, the author claims that this primarily addresses the responding side (i.e., required needs) of OA. Sensing capabilities (i.e., potential needs) are provided by other information systems, such as ERP, CRM and SCM [23,29,26]. However, the ability to support the anticipation of future needs by BPMS lies within every business process and within the knowledge of IT-personnel [7]. The latter was shown by Fink and Neumann (2007), who contributed an approach regarding the "relationships between IT personnel capabilities, IT infrastructure capabilities, and IT-dependent organizational agility" [7].

Scholars have already developed a measurement method for OA as the contribution of Overby et al. (2006) evinces [20]. They have depicted a measurement for OA with an underlying direct effect of IT to OA [20] and an assumed indirect effect of IT to OA through digital options [20,23]. This measurement is designed to use scales based on other scholars' work [3,16,11], the actual contribution's author claims that measuring business process agility with that approach is hardly possible though.

Consequently, a method regarding the examination of business process agility has to be evolved. An adequate method may require an empirical study or other scientific methods to determine measured variables of BPA. However, the author contributes requirements for BPMS supporting business process agility, based on a innovative thinking process as a first step. Table 2 lists the resulting items, which are considered to be of a qualitative type. The requirements are deduced by the findings of Chap. 2.3, whereas the stages of the BPM lifecycle are abbreviated as follows: process design (PD), system configuration (SC), process enactment (PE) and diagnosis (D).

As has been noted, Table 2 depicts *only* aspects of the chosen definition of business process agility. However, this determines a first step to examine BPMS concerning this matter. The suggested items will be evaluated in the near future,

Table 2. Requirements for BPMS supporting business process agility

Stage of BPM lifecycle	Requirement	Description
PD	Reconfigurability	Integrated reflection of business process models
		Models of already implemented and managed business processes have to support reconfiguration of used data (input, output) and parameters, such as key performance indicators (KPI)
	Responsiveness	Ability to directly transform the modified model in a machine-readable and -executable format
		Ability to test and simulate business process models
	Flexibility	Support of designing (un-)predicted exceptions
SC	Reconfigurability	Support of modularity of dependent information systems
	Responsiveness	Changes have to be instantly integrated into business process models and their executable formats
	Flexibility	Support of *Inversion of Control*
PE	Reconfigurability	BPMS have to support different ways to achieve the goal of a business process. Dynamic needs cannot generally be integrated by PD. The model has to allow different paths, not modelled paths too, e.g., *model while you go*
	Responsiveness	PE requires the ability to change instances instantly
	Flexibility	Dynamic support of changes, e.g., AdHoc process
D	Reconfigurability	KPI and monitored data in general has to able to be modified instantly, and this modification has to be tracked back by the business process model (PD).
	Responsiveness	Reconfigure diagnosis based on sensed needs, e.g., flexible alignment of planning cycles
	Flexibility	Alter bundles of KPI, ability to diagnose based on different metrics and statistical methods

additional items will also be introduced to cover all facets of OA. Furthermore, the author will review literature on organizational development to determine specific requirements concerning BPA. Chapter 4 summarizes the contribution's findings and points out further work.

4 Conclusion and Further Work

This contribution provides essential requirements for BPMS to support business process agility. These requirement were derived by the confrontation of the concept of business process agility with van der Aalst et al.'s BPM lifecycle. It has been reviewed that business process agility as well as information systems facilitate OA, whereas the missing evidence of the supporting link between BPMS and business process agility/OA has been identified. Accordingly, requirements regarding the supporting link were introduced.

On the contrary, several questions remain unanswered, which determines the author's further work in the near future. Firstly, several questions in terms of business process agility have not been answered, such as business process responsibility and agility knowledge. Secondly, it has also already been pointed out that scholars revealed further facets of OA (e.g., [24]), which have to be deliberated and included in the requirement's list.

Finally, a specific BPMS has to be examined to prove the significance of the proposed requirements. Due to the postulated ability to provide directly transferable business process models, a BPMS based on the subject oriented business process method [8] might be chosen and investigated. This might reveal the validity of the contribution's findings and hence lead BPMS to achieve a great deal of OA.

References

1. van der Aalst, W.M.P., ter Hofstede, A.H.M., Weske, M.: Business Process Management: A Survey. In: van der Aalst, W.M.P., ter Hofstede, A.H.M., Weske, M. (eds.) BPM 2003. LNCS, vol. 2678, pp. 1–12. Springer, Heidelberg (2003)
2. Barua, A., Kriebel, C.H., Mukhopadhyay, T.: Information technologies and business value: An analytic and empirical investigation. Information Systems Research 6(1), 3–23 (1995)
3. Chan, Y.E., Huff, S.L., Barclay, D.W., Copeland, D.G.: Business strategic orientation, information systems strategic orientation, and strategic alignment. Information Systems Research 8(2), 125 (1997)
4. Davenport, T.H.: Process innovation: reengineering work through information technology. Harvard Business Press (1993)
5. Dove, R.: Knowledge management, response ability, and the agile enterprise. Journal of Knowledge Management 3(1), 18–35 (1999)
6. Erl, T.: Service-Oriented Architecture: A Field Guide to Integrating XML and Web Services. Prentice Hall PTR, Upper Saddle River (2004)
7. Fink, L., Neumann, S.: Gaining agility through IT personnel capabilities: The mediating role of IT infrastructure capabilities. Journal of the Association for Information Systems 8(8) (August 2007)

8. Fleischmann, A., Schmidt, W., Stary, C., Obermeier, S., Börger, E.: Subjektorientiertes Prozessmanagement: Mitarbeiter einbinden, Motivation und Prozessakzeptanz steigern. Carl Hanser Verlag GmbH & CO, KG (2011)
9. Gadatsch, A.: Management von Geschäftsprozessen.: Methoden und Werkzeuge für die IT-Praxis. Eine Einführung für Studenten und Praktiker. Vieweg (June 2002)
10. Ganguly, A., Nilchiani, R., Farr, J.V.: Evaluating agility in corporate enterprises. International Journal of Production Economics 118(2), 410–423 (2009)
11. Grewal, R., Tansuhaj, P.: Building organizational capabilities for managing economic crisis: The role of market orientation and strategic flexibility. Journal of Marketing 65(2), 67–80 (2001)
12. Hammer, M., Champy, J.: Reengineering the Corporation: A Manifesto for Business Revolution. HarperBusiness (April 1994)
13. Heftberger, S., Stary, C.: Partizipatives organisationales Lernen. DUV (September 2004)
14. Hobbs, G.A.: Enabling agility in existing information systems: a capability structure for the IT function. Ph.D. thesis, Department of Information Systems, The University of Melbourne (2010)
15. Iacocca Institute of Lehigh University, Nagel, R.N., Dove, R., of Defense. Office of Managing Technology, U.S.D.: 21st Century Manufacturing Enterprise Strategy: An industry-led view. DIANE Publishing (November 1991)
16. Kohli, A.K., Jaworski, B.J., Kumar, A.: MARKOR: a measure of market orientation. Journal of Marketing Research (JMR) 30(4), 467–477 (1993)
17. Luftman, J., MacLean, E.R.: Key issues for IT executives. MIS Quarterly Executive 3(2), 89–104 (2004)
18. Meyer, N., Feiner, T., Radmayr, M., Blei, D., Fleischmann, A.: Dynamic Catenation and Execution of Cross Organisational Business Processes - The jCPEX! Approach. In: Fleischmann, A., Schmidt, W., Singer, R., Seese, D. (eds.) S-BPM ONE 2010. CCIS, vol. 138, pp. 84–105. Springer, Heidelberg (2011), doi:10.1007/978-3-642-23135-3_5
19. Meyer, N., Radmayr, M., Heininger, R., Rothschädl, T., Fleischmann, A.: Platform for Managing and Routing Cross-Organizational Business Processes on a Network Router. In: Schmidt, W. (ed.) S-BPM ONE 2011. CCIS, vol. 213, pp. 175–189. Springer, Heidelberg (2011), doi:10.1007/978-3-642-23471-2_13
20. Overby, E., Bharadwaj, A., Sambamurthy, V.: Enterprise agility and the enabling role of information technology. European Journal of Information Systems 15, 120–131 (2006)
21. Raschke, R.L.: An empirical analysis of business process agility: Examining the relationship of IT on business process agility and the effects of business process agility on process outcomes. Dissertation, Arizona State University (2007)
22. Raschke, R.L., David, J.: Business process agility. In: AMCIS 2005 Proceedings (January 2005)
23. Sambamurthy, V., Bharadwaj, A., Grover, V.: Shaping agility through digital options: Reconceptualizing the role of information technology in contemporary firms. MIS quarterly, 237–263 (2003)
24. Sambamurthy, V., Wei, K., Lim, K., Lee, D.: IT-Enabled organizational agility and firms' sustainable competitive advantage. In: ICIS 2007 Proceedings (December 2007)
25. Scheer, A., Kruppke, H., Jost, W., Kindermann, H.: Agilität durch ARIS Geschäftsprozessmanagement: Jahrbuch Business Process Excellence 2006/2007. Springer (May 2006)

26. Seethamraju, R., Seethamraju, J.: Enterprise systems and business process agility -
    a case study. In: 42nd Hawaii International Conference on System Sciences, HICSS
    2009, pp. 1–12. IEEE (January 2009)
27. Seo, D., La Paz, A.I.: Exploring the dark side of IS in achieving organizational
    agility. Commun. ACM 51(11), 136–139 (2008)
28. Tallon, P.P., Pinsonneault, A.: Competing perspectives on the link between strate-
    gic information technology alignment and organizational agility: Insights from a
    mediation model. MIS Quarterly 35(2), 463–486 (2011)
29. Trinh-Phuong, T., Molla, A., Peszynski, K.: Enterprise systems and organisational
    agility: Conceptualizing the link. In: 21st Australasian Conference on Information
    Systems (ACIS 2010), pp. 1–10 (2011)

S-BPM Education on the Dalton Plan: An E-Learning Approach

Georg Weichhart

Johannes Kepler University Linz
Department of Business Information Systems - Communications Engineering
Freistaedterstrasse 315, 4040 Linz, Austria
georg.weichhart@jku.at

Abstract. S-BPM (Subject-oriented Business Process Management) is a new communication oriented approach to Business Process Management. Because of its novelty, good approaches to education are required. Guided by theory in this paper a didactic approach is identified. It is argued that the chosen Dalton Plan pedagogic is suitable to form a basis for modern constructivist e-learning. The paper showcases the e-learning platform *nymphaea* which integrates Dalton Plan assignments and exemplifies the presented approach and tool using the s-bpm live cycle.

Keywords: s-bpm, e-learning, progressive education, assignment, dalton plan.

1 Introduction

One the one hand, „there is a significant need for BPM skilled people" [12, P. 789], on the other hand the „lack of appropriate BPM education is still a topic that is raised as a perennial issue" (ibidem). Subject-oriented Business Process Management (S-BPM) is a new approach to BPM, and as such, it is even more evident that appropriate education about this topic is missing [23]. It has been observed that BPM education happens to a large extend using traditional methods: teachers presenting selected topics on a regular basis. However, this method has proven to be ineffective, not only with respect to BPM education [12], but also with respect to education in general [20,5]. E-learning environments are used to support education, but often lack a paedagogical basis [1]. In combination with traditional class-room settings, e-learning platforms are used only as file-sharing tools, where teachers make presentation slides available online.

In the following, an approach for educating S-BPM on the web is developed. We argue for using a particular didactic approach called the Dalton Plan. We review existing approaches integrating the Dalton Plan pedagogy in e-learning environments. In order to demonstrate the integration of this didactic approach in e-learning we exemplify a Dalton Plan assignment integrated in an e-learning environment for educating the S-BPM cycle of activites.

S. Oppl and A. Fleischmann (Eds.): S-BPM ONE 2012, CCIS 284, pp. 181–193, 2012.

2   E-Learning Didactics

For e-learning environments, didactic approaches related to constructivism have been found to be effective[4,18]. Constructivist didactics requires a changed role of the teacher compared to traditional means of teaching[16]:

> „The task of the teacher consists of setting up, or staging, learning environments in which learning as co-constructing and restructuring in social and situated context becomes more probable. The learning environments particularly suited for this purpose are those that take into account the situation-bound and constructive character of any kind of learning in which learners can independently make their own way" [24, P. 32f].

The same view is promoted in reform-pedagogical didactics (aka. progressive education) [16,7]. Helen Parkhurst's Dalton Plan [15] is one prominent example, used in the following.

2.1   Dalton Plan Laboratory

The Dalton Plan provides teachers with methods inline with principles offered by the constructivist didactics. The assignments focus not on direct instruction but on guiding students during practical exploration and acquisition of knowledge by themselves and within groups. Research has shown that this is important and effective [18]. We expect that the Dalton Plan is equally effective for e-learning as constructivist didactics in general. The three basic principles of the Dalton Plan are [6,15]:

- Freedom - Students enjoy the freedom to choose (and manage) their own learning paths and times
- Co-operation (interaction of group life) - Students are required to co-operate on subject matters to fulfil their learning goals
- Self-management (budgeting time) - Students are in charge to mange their own learning to get task done within a given time-frame

Parkhurst has developed two means supporting teachers and students. Assignments are used to guide students through the work. Graphs are used to provide feedback to students and teachers about the progress made by students on learning tasks [15].

Education using the Daltonplan supports and facilitates self-organised learning and help students to develop the advanced learning skills including critical thinking, problem solving and reflective skills, which is found currently missing in BPM education [12]. The Dalton Plan approach allows to learn on all four competence levels identified by the German Bildungsrat (see Table 1).

In this first attempt to support SBPM education using e-learning rooted in a didactic approach we focus on the Daltonplan assignments in the following.

Table 1. Levels of Competence (Deutscher Bildungsrat 1970, in [11])

Quality	Name	Competence
Highest	Problemsolving	Apply lessons learned in novel situations
	Transfer	Transfer lessons learned to similar situations
	Reorganisation	Reproduction of lessons learned from a different point of view
Lowest	Reproduction	(Exact) Reproduction of lessons learned

Preface (Orientation Section). The preface section of the assignment motivates the learning task. It provides the context and orientation to let students understand why a particular assignment is usefull and where it can be used. Additionally this section should be given in a form that is motivating for students to work on these tasks.

Topic / Objectives. This section clearly states the central idea of the subject to be learned. This helps students to stay focused and reflect about their own work on/about this topic.

Problems and Tasks. This section includes all tasks students work within the frame of the current assignment. The tasks given should allow students with different levels of competence to work on the assignment. In order to meet different abilities of students, teachers should try to create tasks that cover all four competence levels identified above (see table 1). Rozendaal and others have identified four categories of learners by identifying 'surface-level processing' and 'deep-level processing' not as different ends to the same dimension but two independent dimensions [19]. Their empirical work supports these four categories: Students that mainly use deep-learning methods. Students that mainly reproduce learning content. Learners that are able to actively choose between reproduction and deep-learning methods. Learners, that without knowing, mix strategies and learning methods.

Written Work. This section identifies the documentation provided by the student. According to Parkhurst, it is advisable to provide a date for each step [15]. At that date teachers are taking a look at the particular written work. This might be done within a meeting/conference (see below).

Work can be done individually or within a group of learners. This group could be the whole class, or smaller learning (peer) groups may be created for the tasks at hand. In e-learning environments a forum facilitating interactions in the learning group should be created.

Memory Work. In this part of the assignment the cognitive work is stated. Reproduction tasks should be given as well as deep level processing tasks [19] in order to reach different kind of information processing student types.

Conferences / Meetings. While students are required to manage their own (learning) time, it is often advisable to schedule meetings and check the intermediate progress. For each meeting, the topics, participants and dates have to be provided. At least two meeting are advisable, before starting an assignment it should be introduced by the teacher. In order to hand in and discuss the documented work with the teacher one meeting should be scheduled at the end of the work period.

References. All articles and books used to prepare the assignment are listed in this section. Also literature required by students to finish the assignment is referenced here.

Equivalents. The planned effort for this assignment is provided here. It helps students „budgeting time" and is used also with the graphs of the dalton plan. The effort might be given for each problem/task on which students work.

Bulletin Study. This shows students the place where they find up-to-date information with respect to their work.

Departmental Cuts. Sometimes work is done used for two different courses. For example work for the Lecture Communications Engineering might be done in English and used to cover parts of an English course as well.

2.2   E-Learning Assignments

The above described didactic approach is of such general nature, that it easily can be used within e-learning environments. Assignments are already supported by e-learning platforms. Stary has adopted assignments (termed Intelligibility Catchers - ICs) to guide users not only with respect to a certain topic, but showing them effective use of features of the e-learning platform „Scholion" [21,22]. This specific implementation of assignments marks all features of the platform in the assignments and hence constraints users in how documented work elements are made available in the platform. The following table shows the documented work section of such an intelligibility catcher (table 2).

The assignments themselves are provided in separate documents and not integrated in the electronic web-plattform.

Another use of assignments are made in the COOL project and its eCOOL platform. COOL (COoperatives Offenes Lernen, [13]) is a teaching approach grounded in the Dalton plan which uses learning-contracts extensively. The eCOOL platform, built on moodle, supports students and teachers managing contracts and documented work by using an ePortfolio [9]. These assignments are implemented as forms (fig. 1 bottom) tailored to the COOL approach and stored in the portfolio system (fig. 1 top).

Access to the general public may be given to the portfolio in order to allow students to showcase their own work. The COOL approach focuses not only on assignments but also views teacher education, and active teacher collaboration as inherent part of the approach.

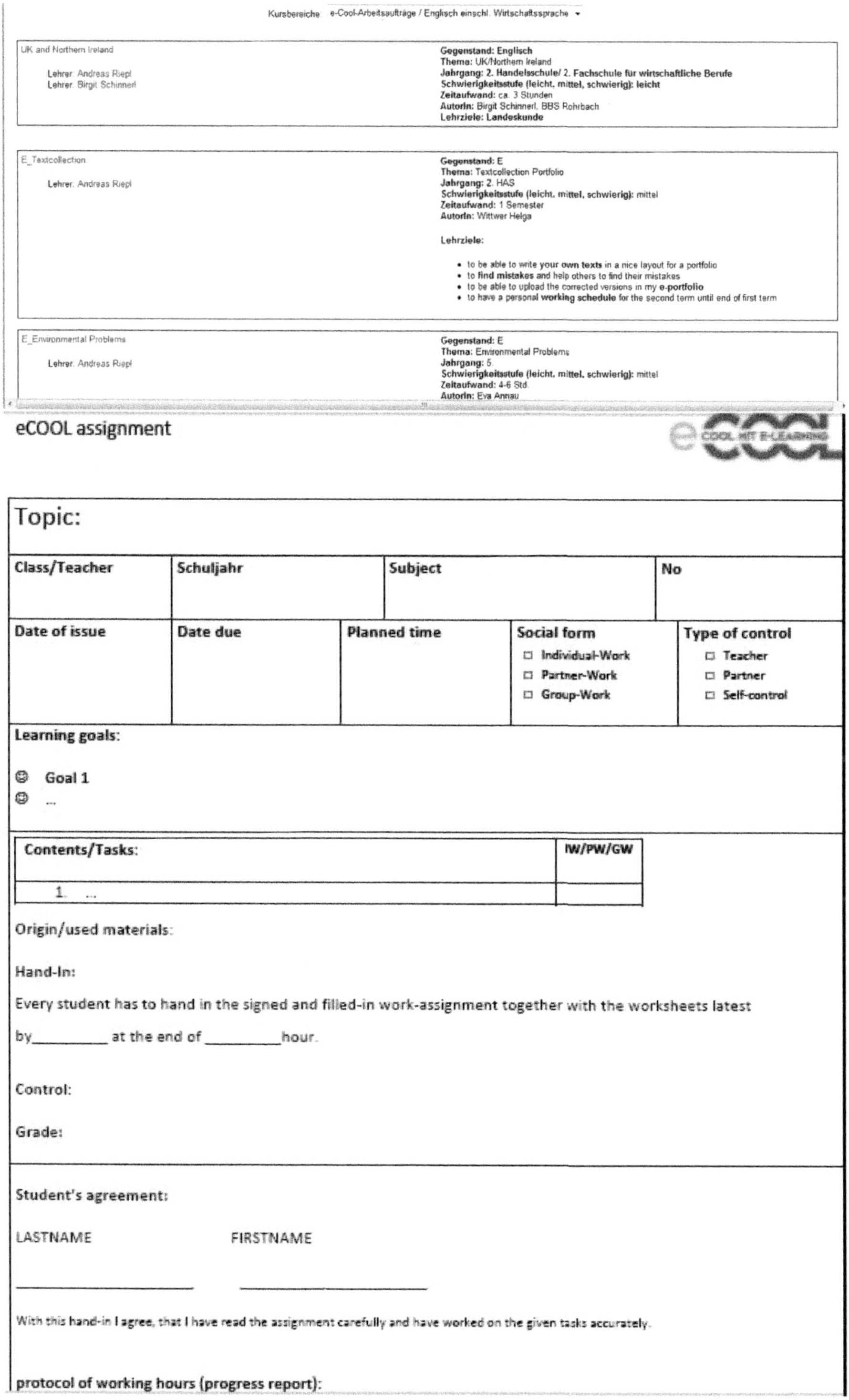

Kursbereiche: e-Cool-Arbeitsaufträge / Englisch einschl. Wirtschaftssprache

UK and Northern Ireland

Lehrer: Andreas Riepl
Lehrer: Birgit Schinnerl

Gegenstand: Englisch
Thema: UK/Northern Ireland
Jahrgang: 2. Handelsschule/ 2. Fachschule für wirtschaftliche Berufe
Schwierigkeitsstufe (leicht, mittel, schwierig): leicht
Zeitaufwand: ca. 3 Stunden
AutorIn: Birgit Schinnerl, BBS Rohrbach
Lehrziele: Landeskunde

E_Textcollection

Lehrer: Andreas Riepl

Gegenstand: E
Thema: Textcollection Portfolio
Jahrgang: 2. HAS
Schwierigkeitsstufe (leicht, mittel, schwierig): mittel
Zeitaufwand: 1 Semester
AutorIn: Wittwer Helga

Lehrziele:

- to be able to write **your own texts** in a nice layout for a portfolio
- to **find mistakes** and help others to find their mistakes
- to be able to upload the corrected versions in my **e-portfolio**
- to have a personal **working schedule** for the second term until end of first term

E_Environmental Problems

Lehrer: Andreas Riepl

Gegenstand: E
Thema: Environmental Problems
Jahrgang: 5.
Schwierigkeitsstufe (leicht, mittel, schwierig): mittel
Zeitaufwand: 4-6 Std.
AutorIn: Eva Annau

eCOOL assignment

Topic:

Class/Teacher	Schuljahr	Subject	No

Date of issue	Date due	Planned time	Social form	Type of control
			☐ Individual-Work ☐ Partner-Work ☐ Group-Work	☐ Teacher ☐ Partner ☐ Self-control

Learning goals:

☺ **Goal 1**
☺ ...

Contents/Tasks:	IW/PW/GW
1. ...	

Origin/used materials:

Hand-In:

Every student has to hand in the signed and filled-in work-assignment together with the worksheets latest by_________ at the end of _________hour.

Control:

Grade:

Student's agreement:

LASTNAME FIRSTNAME

____________________ ____________________

With this hand-in I agree, that I have read the assignment carefully and have worked on the given tasks accurately.

protocol of working hours (progress report):

Fig. 1. eCool Assignments in portfolio (top) and Assignment (bottom) [17]

Table 2. Intelligibility catcher - documented work section (excerpt) [22, p. 205]

3.a Documented Work (platform features are in *Italics*)	— *Filter* content for <u>directives</u> (a content type in Scholion) on model-based design — Set up *view* '<your name> MyFirstModel-based Design' — *Search* for examples for UML class and behavior diagrams being used for designing interactive distributed systems in a model-based way. You might use the learning material provided in Scholion or search in the web. — Supplement (*annotate*) in your view each diagram with the information found, e.g., a design class diagram in Scholion with an UML model capturing work tasks ... — Establish a design dialog by reflecting your results in dedicated entries of the *discussion forum*. Search for a peer via the Scholion *buddy list*. The forum entries need to be *linked* to the application model *annotation*. Your model-based representation needs to be *linked* to the feedback provided by your peer. ...

3   Nymphaea Assignment for Understanding the S-BPM Live-Cycle

In our e-learning platform „nymphaea" we have implemented an editor supporting the creation of assignments based on the Dalton Plan. The editor supports teachers writing assignments. In the current version it integrates the structures of the dalton plan pensum in the e-learning platform. It has separate views for each part of the dalton plan assignment. On top of each view Parkhurst's description of the particular part is given. The editor allows rich text descriptions with embedded images, videos or flash elements. Multi-media elements support learning by making assignments more motivational and interactive (in the case of flash).

Additionally there is a need for teachers to learn from existing assignments. Therefore the editor allows sharing existing assignments in the group of teachers working on assignments. On bottom of the editor, selected parts of other assignments are given (see fig. 2).

The editor supports intra-assignment links allowing to provide explicit connections between elements of the work sections and problems, tasks. In figure 3, the Infobox containing Parkhurst's description is closed. Below this closed box a list of all problems in the assignment is given. This list is followed by the text box supporting users in writing a written work.

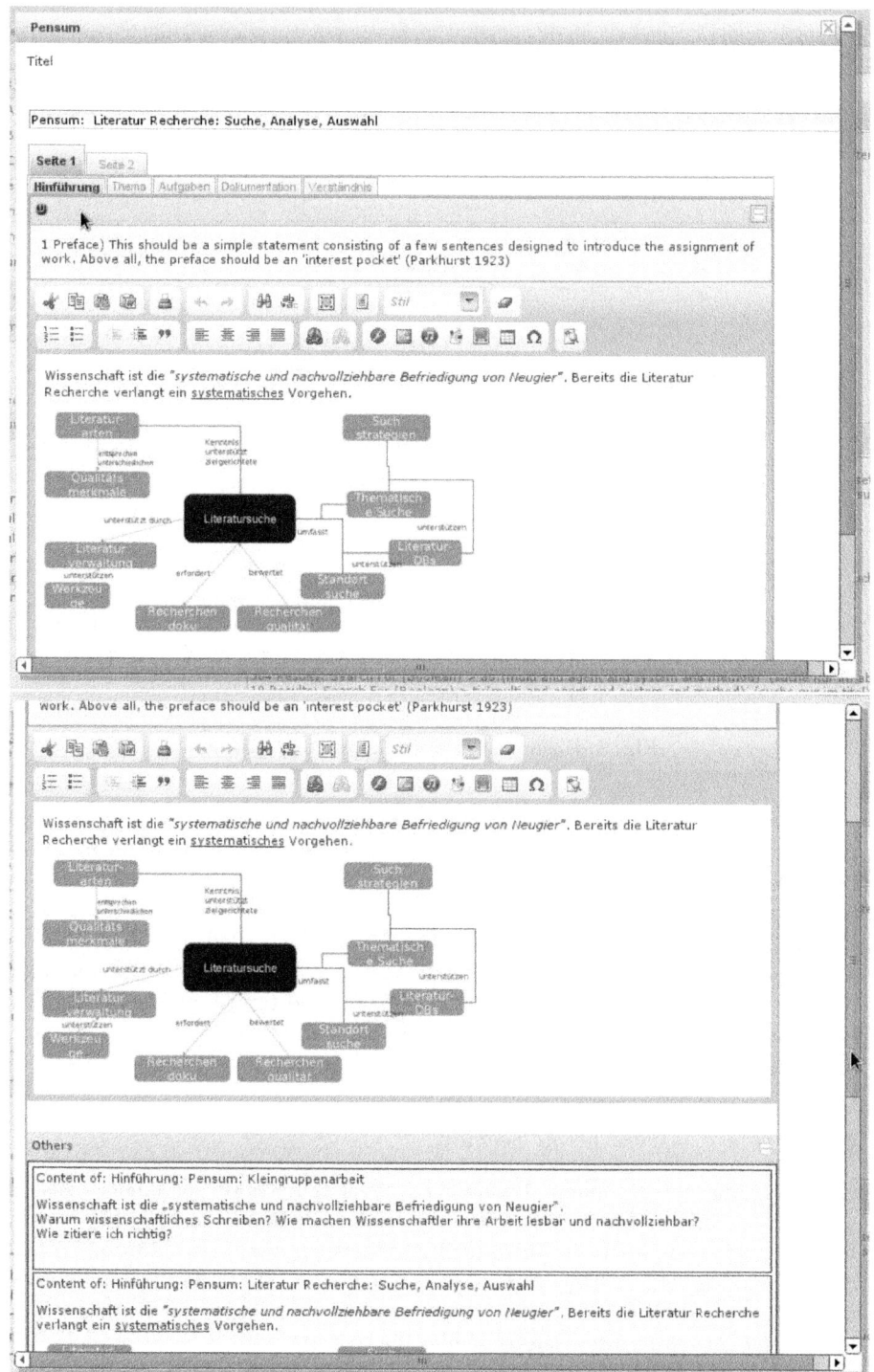

Fig. 2. Nymphaea assignment editor

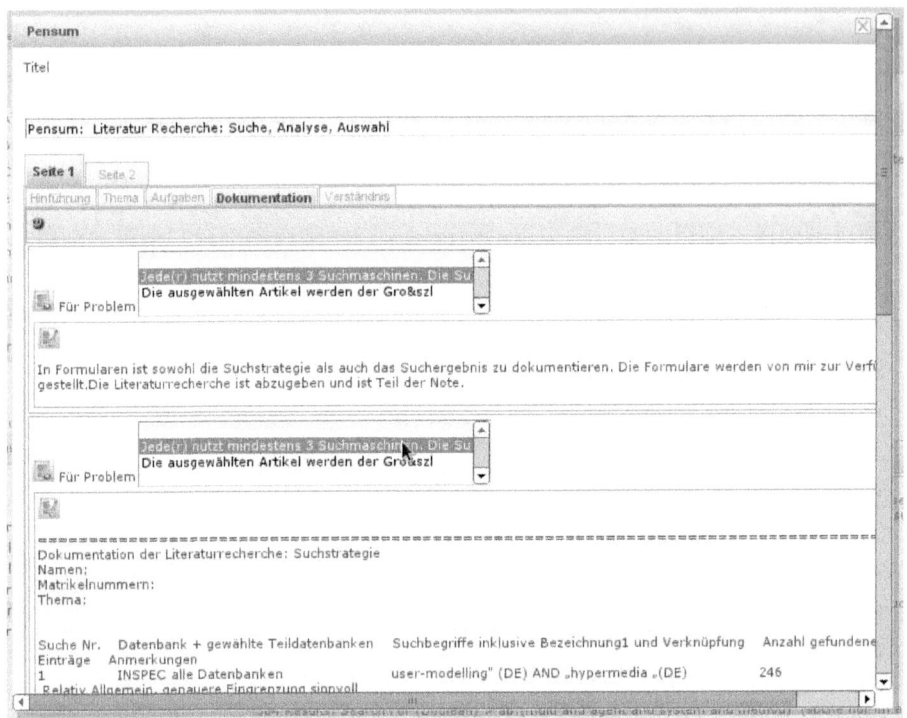

Fig. 3. Documented work linking to problems

Having introduced Dalton Plan assignments in e-learning, we apply this approach to S-BPM eduction. In order to make the S-BPM assignment better readable we refrain from presenting screenshots. This has the consequence that hyperlinks do not work. Therefore in the following we annotate the text using „[-> Hypertextlink description]". The book which used as a basis for the assignment is „Subjektorientiertes Prozessmanagement - Mitarbeiter einbinden, Motivation und Prozessakzeptanz steigern" [8]. The text is online available in nymphaea. Additionally the assignment itself makes use of features of the e-learning platform. These features are marked in italics letters.

3.1   Preface (Orientation Section)

Organisations are complex, dynamic Systems [2]. These systems consist of autonomous interacting agents. Business Process Management (BPM) aims at handling this complexity by introducing models (of work). In addition to this, S-BPM models use as basis the subjects (agents) of the organisation. Assuming a dynamic environment these models need to be adapted on a regular basis to reflect changed reality. Before being able to work with S-BPM models, it is necessary to learn about the process that leads to these models. It is therefor necessary to understand the continuous cycle of activities that leads to S-BPM models and their adaptation (see figure 4).

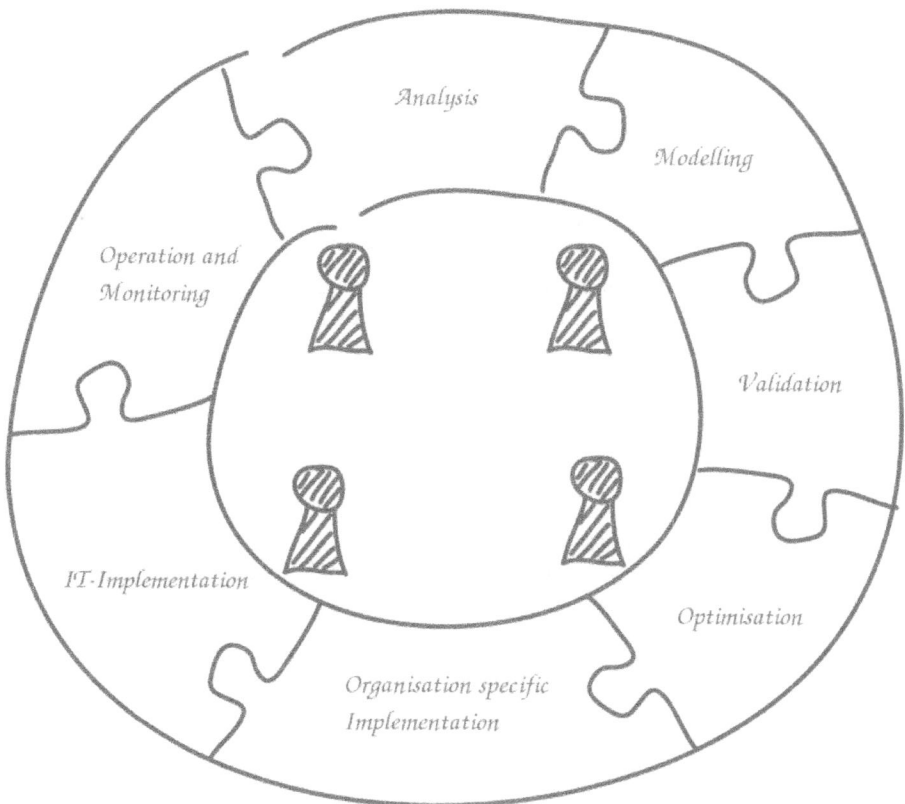

Fig. 4. S-BPM cycle of activities [8, p. 48]

3.2   Topic / Objectives

Understand the S-BPM activities that lead to S-BPM models.

3.3   Problems and Tasks

1. Identify and understand the activities and key players acting in the S-BPM developmentprocess
2. The peer group describes all activities of the S-BPM developmentprocess (open control loop) in their own words
3. Identify key elements of S-BPM Models and their connections
4. The peer group draws a S-BPM Model of the open control loop

3.4 Written Work

Nymphaea features are marked in *italics*.

- Open the book in nymphaea [-> Hypertextlink to Book].
- Create a new *Notes Layer* named <your name - activities>.
- Mark key activities and players discussed in the book using the *highlighting* feature.
- *Share* your *notes-layer* with your peer-group members.
- Open a *forum* for your peer-group.
- Create a new *discussion thread* and *link* all activities, players mentioned to the book.
- Create a new *Notes Layer* named <your name - elements>
- Mark key elements discussed in the book using the *highlighting* feature.
- *Share* your *notes-layer* with your peer-group members.
- Use the Suite and draw a S-BPM model of the S-BPM development process.
- Export your model as set of images.
- Crate a new *module*, upload the images as content and briefly discuss the results of your group work in the *content nodes*.

3.5 Memory Work

- Understand the activities related to S-BPM and their interdependencies
- Understand the key elements of S-BPM models and their interdependencies

3.6 Conferences /Meetings

- Presentation of Assignment; Participants: all; Preparation: Students: none, Teacher discusses details
- Presentation of Group Work; Participants: all; Preparation: Students: Images and Discussions in nymphaea

3.7 References

- Albert Fleischmann and Werner Schmidt and Christian Stary and Stefan Obermeier and Egon Börger, "Subjektorientiertes Prozessmanagement - Mitarbeiter einbinde, Motivation und Prozessakzeptanz steigern", Carl Hanser Verlag, München (2011), 434.[8] [-> Hypertextlink to Book]
  - For this assignment Chapter 2.8 and 3 of the S-BPM book are essential [-> Hypertextlink to book chapters]
- Philip Anderson, "Perspective: Complexity Theory and Organization Science", Organization Science (1999), 216-232. [2][-> Hypertextlink to Paper]

3.8 Equivalents

For working on this assignment about 36 hours of work are needed.

3.9   Bulletin Study

The following Forum in nymphaea provides a place where the discussions with respect to this assignment should take place:
[-> Hypertextlink to nymphaea forum]

3.10   Departmental Cuts

Departmental Cuts are not considered in this assignment.

3.11   Discussion of the Assignment

First the topic was selected a-priori. The preface section provides a motivation from a more general and applied point of view for the given topic. The problems section contains tasks that require different levels of competence: (1) is a retrieval task; (2) is a reorganisation task; (3) is a retrieval task; (4) is a transfer task. Learners have to show competences on three of four competence levels mentioned above (table 1). The documented work contains work done by learners individually and by the peer group in which every learner is member. Similar to ICs [21], letters in *italics* are used to mark platform features that have to be used for documenting the work. The memory work section identifies cognitive work load. In the current assignment only two meetings are scheduled. In both, all class members take part. The reference section contain links to digital versions of books or articles required for learning. A brief estimation of the work load is given by the teacher. The forum in the bulletin study section is created automatically.

4   Conclusions

It has been identified by academics and practioniers, that there is a) a need for BPM skilled people, and b) that traditional approaches to teaching are not effective [12,23,18]. This paper presents a didactic approach supported by the e-learning platform *nymphaea* for S-BPM education. The overall approach builds on constructivist didactics, which has been found to be effective for e-learning environments [4], and which supports acquisition of creative problemsolving skills by students [3].

Further research has to take a look at the two involved roles in learning: teacher and student. Currently a few features exist to support teachers in writing assignments. Further work is required to understand the need of teachers and provide better support for creating assignments. With respect to affects of assignments on students' learning, research from the field of psychology or pedagogy is missing. However, there is evidence that constructivism and reform pedagogy is superior to traditional means of education [12,10,16,14].

References

1. Adams, A.M.: Pedagogical underpinnings of computer-based learning. Journal of Advanced Nursing 46(1), 5–12 (2004), http://www.blackwell-synergy.com/links/doi/10.1111%2Fj.1365-2648.2003.02960.x
2. Anderson, P.: Perspective: Complexity theory and organization science. Organization Science 10(3), 216–232 (1999)
3. Aqda, M.F., Hamidi, F., Ghorbandordinejad, F.: The impact of constructivist and cognitive distance instructional design on the learner's creativity. Procedia Computer Science 3, 260–265 (2011), http://www.sciencedirect.com/science/article/pii/S1877050910004199, World Conference on Information Technology
4. Auinger, A., Stary, C.: Didaktikgeleiteter Wissenstransfer - Interaktive Informationsräume für Lern-Gemeinschaften im Web. Deutscher Universitäts-Verlag / GWV Fachverlage GmbH, Wiesbaden (2005)
5. Dean Jr., D., Kuhn, D.: Direct instruction vs. discovery: The long view. Science Education 91(3), 384–397 (2007)
6. Eichelberger, H. (ed.): Eine Einführung in die Daltonplan-Pädagogik. StudienVerlag (2002)
7. Eichelberger, H., Laner, C., Kohlberg, W.D., Stary, E., Stary, C.: Reformpädagogik goes E-Learning - neue Wege zur Selbstbestimmung von virtuellem Wissenstransfer und individualisiertem Wissenserwerb. Wien, Oldenbourg (2008)
8. Fleischmann, A., Schmidt, W., Stary, C., Obermeier, S., Börger, E.: Subjektorientiertes Prozessmanagement - Mitarbeiter einbinden, Motivation und Prozessakzeptanz steigern. Carl Hanser Verlag, München (2011)
9. Hölbling, R., Wittwer, H., Neuhauser, G.: Cool cooperatives offenes lernen: Eine initiative für mehr selbständigkeit, eigenverantwortung und kooperation an unseren schulen. Booklet to Video, Kullmann und Berger Filmproduktion (2008), http://www.abc.berufsbildendeschulen.at/upload/1373_Cool_Booklet_Letztversion_lr_081014.pdf
10. Lillard, A.S.: Montessori - The Science behind the Genius, 2nd edn. Oxford University Press (2007)
11. Mankel, M.: Lernstrategien und E-Learning - Eine empirische Untersuchung. Verlag Dr. Kovac (2008)
12. Marjanovic, O., Bandara, W.: The Current State of BPM Education in Australia: Teaching and Research Challenges. In: zur Muehlen, M., Su, J. (eds.) BPM 2010 Workshops. LNBIP, vol. 66, pp. 775–789. Springer, Heidelberg (2011), http://dx.doi.org/10.1007/978-3-642-20511-8_69
13. Neuhauser, G., Wittwer, H.: Das cool*-projekt - der daltonplan in der sekundarstufe ii - ein dalton-inspirierter schulentwicklungsprozess an der bhak/bhas-steyr. In: Eichelberger, H. (ed.) Eine Einführung in die Daltonplan-Pädagogik, pp. 161–203. StudienVerlag (2002)
14. Osborne, J., Dillon, J.: Science education in europe: Critical reflections a report to the nuffield foundation (2008)
15. Parkhurst, H.: Education On The Dalton Plan. Nabu Press (1923, 2010)
16. Reich, K.: Konstruktivistische Didaktik - Lehr- und Studienbuch mit Methoden-pool. Beltz Verlag, Weinheim und Basel, 4., durchgesehene auflage edn. (2008)
17. Riepl, A.: ecool concept. Tech. rep., gtn-solutions (2010), www.cooltrainers.at/uploads/media/ecool_concept_english.pptx

18. Rovai, A.P.: A constructivist approach to online college learning. The Internet and Higher Education 7(2), 79–93 (2004),
    http://www.sciencedirect.com/science/article/pii/S1096751604000144
19. Rozendaal, J.S., Minnaert, A., Boekaerts, M.: Motivation and self-regulated learning in secondary vocational education: information-processing type and gender differences. Learning and Individual Differences 13(4), 273–289 (2001),
    http://www.sciencedirect.com/science/article/B6W5P-48643G6-3/
    2/4892c32dea15742675984a556c9df75c
20. Schmidt, H., Cohen-Schotanus, J., van der Molen, H., Splinter, T., Bulte, J., Holdrinet, R., van Rossum, H.: Learning more by being taught less: a "time-for-self-study" theory explaining curricular effects on graduation rate and study duration. Higher Education 60(3), 287–300 (2010)
21. Stary, C.: Intelligibility catchers for Self-Managed knowledge transfer. In: Seventh IEEE International Conference on Advanced Learning Technologies, ICALT 2007, pp. 517–521 (July 2007)
22. Stary, C.: The design of e-Learning contracts: Intelligibility catchers in praxi. In: IEEE/WIC/ACM International Joint Conferences on Web Intelligence and Intelligent Agent Technologies, WI-IAT 2009, vol. 3, pp. 203–206 (September 2009)
23. Stary, C.: Evidence-Based (S-)BPM Education. In: Schmidt, W. (ed.) S-BPM ONE 2011. CCIS, vol. 213, pp. 3–15. Springer, Heidelberg (2011)
24. Terhart, E.: Constructivism and teaching: A new paradigm in general didactics? Journal of Curriculum Studies 35(1), 25–44 (2003),
    http://www.tandfonline.com/doi/abs/10.1080/00220270210163653

Smart4sense2act: Introducing an Organic Approach to Task and Process Design

Fritz Bastarz and Patrick Halek

smart4sense2act
Rosenbursenstrasse 4, 1010 Vienna, Austria
{fritz.bastarz,patrick.halek}@infomedia.at
www.smart4sense2act.com

Abstract. Circumstances in our society and economy are far more complex and interconnected today than they were years ago. But still we focus on a very traditional way of working on tasks: a linear and mechanistic way of thinking and acting. Ignoring that modern, complex and highly developed systems need a different way of dealing with organisations, tasks and processes, we wonder more and more why goals can be achieved less and less. Leaving the mechanistic point of view and introducing an organic approach, *smart4sense2act* (read: *smart-for-sense-to-act*) offers a computer-supported approach and procedure (including a set of methods) ready to use for displaying, analysing and working on complex tasks and processes. Be it strategic planning, organisational development, process- or project-mangement, *smart4sense2act* offers one set of methods and one web-based tool for different tasks. *smart4sense2act* is barrier-free as well as quick and easy to use. Based on subject-oriented process-management, the principle of *smart4sense2act* is a stakeholder oriented systemic analysing and arranging of tasks. Aiming on the quick and direct implementation of results within the organisation, the goal of *smart4sense2act* is to support organisations in gaining a more realistic and value-oriented performance facing the actual needs of today and tomorrow.

Keywords: complexity, corporate governance, holistic management, lateral thinking, organic management, performance management, stakeholders, systemic thinking.

1   Performance through Organic Management

During the past 150 years, we have been brought up to understand organisations being mechanistic systems based on linear connections and simple input-output-relations. But those times are over because circumstances in our society and economy are far more complex and interconnected today than they were years ago [1]. Though, still quite a few among us thinking challenges of today and tomorrow can be met with the knowledge and the methods of yesterday focus on this very traditional, linear and mechanistic way of thinking and acting [2]. Ignoring that modern, complex and highly developed systems need a different way of dealing with organisations, tasks

S. Oppl and A. Fleischmann (Eds.): S-BPM ONE 2012, CCIS 284, pp. 194–201, 2012.

and processes, many among us wonder more and more why goals can be achieved less and less. This is understandable from the human point of view, because the mechanistic point of view has catered to an enormous economical development based on industrial production and its linear approach. But the industrial age was yesterday. Today, we have already entered a new age: the age of knowledge. So, for many of our traditional ways of thinking and acting are based on linear and hierarchical approaches they are not suitable for solving modern knowledge-based, complex and multidimensional tasks successfully [3]. In other words: on the one hand we have been to the moon already but on the other hand we still don't want to give the flintstone away.

Therefore, companies and their performance management are challenged increasingly. Because they want to remain competitive, they need to abandon ways of thinking and managing they have practised for decades. The message is that companies today must obey and take into account much more than it was the case until now. Companies have to balance a turbulent environment, heterogeneous markets, different stakeholders, new social rules and new patterns of thinking and behaviour. The interdependencies between organisations, markets and society have to be seen in a new, different light [4].

Dealing with knowledge and information is *the* crucial basis for managing businesses and *the* resource for their competitive position. Though, it is still widely ignored that not moving figures and managing databases, but creating and managing a sustainable competitive perspective is the essential discipline of entrepreneurship [5]. Therefore, performance management is about managing an ongoing creative process focussing on a sustainable competitive position [6]. But how is this supposed to work?

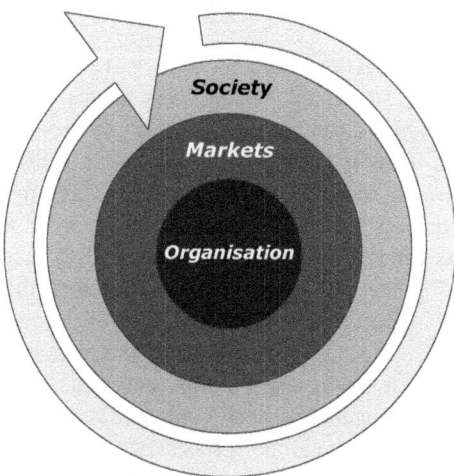

Fig. 1. Interdependence of organisation, markets and society

A linear, mostly one-dimensional thinking is standing in our way, because it results in methods and tools that cannot meet the multi-dimensional requirements we have to deal with when managing an organisation in the age of a knowledge based society. Newer approaches, such as Lateral Thinking and Systemic Thinking introduce enormous potential, because they can develop unknown dimensions of high quality solutions in a very pragmatic way. But humans have limited capabilities in dealing with abstract thinking. Therefore, when managing an organisation we need a barrier-free approach to be able to manage understanding, analysing and designing complex tasks and processes in every-day-business. Organisational development means improving both the effectiveness and the efficiency in defining and managing tasks [7]. This requires clarity, agility, transparency and compliance. Therefore, the goals must be the following:

- improving the quality of decisions
- improving both the effectiveness and efficiency of communication
- saving the setup of actions
- accelerating of task-implementation
- adapting of new circumstances more flexibly

But how can a solution look like that can actually be used in every-day-business?

Based on the grounds of a network-approach, linear processes and connectivities as well as simple input-output-relations are being replaced by an organic approach. This means, that factors like *big picture, overall goals, multilateral interdependencies, cooperation* and a *relevant stakeholder focus* need to be in the centre of interest. It's not the linear connectivity, that counts anymore. It's the question, who and what has to be related to eachother in which way to make a system work successfully.

2   Re-focussing on Value Creation

To put it very clearly, many organisations have to re-learn what their game is all about: it's about creating sustainable value. This means creating sustainable value within and through an organisation within a complex environment calls for a new and different approach. Re-focusssing on value-chains or -circles, both internal and external processes have to focus on creating value according to the organisational goals – and those processes have to be interlinked in order to make sense. Tasks, processes and projects cannot be considered as an end in themselves anymore, but being part of an overall process of value creation. Therefore, the knowledge society is creating a lot of new opportunities but also forcefully calls for new patterns of thinking and acting [8]. Relevant internal and external stakeholders have to be consolidated as well as their stakes, expectations and needs. The usual homogeneity is getting replaced by heterogeneity and complexity increasingly. Thereby, the transparency of social and economic processes increases apparently. But just apparently. The truth is it's the complexity of these processes which dramatically increases. Conclusion: We can see more but we understand less and less. Therefore, it is increasingly difficult to understand coherences and to predict or shape trends [9]. The big picture (overall view, key-elements & their relations) is getting lost more and more and we seek refuge in details. This creates a downward spiral. The problem is that this danger creeps up almost unnoticed and then suddenly and inevitably breaks open. At that time an effective response in many cases is not possible anymore. So, the all-important question is: How can organisations remain competitive in such an environment at all – and most important: in a sustainable way? The answer is: leaving the linear and mechanistic approach and entering into an organic way of creating and managing organisations, tasks and processes [10].

Focussing on value creation and entering the organic approach means introducing a different way of thinking and acting in solving tasks and creating processes. This is exactly *smart4sense2act's* goal. Creating and displaying relations between elements on the grounds of a subject-oriented process-modelling, the question is not anymore: "What follows or triggers what?" (state-of-the-art-way until today). The question is: "Who or what is related to whom or what in which way and which impact does it have?". This allows not only displaying and recognising linear relations between two elements, but displaying and recoginsing entire networks, their interdependencies and their impact on a specific task, a process or the entire organisation.

3   smart4sense2act

Multidimensional tasks being subject to the principles of networking and complexity cannot be solved with the tools of a hierarchically structured and linear world anymore [11]. That's why *smart4sense2act* was created. It was developed based on the findings that the knowledge society cannot be implemented with previously lived patterns of thinking and acting [12]. It is a novel method development providing a specific approach and a web-based tool for networks and complex environments, not only to meet complexity and enable knowledge-orientation, but especially to facilitate organisational changes and managing systemic performance in every-day-business.

smart4sense2act enables introducing an organic approach to every-day-busines, as it works in a context-sensitive (systemic) while focussed way based on subject-oriented and semantic process-modelling. *smart4sense2act* only takes elements into account that can be implemented in every-day-business, as they lay ground to competitive advantages [13]. Therefore, the key to defining processes is to focus on the subject, on stakeholders and their expectations involved [14] . Since organisations are not only driven by formal structures and processes, but also strongly by informal processes, values and the implicit knowledge of the people who are in touch with these organisations have significant impact on an organisation's success. [15]. The latter allow discovering and developing enormous organisational potential.

Since every theory is only as good as effectively it can be implemented, *smart4sense2act* offers a specific IT-supported tool ready to use without the need of special skills. The focus of the development is on barrier-free accessibility and integration into every-day-business because the needs of today demand a proper procedure. Tasks and processes can be designed as a part of daily business and adapted quickly and flexibly on a continous basis to meet new requirements – without the need of opening the "entire package" again. In doing so, *smart4sense2act* helps creating a long term flow. This means there are no obstacles that usually could make it difficult to adapt processes to new challenges - obstacles that often stand in the way

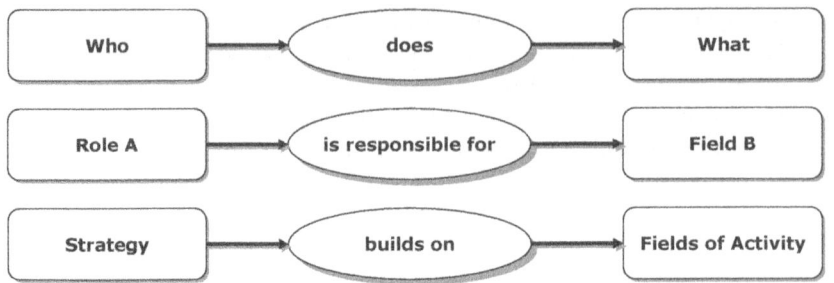

Fig. 2. Who or what is related to whom or what in which way and which impact does it have?

of the future and a sustainable perspective. Based on subject-oriented modelling, interconnections between all elements taken into account create a much more valid picture of real needs and actual impacts. The term *"smart"* was created by the 1st letters of the following expressions:

- *SYSTEMIC*: holistic, in order to allow the basical understanding of a situation and recongnising of principles, patterns and dependencies.
- *MODEL-DRIVEN*: a structured description / interpretation of relevant realities.
- *ACHIEVABLE*: really feasible, thus to be implemented effectively.
- *RELATED*: not only linear hirarchies but relations and their impacts are part of success. Not only formal, certified processes are considered, but also informal and human motives of relevant stakeholders that determine success or failure.
- *TIMELY*: up to date and meeting today's requirements. Everywhere we hear of creating networks, even across company boundaries. But how to deal with

Following these definitions, the focus is on the terms "*sense*" and "*act*", which clearly express that all states from capturing the situation to executing the solution are considered and integrated.

Sense: *SENSING* means the capturing, perceiving and recognising of important events and factors when managing an organisation – it means to feel and to interpret. In the corporate meaning it is like putting out the feelers in order to understand the environment, its relevant stakeholders, their expectations and to properly interpret their actions [16].

Act: *ACTING* means acting as a result of a need for action that arises from different perceptions (sensing) and calls for clearly defined and structured activities when managing an organisation. The quality of action depends on the players' abilities and the functionality of the chosen tools.

4   The 6 Pillars of *smart4sense2act*

smart4sense2act was created to introduce an organic approach, task and process design to organisations. Therefore, a solution was created in order to follow the concept of a barrier-free and ready to use tool based on a clear and structured method. *smart4sense2act* has 6 pillars:

Web-Based: The tool *smart4sense2act* uses is web-based. This creates the opportunity for different users to work on the same task at different places. Since focussing on the subject, different perspectives create a much more diverse and therefore valid model of reality.

Semantic: No special process-language is needed. *smart4sense2act* is based on free semantic modelling. Processes are created on the basis of our natural language, which means the language we speak, following the way we build sentences: subject - predicate - object.

Subject-Oriented: The focus of modelling is on the subject and its clearly defined realtions. The question *smart4sense2act* answers is not "What has to follow what?", it is "Who or what is related to whom or what in which way and which impact does it have?"

Interconnected: Since the focus is on the subjects, modellig can be done on various and different levels which can be linked through just a mouse click. This way, the overall view (Big Picture) never gets lost even when modelling details.

Multi-usable: Be it strategic planning, organisational development or one single project – *smart4sense2act* offers one tool for different tasks. Modelling different tasks can be done and linked to eachother as well as to documents and websites barrier-free.

Just-in-Time-Documentation: The documentation of tasks and process does not have to be a separate procedure anymore. Working on tasks or processes, the tool saves every step and all changes. So: whatever has been created is saved and documented automatically.

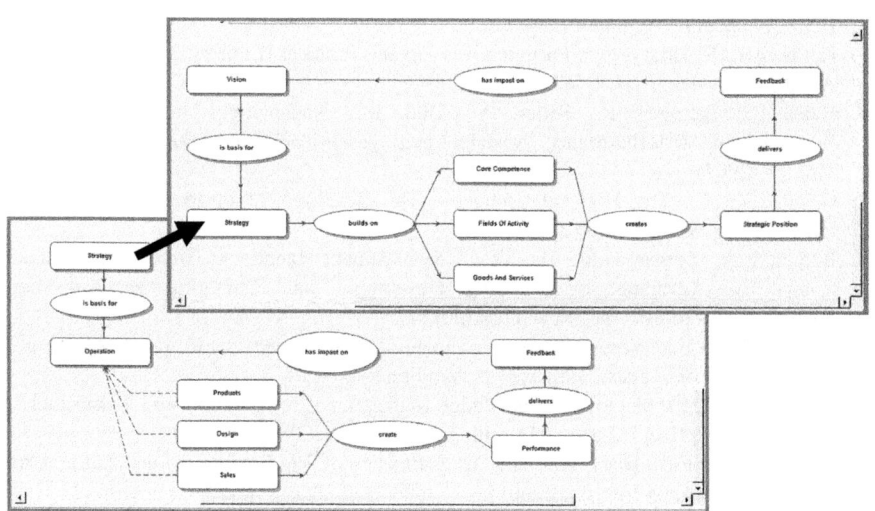

Fig. 3. Linking different levels through just a mouse click (showing a case)

5   Summative Conclusions

smart4sense2act introduces an ontology driven, organic approach to task and process design by offering a computer-supported procedure (including a set of methods). *smart4sense2act* is ready to use for displaying, analysing and working on complex tasks and processes. It is quick and easy to use as well as multi-usable for different kinds of tasks which can be linked to each other through just a mouse click. Based on subject-oriented and semantic modelling, it enables individuals and organisations to recognise interconnections between elements in order to use so far unseen potentials. Stakeholders and their expectations create networks of tasks being solved and processes being designed and implemented. The direct import into the *Process-Management System MetaSonic* makes it possible to deliver the developed processes directly on the communication level, complete them with process-specific functionality, validate them with all parties, implement them, and use them in everyday work immediately [17]. These features and attributes support catering to a more systemic, impact-oriented and sustainable performance in everyday business.

Acknowledgments. The research leading to these results has received funding from the Austrian Research Promotion Agency (FFG) within the General Programme (Basisprogramm) under grant agreement n° 828238 (SMARTtransformation).

References

1. Vester, F.: The Art of Interconnected Thinking. Ideas and Tools for tackling complexity. MCB-Verlag, Munich (2007)
2. Williams, B.A.O.: Descartes: Das Vorhaben der reinen philosophischen Untersuchung. Beltz Athenäum, Weinheim (1996)
3. Heftberger, S., Stary, C.: Partizipatives organisationales Lernen; Ein prozessbasierter Ansatz. GWV-Fachverlag, Wiesbaden (2004)
4. Haas, B., Oetinger, R., Ritter, A., Thul, M.: Nachhaltige Unternehmensführung. Verknüpfung wirtschaftlicher, sozialer und gesellschaftlicher Forderungen. Hanser, Munich (2007)
5. Grimberger, G.: The High-IQ Company: The Development of the Organisational IQ. VDM Verlag, Saarbrücken (2009)
6. Berger, L.A., Berger, D.R.: The Talent Management Handbook: Creating a Sustainable Competitive Advantage by Selecting, Developing, and Promoting the Best People. McGraw-Hill Professional, New York (2011)
7. Lawler III, E.E., Worley, C.G., Creelman, D.: Management Reset: Organizing for Sustainable Effectiveness. Jossey Bass, San Fransisco (2011)
8. Koskinen, K.U., Pihlanto, P.: Knowledge Management in Project-Based Companies: An Organic Perspective. Palgrave Macmillan, New York (2008)
9. Senge, P.: The Fifth Discipline: The Art & Practice of The Learning Organization. Crown Business, New York (rev. ed. 2006)
10. Malik, F.: Strategie: Navigieren in der Komplexität der Neuen Welt. Campus Verlag, Frankfurt am Main (2011)

11. Yeo, R.K.: Organisational Development in the 21st Century: Learning for Success - Lessons from Singapore's Learning Organisations. VDM-Verlag, Saarbrücken (2009)
12. Varela, F., Thompson, E., Rosch, E.: Der mittlere Weg der Erkenntnis: die Beziehung von Ich und Welt in der Kognitionswissenschaft - der Brückenschlag zwischen wissenschaftlicher Theorie und menschlicher Erfahrung. Goldmann Wilhelm, Munich (1995)
13. Jeston, J., Nelis, J.: Management by Process: A practical road-map to sustainable Business Process Management. Butterworth-Heinemann, Burlington (2008)
14. Nel, R.: Puppets Or People: People And Organisational Development: An Integrated Approach. Juta Academic, Claremont (2008)
15. Allee, V.: The Future of Knowledge: Increasing Prosperity through Value Networks. Butterworth-Heinemann, Burlington (2003)
16. Halek, P.: Die Marke lebt! Das All-Brand-Concept. Die Marke als Kern nachhaltiger Organisationsführung. Facultas.wuv, Vienna (2009)
17. Fleischmann, A., Schmidt, W., Stary, C., Obermeier, S., Börger, E.: Subjektorientiertes Prozessmanagement: Mitarbeiter einbinden, Motivation und Prozessakzeptanz steigern. Carl Hanser Verlag, München (2011)

SMART - Knowledge Enriched S-BPM

Ricarda Vierlinger

Johannes Kepler University Linz
Department of Business Information Systems - Communications Engineering,
Freistaedterstrasse 315, 4040 Linz, Austria
ricarda.vierlinger@jku.at

Abstract. The SMART approach is a socio-technical approach towards holistic performance management and corporate governance. Supported by the modeling tool *SMARTmodeler*, the described methodology provides a generic method that can be applied to various problem domains in the context of strategic planning, organizational development, and project management. Although the SMART approach is supported by a semantically open modeling tool, people have difficulties applying it. Addressing these difficulties, three issues regarding the people's unwillingness or inability to apply the approach are identified and explored in the course of this paper. Concerning the results gained through the exploration of each of these issues, proposals to resolve these issues improving the application of the SMART approach are developed.

Keywords: change process, complexity, knowledge, knowledge sharing, modeling, SMART approach, subject-orientation, systemic thinking.

1 Introduction

Organizational change processes are complex and are hardly comprehensible by single actors within an organization [13]. To deal with complexity, key aspects of organizational situations have to be identified [1]. Reflecting on these aspects from a global point of view enables process evaluation which may lead to organizational change processes, that eventually have to be communicated in order to put them to practice [14].

Graphical representations enable reflection and communication of organizational situations [9]. Perceptions of complex organizational issues, however, can be vague and incomplete and thus can hardly be represented in a formalized way [3]. Semantically open modeling approaches enable people to visualize and reflect their individual views of an organization without restricting them in terms of representational flexibility [5]. Existing approaches, such as ARIS [15] and Bonapart [12], do not provide this kind of flexibility and thus do not support triggering of organizational change processes by the people who are directly involved in the actual work processes.

To meet these requirements, the SMART approach was developed based on the idea of supporting or triggering activities leading to organizational change processes. The term *SMART* is an acronym built from the following expressions:

S. Oppl and A. Fleischmann (Eds.): S-BPM ONE 2012, CCIS 284, pp. 202–213, 2012.

- *SYSTEMIC*: holistic, in order to allow fundamental understanding of a situation and recognition of principles, patterns and dependencies
- *MODEL-DRIVEN*: built upon a structured description of significant realities, processes and issues
- *ACHIEVABLE*: feasible, i.e. to be implemented effectively
- *RELATED*: linear hierarchies as well as relations and their impacts are part of success. Not only the formal, certified processes are considered, but also the informal processes and stakeholder's motives determine success or failure
- *TIMELY*: enabling continuos and fast adaptation to permanently changing requirements. People talking about creating networks, even across company boundaries. But how to deal with networks, that are changing constantly? [1]

Applying this methodology means focusing modelling on the subject and its relations to others while, continuously reflecting the core question *"Who or what is related to whom or what in which way"*. The SMART approach is a modeling approach for sociotechnical systems. It enables the integration of different knowledge and perspectives of various stakeholders in an organization and thus supports organizational knowledge sharing. The main objective applying the approach in organizational structures is to facilitate subject-oriented modeling processes that link all the stakeholders involved in a certain organizational process [1].

The SMART approach is supported by the semantically open, semi-structured modeling tool *SMARTmodeler*, enabling the modeling of cooperative processes [6]. This tool picks up the SMART approach and provides a modeling environment designed for collaboratively developing and mapping organizational processes represented by semantically open models. The representation of individual views (subject-orientation) is enabled to involve all stakeholders and their interrelation required for an organizational process [1]. The provided tool is web-based and therefore accessible for all users working on the same task. During modeling, no specific modeling language is prescribed.

By means of integrated information and subject-oriented process-management, processes can be created and reflected in a quick an direct way as well as integrated into organizational every-day business on the ground of current needs. An increased transparency and a common understanding of organizational processes can be achieved [1].

Experiences in applying the modeler in different real-world use cases showed a gap between the intended use of the modeler as specified by the SMART approach and the way people actually perceived the support provided by the SMARTmodeler. People could not use the modeling tool in terms of supporting the SMART approach without guidance. The project *smartTransformation* was initiated to identify the reasons for the inability of users to effectively use the SMARTmodeler and eventually to develop a methodology that enables people to use the modeling toolset to facilitate continuos reflection and change from within an organization.

The goal of this paper is to reflect on the processes of SMARTtransformation that led to the development of the stakeholder-oriented methodology to facilitate organizational change processes. The documentation of the project's articulation and operative work processes can act as a reference for other projects in similarly complex situations, where both, the desired outcome and the steps to be performed are refined and evolve over time.

The paper is structured along issues that were examined in ongoing end-user studies and guided the research process. The main research interest was to explore whether the examined issues contribute to the lack of user acceptance and to propose potential solutions for the shortcomings. The identified issues, their exploration are discussed in more detail in the following sections. Considering the results of the exploration, further research topics and open issues are presented at the end of this paper.

2   Enabling Subject-Oriented Knowledge Elicitation

As mentioned above, practical experiences with end users showed that people had problems using the SMART approach. The main objective of the SMART approach is to facilitate subject-oriented modeling processes. It is intended to let people use the methodology and the toolset in an unguided or at most semi-guided way. This means that people using the approach are only provided assistance to the basic functions and steps of the approach but should not be influenced in externalizing their individual models. At the beginning of the project, the reasons for people's unwillingness to apply or their inability to comprehend the approach was unclear. Existing literature on requirements on instruments for similar use cases was thus examined to identify starting points for the exploration of potential shortcomings.

Herrmann et al. have proposed an approach to attain a common view on cooperative work processes. They use a flexible modeling methodology to externalize and combine the viewpoints of different individuals [6].

The methodology used in this modeling approach is the socio-technical walkthrough (STWT) [8] [7]. The STWT focuses on facilitating communication processes within several workshops to enable representation of the concept or outline of a socio-technical system by a diagrammatic model [7]. Subject-oriented processes have to be carefully prepared and the facilitation has to be supported by some methodical and technical tools [7].

Herrmann et al. emphasize three aspects which are relevant for the success of knowledge sharing and integration. They start with the visual presence of a tool's feature as well as the option to add further details and comments if necessary [8]. As as a second point he points out that hence formalisation can lead to misleading representations, a modeling method for socio-technical systems must be able to present a contingent as well as highly determined structures and processes [8]. Elements available for modeling activities have to be clearly revealed [7]. In accordance to the second issue, Herrmann lists levels of abstractions that require a certain amount of effort to compare models created by different persons [8]. Appropriate training of the approach is the considered the third requirement as the abstractness of models can lead to differing interpretations of the depicted process [7]. Providing material like photographs, documents, prototypes etc, which are of relevance for modeling process and might be integrated into the models [7] can support the interpretation activities. To subsume Herrmann asserts that a detailed visualization and guided step-by-step development of models has a significant positive effect on knowledge integration and on the participants' ability and willingness to use a recently developed system [7].

Summarizing, Herrmann et al. adress the issues as potential obstacles to successfully deploy socio-technically supported modeling methods.

Issue 1: Lack of technical support (missing or incomplete tool support)
Issue 2: Lack of conceptual support (ambiguous or misleading model interpretation)
Issue 3: Lack of procedural support (uncertainty in how to apply the methodology)

Another reference justifying the identification of these issues can be found in the *Guidelines of Business Process Modeling (GoM)* [2], where design proposals concerning modeling activities are explained. GoM aim at increasing the quality of models beyond fulfillment of six syntactic guidelines: *Correctness, Relevance, Economic Efficiency, Clarity, Comparability, Systemic Design* [2]. *Comparability & Relevance* can be related to the usability issue (1) of the SMART approach. The selection of the relevant object system as well as supporting the application of relevant modeling techniques and the consistent usage of all guidelines including a conform naming/layout convention [2] is covered. *Clarity & Correctness* include the consistent and syntactically correct modeling against an explicit meta model. Readable, understandable, useful models are required [2]. Thus this guidelines can be attributed to the required conceptual support (2) while applying the SMART approach. *Systematic Design & Economic Efficiency* can be related to the required procedural support (3). This guidelines determines the need of a appropriate modeling tool or the re-use of models, as well as well-defined relationships between information models, which belongs to different views [2].

These issues can be used to as a starting point to examine why people are not able to apply the SMART approach and to use the SMARTmodeler in the way it is supposed to. User studies were initiated to closer examine and find resolutions regarding these issues. The exploration of each issue is described in the following sections, including motivation of why exploring this issue (*motivation*) as well as a detailed description of the exploration design (*implementation*). Furthermore an interpretation of theses results, gained through exploration (*reflection*) is given. An approach to resolve each of these issues is made to meet the requirements on appropriate methodological and technological support of enabling individuals to apply the SMART-approach in organizational structures.

2.1   Technical Support for the SMART Approach

People often could not be convinced to use the SMARTmodeler. This lack of acceptance was attributed to usability issues in informal feedbacks. Herrmann states, that learning to use a system represents the foundation of every modeling approach, going to be applyied in an organization [8]. It had to be scrutinized on how the individual elicitation of organizational process models, as well as enabling organizational knowledge sharing can be technically supported. Thus the examination of the usability of the SMARTmodeler in the context of individual elicitation of organizational process models was required.

Implementation. A user study was set up to gather more information about the usability of the SMARTmodeler. A group of three people was requested to map an arbitrary chosen process using the tool. None of these persons had prior knowledge with respect to modeling. The persons got no specific introduction besides questions that they had to keep in mind while modeling. These questions (cf. Figure 1) guide users while modelling according to the SMART approach.

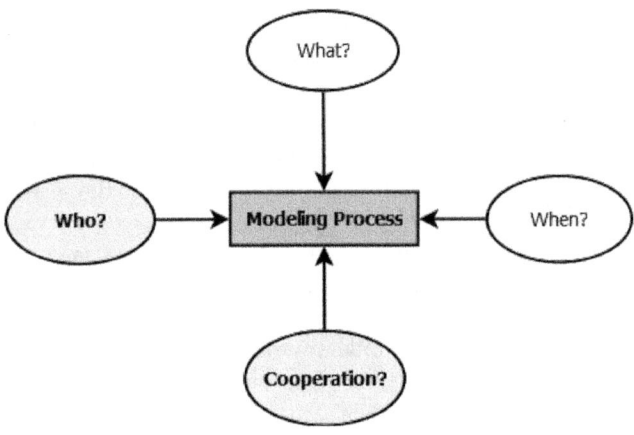

Fig. 1. Questions to Keep in Mind While Modeling

Core aspect *"Who?"* focus on the subjects involved in the process and thus is emphasized on the map. Even process-related communication between different subjects (*"Cooperation?"*) has to be taken into account, as the interrelation between SMART and the subject-oriented business process modeling (S-BPM) gets apparent. Figure 1 is a visualization of the SMART approach based on the terms (*Systemic, Model-Driven, Achievable, Related, Timely*) mentioned in section 1 [1].

The usability study focused on the elaboration of proposals based on the evaluated results to get people to implement the SMART approach in organizations through improved usability. In this context, the objective was to assess the capabilities of the SMARTmodeler to enable intuitive modeling without intervention to subsequently determine the comprehensibility of the tool.

In order to document the modeling process, the entire modeling session was video-recorded. Following the active part of the study, an ex-post survey reflecting the previous modeling process using the SMARTmodeler was accomplished.

As part of the video-analyzing activities, the occurrence of usability difficulties as well as the need for explicitly required intervention while modeling was collected and documented. The resulting documentation showed a number of additional interventions by the developers of the toolset explaining how to handle the tool in order to perform the intended modeling steps.

Survey results include the identification of positive and negative aspects concerning the outcome in terms of the SMARTmodeler's usability and the perceived mapping accuracy between the real organizational world and the model.

The survey results show that the SMARTmodeler is perceived to enable creativity, flexibility and freedom of scope of an individual. As already observed during the user study, the modeling tool also is perceived to support cooperative modeling. The persons indicated that providing example-models before starting modeling would be helpful in order to understand the intention of the modeling tasks.

The usability of the SMARTmodeler was heavily criticized. Partly the user expectations were not met and thus ongoing interventions were required to convey the handling of the tool. Furthermore, a focus on a certain type of relation within the models, the *"part-of"* relation, was identified. Any other relation to be displayed thus has to be defined by using a generic mechanism. This *"part-of"* relation is used to create hierarchical structures. In the scope of the assessed study, semantic relations were not defined at all until an intervention was made.

Reflection. The untrained use of the modeling tool induced difficulties in ensuring the unobstructed flow of the modeling process, as well as focusing on an approach that does not meet the intended use of models. Furthermore, the global process model (aspects to be modeled and modeling targets) has to be increasingly communicated. Once the problem areas concerning the SMARTmodeler's usability were identified, the major issues were selected. A proposal to counteract the negative implications of the SMARTmodeler and to enable appropriate user support is to develop a model approach that enables individual step-by-step modeling realized by an online training using a web-based platform [7].

2.2   Conceptional Support for the SMART Approach

When implementing SMART, one fundamental step is to recognize common concepts underlying recurring issues in order to trigger fundamental change processes. People using the SMARTmodeler, however, hardly generalized their examples to identify their common core issue. Generalization is a core requirement of conceptual modeling [4]. People using the SMARTmodeler to implement the SMART methodology, however, were hardly able to perform this step. The inability of people to perform generalization of designed models and the missing documentation of the model element semantics lead to misinterpretation of these models.

The SMARTmodeler intends to enable subject-oriented visualization of organizational issues [18]. An organization-wide consistent modeling notation including the usage of common elements while modeling aims at gaining transparency and traceability of the resulting models. Experiences made in different projects illustrate that people start modeling in their own way creating individual semantics of elements and therefore not considering an uniform notation of modeling. Before starting the project *SMARTtransformation*, users assigned individual semantics to the models' elements in most cases and did not communicate the meanings. Due to missing knowledge of contextual information, the interpretation of created models by other users was not possible. In other words, persons who were not actively involved in the creation process were not able to determine the context of the models and hence the meaning of the elements. The main reason identified in end user studies is the users' ad hoc creation of models using their individual semantics, not considering potentially existing global meta-models (i.e. predefined language constructs). In reflective interviews, the avoidance of building upon existing meta-models was attributed to the lack of communicated meta-models and/ or the incomprehensibility of model element semantics [18]. To closer examine this issue, task was to develop a procedural model to derive meta-models from a pool of existing models created in the SMARTmodeler.

Implementation. Based upon existing approaches in literature [11] [10], we have developed a procedural model to derive meta-models, specifically tailored to the SMART approach. A precondition to derive meta-models is the availability of already modeled processes in the SMARTmodeler. If this is not the case, these models have to be built a-priori to the next step. Next, an initial coarse-grained analysis of existing models had to be accomplished. This analysis included a categorization of models, serving as an indicator for possible classes of existing meta-model types behind. In a next step, each model was reflected in more detail to gain a set of feasible characterizing properties of the model at hand. After this overall analysis phase (coarse-grained and detailed analysis) was completed, a consultation between the project's partner happened in order to tune the results of this phase. As a final step the different meta-models were derived. An overview of the general process described in this section is given in Figure 2.

Applying this procedural model to existing models created in the SMART-modeler, three different types of meta-models were derived. Additionally a common meta meta model was created [18]. Existing inconsitencies between models were fixed in tuning the results of the catigorization using a semi-structured questionnaire. To gain further information about the meta model extraction process see [18].

Reflection. The application of the procedural model to derive meta models leads to an increased awareness with respect to the use and misuse of meta models. Thus, meta models are vital in order to improve comprehensibility of model element semantics [18]. Herrmann determined that a detailed visualization, including conscious use of meta-models positively effects knowledge integration and the participants' ability and willingness to use a new system [8]. This meta-model examination enables the adaption and modification of the models at any time. It also facilitates the creation of new instances of the current model.

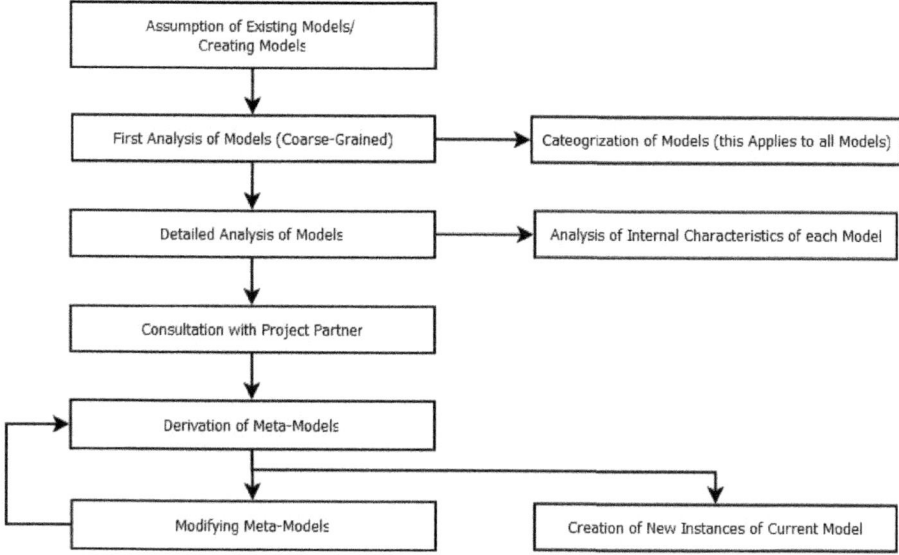

Fig. 2. Bottom-Up Meta Model Creation Process

Elaborating the task of developing a procedural model to obtain meta models should stimulate users' awareness of existing meta models. This enables the development of a common understanding of the concepts represented in a model, created in the SMARTmodeler. Regarding initial practical results, persons using the SMARTmodeler are now enabled to model element legends (explicitely reveal what is depicted) to improve comprehensibility of their models.

2.3   Procedural Support for the SMART Approach

Regarding the indivdidual representation of organizational processes that probably can lead to differing interpretations of the depcited processes [7] and the people's inability to perform the generalization steps necessary to apply the SMART methodology, an applicable guidance throughout the entire modeling process to get people to apply this approach has to be provided. Practical experiences with end users showed that people, intended to use the SMART approach, had difficulties at the very beginning of the modeling process. As an entry point of conveying people to apply the SMART approach using an appropriate procedural model and to facilitate the introduction in the SMART methodology, the support process is triggered by a (generalized) key question. This key question have to be designed in a way that they appeal to people, involved in the modeling process.

Implementation. The first step of developing a SMART-specific training concept was to define possible entry points that could trigger a respective process.

The entry points were recurring stereotypical statements issued by people involved in different organizational change projects. The selection of theses stereotypical statements, were predicated on practical experiences of the project partner. In a user study, the comprehensibility and the potential to trigger examples representing the respective statement were identified. Main interest of this study was to evaluate whether one or more of these core questions contribute to a successful introduction of the SMART approach in organizational structures. The user study was conducted as part of *"S-BPM ONE 2011"* [16], an international conference on business process modeling.

The study was divided into two parts and was split over two days. First people were provided six stereotypical problem-oriented statements to discover whether one or more of these statements could provide an entry point in an organizational change project.

In the second part, participants were provided additional solution-oriented statements in combination with problem-oriented statements of the first day. Thus main objective of the second day was to check whether the connection between the problem-oriented (first part of survey) and solution-oriented statements can be made. Moreover the contribution to organizational changing processes had to be determined subsequently.

The following questions have been used:

Problem-Oriented Part

> We need to focus on details increasingly!
> We've always done it that way!
> We don't have time for experiments or new stuff.
> We have to try harder.
> I am sure all the required information is available
> There should not be a problem.

Solution-Oriented Part

> Do we care about the big picture?
> Do we still deal with the same requirements?
> The solutions we created yesterday might not help us solving our current and future tasks
> (Even) More of the same?
> Which information do we actually need for problem solving?
> What about the effectiveness of our so-called solutions?

Participants were asked to rate the problem-oriented questions once again, to evaluate the solution-oriented part under consideration of the problem oriented part subsequently. Storytelling [17], as a narrative method, was used to gather further information about these statements. Therefore the participating people were asked to tell a self-experienced story regarding one or more of the statements (no matter if problem-oriented or solution-oriented). So information about the capability of the statements contributing to organizational problem solving and the capability of triggering a story recently experienced had to be collected.

Regarding the future tasks of providing an applicable guidance throughout the entire modeling process to get people to use the SMARTmodeler in the intended way, the statements' relevance was evaluated. Reflecting on these results, it got apparent that certain statements are more suitable triggering individual user stories, than others. In a second round of interviews, users were asked to tell a story while keeping in mind a certain statement. These user stories are intended to be a trigger for organizational change processes.

Reflection. The application of the SMART approach supporting the individual modeling of organizational processes fosters the elicitation of organizational knowledge in a setting focusing on individuals, and hence, leading to an increased transparency and comprehensibility of these organizational issues. Establishing key statements supports users in focusing on the core issues while modeling. Since possible entry points could be defined by means of the realized user study, a procedural model of how to successfully implement the SMART approach in organizations has to be developed in future tasks. This procedural model is intended to enable an unguided implementation of the SMART approach in organizational structures, focusing on subject-oriented modeling processes.

3 Conclusions

The SMARTmodeler is intended to be an intuitive instrument facilitating subject-oriented modeling of organizational processes. In order to enable the use of this instrument for modeling, appropriate tools support has to be provided. In its initial version, the use of the SMARTmodeler was largely avoided by users. To identify reasons for this phenomenon and to propose possible solutions, literature on socio-technical system design was examined. Three potential issues were identified, referring to required technical support, conceptual support, and procedural support.

Technical issues have beed adressed by the identification and resolution of of major usability issues. To enable people using the SMARTmodeler, a specific training concept concerning usability issues has to be developed. On a conceptual level, the comprehensibility of model element semantics was adressed by proposing an approach to make people aware of their implicit meta-models and to facilitate the externalization of these meta-models.

Based on the results of the explorations, further research is necessary to adress the third issue and to develop an appropriate procedural model to support the application of the SMART approach.The key statements described in the previous section are a starting point in the development of the procedural model. They are intended to act as anchors in organizational change processes. People should be able to identify a statement appropriate to their current situation and then can refer to at any time while applying the SMART methodology.

Starting from one of the key question, narrative methods [17] could be used to elicit a self-experienced story which in turn facilitates the identification of the concepts relevant to the organizational situation. The application of a narrative method provides people with a starting point to visualize the relevant organizational information and problem issues using the SMARTmodeler. The visualization of all core elements supports the identification of a core statement for the examined organizational situation. According the the SMART approach, such a core statement is necessary to represent the background of organizational change processes and to serve as an anchor while modeling. The development of the procedural model guiding individuals through the entire SMART process is still in its early stage and has to be iteratively refined via experiences in practical use-cases.

The proposed solutions not only enable putting the SMART approach to practice but also have the potential to augment it with additional, subject-specific knowledge. This knowledge can be use to situate SMART-models in their real-world organizational context. It also enables communication of and about models with other stakeholders and facilitates the transfer of both problem awareness and potential solutions. Starting from a stakeholder-centric perspective, the proposed approaches thus directly contribute to trigger and facilitate organizational change processes, which is the ultimate goal of the SMART approach.

Acknowledgments. The research leading to these results has received funding from the Austrian Research Promotion Agency (FFG) within the General Programme (Basisprogramm) under grant agreement n° 828238 (SMARTtransformation).

References

1. Bastarz, F., Halek, P.: smart4sense2act: A Smart Concept for Systemic Performance Management. In: Schmidt, W. (ed.) S-BPM ONE 2011. CCIS, vol. 213, pp. 109–114. Springer, Heidelberg (2011)
2. Becker, J., Rosemann, M., von Uthmann, C.: Guidelines of Business Process Modeling. In: van der Aalst, W., Desel, J., Oberweis, A. (eds.) Business Process Management. LNCS, vol. 1806, pp. 30–262. Springer, Heidelberg (2000)
3. Borgi, A., Akdag, H.: Knowledge based supervised fuzzy-classification: an application to image processing. In: Annals of Mathematics and Artificial Intelligence. Kluwer Academic Publishers (2001)
4. Davies, I., Green, P., Rosemann, M., Indulska, M., Gallo, S.: How do practitioners use conceptual modeling in practice? Data & Knowledge Engineering 58(3), 358–380 (2006)
5. Goguen, J.A.: Keynote: On notation. In: TOOLS (10), pp. 5–10 (1993)
6. Herrmann, T., Hoffmann, M., Kunau, G., Loser, K.: Modelling cooperative work: Chances and risks of structuring. In: Proceedings of Cooperative Systems Design, A Challenge of the Mobility Age, COOP 2002, pp. 53–70. IOS press (2002)
7. Herrmann, T., Kunau, G., Loser, K., Menold, N.: Socio-technical walkthrough: designing technology along work processes. In: Proceedings of the Eighth Conference on Participatory Design, Artful Integration: Interweaving Media, Materials and Practices, pp. 132–141. ACM Press, New York (2004)
8. Herrmann, T., Loser, K., Jahnke, I.: Sociotechnical walkthrough: a means for knowledge integration. The Learning Organization 14(5), 450–464 (2007)

9. Herrmann, T., Hoffmann, M., Kunau, G., Loser, K.U.: Modelling cooperative work: Chances and risks of structuring. In: Cooperative Systems Design, A Challenge of the Mobility Age (Coop 2002) pp. 53–70 (2002)

10. Himsl, M.: Adaptives Modellierungswerkzeug für Metamodelle und deren Instanzen (I): Analyse von Werkzeugen zur Unternehmensmodellierung sowie Design und Implementierung einer Benutzer- und Rechteverwaltung. Master's thesis, Johannes Kepler University, Linz (2006)

11. Kern, H.: Metamodellierung aus Sicht von ARIS. In: Fähnrich, K.P., Thränert, M., Wetzel, P. (eds.) Integration Engineering: Motivation – Begriffe – Methoden – Anwendungsfälle, pp. 77–90. Leipziger Beiträge zur Informatik, Eigenverlag Leipziger Informatik-Verbund (LIV), Leipzig, Germany (2007)

12. Krallmann, H., Schönherr, M., Trier, M.: Systemanalyse im Unternehmen - Prozessorientierte Methoden der Wirtschaftsinformatik, 5th edn. Oldenbourg Wissenschaftsverlag GmbH (2007)

13. Luhmann, N.: Einführung in die Systemtheorie, 5th edn. Carl-Auer-Verlag, Heidelberg (2008)

14. Nonaka, I., Takeuchi, H.: The knowledge creating company. Oxford University Press, Inc. (1995)

15. Scheer, A.-W.: ARIS - vom Geschäftsprozess zum Anwendungssystem, 4th edn. Springer (2002)

16. Schmidt, W. (ed.): S-BPM ONE 2011. CCIS, vol. 213. Springer, Heidelberg (2011)

17. Thier, K.: Storytelling - Eine narrative Methode. Springer (2006)

18. Vierlinger, R.: Verfahrensentwicklung zur Metamodellerhebung. Bachelor's thesis, Johannes Kepler University, Linz (2011)

Subjective Security and Safety – S-BPM as a Base for the Description of Security and Safety Objectives

Max Dirndorfer, Barbara Handy, Josef Schneeberger, and Herbert Fischer

HDU – Hochschule Deggendorf
Edlmairstraße 6+8, 94469 Deggendorf, Germany
{max.dirndorfer,barbara.handy,josef.schneeberger,
herbert.fischer}@fh-deggendorf.de

Abstract. Security and privacy in computer systems is a major issue and it is hard to find a good compromise between necessary protection and desirable open access to the internet. We propose a subject-oriented approach to computer security analysis in order to comply with the users' needs.

Keywords: security, safety, privacy, electronic government, subject-oriented modeling, notaries, business process modeling, subject, object, action.

1   Motivation: Security and Safety in Current IT

Electronic transactions and electronic networking have become a part of our everyday lives. More and more activities and in particular communication is happening via IT systems. The benefits are improved economic efficiency, reduced turnaround times, or independence of location and time. However, electronic transactions imply an increased vulnerability of communication and information (see [1] or [2]). Some content such as personal data requires particular protection. Often security provisions are introduced into an IT infrastructure for purely subjective reasons decided by network administrators with respect to their perception of menace. These provisions may not meet the actual needs of the users and insignificant components are secured while crucial parts remain unprotected. IT security provisions certainly create costs and unnecessary protection is a waste of money. To identify security needs more precisely, we need a suitable concept for the evaluation and description of the respective requirements. We propose a new concept to analyze security requirements in a subjective way using S-BPM.

Our application domain is electronic communication in the context of public administration. In particular, we investigate the communication needs of German notaries in the STERN[1] project. Fig.1 depicts possible interactions between communication partners and the notary. Some of the communication relationships demand strict rules concerning confidentiality and authenticity. In other cases the notary is free to choose a suitable protection level on his own.

---

[1] The STERN Project is funded by the State of Bavaria, Germany. For details see:
http://www.stern-projekt.de/

S. Oppl and A. Fleischmann (Eds.): S-BPM ONE 2012, CCIS 284, pp. 214–219, 2012.
© Springer-Verlag Berlin Heidelberg 2012

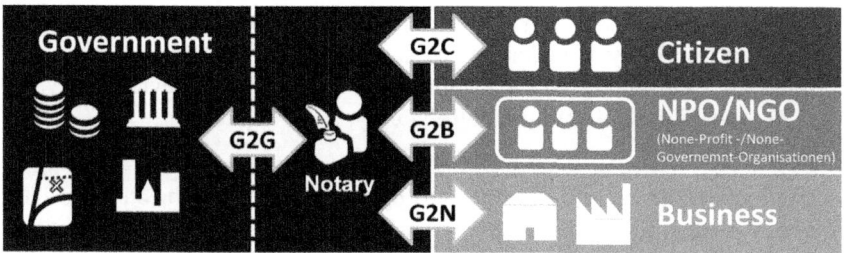

Fig. 1. Communication relations of notaries according to [3]

In the context of the STERN project, we enveloped a *reference model for the no-tarial communication* [4]. It describes notarial communication systems by seven views, e.g. for processes or communication partners. The view *Security, Safety and Quality* plays a vital role in notarial communication. In order to provide a crisp speci-fication we chose a subjective approach which will be presented and discussed in Section 2.

In the literature, the term security describes provisions to prevent cyber attacks while safety measures serve to prevent accidental events. Our model focuses on secu-rity, but we are confident that it may be adapted to safety requirements or even quality requirements in general.

2   The OSA Model

The objective of S-BPM is the division of business processes into subject, predicate (or action [5]), and object. This concept is called OSA model and it is widely used in analogy to the basic structure of natural language sentences [6]. It can be found also used in the IT security literature, for example illustrating the access rights of a com-puter file system (see Fig. 2). Concerning in a communicative act *subjects* are the actors while *actions* are activities and *objects* represent the contents. The subject may be a sender or receiver of the message exchanged.

Fig. 2. A user (subject) reads (action) a file (object) [7]

2.1   Security Objectives in the OSA Model

In the literature on IT security three basic objectives are specified (see [8], [9] or [10]). Furthermore, additional concerns are discussed which may be interpreted as sub-concepts of the basic security issues:

— **Confidentiality:** Anonymity, Pseudonymity, Obscurity, Deniability, Unobservability, Untraceablitiy, Unlinkability
— **Integrity:** Authenticity, Accountability, Non-Repudiability, Reviewability, Liabili-
   ty, Dependability, Reliability, Controllability, Non-Propagation
— **Avalibility**

Federrath and Pfitzmann [11] propose to map these security objectives to the OSA
scheme. We adopt this proposal and introduce a table–the OSA-CIA-matrix[2]–to combine the security objectives with the concepts of subjectivity. For comprehensibility,
we start with a reduced set of security objectives (see Table 1). Each of these objectives may then be analyzed with respect to subject, action, and object.

Table 1. Object, subject, and action in relation to confidentiality, integrity, and availability

	Confidentiality	Integrity	Availability
Objekt (O)	Confidentiality	Integrity	Availability
Subjekt (S)	Anonymity	Authenticity	Availability
Aktion (A)	Unobservability	Accountability	Availability

If, for example, confidentiality of a communication is required the object concerning the communicative act has to be handled confidentially in particular. The subject
of the communicative act is the sender or the receiver and in very confidential cases
the sender and/or receiver may want to remain anonymous. Anonymity here is just
one possible property. Another possibility to protect the subject in a confidential
communication may be the unobservability by transmitting agents. Finally, the action
in a confidential communicative act should not be observable by observing parties.

2.2   Scales for Assessing Security Objectives

To analyze the security objectives in more detail it is helpful to introduce a finer
scale. For example, confidentiality may be interpreted with respect to an organization.
A communicative act may then be confidential with respect to a single person, but
also with respect to a department. A grading may be introduced as follows.

1. *Public*: The contents of a message may be acknowledged by everyone.
2. *Internal*: Only members of an organization may see the message.
3. *Limited*: The content of the message is restricted to the members of a specific
   group.
4. *Confidential*: Access to the message content is restricted by a contract.
5. *Top secret*: The message content is available for named subjects.

Similar scales have to be defined for the other security objectives. We are currently
elaborating corresponding scales for other security objectives [12]. A similar approach in this direction is taken by [8].

---

[2] OSA-CIA-matrix – Subject-Object-Action-Confidentiality-Integrity-Availability Matrix.

2.3   Application of the OSA-CIA Matrix

To illustrate the usage of the OSA-CIA matrix we consider a scenario in which a notary sends a draft contract to his client (Fig. 3). After all subjects, objects, and actions have been identified the entries of the OSA-CIA matrix are rated with respect to security needs.

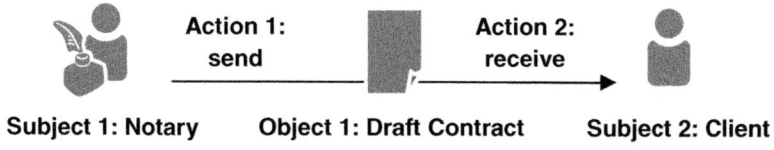

Subject 1: Notary   **Object 1: Draft Contract**   **Subject 2: Client**

Fig. 3. A notary sends a draft contract to his client

In Table 2 we elaborate the objective *Confidentiality*. Due to subject-orientation, every participating subject has to decide which level of security is needed. For the notary the draft is rated internal which means that the notary's staff is allowed to see it. For the client the rating may be confidential, i.e., that only a defined group of people in the company may see it. Anonymity of the notary and the client has to be maintained for the observing public. The unobservability of the sending and receiving actions is internal, i.e. the staff of the company may notify those actions.

Table 2. Possible rating for the example from Figure 3

Confidentiality	Objects (Confidentiality)	Subjects (Anonymity)		Actions (Unobservability)	
View of subject:	Draft Contract	Notary	Client	Send	Receive
Notary	Internal	Public	Public	Internal	Internal
Client	Confidential	Public	Public	Internal	Internal

3   Assignment S-BPM with Security Requirements

Like S-BPM for business processes, the OSA model offers an improved comprehensibility and completeness to analyze security requirements. In S-BPM, a Subject-Interaction-Diagram (SID) exhibits that only authorized subjects may exchange particular objects and the Subject-Behavior-Diagram (SBD) shows the actions that may be taken by a subject. Modeling security requirements in an S-BPM model requires the following three steps:

1. The subjects and objects have to be identified.
2. The object exchange (interaction) of the subjects is modeled in the SID.
3. For each subject the actions (behavior) are modeled and combined in the SBD.

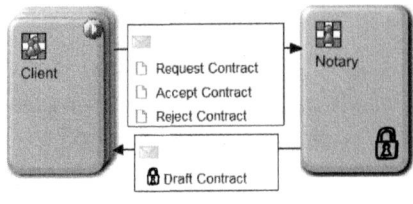
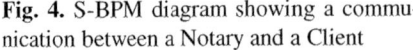
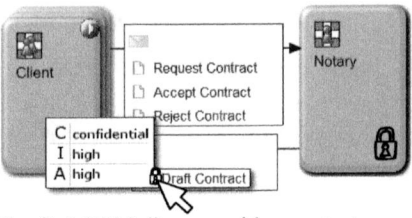

Fig. 4. S-BPM diagram showing a communication between a Notary and a Client

Fig. 5. S-BPM diagram with a context menu for security requirements

Fig. 4 presents the SID as a result of the first step. In the SID two subjects (client and notary) are exchanging objects (the draft contract). In the SBD the actions of the notary are presented. In the following step, the process model and the OSA-CIA matrix will be combined:

— Assign security requirements to each subject, object, and action of the S-BPM model.
— Rate these requirements using adequate scales. If one requirement has multiple different ratings (as shown in Table 2), the highest or strongest security level is chosen.

To provide an integrated illustration of business processes and security requirements, we propose to extend S-BPM diagrams which is shown in Fig. 4 and Fig. 5. Each element with defined security requirements exhibits an icon, e.g. a lock. This allows identifying security critical components easily while retaining the simple and clear appearance of S-BPM diagrams. Using modeling software, clicking on the lock icon may display the specified security requirements.

S-BPM models integrating security requirements may also be exploited by a workflow engine [13]. During the execution of a model, security ratings can be used as a rule set to control the workflow engine and to enforce appropriate security provisions. Additionally, the workflow engine may provide support to select adequate communication channels and necessary technicalities to access them. This approach seems to make it possible to implement a workflow engine that automatically chooses appropriately secured communication channels for the needs of the subjects.

4   Conclusion

We presented an approach to integrate S-BPM with security requirements needed in electronic communication. The results strongly suggest that S-BPM is not only helpful for business processes but can also for security, safety, or quality assessment. Starting from these results, we intend to provide a more detailed OSA-CIA matrix for security objectives. Furthermore, we will evaluate the concept in practice using a lab environment but also on real word scenarios in cooperation with notaries.

Further research on the subject will compare our approach with other approaches integrating security requirements into models EPC, BPMN, and UML (see [14] or [15]). Monacova et al. [16] identifies five requirements for business process models that deal with security and safety: awareness, visibility, consistency, excitability, and provability. All these objectives can be fulfilled by the use of our approach, however, a more detailed elaboration is desirable.

Finally, we would like to express our gratitude to the Bavarian Ministry of Research for founding this research and to the anonymous reviewers of S-BPM-ONE who helped to improve this paper.

References

1. Bettendorf, J.: Dienstordnung und Büro. In: Brambring, G., Jerschke, H.-U. (eds.) Beck'sches Notar-Handbuch, pp. 1665–1711. Beck Juristischer Verlag, München (2009)
2. Armbrüster, C., Preuß, N., Renner, T.: Beurkundungsgesetz und Dienstordnung für Notarinnen und Notare: Kommentar. Gruyter (2008)
3. Wirtz, B.W.: E-Government: Grundlagen, Instrumente, Strategien. Gabler Verlag (2010)
4. Dirndorfer, M.: Konzeption eines Referenzmodells für die notarielle Kommunikation. Unpublished master thesis (2011)
5. Eckert, C.: IT-Sicherheit: Konzepte - Verfahren - Protokolle. Oldenbourg Wissenschaftsverlag (2009)
6. Fleischmann, A.: What Is S-BPM? In: Buchwald, H., Fleischmann, A., Seese, D., Stary, C. (eds.) S-BPM ONE 2009. CCIS, vol. 85, pp. 85–106. Springer, Heidelberg (2010)
7. Johansson, J.M.: Sicherheit auf dem Prüfstand Subjekte und Sicherheitsprinzipale, http://technet.microsoft.com/de-de/query/dd297621
8. Kersten, H., Klett, G.: Der It Security Manager: Expertenwissen für jeden It Security Manager- von namhaften Autoren praxisnah vermittelt. Vieweg + Teubner (2008)
9. Bedner, M., Ackermann, T.: Schutzziele der IT-Sicherheit. Datenschutz und Datensicherheit, 323–328
10. Schumacher, M.: Security patterns: integrating security and systems engineering. John Wiley & Sons (2006)
11. Federrath, H., Pfitzmann, A.: Gliederung und Systematisierung vonSchutzzielen in IT-Systemen. Datenschutz und Datensicherheit, 704–710 (2000)
12. Dirndorfer, M., Handy, B.: Internalpaper on Describing and Documenting IT Security Objectives in the Notarial Context (2011)
13. Fleischmann, A., Stary, C.: Whom to talk to? A stakeholder perspective on business process development. Universal Access in the Information Society (2011)
14. Heinrich, R., Kappe, A., Paech: Modeling Quality Information within Business Process Models. Tagungsband 4. Workshop zur Software-Qualitätsmodellierung und -bewertung, pp. 4–13. Institut für Informatik der TU München (2011)
15. Jensen, M., Feja, S.: A Security Modeling Approach for Web-Service-based Business Processes. In: 16th Annual IEEE International Conference and Workshop on the Engineering of Computer Based Systems, pp. 340–347 (2009)
16. Monakova, G., Brucker, A.D., Schaad, A.: Security and Safety of Assets in Business Processes. In: ACM 27th Symposium on Applied Computing. ACM Press, New York (2012)

TAPIR: Wiki-Based Task and Personal Information Management Supporting Subjective Process Management

Uwe V. Riss

SAP Research
Vincenz-Priessnitz-Str. 1, 76131 Karlsruhe, Germany
uwe.riss@sap.com

Abstract. We introduce a subject-driven approach to integrated process, task, and information management for knowledge workers. This approach is realized in the Task and Personal Information Rendering (TAPIR) extension of the Semantic Mediawiki that we present in this paper. The focus is placed on eliciting subjective process information from daily task management. The approach starts from the insight that individuals' motivation to provide relevant process information can be increased if they directly benefit from their contributions. TAPIR uses process relevant information to support users in their task management. Hereby it fosters S-BPM by gathering subjective process information that can be used for organizational purposes.

Keywords: task management, subject-orientation, personal semantic desktop wiki.

1   Introduction

The increasing importance of Knowledge Work (KW) [11,25] leads to the question how information systems can better support knowledge workers in their work processes. It is the highly dynamic and information centric working style of knowledge workers [8] that determines the central barrier for process support in KW. Business Process Management (BPM) has not become obsolete in KW since it still encompasses a considerable portion of recurring activities. However, the costs for traditional upfront modeling are increasing while the resulting models regularly encounter outdatedness [17]. In addition, more dynamic work styles lead to increasing task complexity and need for task related information [4].

Several approaches have been proposed to overcome the current limits of BPM, aiming at a Subject-oriented Business Process Management (S-BPM) [12]. Many of them involve end-users in process modeling, referring to the paradigm of End-user Development (EUD) [20]. Thus, EUD has become an acknowledged paradigm in S-BPM. However, EUD faces a gap between actual individual performance and subjective modeling. Moreover, it has to deal with issues of the users' motivation to contribute to modeling as well as users' modeling competence. The

S. Oppl and A. Fleischmann (Eds.): S-BPM ONE 2012, CCIS 284, pp. 220–235, 2012.
© Springer-Verlag Berlin Heidelberg 2012

former issue originates from the fact that modeling is always a peripheral activity that suffers from the well-known knowledge sharing dilemma [6]. Consequently, EUD activities must visibly help users accomplish their ordinary work [12].

In the current approach we refer to the idea of process-oriented Knowledge Maturing where the latter aims at organizational learning as a seamless process from individual performance to formalized representations at the organizational level [31]. More concretely, users provide task information that is then aggregated to process knowledge and checked by recurring application. This knowledge life-cycle constitutes a maturing process. This view is in line with that of Fleischmann and Stary, who have stressed the importance of increasing the organization's learning capacity to meet the demands of knowledge-intensive processes [12]. The crucial point is how such a lifecycle can be efficiently established.

The proposed solution integrates (organizational) Process and (personal) Task Management [28]. In the same way as EUD, it aims at involving users in process development by integration of task and process handling. Here processes are to be automatically derived from task handling so that an elaborate process modeling environment is not required. In addition, we assume that all task handling in KW is interwoven with Personal Information Management [34]. To address all of these demands we propose a lightweight wiki-based tool that is realized as a Task and Personal Information Rendering (TAPIR) extension of the popular Semantic Mediawiki [19].

The paper is organized as follows. In Section 2 we recapitulate some of the central requirements of knowledge-intensive process compiling results of existing literature. In Section 3 we described the TAPIR approach in more details and explain how it is related to existing solutions. In Section 4 we describe the implementation of the TAPIR extension. Section 5 explains how it addresses the mentioned challenges and we provide some quantitative results of a 6 month test phase. In Section 6 we discuss the similarities and differences to other approaches. In Section 7 we conclude the presentation with a discussion of the solution and give some outlook on the next development steps.

2   State of the Art in Knowledge Work Support

In the following we will compile the central KW requirements and their relevance for subjective process management. Recently Grebner [13] determined 6 topics that support tools for KW should cover:

- *Task Management*: Planning and structuring individual tasks.
- *Time Management*: Controlling the order and priority of work.
- *Personal Social Network Management*: Maintaining and overlooking one's personal network of collaborators.
- *Event Management*: Organizing one's meetings and events.
- *Information Management*: Collecting, organizing, and navigating through one's personal information.
- *Collaboration Management*: Communicating and collaborating with others.

These requirements are strongly influenced by the overlap of process, task, and information management in KW mentioned before. Similar requirements can be found for the Semantic Desktop as another solution that supports KW (see Sauermann et al. [30]). It addresses the problem of a disintegrated desktop environment for KW. Hereby they mean that information is spread over various desktop applications and repositories, requiring user interventions that consume a considerable amount of time. The respective requirements are described as:

- *Application Integration*: Integration of information objects over different desktop applications.
- *Networked Navigation*: Providing a networked navigation structure over these information objects.
- *Openness*: Possibility of personal extensions of the information model.

Völkel, Schaffert, and Oren [35] argue for a semantic-web solution for KW support and specify following requirements:

- *Acceptable Costs of Use*: Minimizing the effort for maintaining the support system and its semantic metadata.
- *Individual Focus*: Freeing knowledge workers of undue restrictions.
- *Flexible Classification*: Adaptable information objects for different purposes.
- *Link Following*: Enabling networked information navigation instead of offering advanced search.
- *Contextuality*: Adapting information to the context in which it is needed.
- *Value of Paper and Free Notes*: Allowing users to take notes in a simple way.
- *Simplicity*: Providing an easy-to-use tool that does not hamper the core work.
- *Keeping the Flow*: Avoiding interrupts in KW core activities.

Although process management does not directly appear in these requirements, it is always affected due to the described relatedness of information, task, and process management in KW. This also holds for email integration, a KW demand that is known for a long time [37,36]. In Section 6 we will come back to these requirements and discuss how TAPIR fulfills them.

3 Approach

The TAPIR approach combines wiki-based personal information management with task and process management based on a common semantic infrastructure. Its primary design goal is support of personal task and information management. However, this approach also opens up opportunities for handling subjective processes. A central goal is to enable knowledge workers to organize their personal tasks and monitor the implicitly evolving processes. Since processes are usually not in the focus of individual users it is helpful to educe added value of subjective process handling. Indeed, user motivation plays an eminent role [27]. Here we face especially one central problem: How can we overcome the barrier imposed by the necessary abstraction from individual tasks to recurrent activities? This problem is addressed by the use of Task Patterns [32,26]. However, before we go into details we first describe how TAPIR handles personal information, objects, tasks, and subjective processes.

3.1 Personal Information Management

We have pursued the idea of Personal Semantic Wikis [24,23] since they provide a number of interesting features. First, they allow for the integration of unstructured text and structured semantic annotations. While free text makes it easy for users to produce content at low costs, semantic representation is indispensable for intelligent information retrieval and process extraction. Even if wikis as primarily used for collaborative purposes this does not exclude a personal use but rather assists it. This combination of properties renders the Personal Semantic Wiki an ideal platform for S-BPM.

Another idea that influenced the current development is that of the Semantic Desktop [9,30]. The semantic desktop describes a user interface that allows users to define metadata about information objects on the desktop between different desktop applications. The idea to bring Personal Semantic Wiki and Semantic Desktop together has been brought up by Kiesel and Sauermann, who suggested the idea of a combined Semantic Desktop Wiki [18]. The TAPIR approach realizes this idea. Additionally we have integrated the handling of email which essentially contributes to the lightweight character of the solution.

3.2 Task and Process Management

Conceptualizing the task-enabled wiki we could profit from the experience gained from the integration of Task Management in the Nepomuk Semantic Desktop that we have called Semantic Task Management [22]. It provides the technical basis for Task Patterns as shared representations for a set of similar tasks. We have reused this concept in TAPIR to support the transition from individual task to collaborative process handling.

Talking about integration in these various facets it is to be emphasized that integration has not been considered as a goal in itself but as a means to realize Knowledge Maturing. Hereby we mean the continuous enhancement of knowledge and the artifacts representing it by suitable technology [31]. In fact, it has been argued that especially Wikis provide a favorable framework for supporting the maturing process [21]. The reason is that they allows for the coexistence of and gradual transition between maturing phases with individual and organizational focus. They are suitable for capturing personal notes as well as structured tasks, describing singular work activities and fostering collaborative and organizational knowledge sharing. Regarding the latter aspect wikis have also been suggested as platform for collaborative business process management [10].

A crucial step in the approach is still the transition from individual task handling to process descriptions. The use of Task Patterns mitigates this problem since they provide intermediate artifacts for capturing process knowledge, allowing for a smoother transition from tasks to processes. Consequently the system design aims at making the Task Pattern definition for users as easy and straightforward as possible. This will be explained in the next section.

4   Implementation

TAPIR has been implemented as an extension of the Semantic Mediawiki (SMW), which again is an extension of Mediawiki [2]. Mediawiki is one of the currently most popular wiki implementations worldwide and the technical platform of Wikipedia. Its basic wiki functionality allows providing information in the form of texts on wiki pages. The semantic extension enables structured information handling, mainly by semantic annotating the content of wiki pages by additional metadata. The TAPIR extension, finally, supports advanced task handling including subjective process management.

4.1   Information Management

The TAPIR extension includes certain categories for personal information objects such as events, documents, tasks, persons, emails, tags and others. Each of these objects is represented by a wiki page. These categories are inspired by PIMO, a data format for KW information objects developed in the Nepomuk project [29]. In contrast to the Nepomuk approach TAPIR omits a dedicated ontology for information objects in favor of a view concept. This means that all objects (or pages) are endued with a common set of properties such as *HasTitle*, *HasAuthor* etc. that can be specifically interpreted in different contexts. For instance, the property *HasTitle* appears as Subject if the information object is displayed in an email view but can also appear as Title in a document view. TAPIR determines a meaningful view, based on the set properties, and renders the corresponding views. To this end it considers the context of an object, for instance, whether it is specified as a resource on some page, and offers the respective view. In case that several views are possible TAPIR offers all of them. Every view possesses a specific semantic form that allows users to easily edit the information object (e.g., a task edit form, or a person edit form). It has been an early experience of the implementation that such view-based information architecture better suits the flexibility requirements of KW since it allows objects to implicitly change their category if suitable. For example, a person can become a tag when it is used as such on any page.

In Fig. 1 we see an example of a page representing a task. Such pages generally show three parts. The upper part offers a set of *actions* to be performed on the task (one of TAPIR's main contributions to SMW). Here users can create new objects such as subtasks or related emails, or request additional information about the process instance to which the task belongs. The middle section in Fig. 1 (indicated by the headline Task View) provides structured information about the information object. Only the most important properties are displayed by default while other properties (e.g., about used task patterns) are only displayed if they

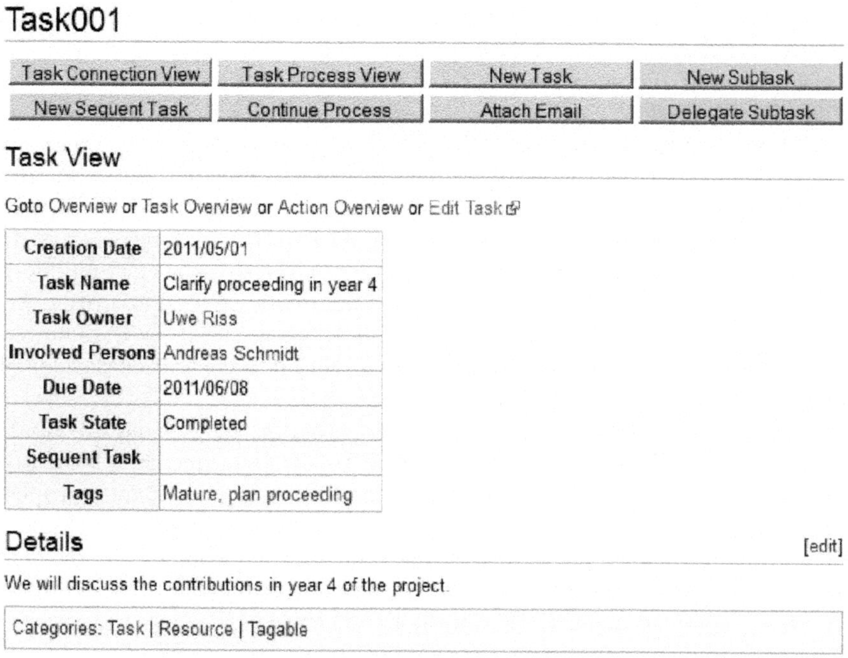

Task001

| Task Connection View | Task Process View | New Task | New Subtask |
| New Sequent Task | Continue Process | Attach Email | Delegate Subtask |

Task View

Goto Overview or Task Overview or Action Overview or Edit Task &

Creation Date	2011/05/01
Task Name	Clarify proceeding in year 4
Task Owner	Uwe Riss
Involved Persons	Andreas Schmidt
Due Date	2011/06/08
Task State	Completed
Sequent Task	
Tags	Mature, plan proceeding

Details   [edit]

We will discuss the contributions in year 4 of the project.

Categories: Task | Resource | Tagable

Fig. 1. Information objects displayed in the *Task View*

are actually set. The bottom section in Fig. 1 (indicated by the headline 'Details') shows a text area that users can edit to scribble down their personal notes about the information object. Throughout the page links to related information objects are provided (following the network idea of the Semantic Desktop).

We have integrated email via a connection to MS Outlook. By a click in the context menu an email is transferred from MS Outlook to TAPIR. It is also possible to create emails in TAPIR, which can then be sent by an additional click via MS Outlook to the recipients. Users are only supposed to include emails in TAPIR if these contain information to which they are likely to revert later, for instance, as part of task execution. Finally, TAPIR offers knowledge workers aggregating overview pages for different information object categories such as a *Task Overview*, an *Event Overview*, an *Email Overview* and others. These overview pages are realized by using the inline query language (*ASK* syntax) offered by SMW so that users can modify them.

4.2   Task Management

The used task model is derived from that of the Nepomuk Semantic Desktop [14]. In addition to the usual task attributes such as due date, task state or tags, TAPIR supports the assignment of task patterns, involved persons, and resources. An included free text area (the bottom area in Fig. 1) can be used for task protocols. Users cannot only assign persons, resources and subtasks but also specify their roles in the task. For examples, a task can contain a *Hotel Booking* subtask or a *Booking Confirmation* resource. These role assignments help users in task planning and understanding and motivate the use of such roles.

The TAPIR Task View (Fig. 1) offers specific task functionality, implemented as PHP-based extensions of the SMW. Thus, users can immediately create tasks in all work situations. For example, receiving an email they add it to TAPIR and create a new task. TAPIR automatically transfers specific context information (e.g., involved persons or tags) from the email to the task template and frees users from copy and paste activities. Semantic relationships to existing information objects (e.g., the original email) are automatically created according to the current work context. This reduces the annotation overhead for the knowledge workers. Here we refer to the idea of implicit metadata generation developed in Nepomuk [15].

Relationships between tasks play a central role in TAPIR and are used for process analysis. We distinguish two central types: (1) sequence relations, and (2) subsidiary relations. They are implemented by different semantic properties [[*SequentTask* ::< wiki page name >]] and [[*Subtask* ::< wiki page name >]], respectively. The first type describes the temporal sequence of loosely related tasks. For instance, a user has a accomplished a task but later starts follow-up activities. Therefore sequence relationships can be used for reoccurring tasks such as regular meetings. Subsidiary (or subtask) relationships reflect the fact that the completion of the superior task depends on the execution of the subsidiary task as in the case of going on a business trip and booking the necessary flight.

Currently, TAPIR supports 6 different actions on task, displayed in the top section of Fig. 1: (1) creation of new independent tasks; (2) creation of new subtasks; (3) creation of new sequent tasks; (4) process continuation (see process section below); (5) creation of related emails; (6) delegation of subtasks (via email). The two latter actions are related to email handling and reflect the importance of email in KW. In operation (5) an email template is prefilled with context information. By submitting the template users get a prefilled email form including a link that creates the corresponding email in MS Outlook. This reduces the additional effort for the user and fosters semantic integration. When a reply email arrives in MS Outlook the user can directly transfer the email information to TAPIR by a click in the email's context menu. Assignment of incoming emails to tasks is immediately possible. Thus, the entire delegation process is handled via emails and covered by corresponding tasks in TAPIR.

4.3   Process Management

We now come to the S-BPM relevant process management aspects of TAPIR. The traditional way to extract such information is Process Mining [1]. TAPIR aggregates users' task information and relations to derive subjective process descriptions. The existing relationships between tasks yield the required information about process instances. However, general processes require a more abstract description than individual process instances. Unfortunately Process Mining still requires a process engineer to interpret the mined data. In knowledge work this becomes especially tricky since task structures are often rather blurry [7]. This makes the identification of abstract activities rather difficult.

The central support in abstracting processes consists in introducing Task Patterns [32,26], which serve to aggregate process knowledge [12,3]. Hereby we mean that they are designed for sharing common task experience as well as for application to individual tasks. This goal requires a seamless integration of task and task pattern management and support for abstraction; Task Patterns contain person roles, object roles, and subtask roles (also called Sub-Task Patterns since they are represented by task patterns) rather than concrete persons, objects, and subtasks. This is the point where TAPIR's role concept comes into play. To motivate the definition and assignment of roles the system offers them to better explain subjective processes giving them a general and reusable structure. In this way Task Patterns become helpful even if they are only used privately and for personal purposes.

While object and person roles are explicitly defined, subtask roles are identified with assigned task patterns. For instance, let us assume that a user has specified $TaskA$, for which she has defined a subtask $TaskB$. Let us further assume that both tasks are associated with Task Patterns $TaskPatternA'$ and $TaskPatternB'$, respectively. TAPIR interprets the specified relationships as a relationship between the two Task Patterns, as depicted in Fig. 2. First results of daily use have shown that this procedures works quite well. The crucial point is that this procedure yields elementary process chunks, which can be then connected to larger processes.

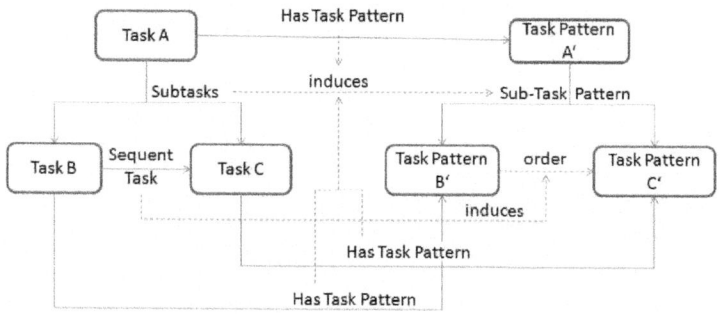

Fig. 2. Induction of elementary process relations via Task Patterns

4.4   Subjective Process Support

Three views realize process support: (1) a *Task Connection View*, (2) a *Task Process View*, and (3) a *Process View*. Task pages only offer the *Task Connection View* and the *Task Process View* (see Fig. 1). The *Task Connection View* (Fig. 3) presents the depending subtask and sequent tasks of a task, including descriptions, such as associated task patterns and tags. In contrast, the *Task Process View* (Fig. 4) is exclusively process oriented.

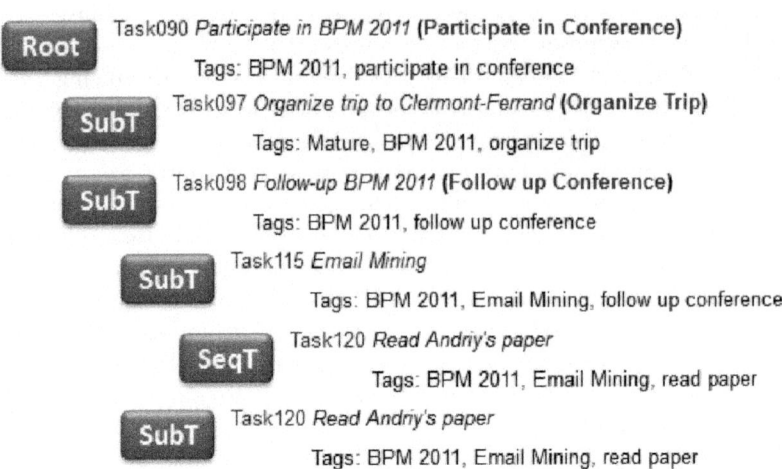

Fig. 3. Task Connection View

Fig. 3 depicts the Task Connection View. It shows the task hierarchy for a task its sequence and subsidiary relationships to other tasks. It explains how a task is connected to others. It also indicates whether the user has already created a task for a specific process activity. The displayed sequence of relationships describes the order of tasks in the process. Each task pattern associated with a task is displayed but the view also shows relationships to tasks that are not (yet) assigned to task patterns and therefore do not fit into an abstract process descriptions.

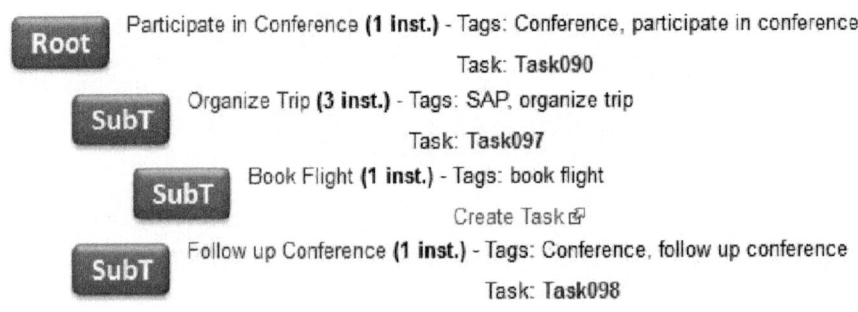

Fig. 4. Task Process View

In contrast to the previous view, the *Task Process View* takes a process centric perspective but relates it to the task, from which the view has been called. It shows how this task fits into the process and for which process activities (represented by task patterns) the user has already defined tasks. Activities, for which the user has not yet created a task, show a link that allows the user to create such task. If the user creates this task the context information regarding the respective superior task, involved persons, and tags is transferred to the new task and the sequence relation between the task, from which the view has been called, and the new task is automatically defined. In this way the new task is properly embedded in the process without additional effort for defining the respective metadata. Finally the view gives users additional information about the tags assigned to a task and how often a specific activity has been executed in previous processes in order to show its relevance.

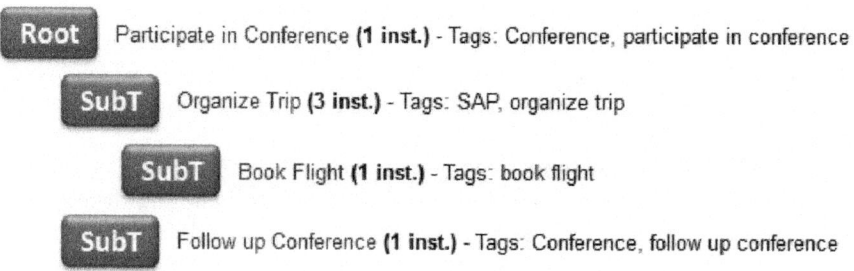

Fig. 5. Process View

On the Task Pattern page a third function is offered that does not contain any (private) task information at all. It represents a public view of the respective process that can be shared among users. This demonstrates the advantage of generalization and depersonalization, which, however, usually comes along with considerable maintenance costs. The view also displays additional individual information, namely, which of the user's task is assigned to this pattern. From here users can switch to the respective tasks and use the two task-centric views that are more suitable for task handling.

The embedding of a task also offers another advantage for the user. This is the transfer of person and resource related information from one task in the process to another task. For instance if a user defines a resource with a specific role in a task that belongs to a process, this resource including its role can be transferred to another task created in this process. The same abstraction principle then tells which resource types are used throughout the process. In this way the system guides users how to continue a process and supports this continuation by data transfer.

5   Evaluative Results

First, we briefly discuss to which extent TAPIR addressed the requirements that we have compiled in Section 2. We find the following features: (1) *Task Management*: TAPIR provides a seamless integration of information, task, and process management. (2) *Time Management*: TAPIR supports the sequencing of tasks and thus indirectly also sequences in processes that help users in their time management. Additionally it provides a task overview that simplifies activity planning. (3) *Event Management*: For every event corresponding tasks (e.g., preparation or follow-up activities) can be defined and directly related to the event. (4) *Information Management*: TAPIR allows users to start tasks from information objects and to assign information objects to roles. The respective information is depersonalized so that it can augment process descriptions and increase their value for the individual user. (5) *Collaboration Management*: Collaboration via email is supported and the respective information is used in process derivation.

Regarding the second set of requirements we find: (1) *Application Integration*: Process management is realized as part of integrated task and information management. (2) *Networked Navigation*: TAPIR allows seamless navigation between all information objects. (3) *Openness*: The SMW is framework in which openness is realized. As we said before, however, there are certain limits of flexibility in process management.

The final set of requirements is supported in the following way: (1) *Acceptable of Cost of Use*: TAPIR reduces the costs of metadata handling decisively and makes process management part of a setting to reduce individual task management costs. (1) *Individual Focus*: User can define their own proceedings. Streamlining of individual procedures is not the focus of the current project. (2) *Contextuality*: This is realized by the integration of task and process management, in which tasks provide the required context. (3) *Value of Paper and Notes*: This is only supported by the possibility to provide free-text notes. (4) *Simplicity Keeping the Flow*: First experience in using TAPIR has shown that especially the integration of task and process management helps keep the flow of work. Implicit metadata generation in transitions between task and process management also help in this respect. This also concerns the handling of task patterns, which has been a distractive activity in previous solution such as *Kasimir*. In TAPIR their handling becomes easier since considerable information is automatically transferred between tasks to task patterns. The simple assignment of a task pattern is often enough to enhance the process perspective.

After these rather qualitative results we also provide some quantitative results for the use of TAPIR. These are based on the author's use of TAPIR for 6 months. Within this period 250 tasks have been created. The number of tasks created per day might appear rather low but we also have to take the duration of these tasks into account. Therefore we investigated those 218 tasks that have already been finalized regarding their duration and found that the average duration of each task is 26,7 days (from creation to closing). This means that on average users deal with more than 7 open tasks in parallel. Moreover, we have to take into account that mainly complex tasks appear in TAPIR's task management while most simple tasks are executed directly. However, there is one interesting aspect to note: While the average duration for the first 100 tasks was 35,5 days, duration for the second 100 tasks was only 17,9 days. This means that in the course of time TAPIR has been used in a more targeted way. Concerning the use of task patterns there are also significant differences between these two groups. During the first 100 tasks there were only 12 tasks to which task pattern had been assigned. The reasons were a missing selection of task patterns as well as missing functionality that supported the use of task patterns. This changed in the course of time so that in the second 100 tasks task patterns were assigned to 52 tasks. The average duration of these tasks were 21,0 days, that is, longer than on average. Obviously that they were mostly used for more complex tasks. The total number of task patterns was 36 after 6 months; in general 15% of all tasks were assigned to task patterns. 28% of them describe tasks that belong to complex hierarchical process while 72% belong to reoccurring individual tasks. For each task pattern we find 1,76 tasks on average that are assigned to it. 6 task patterns that belong to hierarchical processes are root tasks, that is, they can be regarded as proper processes. The average number of process step in there is 5.2, that is, these processes are far from trivial. One of the reasons for their definition has been to remember the reoccurring steps in further applications. To summarize the results we can say that after an initial phase the features were better understood and used. Task patterns became a regularly used feature that were applied to more than 50% of all tasks. Further evaluation might be necessary but we can already say that TAPIR has provided some insight into the structure of daily KW and helped reveal relevant KW processes including the aggregation of related process information.

6   Connections to Related Approaches

Central ideas of TAPIR are inspired by the Nepomuk Semantic Desktop (NSD) [16] and its task management component *Kasimir* [14]. The NSD also gives users the freedom to structure their information space according to their needs. However, there are decisive differences. *Kasimir* and the NSD are mainly Java-based and there is no wiki as core component. Moreover, the NSD relies on various ontologies based on the personal information model PIMO. TAPIR tries to realize semantic technologies without formal ontologies. All central objects share the same set of properties and only differ with respect to specific views (see above). Another related application based on the NSD is SPONGE [5]. It is a collection of gadgets that offer functionalities to manage personal information and to seamlessly share such information within knowledge networks. However, as other Nepomuk-based tools it does not possess a dedicated focus on task management although it sees task handling as a central requirement. A direct extension of *Kasimir*, developed in the MATURE project, is the more process adapted *KISSmir* application [38]. It uses Task Management to enhance knowledge-intensive process management. *KISSmir* also uses task patterns as flexible extensions of process activities but lacks semantic information integration and treats modeled processes and individual tasks separately.

Another process oriented solution that uses task patterns is *Collaborative Task Management* (CTM) [33]. With *Kasimir* and TAPIR it shares the idea that process management in KW should be based on end-user contributions. However, CTM follows the strategy of End-user Development (EUD), that is, the inclusion of end-users in process modeling activities. TAPIR avoids imposing process development on end-users and aims at implicit process extraction from tasks and task patterns. In TAPIR process-relevant steps (e.g., task pattern definition) are supported by the system and embedded in other activities. All approaches share the idea of subject-oriented Business Process Management (S-BPM) [12] including user participation and the avoidance of program changes.

Naturally TAPIR resembles other personal wikis such as *SemperWiki* (see [23] and reference of other examples in there). With these approaches we share the idea that wiki technology is not only beneficial for collaboration but also for individual use in KW. However, in contrast to TAPIR, these wikis are primarily focusing on Personal Information Management and neglect task and process management. An exception is *Wikiing Pro* that also strives for collaborative process management and is also based on SMW, [10]. It follows the same maturing idea as TAPIR but does not involve a task management from which processes can be derived.

7   Discussion

This paper has presented the TAPIR extension of the SMW as a task and process enabled personal Wiki. It incorporates MATURE's Knowledge Maturing idea that the development of process knowledge starts from individual tasks by information aggregation in task patterns. A central advantage of this approach is the immediate update of process information and the seamless transition from tasks to processes. There is no intermediate process mining and modeling step through which process information has to pass. Process engineers can work with aggregated processes that actually take place and compare them to modeled processes. The TAPIR approach cannot replace modeled processes, which additionally contain organizational aspects not covered by the described bottom-up processes, but it can definitely provide relevant process information to individual users as well as process designers.

TAPIR has not been designed as a substitute for existing subject-oriented BPM approaches that often focus on End-user Development but it aims at supporting such bottom-up design activities by exploiting the knowledge workers' daily task handling. This is done without violating the privacy of these knowledge workers. Furthermore, users are motivated to partake in process modeling activities since they can directly profit from such activities.

In a preliminary user test TAPIR has been used for task and personal information management for 6 months in order to identify and remove the main barriers for its application. In the course of this preliminary use it has become clear that the smooth integration of email is an importaqnt step towards unintrusive task mangement that fundamentally relies on the use of email. Thus, 170 emails have been added to tasks to show where a task comes from or to demonstrate the execution by emailing information; on average 63% of the tasks are related to emails. A second insight has been that the use of ontologies rather hampers the efficiency of the system than increasing it. Nevertheless TAPIR clearly is a semantic application. Another identified benefit is that users get an overview of relations between their previously and currently executed subjective processes.

This is reflected in an increasing use of the sequence relationship between tasks: 39% of the first 100 tasks used it while 53% of the second 100 tasks. The offered task management functionality outpaces simple to-do lists. New tasks can be created within a given process and context that information helps enrich newly created tasks. In particular, implicit metadata creation reduces the effort of annotation and increases the attractiveness of the approach.

Although the use of process features in TAPIR is already quite smooth there is still potential for further improvement, especially regarding the exploitation of process information. Implicit metadata creation can still be extended. One additional step could be a better integration of event and meeting management. Many events require quite specific and extended processes with respect to their preparation and follow-up activities. Although the explication of process models is central for reflection the methods how to come up with these are not yet fully developed. Users appreciate more transparence of their work, which can only be realized by better bridging the gap between concrete (subjective) tasks and abstract (objective) process models. Here further support appears to be valuable.

Acknowledgments. The conceptual part of this work has been supported by the European Union IST fund through the EU FP7 MATURE Integrating Project (Grant No. 216356).

References

1. van der Aalst, W.M.P., Weijters, A.J.M.M.: Process mining: A research agenda. Comput. Ind. 53(3), 231–244 (2004)
2. Barrett, D.J.: Mediawiki. O'Reilly Media (2008)
3. Brown, J.S., Duguid, P.: Organizing Knowledge. California Management Review 40(3), 90–111 (1998)
4. Byström, K., Järvelin, K.: Task complexity affects information seeking and use. Information Processing and Management 31(2), 191–213 (1995)
5. Christidis, K., Papailiou, N., Apostolou, D., Mentzas, G.: Semantic Interfaces for Personal and Social Knowledge Work. Int. J. of Knowl.-Based Org. 1(1), 61–77 (2011)
6. Cress, U., Barquero, B., Buder, J., Hesse, F.W.: Social dilemmas in knowledge communication via shared databases. In: Bromme, R., Hesse, F.W., Spada, H. (eds.) Barriers and Biases in Computer-Mediated Knowledge Communication - and How they may be Overcome, pp. 143–167. Springer, New York (2005)
7. Czerwinski, M., Horvitz, E., Wilhite, S.: A diary study of task switching and interruptions. In: Proc. of the SIGCHI Conference on Human Factors in Computing Systems, CHI 2004, pp. 175–182. ACM, New York (2004)
8. Davenport, T.H.: Thinking for a Living: How to Get Better Performances And Results from Knowledge Workers. Harvard Business Press (2005)
9. Decker, S., Frank, M.: The Social Semantic Desktop. Tech. rep., DERI Galway (2004)
10. Dengler, F., Vrandečić, D.: Wiki-Based Maturing of Process Descriptions. In: Rinderle-Ma, S., Toumani, F., Wolf, K. (eds.) BPM 2011. LNCS, vol. 6896, pp. 313–328. Springer, Heidelberg (2011)
11. Drucker, P.F.: The new productivity challenge. Harv. Bus. Rev. 69(6), 69 (1991)

12. Fleischmann, A., Stary, C.: Key Features of Subject-Oriented Modeling and Organizational Deployment Tools. In: Stephanidis, C. (ed.) UAHCI Part IV, HCII 2011. LNCS, vol. 6768, pp. 205–214. Springer, Heidelberg (2011)
13. Grebner, O.: Using Personal Information Management Infrastructures to Facilitate User-Generated Services for Personal Use. In: Dan, A., Gittler, F., Toumani, F. (eds.) ICSOC/ServiceWave 2009. LNCS, vol. 6275, pp. 560–569. Springer, Heidelberg (2010)
14. Grebner, O., Ong, E., Riss, U.V.: KASIMIR – Work process embedded task management leveraging the Semantic Desktop. In: Multikonferenz Wirtschaftsinformatik (MKWI 2008), pp. 715–726. GITO-Verlag, Berlin (2008)
15. Grebner, O., Riss, U.V.: Implicit Metadata Generation on the Semantic Desktop Using Task Management as Example. In: Borgo, S., Lesmo, L. (eds.) Formal Ontologies Meet Industry. Frontiers in Artificial Intelligence and Applications, vol. 174, pp. 33–44. IOS Press, Amsterdam (2008)
16. Grimnes, G.A., Sauermann, L., Bernardi, A.: The Personal Knowledge Workbench of the NEPOMUK Semantic Desktop. In: Aroyo, L., Traverso, P., Ciravegna, F., Cimiano, P., Heath, T., Hyvönen, E., Mizoguchi, R., Oren, E., Sabou, M., Simperl, E. (eds.) ESWC 2009. LNCS, vol. 5554, pp. 836–840. Springer, Heidelberg (2009)
17. Kemsley, S.: Enterprise 2.0 Meets Business Process Management Handbook on Business Process Management 1. In: vom Brocke, J., Rosemann, M. (eds.) Handbook on Business Process Management 1. International Handbooks on Information Systems, ch. 26, pp. 565–574. Springer (2010)
18. Kiesel, M., Sauermann, L.: Towards Semantic Desktop Wikis. Upgrade VI(6), 30–34 (2005)
19. Krötzsch, M., Vrandečić, D., Völkel, M.: Semantic MediaWiki. In: Cruz, I., Decker, S., Allemang, D., Preist, C., Schwabe, D., Mika, P., Uschold, M., Aroyo, L.M. (eds.) ISWC 2006. LNCS, vol. 4273, pp. 935–942. Springer, Heidelberg (2006)
20. Lieberman, H., Paternò, F., Wulf, V.: End User Development. Human-Computer Interaction Series. Springer (2006)
21. Maier, R., Schmidt, A.: Characterizing Knowledge Maturing: A Conceptual Process Model for Integrating E-Learning and Knowledge Management. In: 4th Conference Professional Knowledge Management, pp. 325–334. GITO-Verlag (2007)
22. Ong, E., Riss, U.V., Grebner, O., Du, Y.: Semantic Task Management Framework: Bridging Information and Work. In: Pellegrini, T., Auer, S., Tochtermann, K., Schaffert, S. (eds.) Networked Knowledge - Networked Media. SCI, vol. 221, pp. 25–43. Springer, Heidelberg (2009)
23. Oren, E.: SemperWiki: a semantic personal Wiki. In: Semantic Desktop Workshop, ISWC (2005)
24. Oren, E., Völkel, M., Breslin, J.G., Decker, S.: Semantic Wikis for Personal Knowledge Management. In: Bressan, S., Küng, J., Wagner, R. (eds.) DEXA 2006. LNCS, vol. 4080, pp. 509–518. Springer, Heidelberg (2006)
25. Pyöriä, P.: The concept of knowledge work revisited. Journal of Knowledge Management 9(3), 116–127 (2005)
26. Riss, U.V.: Pattern-Based Task Management as Means of Organizational Knowledge Maturing. Int. J. of Knowl.-Based Org. 1(1), 20–41 (2011)
27. Riss, U.V., Cress, U., Kimmerle, J., Martin, S.: Knowledge transfer by sharing task templates: two approaches and their psychological requirements. Knowledge Management Research & Practice 5(4), 287–296 (2007)
28. Riss, U.V., Rickayzen, A., Maus, H., van der Aalst, W.M.P.: Challenges for Business Process and Task Management. JUKM (2), 77–100 (2005)

29. Sauermann, L., van Elst, L., Dengel, A.: Pimo - a framework for representing personal information models. In: Proc. of I-MEDIA 2007 and I-SEMANTICS 2007, Graz, Austria, pp. 270–277 (2007)
30. Sauermann, L., Kiesel, M., Schumacher, K., Bernardi, A.: Semantic Desktop. In: Blumauer, A., Pellegrini, T. (eds.) Social Semantic Web, ch. 17, pp. 337–362. X.media.press, Springer, Berlin, Heidelberg (2009)
31. Schmidt, A.: Knowledge Maturing and the Continuity of Context as a Unifying Concept for Knowledge Management and E-Learning. In: Proc. of I-KNOW 2005, Graz, Austria (2005)
32. Schmidt, B., Riss, U.V.: Task Patterns as Means to Experience Sharing. In: Spaniol, M., Li, Q., Klamma, R., Lau, R.W.H. (eds.) ICWL 2009. LNCS, vol. 5686, pp. 353–362. Springer, Heidelberg (2009)
33. Stoitsev, T., Scheidl, S., Flentge, F., Muhlhauser, M.: Enabling end-user driven business process composition through programming by example in a Collaborative Task management system. IEEE Computer Society, Los Alamitos (2008)
34. Teevan, J., Jones, W. (eds.): Personal Information Management. University of Washington Press (2007)
35. Völkel, M., Schaffert, S., Oren, E.: Personal Knowledge Management with Semantic Technologies. In: Rech, J., Decker, B., Ras, E. (eds.) Emerging Technologies for Semantic Work Environments, ch. 9, pp. 138–153. IGI Global (2008)
36. Whittaker, S., Bellotti, V., Gwizdka, J.: Everything through Email. In: Teevan, J., Jones, W. (eds.) Personal Information Management, pp. 167–189. University of Washington Press (2007)
37. Whittaker, S., Sidner, C.: Email overload: exploring personal information management of email. In: Proc. of the SIGCHI Conference on Human Factors in Computing Systems: Common Ground, CHI 1996, pp. 276–283. ACM, New York (1996)
38. Witschel, H.F., Hu, B., Riss, U.V., Thönssen, B., Brun, R., Martin, A., Hinkelmann, K.: A Collaborative Approach to Maturing Process-Related Knowledge. In: Hull, R., Mendling, J., Tai, S. (eds.) BPM 2010. LNCS, vol. 6336, pp. 343–358. Springer, Heidelberg (2010)

The Effect of Process-Oriented Organizational Design on Firm Performance: A Comparison of Manufacturing and Service Organizations

Doris Weitlaner

Graz University of Technology
Institute of General Management and Organization
Kopernikusgasse 24/IV, 8010 Graz, Austria
doris.weitlaner@student.tugraz.at

Business process orientation (BPO) is a concept where the firm's organizational design focuses on business processes ranging from customer to customer rather than on the functional structure. Various authors and studies refer to a positive impact of BPO on firm performance, building the study's underlying research hypothesis. Although literature in this field is growing, certain gaps still remain. The Master's Thesis contributes to a greater clarity and better understanding of how BPO influences firm performance in two ways. First, the study respects the multidimensional nature of BPO. The firm's exhibited BPO degree is measured along the dimensions process knowledge/documentation, continuous process improvement, corporate culture, process owner, management commitment, and process performance measurement. Second, the investigation is performed as a function of industry type in order to identify differences between manufacturing and service companies. For this purpose, Austrian manufacturing and service firms with at least 50 employees were examined on the basis of an online survey. Marketing data served as primary data basis. A pilot test was conducted at the beginning of May 2011 including 500 randomly drawn firms. Due to the rather low response rates, it was decided to directly contact key informants like managing directors or heads of quality management. Data collection finished in the first week of August 2011 with 898 (18.79%) completed questionnaires. As dependent and independent data rely on single-source ratings and therefore potentially suffer from common method bias, a follow-up survey was conducted in October 2011 focusing on the outcome variables financial performance, customer satisfaction, and innovation. This led to a final sample size of 483. After assessing the construct's unidimensionality, reliability and validity, hierarchical regression analyses were performed. The findings indicate that the culture in line with the process approach is a positive driver of financial performance and customer satisfaction. Furthermore continuous process improvement, the process owner role and management commitment are positively related with certain types of innovation. However, also a negative effect of process knowledge and documentation was discovered. Especially service innovation processes are rather unformalized and unstructured which is grounded in the service nature. Since customers and their needs are directly involved in these processes requireing larger amounts of communication, subject-oriented business process management (S-BPM) could help making these processes more systematic in order to enhance performance.

S. Oppl and A. Fleischmann (Eds.): S-BPM ONE 2012, CCIS 284, p. 236, 2012.
© Springer-Verlag Berlin Heidelberg 2012

Using Concurrent Task Trees
for Stakeholder-centered Modeling
and Visualization of Business Processes

Jens Kolb[1], Manfred Reichert[1], and Barbara Weber[2]

[1] Institute of Databases and Information Systems, Ulm University, Germany
{jens.kolb,manfred.reichert}@uni-ulm.de
[2] Quality Engineering Research Group, University of Innsbruck, Austria
barbara.weber@uibk.ac.at

Abstract. The different stakeholders in Business Process Management have to deal with various process models in order to understand the business processes being relevant for them. Especially inexperienced stakeholders often have difficulties in comprehending large and complex process models. In this paper a stakeholder-centered approach for modeling, changing and visualizing business processes is introduced. It is based on the Concurrent Task Tree (CTT), which constitutes a task modeling language widely applied in the field of end-user development. In particular, CTT considers stakeholder needs in modeling the behaviour of user interfaces. In the context of our work we apply CTT for modeling, changing and visualizing business processes. To evaluate whether CTT is appropriate for stakeholder-centered process modeling we compare it with imperative process modeling, and introduce a mapping between CTT process models and imperative process models expressed in terms of the Business Process Modeling Notation (BPMN). Finally, we provide an advanced stakeholder-centered visualization concept based on CTT.

Keywords: stakeholder-centered process modeling, process visualization, concurrent task tree.

1 Introduction

When developing an information system a precise specification is required to describe the system's behaviour. For this purpose, requirements' engineers interview stakeholders and end-users, and try to capture elicitated requirements in these software specifications. As a common problem such specifications do not always meet the actual requirements of the stakeholders. In particular, this results from communication problems between stakeholders and software engineers due to the different backgrounds and goals these two groups have. *End-User Development (EUD)* has tackled this challenge by enabling stakeholders to create software specifications on their own [8]. Usually, this is addressed by providing easy to understand specification techniques. One of them is the *Concurrent Task*

S. Oppl and A. Fleischmann (Eds.): S-BPM ONE 2012, CCIS 284, pp. 237–251, 2012.

Tree (CTT), which constitutes a widely applied task modeling language for describing the behaviour of end-user interfaces [14]. More precisely, a stakeholder may specify a *hierarchical task model*, where lower level tasks refine upper level ones. Furthermore, *temporal relations* between tasks being on the same level may be introduced specifying the order in which these tasks shall be executed. A corresponding development environment is provided by the *Concurrent Task Tree Environment (CTTE)* [10]. In addition to its CTT modeling component, CTTE comprises a simulation component enabling stakeholders to check whether or not a CTT-based task model behaves as desired.

In *Business Process Management (BPM)* or – to be more precise – in the field of *Business Process Modeling* one has to deal with similar problems. Typically, numerous stakeholders are involved in the performance of a business process (i.e., its process instances and business cases respectively), whereas only few stakeholders are actually able to define respective process models. Furthermore, in practice process models often become very large and complex, and are not understandable to non-experts [30,25].

When executing process models using a *Business Process Management System (BPMS)* it is desirable that all stakeholders are able to understand these process models or at least selected views on them [29]. Further they should be able to (dynamically) adapt process models if required, e.g., to deal with a changing environment or exceptional situations [23,31]. Partially, the *Business Process Modeling Notation (BPMN) 2.0* tries to foster model comprehensibility by establishing an industry-wide and well-founded standard for process modeling [12]. Furthermore, it introduces advanced modeling elements and patterns in order to reduce model complexity for non-experts as well. Still, the problems coming with large process models remain and advanced visualization concepts are missing [2]. Respective concepts are required since process-aware information systems become increasingly adaptive and stakeholders need assistance in adapting their processes and process models respectively [24].

This paper addresses these issues and introduces a CTT-based approach for specifying, visualizing and changing process models at a higher level of

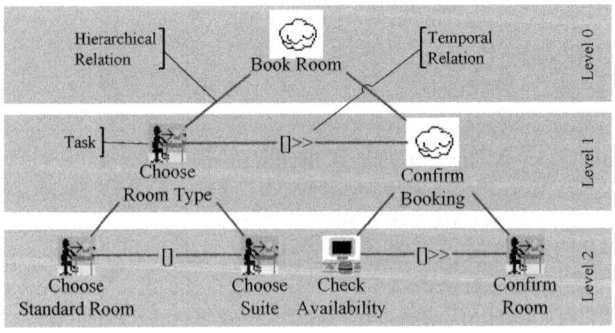

Fig. 1. Room Booking modeled in CTT [13]

abstraction. It therefore provides a mapping of CTT modeling elements to BPMN elements and investigates how model changes can be accomplished in either one of these two formalisms. Further, a visualization concept is introduced to support stakeholders in viewing their process models.

This work was done in the context of the *proView* project, which enables stakeholders to adapt business process models based on personalized process views [22]. Such a personalized process view abstracts a business process model in a stakeholder-centered way, e.g. by only displaying those activities to a stakeholder he or she is involved in. Furthermore, *proView* provides alternative process representations to stakeholders (e.g., process graphs, forms or trees) such that they can choose the one being most favorable in their current work context. The overall goal is to assist stakeholders in understanding and adapting the business processes they are involved in.

The remainder of this paper is organized as follows: Section 2 introduces the structural modeling elements of CTT and then maps them to BPMN 2.0 elements. This mapping is required to support process modelers with a high-level specification approach on the one hand and to be still able to execute CTT process models in traditional BPMSs on the other hand. Opposed to [5] we do not provide a proprietary execution engine for CTT process models, but rather use CTT as stakeholder interface. Furthermore, we investigate what effects the changes of a CTT process model have on the corresponding BPMN model, and vice versa. Section 3 discusses how stakeholders may benefit from the use of CTT as process modeling language. In this context we also introduce CTT-specific visualization concepts. Section 4 discusses related work. The paper concludes with a summary and outlook in Section 5.

2 Using Concurrent Task Trees for Process Modeling

Section 2.1 first introduces basic modeling elements of CTT and shows how they can be mapped to BPMN elements. Section 2.2 then discusses how complex CTTs can be mapped to BPMN process models. Finally, Section 2.3 deals with changes on CTT process models.

2.1 Basic Modeling Elements

Concurrent Task Trees (CTTs) use *tasks* to describe changes of the state of the underlying information system. Thereby, a *task* represents work accomplished by the stakeholder or the underlying information system. Furthermore, tasks can be ordered and be structured hierarchically. Basically, there exist two kinds of relations between tasks: *Hierarchical Relations* and *Temporal Relations*. Figure 1 illustrates this using a room booking example. It describes the tasks to be accomplished in order to book a hotel room. Hierarchical relations connect tasks belonging to different tree levels, i.e., tasks having different granularity. Temporal relations, in turn, describe order and execution constraints of tasks belonging to the same level. We first consider tasks as basic building blocks of CTT. Generally, tasks are comparable to activities in a BPMN process model. As shown in Figure 2, CTT distinguishes between five different kinds of tasks.

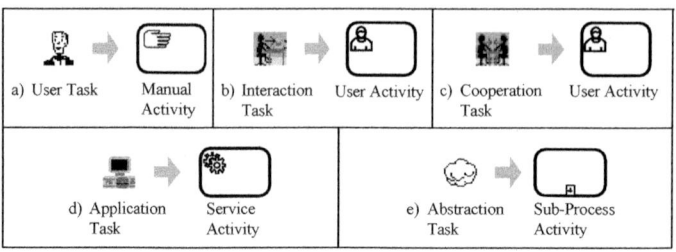

Fig. 2. CTT Task Types and their Mapping to BPMN

We describe these basic CTT task types as well as their mapping to BPMN 2.0 elements [12]. First, a *User Task* represents a task to be performed by a stakeholder without need for interacting with an information system (e.g., a clerk interviewing a customer). This kind of task can be directly mapped to a *Manual Activity* in BPMN. Second, if the stakeholder is interacting with an information system (e.g., filling data into a form), an *Interaction Task* can be used in CTT to express this. In particular, during process execution this kind of task has to be explicitly triggered by the stakeholder. Third, if more than one stakeholder is involved in a particular interaction, a *Cooperation Task* can be used. Both, Interaction and Cooperation Tasks can be mapped to a *User Activity* in BPMN. Note that BPMN does not distinguish between interactions of one or multiple stakeholders with the information system. Fourth, an *Application Task* describes a task to be executed by the information system without need for interacting with any stakeholder (e.g. storing data in a database). In BPMN this can be expressed by a *Service Activity*. Furthermore, BPMN offers specific alternatives to which a CTT Application Task may be mapped depending on what is done during the execution of the task. Either the BPMN *Send/Receive Activity* (e.g., if the task sends or receives messages) or the *Script Activity* (e.g., the task interprets a script) can be used. Fifth, an *Abstraction Task* covers activities not matching to any of the aforementioned task types. The semantics of an Abstraction Task is specified by refining it through child tasks. In BPMN this corresponds to a *Sub-Process Activity*. If an Abstraction Task has no child tasks, in turn, an *Abstract Activity* can be used in the corresponding BPMN process model instead.

Creating a task tree model based on CTT constitutes a top-down approach. The root task describes the name of the process and may be refined by lower-level tasks. The different levels are connected by *Hierarchical Relations*. In this context the type of a parent task is determined by the types of its child tasks. If all child tasks have the same type (e.g. Interaction Task) this type is assigned to the parent task as well. If the child tasks do not have the same type, however, the parent task will be an *Abstraction Task* (cf. *Confirm Booking* in Figure 1). We discuss how such task hierarchy can be mapped to a BPMN process model in Section 2.2.

After specifying the *Hierarchical Relations* between the tasks belonging to different tree levels, the *Temporal Relations* between the tasks referring to the same tree level have to be specified. Such relations describe the order in which the tasks of a particular level shall be executed. CTT offers eight kinds of temporal relations (cf. Figure 3). Relations *Enabling* and *Enabling with Information Passing* correspond to the *Sequence Flow* in BPMN. The latter relation sends additional information (i.e. data objects) to its target task (cf. Figure 3a+b). Furthermore, Figure 3c visualizes the temporal relation called *Iteration*, which can be mapped to a *Loop Activity* in the corresponding BPMN model. As specialization of Iteration, *Finite Iteration* can be used in CTT. It pre-specifies the number of iterations at design time.

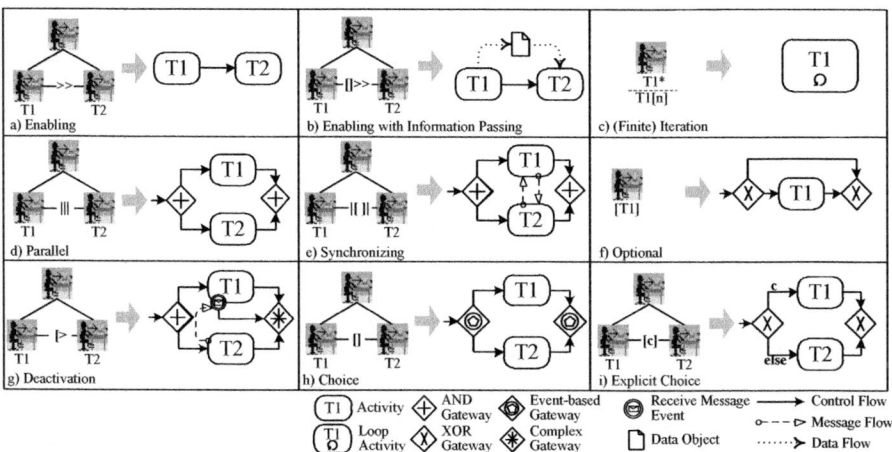

Fig. 3. Mapping CTT Temporal Relations to BPMN Model Elements

Three vertical lines between two tasks (cf. Figure 3d) express *Parallel* execution. Consequently, in the corresponding BPMN process model, the respective activities are surrounded by a splitting and joining AND-gateway. Since CTT realizes a task tree structure, CTT process models can be always mapped to a well-structured BPMN model, i.e., a BPMN process model for which every split gateway has a unique join gateway of the same type and vice versa. We denote such pair of gateways and their enclosed activities as *SESE* (Single-Entry-Single-Exit) block. SESE blocks may be nested, but must not overlap [21].

A special case of the aforementioned parallel relation is provided by the *Synchronizing* relation. It executes tasks in parallel, but these may exchange certain information with each other as well. In a BPMN process model this can be realized by sending messages from one activity to another.

An *Optional* CTT task (cf. Figure 3f) has to be mapped to a BPMN process fragment using an XOR-gateway, which then allows deciding whether or not the respective task shall be executed. *Deactivation*, in turn, executes the first task (cf. Figure 3g, task T1) as long as the second one is not started. However, when starting the second task the first one is aborted. A use case of this temporal relation is a user form that may be edited until the submit button is pressed. In a BPMN process model we can use an AND-gateway for expressing this scenario, i.e., both activities T1 and T2 become activated and hence may be started. Once T2 is started, it sends an event to T1 in order to abort its execution. Since it is *a-priori* not clear whether T1 is terminated normally or aborted, a complex gateway has to be used, allowing for the specification of respective join behaviour [12]. Finally, CTT offers a *Choice* relation between tasks; e.g. a user may decide whether T1 or T2 is executed. Once one of the two tasks is selected, the other one is no longer offered to the user. This behaviour can be mapped to an *Event-based* gateway in BPMN (cf. Figure 3h). Since this is the only way to express an alternative relation CTT offers, we extend the set of temporal relations by an *Explicit Choice* relation (cf. Figure 3i). The latter is needed in order to be able to express an alternative path based on data objects. In this context, we use a branching condition c within the square brackets between T1 and T2. The Explicit Choice relation can be mapped to an *Exclusive* gateway in BPMN.

2.2   Mapping Complex CTT Process Models to BPMN

Section 2.1 has shown how to map basic CTT elements to corresponding BPMN elements. Based on these elementary mappings, we informally show how CTT process models can be transformed into a behavior-equivalent[1] BPMN model. Obviously, the opposite mapping is not always possible, since not all BPMN models are well-structured or cannot be transformed into a behavior-equivalent, well-structured process model [9]. Besides, not all BPMN elements can be mapped to corresponding CTT elements (e.g. message flows, attached events).

When building and interpreting CTT process models, ambiguities might occur, particularly when introducing different kinds of temporal relations at the same level. As example assume that there are three tasks $T1$, $T2$ and $T3$ on the same tree level with: $T1 \; [] \; T2 \; ||| \; T3$; i.e., $T1$ and $T2$ are connected by a Choice relation, and $T2$ and $T3$ are connected by a Parallel relation. There are two ways to interpret these relations: $((T1 \; [] \; T2) \; ||| \; T3)$ or $(T1 \; [] \; (T2 \; ||| \; T3))$ (cf. Figure 4). This ambiguity has to be resolved since it affects both process semantics and the transformation of the CTT to the BPMN process model. CTT offers two options in this context [14]: First, the priority order defined in the ISO standard LOTOS may be used [7]; e.g., Choice > Parallel composition > Disabling > Enabling. Second, another tree level may be added to resolve the ambiguity, e.g. $T1 \; [] \; (T2 \; ||| \; T3)$. To support stakeholders in understanding CTT process models we prefer the second option since it requires no additional modeling knowledge.

When dealing with complex CTT process models the tree hierarchy needs to be transformed into the BPMN model. Generally, there exist several ways to

---

[1] A CTT process model and a BPMN model are denoted as *behavior-equivalent*, if they have exactly the same sets of producible execution traces. An execution trace reflects the temporal order of events (e.g. start, end activity) related to a process instance [24].

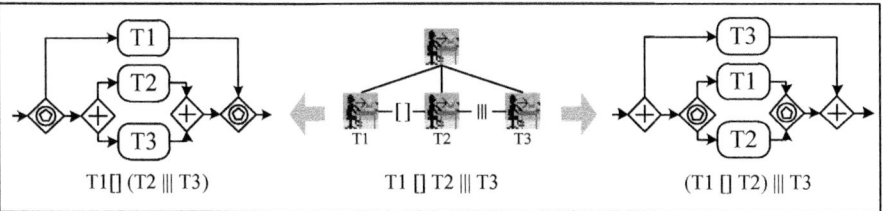

Fig. 4. Ambiguity in the Context of Temporal Relations

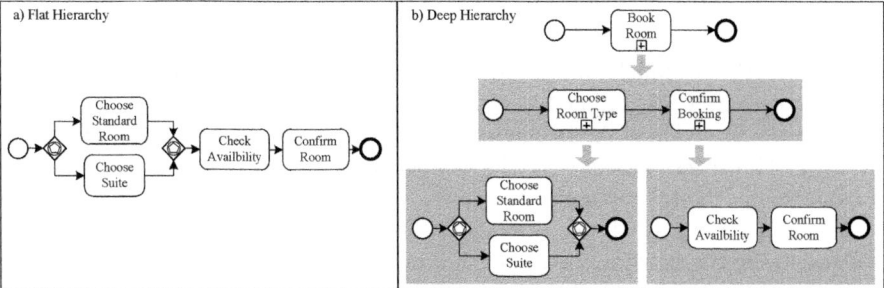

Fig. 5. Mapping the Room Booking CTT Process Model to a BPMN Model

accomplish this. The first one is denoted as **Flat Hierarchy**. Figure 5a shows the result of this transformation applied to the CTT process model from Figure 1. The tasks on the leaf level of the CTT process model are mapped to corresponding BPMN activities. Afterwards, the temporal relations between the tasks are transformed into the respective control flow patterns in the BPMN model. Finally, to connect the different branches the temporal relations of the parent task are used. The second way to map the tree hierarchy is to transform the CTT process model into a BPMN model using a **Deep Hierarchy** (cf. Figure 5b). Here, every tree level and every branch in the CTT process model is mapped to a separate BPMN model. In this context a task of the CTT process model is mapped to a sub-process activity if the task has at least one child task (cf. Figure 3). Finally, the different models are assembled to a process hierarchy by connecting sub-process activities to the respective (sub-)process models.

Which of the two approaches for transforming a complex CTT process model into a BPMN model is more favorable depends on the concrete use case of the resulting BPMN model. For example, if one wants to integrate the model into a BPMS with the purpose to execute it, a flat hierarchy should be chosen. If the BPMN model is used to visualize the process for individual stakeholders, in turn, a deep hierarchy should be chosen. We discuss the second use case in more detail in Section 3.

2.3   Changing a CTT Process Model

Stakeholders should not only be supported in understanding process models, but also in changing and evolving them over time [31]. In this context, the use of CTT in the field of End-User Development has already shown promising perspectives. This section gives some insights into whether building and changing CTT process models is actually that easy as expected. Changes of a CTT process model can be categorized into three types. First, a change may concern *Temporal Relations*. Second, it may change the *Depth* of the CTT. Third, it may affect the *Breadth* of the tree. This is illustrated by Figure 6, which shows the progress during the modeling of a simple CTT process model as well as the respective modeling stages in the corresponding BPMN process model.

Changing the type of the **Temporal Relation** in the CTT process model influences the execution order of the respective tasks. This simple change of a CTT process model, however, might require complex adaptations of the corresponding BPMN model. In our example from Figure 6 the sequential ordering of tasks T1 and T2 is changed to a parallel one. While in the BPMN model this requires the insertion of AND-gateways for splitting and joining the control flow, in the CTT process model only the temporal relation is changed without need for modifying the tree structure.

The **Depth** of a CTT process model (i.e., the depth of its tree) may change when refining a task. More precisely, new child tasks may be added to a task and a new level be introduced in the tree. Depending on the level of the refined task, either the overall depth of the CTT process model or the depth of a specific sub-tree of the CTT process model increases. Generally, there are two alternatives to transfer a CTT process model change to the corresponding BPMN model depending on whether a flat or deep hierarchy is used (cf. Section 2.2). When using a flat hierarchy the activity of the refined task in the BPMN model is replaced by its newly added child tasks (cf. Figure 6). Using a deep hierarchy, in turn, the type of the refined task in the corresponding BPMN model is changed to a sub-process activity and a new sub-process is added to the BPMN process model hierarchy.

When deleting child tasks of a complex task in a CTT process model and only one or no child task remains, the respective child level is removed. Furthermore at least the depth of the affected sub-tree in the CTT process model is decreased by one. Depending on the chosen CTT-to-BPMN transformation, the sub-process activity will be removed or replaced by the parent task.

The **Breadth** of a sub-tree in a CTT process model changes when adding a new task to the respective level; e.g., when adding T5 to the CTT process model depicted in Figure 6. In general, adding a task requires adding a new hierarchical relation to its parent task as well as temporal relations to selected sibling tasks. To transfer the CTT process model change to a change of the corresponding BPMN process model, an activity needs to be added. Depending on the newly created temporal relations in the CTT process model, this activity is added sequentially or as new branch to existing split/join gateways. Obviously, when deleting a task in a sub-tree of a CTT process model, the breadth of this sub-tree is changed accordingly. If the deleted task has child tasks, in turn, these will be removed. In this case, the depth of the sub-tree is affected as well. As opposed to the deletion of a leaf task, deleting a non-leaf task requires the removal of a complete SESE block in the corresponding BPMN model. When using deep

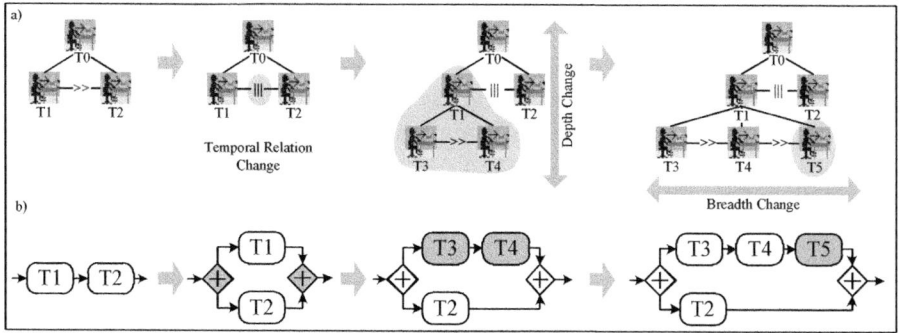

Fig. 6. Evolving Process Models in a) CTT and b) BPMN

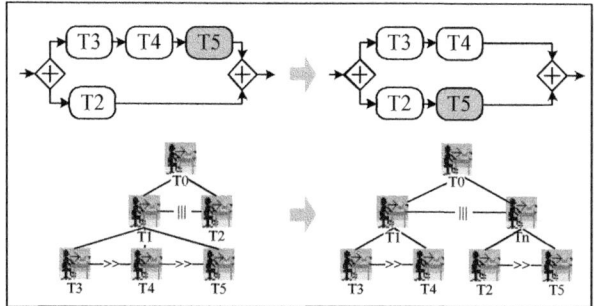

Fig. 7. Changes of a BPMN Process Model and Effects on the Corresponding CTT Process Model

hierarchy (cf. Section 2.2) the sub-process activity as well as the underlying sub-process model are removed. If there is exactly one remaining task left on the tree level the deletion was applied, this level will be removed.

When mapping the effects of changes of a BPMN process model to the corresponding CTT process model, we need to consider whether a flat or a deep hierarchy is used (cf. Section 2.2). As advantage of a deep hierarchy the changes in the respective CTT process model can be kept local; note that each BPMN model represents a tree level in a specific branch of the CTT process model. Consequently, the change of the BPMN process model only concerns this rather small region of the CTT process model.

Using a flat hierarchy, in turn, even a simple movement of an activity from its current position to another one in the BPMN process model might require a complex restructuring of the CTT process model. For example, when moving task *T5* in Figure 7 from its current position to the one following task *T2*, a completely different tree structure results for the corresponding CTT process model. Obviously, the more the structure of a CTT process model is changed, the harder it will become for stakeholders to understand the effects of the change.

3   Supporting Stakeholders by Visualization Concepts

Section 2 discussed how models expressed in terms of activity-based process specification languages like BPMN can be mapped to CTT process models and vice versa. We now want to demonstrate how tree-based CTT process modeling supports stakeholders in understanding and interacting with a process model. Especially when dealing with large process models inexperienced stakeholders often have difficulties with comprehending and changing these models.

To foster model comprehension the tree-structure provided by CTT offers a top-down decomposition of the process model. In particular, any CTT process model can be visualized by folding/unfolding it as illustrated in Figure 8. Starting with Figure 8a the depicted CTT process model can be unfolded step-by-step by the stakeholder, e.g., using a zoom slider to refine the level of detail. Finally, when reaching the leaf level of the CTT process model (cf. Figure 8c), the most detailed level of the process model is shown to the stakeholder. We denote this unfolding as **Leveled Exploration**. In particular, this kind of refinement of CTT process models helps stakeholders in understanding or exploring process models step-by-step. When refining a BPMN process model by navigating to a sub-process, in turn, the related super-processes are no longer displayed to the stakeholder. Thus, the latter might loose the context of the sub-process. By contrast, this context is kept, when using Leveled Exploration in CTT. The second row in Figure 8 shows the BPMN process models corresponding to the respective CTT models. As opposed to other abstraction approaches (cf. Section 4) for each level of detail of the process model the respective sub-process activity labels are provided by the CTT process model; i.e., no label generation is required [19,6].

A second method for exploring a CTT process model is **Depth Exploration**. In Figure 8b the stakeholder may click on one of the tasks *Choose Room Type* or *Confirm Booking*, and the corresponding sub-tree is then unfolded (cf. Figure 9a). Using this exploration method the stakeholder may interactively explore the CTT process model. Starting with an abstract (and small) CTT process model the stakeholder may decide which parts shall be refined. Clicking on the same task again will re-fold this sub-tree. This way the stakeholder may decide which region of the process model shall be explored at which level of granularity. Again a switch from the CTT process model to the corresponding BPMN process model is possible at every point in time during the exploration. As opposed to the use of traditional sub-processes in BPMN, one has the option to visualize selected sub-processes in more detail than others within one and the same process model. This, in turn, allows for a more flexible process visualization.

Our third exploration method provides a different representation of CTT process models to stakeholders. One already introduced example constitutes the **transformation** of a CTT process model to a BPMN process model (cf. Figure 5). As alternative representation of a CTT process model, a corresponding folder structure offers promising perspectives (cf. Figure 9b). In particular, stakeholders are familiar with respective folder structures.

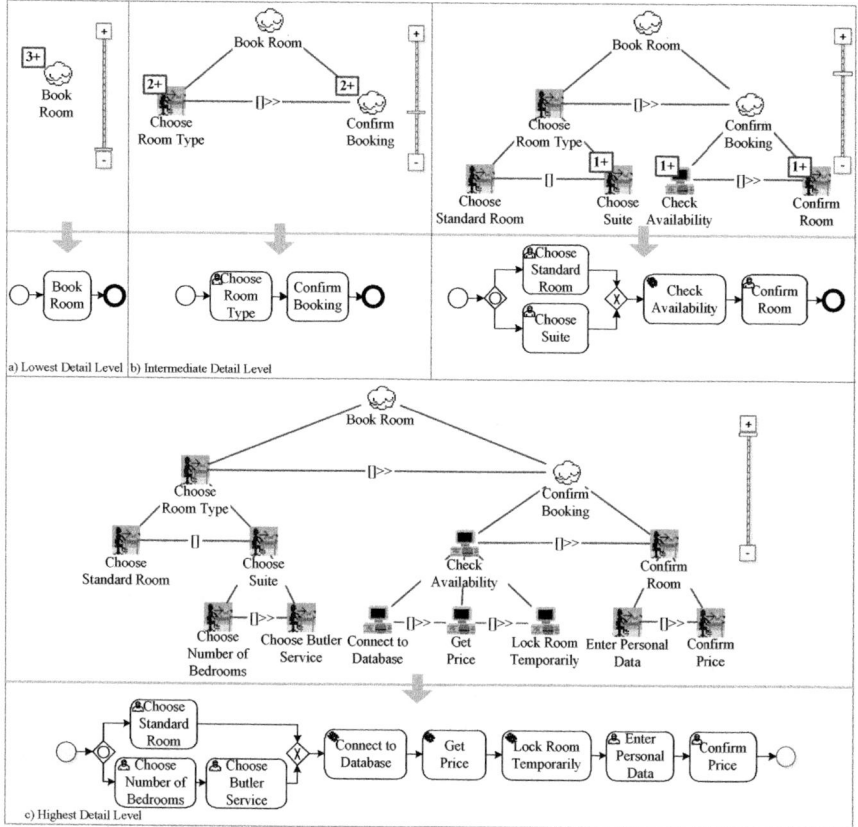

Fig. 8. Leveled Visualization of a CTT Process Model

4   Related Work

Similar to the approach desired in this paper, [11] introduces a mapping of CTT process models to UML 2.0 Activity Diagrams. Although UML provides a rich set of diagram types, none of them is supporting model-based design regarding the behavior of user interfaces. In order to bridge this gap the authors introduce a mapping of CTT modeling elements to UML 2.0 Activity Diagrams. Although UML Activity Diagrams can be used for modeling business processes, the suggested CTT mapping is more complex than in our approach; furthermore the resulting model would be too complex for stakeholders and end-users respectively. A similar approach showing the same drawbacks is introduced in [4].

The approach discussed in [17] uses BPMN for modeling to business processes. However, CTT is used to refine interactive activities in BPMN process models. More precisely, the stakeholder first models the business process using BPMN. Then, the activities requiring user interactions are refined similarly to the definition of a sub-process by defining a respective CTT process model.

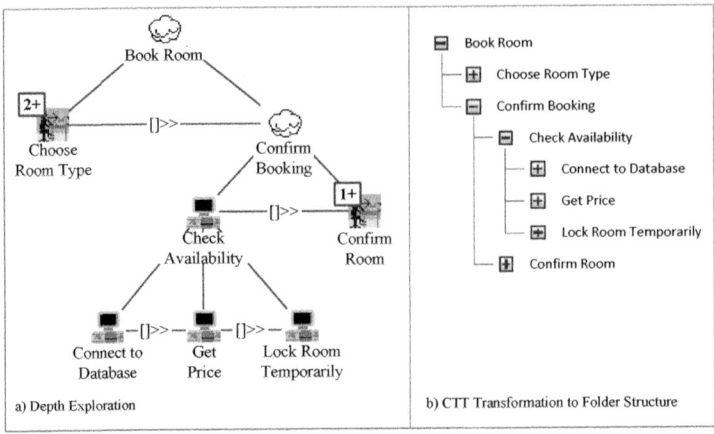

Fig. 9. CTT Process Model Visualization Concepts

Application Tasks (cf. Section 2.1) are mapped to Web Service calls and Interaction Tasks to a specific XML format enabling platform-independent user interfaces [15]. A similar approach is described in [26]. The authors suggest a four-step approach to derive user interfaces from business processes. As in the aforementioned approach, the refinement of an activity within a business process model is accomplished by defining a CTT process model. This CTT model and a domain model are then used to create an abstract user interface.

Another use case for CTT is presented in [5]. The authors introduce a method for modeling business processes based on CTTE (cf. Section 1). Afterwards the resulting CTT process model is transformed into an imperative process model which may be edited using a proprietary process editor (*Task Tree Workflow Management System Editor, TTMS Editor*). This way, the process model can be enriched with explicit choices and execution-relevant aspects. Finally, the process model is exported as XML file to a process engine (*TTMS WfMS*). This transformation described along the tool chain cannot be reversed. However, [5] neither provides an explicit mapping to an existing process modeling language nor does it support appropriate visualizing concepts.

In [27,28] another tree structure, denoted as *Process Structure Tree* (PST), is introduced. On the one hand this tree type is used to analyze a process model in respect to control flow errors, on the other hand the PST structure is applied to detect SESE regions. The latter allows transforming certain classes of unstructured process models to well-structured ones [18]. However, stakeholder needs are not addressed by the PST notion.

Another way to support stakeholders in understanding and modeling business processes is illustrated in [22,1,20]: a powerful approach is introduced to change the visual appearance of a process model by replacing its visual representation by another one, e.g., by changing colors and adding pictographs to selected activities. Furthermore, advanced concepts for abstracting complex process models through hiding and aggregating process fragments is introduced [22,3]. This allows for a more flexible visualization of processes, but also has its limitations. First, when aggregating process fragments, the resulting abstract activity requires an abstracted label, not provided by this approach. Second, the concept does not allow for the automated creation of abstract models as introduced in Section 3.

5   Summary and Outlook

In this paper we applied Concurrent Task Trees to Business Process Management. We showed that it is possible to map CTT to BPMN modeling elements. Especially, temporal relations can be transformed into behavior-equivalent BPMN process fragments. Complex CTT process models, in turn, can be transformed into flat or deep hierarchy process models in BPMN. We further discussed the effects of changes applied to a CTT process model and their translation into a behavior-equivalent BPMN process model. Finally, visualization concepts for CTT process models were presented, which support stakeholders in understanding more complex process models. Since CTTs were designed with the goal to capture user interactions, we particularly suggest using CTTs in the context of human-centric business processes.

We developed a prototype to evaluate our concepts (cf. Figure 10). It extends the Cheetah Experimental Platform [16] and enables CTT-based process modeling. Cheetah is able to measure and log the order of arbitrary modeling steps and the time stakeholders need for accomplishing respective steps. Based on this, we will conduct user experiments for comparing CTT process modeling with BPMN-based modeling in a systematic way.

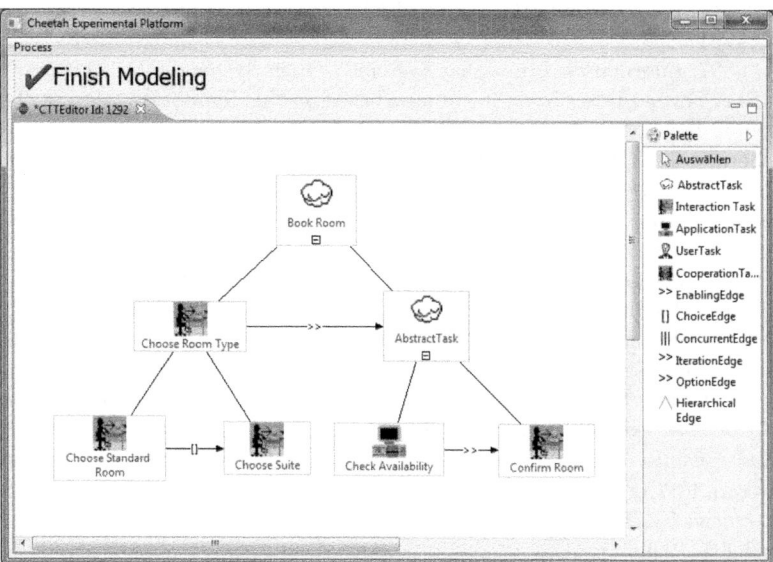

Fig. 10. Prototypical Implementation in Cheetah Experimental Platform

Acknowledgment. The authors would like to acknowledge and thank Thomas Grees for extending the Cheetah Experimental Platform by a CTT process modeling component as well as Yasemin Agbulak for providing first results on this topic.

References

1. Bobrik, R., Bauer, T., Reichert, M.: Proviado – Personalized and Configurable Visualizations of Business Processes. In: Bauknecht, K., Pröll, B., Werthner, H. (eds.) EC-Web 2006. LNCS, vol. 4082, pp. 61–71. Springer, Heidelberg (2006)
2. Bobrik, R., Reichert, M., Bauer, T.: Requirements for the Visualization of System-Spanning Business Processes. In: Proc. DEXA 2005 Workshops , pp. 948–954 (2005), http://ieeexplore.ieee.org/lpdocs/epic03/wrapper.htm?arnumber=1508396
3. Bobrik, R., Reichert, M., Bauer, T.: View-Based Process Visualization. In: Alonso, G., Dadam, P., Rosemann, M. (eds.) BPM 2007. LNCS, vol. 4714, pp. 88–95. Springer, Heidelberg (2007)
4. Brüning, J., Dittmar, A., Forbrig, P., Reichart, D.: Getting SW Engineers on Board: Task Modelling with Activity Diagrams. In: Gulliksen, J., Harning, M.B., van der Veer, G.C., Wesson, J. (eds.) EIS 2007. LNCS, vol. 4940, pp. 175–192. Springer, Heidelberg (2008)
5. Brüning, J., Forbrig, P.: TTMS: A Task Tree Based Workflow Management System. In: Halpin, T., Nurcan, S., Krogstie, J., Soffer, P., Proper, E., Schmidt, R., Bider, I. (eds.) BPMDS 2011 and EMMSAD 2011. LNBIP, vol. 81, pp. 186–200. Springer, Heidelberg (2011)
6. Hipp, M., Mutschler, B., Reichert, M.: Navigating in Process Model Collections: A New Approach Inspired by Google Earth. In: Daniel, F., Barkaoui, K., Dustdar, S. (eds.) BPM Workshops 2011, Part II. LNBIP, vol. 100, pp. 87–98. Springer, Heidelberg (2012)
7. ISO 8807: Information Processing Systems - Open Systems Interconnection - LOTOS: A Formal Description Technique based on the Temporal Ordering of Observational Behaviour (1989)
8. Liebermann, H., Paternò, F., Wulf, V.: End-User Development. Human-Computer Interaction Series. Springer, Dordrecht (2006)
9. Liu, R., Kumar, A.: An Analysis and Taxonomy of Unstructured Workflows. In: van der Aalst, W.M.P., Benatallah, B., Casati, F., Curbera, F. (eds.) BPM 2005. LNCS, vol. 3649, pp. 268–284. Springer, Heidelberg (2005)
10. Mori, G., Paternò, F., Santoro, C.: CTTE: Support for Developing and Analyzing Task Models for Interactive System Design. IEEE ToSE 28(8), 797–813 (2002)
11. Nóbrega, L., Jardim Nunes, N., Coelho, H.: Mapping ConcurTaskTrees into UML 2.0. In: Gilroy, S.W., Harrison, M.D. (eds.) DSV-IS 2005. LNCS, vol. 3941, pp. 237–248. Springer, Heidelberg (2006)
12. OMG: Business Process Management Notation (BPMN) 2.0 (2010), www.bpmn.org
13. Paternò, F.: ConcurTaskTrees: An Engineered Approach to Model-based Design of Interactive Systems. The Handbook of Analysis for Human Computer Interaction, pp. 1–18 (1999)
14. Paternò, F., Mancini, C., Meniconi, S., Maria, V.S.: ConcurTaskTrees: A Diagrammatic Notation for Specifying Task Models. In: Proc. IFIP TC13 Int'l Conf. on Human-Computer Interaction, pp. 362–369 (1997)

15. Paternò, F., Santoro, C., Spano, L.D.: Model-Based Design of Multi-device Interactive Applications Based on Web Services. In: Gross, T., Gulliksen, J., Kotzé, P., Oestreicher, L., Palanque, P., Prates, R.O., Winckler, M. (eds.) INTERACT 2009, Part I. LNCS, vol. 5726, pp. 892–905. Springer, Heidelberg (2009)
16. Pinggera, J., Zugal, S., Weber, B.: Investigating the Process of Process Modeling with Cheetah Experimental Platform. In: Proc. 1st Int'l WS Empirical Research Proc.-Oriented Inf. Sys. Hammamet (2010)
17. Pintus, A., Paternò, F., Santoro, C.: Modelling User Interactions in Web Service-based Business Processes. In: WEBIST 2010, pp. 175–180 (2010)
18. Polyvyanyy, A., García-Bañuelos, L., Dumas, M.: Structuring Acyclic Process Models. In: Hull, R., Mendling, J., Tai, S. (eds.) BPM 2010. LNCS, vol. 6336, pp. 276–293. Springer, Heidelberg (2010)
19. Polyvyanyy, A., Smirnov, S., Weske, M.: Process Model Abstraction: A Slider Approach. In: 12th Int'l IEEE Enterprise Distributed Object Computing Conference, pp. 325–331. IEEE (2008)
20. Reichert, M., Bassil, S., Bobrik, R., Bauer, T.: The Proviado Access Control Model for Business Process Monitoring Components. Enterprise Modelling and Information Systems Architectures - An International Journal 5(3), 64–88 (2010)
21. Reichert, M., Dadam, P.: ADEPTflex - Supporting Dynamic Changes of Workflows Without Losing Control. Journal of Intelligent Information Systems 10(2), 93–129 (1998)
22. Reichert, M., Kolb, J., Bobrik, R., Bauer, T.: Enabling Personalized Visualization of Large Business Processes through Parameterizable Views. In: Proc. 26th Symposium On Applied Computing (SAC 2012), Riva del Garda (Trento), Italy (2012)
23. Reichert, M., Rinderle-Ma, S., Dadam, P.: Flexibility in Process-Aware Information Systems. In: Jensen, K., van der Aalst, W.M.P. (eds.) ToPNoc II. LNCS, vol. 5460, pp. 115–135. Springer, Heidelberg (2009)
24. Reichert, M., Weber, B.: Enabling Flexibility in Process-aware Information Systems - Challenges, Methods, Technologies. Springer (to appear, 2012)
25. Rinderle, S., Bobrik, R., Reichert, M., Bauer, T.: Businesss Process Visualization - Use Cases, Challenges, Solutions. In: Proc. 8th Int'l Conf. on Enterprise Information Systems (ICEIS 2006), Paphos, Cyprus, vol. 2006, pp. 204–211 (2006)
26. Sousa, K., Mendonça, H., Vanderdonckt, J., Rogier, E., Vandermeulen, J.: User Interface Derivation from Business Processes: A Model-Driven Approach for Organizational Engineering. In: SAC 2008, pp. 553–560 (2008)
27. Vanhatalo, J., Hagen, V., Leymann, F.: Faster and More Focused Control-Flow Analysis for Business Process Models Through SESE Decomposition, pp. 43–55 (2007)
28. Vanhatalo, J., Völzer, H., Koehler, J.: The Refined Process Structure Tree. In: Dumas, M., Reichert, M., Shan, M.-C. (eds.) BPM 2008. LNCS, vol. 5240, pp. 100–115. Springer, Heidelberg (2008)
29. Weber, B., Mutschler, B., Reichert, M.: Investigating the Effort of Using Business Process Management Technology: Results from a Controlled Experiment. Science of Computer Programming 75(5), 292–310 (2010), http://linkinghub.elsevier.com/retrieve/pii/S0167642309001701
30. Weber, B., Reichert, M., Mendling, J., Reijers, H.A.: Refactoring Large Process Model Repositories. Computers in Industry 62(5), 467–486 (2011)
31. Weber, B., Sadiq, S., Reichert, M.: Beyond Rigidity - Dynamic Process Lifecycle Support: A Survey on Dynamic Changes in Process-Aware Information Systems. Computer Science - Research and Development 23(2), 47–65 (2009)

Author Index